*The Counterinsurgent's Constitution*

# The Counterinsurgent's Constitution

## Law in the Age of Small Wars

GANESH SITARAMAN

OXFORD
UNIVERSITY PRESS

# OXFORD

UNIVERSITY PRESS

Oxford University Press is a department of the University of Oxford. It furthers the
University's objective of excellence in research, scholarship, and education by publishing worldwide.
Oxford is a registered trade mark of Oxford University Press in the UK and in certain other countries.

Oxford    New York
Auckland    Cape Town    Dar es Salaam    Hong Kong    Karachi
Kuala Lumpur    Madrid    Melbourne    Mexico City    Nairobi
New Delhi    Shanghai    Taipei    Toronto

With offices in
Argentina    Austria    Brazil    Chile    Czech Republic    France    Greece
Guatemala    Hungary    Italy    Japan    Poland    Portugal    Singapore
South Korea    Switzerland    Thailand    Turkey    Ukraine    Vietnam

Copyright © 2013 by Oxford University Press

Published in the United States of America by
Oxford University Press
198 Madison Avenue, New York, NY 10016, United States of America

www.oup.com

Library of Congress Cataloging-in-Publication Data
Sitaraman, Ganesh.
The counterinsurgent's constitution : law in the age of small wars / Ganesh Sitaraman.
p.   cm.
Includes bibliographical references and index.
ISBN 978-0-19-993031-9 (hardback : alk. paper)
1. War (International law) 2. Asymmetric warfare 3. Counterinsurgency. I. Title.
KZ6398.A87S58    2012
341.6'3—dc23      2012006977

1 3 5 7 9 8 6 4 2

Printed in the United States of America
on acid-free paper

# *Contents*

# *Preface*

THIS BOOK IS about law and counterinsurgency strategy, two fields that are rarely combined. Although counterinsurgency strategists and theorists mention the importance of law, few spend much time thinking about legal issues. Perhaps fewer lawyers and legal scholars spend their time thinking about counterinsurgency strategy. One of my goals is that this book will serve as a bridge between these two fields and, in the process, contribute something to each of them. Lawyers and legal scholars can learn a great deal from counterinsurgency, just as soldiers, strategists, and policymakers can learn a great deal from law. In addition to better understanding each other, both sides may even begin to think differently about their own fields. In spanning these two areas, I hope readers will forgive the somewhat introductory explanations of basic concepts that they may take for granted. My aim is to make this book accessible to lawyers, law professors, and others involved in legal issues; members of the military; foreign policy professionals; academics in political science, history, and economics; and the wider public. But in doing so, I have invariably sacrificed some technocratic jargon, depth, and detail.

In some ways, however, this attempt to bridge law and strategy is particularly fitting in a book on counterinsurgency. One of counterinsurgency's most important lessons is that we must integrate seemingly disparate aspects of life: military, political, economic, social, cultural, and legal. Each of these areas is dynamically interconnected with the others, and understanding and addressing their relationships (and the totality) is crucial to success. Indeed, in many ways, "law and counterinsurgency strategy" is even too narrow a description of the fields I seek to unite in this book. Transitional justice raises questions of politics and moral philosophy; the rule of law implicates governance, political theory, and sociology; the political nature of warfare itself requires attention to social movements and mobilization, cultural traditions, and economic factors; and each of these factors necessarily operates with thousands of years of history in the background.

As a result, I draw throughout the book upon insights and lessons from a variety of fields: law, military strategy, political science, political theory and philosophy, political economy, sociology, anthropology, and, of course, history. Specialists in each of these areas will undoubtedly be unsatisfied, and may even take offense, with my treatment of their subjects. The quantitatively minded will no doubt be frustrated by the lack of regressions and empirical work accompanying claims. The comparativist will question the absence of formal case studies, particularly when two, Iraq and Afghanistan, are of so great an interest. And the historian will chafe at my use of "illustrations" based on secondary sources to illuminate theoretical points and contemporary problems. But in venturing across methodological and disciplinary boundaries, I have proceeded on the view that the more we bridge different fields and synthesize ideas, the better we can understand a topic as a whole. I can only ask readers to focus on the insights that emerge from working across fields, rather than on the inevitable defects, errors, and overgeneralizations that arise when treating vast and complex subjects with relative brevity.

Relatedly, my goal has been to write a work of theory and strategy. At present, empirical and experimental research on counterinsurgency operations in Iraq and Afghanistan are proceeding at such a quick pace that any empirical evidence on those two conflicts is likely to be supplanted in a matter of months. But when it comes to the relationship between law and counterinsurgency strategy, there has been little written even from a conceptual perspective. As a result, my goal here is not to make empirical claims on the conditions under which the "population-centric" or "progressive" counterinsurgency strategy will be effective, or the conditions under which certain kinds of legal operations will be effective, but rather to explain what *implications* the current approach to counterinsurgency, popularized by General David Petraeus and the *Counterinsurgency Field Manual*, has for a host of legal issues. Part of my contention is that many have largely misunderstood the general approach to legal issues during counterinsurgency operations—or simply gotten it wrong. In order to get it right, I often rely on "ideal types" to capture the central positions and dispositions that animate debates. Obviously the world is more complicated than such idealized positions, and every position certainly has nuances and caveats. But such facts only make it more essential that we get the general approach right before delving into the technocratic details. Critics may conclude that my generalizations are too stark, but I think our default assumptions, priorities, and mindsets shape the tenor of debate and the main thrust of operations, regardless of how many caveats and exceptions are placed upon them. It is therefore necessary to capture the general mindset as the starting point for any more detailed analysis. In seeking to explain this mindset, my claims should not be taken as empirically proven statements, but rather as theoretical or conceptual arguments, derived from the basic principles of counterinsurgency strategy. Hopefully as current conflicts progress and more scholars turn their attention to legal issues during counterinsurgency, empirical and experimental work will test and demonstrate (or even prove wrong) the conceptual claims made here.

As a matter of methodology, I have adopted a form of applied political theory or public philosophy that was far more prominent in the early and mid-twentieth century in works like E. H. Carr's *Twenty Years' Crisis* or Michael Walzer's *Just and Unjust Wars*. Those books are hard to pigeonhole into a particular academic discipline; they unite political philosophy, history, law, empirical political science, sociology, military strategy, and other fields in order to make an argument. As a practice, applied political theory includes at least three types of activities. First, it explores concepts that pervade popular discourse (such as "the rule of law") in theoretical depth in order to gain clarity as to what the concept means and then to show what implications a clearer understanding of the concept has for practical actions or policies. Second, as all empirical work rests on hypotheses about how the world works, applied political theory often develops theoretical arguments that can be tested by future empirical work. That is, it provides the foundation for empirical research. Finally, in many cases, empirical research is impossible (due to practical constraints) or is irrelevant (because moral or political concerns are preeminent). Applied political theory dominates in these domains. Throughout this book, I engage in all three of these forms of applied political theory.

Afghanistan and Iraq loom large in any contemporary work on counterinsurgency, just as Vietnam and Malaya did for those writing a half-century ago. These campaigns, and the renaissance in writing on counterinsurgency that has accompanied them, are the inspiration for this book. Of course, it is far too soon for definitive histories of these campaigns, and in any event, my interest is less on the history of these particular wars and more on the role law does and can play in counterinsurgency. As a result, I have shied away from original historical research and case studies. Instead, I use examples from these conflicts (and others in history) as illustrations of broader theoretical and strategic points. As much as possible, I have tried to rely upon contemporary reporting and studies of ongoing operations as sources, but participants in these events may have different interpretations than reporters and analysts. My reliance on illustrations rather than case studies is an attempt to expand the significance of this analysis beyond U.S operations in Iraq and Afghanistan.

Although my focus throughout the book is on the United States as a third-party counterinsurgent abroad, the principles of counterinsurgency are not limited to U.S. operations alone. Indeed, at a time when many argue that counterinsurgency is going out of fashion and that the United States will not soon reengage in major counterinsurgency operations like those in Iraq and Afghanistan, understanding the broader principles is perhaps even more important. The basic principles, theories, and strategies outlined here are applicable in a wide range of situations from assistance to governments waging counterinsurgency operations (known as Foreign Internal Defense or FID); to ongoing counterinsurgency operations in India, the Philippines, and Yemen; to insurgencies challenging authoritarian regimes in the Middle East; to conflicts that may arise in the future from the population displacements that are expected as a consequence of climate change. Context is obviously centrally important to determining strategy. But in light of the uncertain future, my hope is that focus on theory and strategy, rather than particular case studies, will make my arguments about the role of law in counterinsurgency more readily portable across contexts.

Given my focus on theory, strategy, and portability across contexts—and in the interest of space—I have simplified some issues worth greater exploration. For example, I often refer to "counterinsurgents" or "the counterinsurgent" as if a monolithic entity. Of course, the reality is far more complicated. When the United States is a third-party counterinsurgent abroad operating as part of a coalition, "the counterinsurgent" may include international partners and the host-nation government—and there may be bargaining, coordination problems, and even conflict between them. Within each of these entities, there are also divergent interests. The State Department, Defense Department, and intelligence community may not see eye to eye on every issue. Within the military, different services may have different views. And even within the top leadership, there may be divergent visions for policy. These conflicts are frequently discussed in work on counterinsurgency and organization design, with particular attention to "the interagency process," "whole of government operations," and "unity of effort." Although it is surely worth unpacking these distinctions and exploring these conflicts in the context of legal issues, for the sake of clarity and scope, I have not pursued this issue except where particularly salient. My hope is that the big-picture conceptual framing will provide a helpful starting point for future work on these nuances.

I have also chosen not to address the question of whether and when a state should engage in counterinsurgency operations. That question is intertwined with the broader questions of when states should intervene and how they should choose between the variety of strategies that are available to them upon intervention. Those questions are far beyond the scope of this book, and they are somewhat (though not completely) separate from the conduct of counterinsurgency operations. My focus here is on the relationship between law and counterinsurgency in the prosecution of the war itself, rather than in the choice to go to war. This should not be taken as an endorsement or criticism of the Iraq or Afghan wars or of counterinsurgency-based interventions generally. Indeed, many students of counterinsurgency are opposed to engaging in such interventions unless absolutely necessary. The path of counterinsurgency is fraught with dangers and uncertainty. It should not be undertaken lightly.

# Acknowledgments

OVER THE YEARS, so many have provided helpful comments and assistance in making this book a reality. Harvard Law School (HLS), my home for most of the writing of this book, provided steadfast support for an unorthodox project. Now Justice, then Dean Elena Kagan appointed me as the inaugural Public Law Fellow at HLS, which provided the time and support to make the book possible. Acting Dean Howell Jackson, Dean Martha Minow, and Assistant Dean Akiba Covitz supported me throughout my fellowship, even when finances were tough—and when I told them I wanted to venture into a war zone. Without the guidance, help, and mentoring of Noah Feldman, Jack Goldsmith, Daryl Levinson, and Elizabeth Warren, the book would never have emerged. Noah first suggested I turn my fragmented thoughts into a single book, and he constantly encouraged me to think more deeply about both underlying themes and practical realities. Jack's energetic enthusiasm, reassuring attaboys, and straightforward advice kept me going at the hardest times. Daryl was patient and insightful every time I bothered him with questions, misgivings, and minutiae, and his wit and wisdom were the best guide to success a young scholar could ever have. And, though counterinsurgency is far from her area of expertise, over the last seven years Elizabeth has been my teacher, coauthor, boss, and friend. The Harvard faculty more broadly provided helpful guidance and characteristically stimulating conversations over the years. Bill Alford, David Barron, Gabby Blum, Rachel Brewster, Jim Cavallaro, Glenn Cohen, Einer Elhauge, Richard Fallon, Jerry Frug, Ryan Goodman, Phil Heymann, Mort Horowitz, Duncan Kennedy, Randall Kennedy, Mike Klarman, Adrianne Lanni, Bruce Mann, Frank Michelman, Bob Mnookin, Gerry Neuman, Ben Sachs, Jed Shugerman, Joe Singer, Matt Stephenson, Jeannie Suk, Cass Sunstein, and Adrian Vermeule all provided helpful thoughts and advice.

The book also benefited from many scholars and policymakers who provided comments, asked thoughtful questions in workshops and presentations, or were otherwise helpful interlocutors. Stanley Hoffmann, my undergraduate thesis adviser, has always been an inspiration—particularly in breaking free of disciplinary constraints and embracing the interconnections between areas of study. Bill Burke-White, Sarah Kreps, Maximo Langer, Jed Purdy, Cindy Skach, and Matt Waxman read chapters and provided helpful suggestions. Portions of the book were presented at the American Society of International Law conference in 2010, the American Political Science Association's annual meeting in 2009, and at workshops at the University of California–Davis Law School, Cardozo Law School, Harvard Law School, the University of Illinois College of Law, the University of Pennsylvania Law School, the University of Southern California Law School, the University of Texas Law School, and Vanderbilt Law School. My colleagues on the *Harvard Law Review* were crucial in improving my first venture into law and counterinsurgency, which was published as my law review note and appears here in revised form as chapter 7. The editors of the *Virginia Law Review* deserve great thanks for editing my article on the laws of war and counterinsurgency—and also, more importantly, for accepting it in the first place. That work appears here in revised form as chapters 1 and 2. Two outside reviewers also provided thorough comments, criticisms, and reflections.

Throughout my research, current and former members of the U.S. military were incredibly helpful. Mark Martins read drafts of virtually everything and provided sage advice. In that crucial early phase, when a single article was but an idea, Tyson Belanger stood with me outside the Science Center, providing his thoughts on counterinsurgency late into the chilly Cambridge night. Rich Gross and Mike Jordan gave me an extraordinary opportunity to test sections of the book on the top lawyers for U.S. Central Command. Ian Brasure, Bob Passerello, Dick Pregent, and Rachel Vanlandingham were all particularly helpful. Ahmed Hashim opened the doors of the Naval War College, where I presented portions of the book.

I had the extraordinary fortune to stay at the Counterinsurgency Training Center at Camp Julien, Afghanistan, in the summer of 2009. John Agoglia was the best host a researcher could ask for. He bent over backward to facilitate my work—and provided colorful commentary along the way. Mike Barry, Simon Cocksedge, Matt Galton, and Tracy Vissia welcomed me with open arms. I also had the great fortune to meet some extraordinary fellow researchers, who provided countless hours of conversation, debate, and friendship then and since: Eli Berman, Mike Callen, Austin Long, and Jay Lyall. Bradley Austin, Fotini Christia, Erica Gaston, Stacia George, Whitney Haring-Smith, Chris Krafchak, Nancy Lindborg, Stephanie McPhail, Todd Stone,

Fred Taylor, Heidi Vogt, and members of the Afghan Independent Human Rights Commission all showed me different sides of Kabul and ongoing operations there. Ashraf Ghani provided the most extraordinary insights into Afghanistan's dynamics. And my trip would never have taken place without the generous support (both financial and intellectual) of Mitch Weiss, Sidharth Shah, and the Tobin Project.

At critical moments, John Nagl proved an invaluable supporter, encouraging the project when it was merely an idea, facilitating my travels to Afghanistan, and hosting me at the Center for a New American Security (CNAS) in the final stages of writing. At CNAS, Dave Barno, Andrew Exum, Nate Fick, Dan Kliman, Kristin Lord, Tiffany Sirc, and many others provided helpful support and comments in addition to a welcoming environment for frantic editing.

Extraordinary friends were with me at every stage of writing, reading successive drafts and providing advice and encouragement even when they had surely heard enough about counterinsurgency. Peter Buttigieg, Tarun Chhabra, Sarah Holewinski, Todd Huntley, Tamara Klajn, Natalie Lockwood, Michael Nitsch, Elizabeth Peterson, Ryan Rippel, J. P. Schnapper-Casteras, Brian Sheppard, Neha Sheth, Erin Simpson, Dan Urman, and Previn Warren all provided helpful comments. In addition to reading multiple chapters, Sabeel Rahman and Dale Stephens were frequent interlocutors, and our conversations always clarified my thoughts. Matan Chorev took the heroic step of reading the entire manuscript with characteristic insight. Jenny Paramonov provided helpful research assistance. Vincent Chiao, Drew Dawson, Deborah Dinner, and Jason Marisam provided moral and social support day-in and day-out in our dark wing of Lewis Library. Judge Stephen Williams, Ira Lindsay, Mary Matera, and Urska Velikonja were supportive in the final stages of editing. Bob Allen, Dan Epps, Sandy Henderson, Adam Jed, Elizabeth Theodore, and David Zionts all read sections with the critical eye of a former law review editor. Rachel Kleinfeld and the Truman National Security Project facilitated important conversations. At Oxford University Press, Dave McBride was a wonderful editor. And I could not imagine writing anything even somewhat intelligent on Afghanistan without the support and feedback of Tarek Ghani, whose understanding of policy and practice was at once grounding and challenging.

Finally, I thank my parents and sister for their encouragement and support over the years. Their help and understanding has been invaluable, so it is to them that I dedicate this book.

*The Counterinsurgent's Constitution*

# Introduction

WE LIVE IN an age of small wars. Around the world, warfare is no longer characterized by amassed armies on pitched battlefields or even by tank battalions maneuvering to break through enemy lines. Rather, insurgents hibernate in the shadows, emerging only when ready for devastating attack; they live among the people, indistinguishable from civilians, as they challenge legitimate and illegitimate governments in a protracted struggle for power. The age of small wars brings with it the risk of secession and separatism. It enables regime change and revolution. And it threatens permanent instability and eternal war. The complexity of small wars is staggering, as their sources are as varied as radical ideologies, tribal dynamics, parochial grievances, convenience and social pressure, and imperial memory. Small wars are wars against insurgents and guerrillas.[1] They are fought among the people and are fought for the people. One side's terrorist is another's freedom fighter, one side's liberator is another's tyrant.

Small wars are not new. They have existed for centuries, playing notable roles in some of the most important periods in history. The American Revolutionaries waged an insurgency against the greatest empire since Rome. Napoleon's troops found themselves bogged down in Iberia by Spanish guerrillas. Americans confronted insurgents when they took control of the Philippines during the Spanish-American War, just as the British met resistance in Southern Africa during the Boer War. In the twentieth century, the Chinese Civil War brought with it Mao Zedong's classic analysis of guerrilla strategy. And the American adventure in Vietnam seared into American minds Lawrence of Arabia's maxim: Waging war against insurgents is "messy and slow, like eating soup with a knife."[2]

Despite their persistence throughout history, small wars have never before seemed so important. In recent years, the world has seen insurgencies in Colombia, Nepal, Sri Lanka, and Chechnya, and the world's attention and resources have been captured by the United States' counterinsurgency operations in Iraq and Afghanistan. Within America, military strategists, historians, soldiers, and policymakers have all taken counterinsurgency strategy seriously, making its principles and paradoxes second nature. Indeed, counterinsurgency has perhaps become the most prominent foreign policy strategy since containment and deterrence dominated Cold War thinking. Military strategists recognize that they cannot ignore the tactics and techniques of small wars in favor of their strengths in conventional warfare. Between radical jihadist ideology, state weakness and failure, democratization movements, and the displacement of populations as a result of climate change, small wars will inevitably remain a staple of the military diet.

And yet waging war against insurgents is radically unconventional. Counterinsurgents speak of "winning hearts and minds" and "population-centric warfare." They argue that killing insurgents may not result in victory and that protecting the civilian population is the best way to defeat the insurgency. Counterinsurgents recommend military officials give greater discretion to subordinates, undermining traditional notions of command hierarchy. They even note that soldiers will have to take on greater short-term risks to their own lives and safety in order to secure an area in the long term. In short, counterinsurgency turns conventional warfare on its head.

Perhaps more surprisingly, counterinsurgency rejects the conventional assumption that law exists in opposition to war. Despite commentators from Cicero to the present arguing that "the law is silent between arms" or that law precariously operates as a constraint on military operations, counterinsurgents of all stripes actually believe that law is *central* to success. British counterinsurgency strategist Sir Robert Thompson once wrote that "the greatest importance should be attached to the Constitution, from which all authority is derived." The Australian counterinsurgency theorist David Kilcullen has stated that a "constitutional path is needed, but lacking, to counter global *jihad*." French counterinsurgent Roger Trinquier argued that "[t]he army must apply the law without hesitation." And the U.S. Army and Marine Corps' *Counterinsurgency Field Manual* declares that "[e]stablishing the rule of law is a key goal and end state," and it mandates that U.S. forces follow domestic and international law in order to maintain their legitimacy.[3]

The vital importance of law to counterinsurgency goes beyond the textbooks of military strategists. Iraq and Afghanistan drafted and ratified constitutions, even as insurgents were plotting against the state. Millions of dollars are spent each year to support law schools and courts, prisons and bar associations, in the name of building the rule of law. The difficulty of distinguishing between civilians and combatants has created legal controversy over the use of force and aerial drone attacks. Corruption among police and government officials threatens to undermine counterinsurgency efforts in Afghanistan. And the failure of lawful procedures at Abu Ghraib and Guantanamo Bay has been a source of motivation for insurgents.

By any account, law plays an important part in counterinsurgency operations. But what is less clear is precisely why law is crucial to counterinsurgency, how law operates during counterinsurgency, and what steps strategists, soldiers, and lawyers should take to incorporate law into counterinsurgency operations. These questions are the subject of this book. I argue that law and counterinsurgency strategy are interconnected, and I explore the consequences of taking counterinsurgency strategy seriously for law and legal operations.

## *The Varieties of Counterinsurgency*

Before venturing into the relationship between law and counterinsurgency, it is necessary to clarify what is meant by the term "counterinsurgency." Despite years of operations in Afghanistan and Iraq, the publication of the U.S. Army/Marine Corps Field Manual 3–24 *Counterinsurgency*, and a veritable renaissance of writing by scholars, historians, and policymakers, there is still considerable debate over what exactly counterinsurgency is. Counterinsurgency is conventionally defined as the "military, paramilitary, political, economic, psychological, and civic actions taken by a government to defeat insurgency."[4] Given the breadth of this formulation, it is probably no surprise that "counterinsurgency operations" often have a kitchen-sink flavor: they include killing and capturing insurgents and also reconciling with them, arming local militias and also training state-run security forces, working with local power brokers and also rooting out corruption. Greater clarity about the varieties of counterinsurgency is therefore essential.

The conventional wisdom is that there are two types of counterinsurgency: enemy-centric and population-centric. The *Counterinsurgency Field Manual* and the United States embrace "population-centric" counterinsurgency, a strategy that focuses on winning over the population by protecting the people, establishing governance, building the rule of law, and stabilizing the economy. Through this range of operations—military, political, and economic—the government can gain the trust, obligation, and support of the people, deny the insurgency that support, and eventually see the insurgency wither. Under a population-centric counterinsurgency strategy, its advocates argue, the insurgency can only be defeated when it has no sanctuary or support from the population.

Population-centric counterinsurgency is traditionally opposed to "enemy-centric" counterinsurgency. An enemy-centric counterinsurgency strategy holds that the best way to defeat an insurgency is to kill or capture enemy forces through traditional military operations. It eschews the idea that counterinsurgents must be nation-builders as well as warriors, that attention to political, social, and cultural factors is the path to success, and that legitimacy is crucial to success. To be sure, population-centric counterinsurgents also recognize that killing and capturing is an important element to their approach, but they do not believe that it can, by itself, create sustainable order in the country. As population-centric counterinsurgents often say, "we cannot kill or capture our way to victory."

As an analytic matter, however, the distinction between enemy- and population-centric counterinsurgency is relatively unhelpful in understanding contemporary counterinsurgency strategy. The central contribution of the distinction is population-centric counterinsurgency's recognition that insurgencies rely upon populations for intelligence, shelter, and other forms of support. Insurgencies operate in a social context, so factors beyond simply killing and capturing insurgents may be relevant to defeating the insurgency. However, the distinction is of limited benefit because there may be many different ways to engage the population. For example, using violence against the population to punish them for supporting the insurgents is quite literally a population-centric strategy. Indeed, indiscriminate bombing campaigns and punitive measures against civilians have been used throughout history as a population-centric approach to defeating insurgents. Moving away from violence, population-control measures are also population-centric, even though they too, in many cases, have few of the humanitarian components that most advocates of contemporary counterinsurgency herald. When the British first placed Malayans into resettlement camps in the early 1950s, the population-centric action actually meant horrid living conditions, little education and public services, and no self-government. In short, the trouble with "population-centric counterinsurgency" as the defining term for modern counterinsurgency is that it only recognizes that the population is relevant. It does not say much about *how* to treat the population.

A second definitional challenge is whether counterinsurgency is a technocratic enterprise, consisting of tactics and operations, or whether it is a policy choice with strategic consequences.[5] The word "counterinsurgency" itself is often used to refer to both, but understanding the difference between counterinsurgency-as-policy and counterinsurgency-as-technocracy requires a more textured understanding of the varieties of counterinsurgency policies and tactics that a state can employ. As policy, counterinsurgency can take three basic forms: repressive counterinsurgency, minimalist counterinsurgency, and progressive counterinsurgency. These categories are ideal types—pure species of counterinsurgency. Any practical counterinsurgency effort is going to incorporate elements from each of these categories in different degrees because every counterinsurgency is different, depending on its context. But it is nonetheless helpful to consider them separately to gain analytic clarity about their central aims and means.

A repressive counterinsurgency policy focuses on defeating the insurgents with little regard for humanitarian concerns. As a policy, repressive counterinsurgency takes a hardline approach: victory is nothing less than a territory in which the insurgency is completely eradicated. To attain this end, the repressive counterinsurgent is willing to adopt brutal means. Force, not persuasion, is the most effective way to counter the insurgency. Repressive counterinsurgency's corresponding tactics and operations center on the power of the counterinsurgent. Population-control measures—from curfews to resettlement—enable the counterinsurgent to control the local environment tightly. Military operations against the enemy are the central tactic for reducing insurgent strength. And military operations against the population punish the people for supporting the insurgency and encourage them to stop providing intelligence, sanctuaries, and support to the enemy.

A minimalist counterinsurgency policy seeks not to eradicate the insurgency completely but instead to manage the insurgent problem in the short to medium term. It pursues limited and potentially transient action in order to counter the insurgency. Its vision of victory is not permanent, and its approach may not be sustainable in the long run. Success simply means reducing violence *now*. Minimalist counterinsurgency may be particularly appealing to foreign counterinsurgents, who often face domestic political pressure to end involvement in the conflict. Minimalist counterinsurgency enables them to reduce violence in the short run, declare victory, and return home. The primary means of minimalist counterinsurgency, therefore, focus on the counterinsurgent reducing its ambitions by accepting some level of insurgent presence. Reconciliation and reintegration are perhaps the most important tactics for minimalist counterinsurgency: they seek to end the insurgency by co-opting the insurgents. But they are a shallow form of victory because they inevitably require making limited concessions to the insurgents. Corporatism is another tactic: counterinsurgents can buy off powerful local actors or insurgent groups in order to gain their support in the short run. When funds run dry, the insurgents may again take up arms, but in the short term, peace can come at a manageable price. Finally, counterterrorism is a crucial tactic of minimalist counterinsurgency. Either through law enforcement or military operations by special forces, counterterrorism can manage the worst excesses of an insurgency: violence against the people and the state. However, counterterrorism alone is less likely to address the root causes of the insurgency or bring an end to the insurgency as a whole.

Progressive counterinsurgency embraces the idea that warfighting is state-building and that the only way to achieve a sustainable order in a territory is to gain the trust, obligation, and support of the population. As a policy, progressive counterinsurgency aims for complete victory, but it seeks victory primarily through persuasion rather than force. It imagines a state in which the political community remains intact, with every citizen feeling an obligation to the government and to each other. As a result, repressive tactics can often be counterproductive, because they risk alienating groups within the population rather than persuading them to join forces with the government. While progressive counterinsurgency does recognize the need for force, its central thrust consists of operations designed to win over the population. Tactically and operationally, progressive counterinsurgency focuses on (re)building the institutions of the state. Programs in security, governance, the rule of law, and economic stability—the theory goes—can help win the support of the population for the government, and thereby reduce the support the people provide to the insurgents. As a result, progressive counterinsurgency is decidedly evolutionary: it operates over an extremely long period of time precisely because it is very difficult to win over the obligation of a people who fear, distrust, or have little faith in the government's ability to provide the basics of a desirable social and political order.

Some might object to calling this last form of counterinsurgency *progressive*, given that term's connotations in American politics. But the term is faithful to this strand of counterinsurgency's aims. The central goals of the American Progressives of the early twentieth century are not so dissimilar to those of the progressive counterinsurgent: building a robust national community, developing and modernizing the institutions of state to deal with complex changes and powerful interests within society, regaining mastery over social forces through political self-determination, and being willing to reform and innovate. The American Progressives thus focused on making police less corrupt and more professional, creating a melting pot that would build national identity, and increasing self-determination through the direct election of senators and expansion of suffrage to women. Progressive counterinsurgents are surprisingly similar in their overarching approach.

Throughout the book, I consider all three types of counterinsurgency policies and their corresponding tactics and operations, though I focus primarily on the progressive approach. Some critics might argue that this focus is misguided if the repressive approach is more effective at defeating insurgencies. But efficacy does not alone define strategy. Strategy is a function of goals and the means to achieve those goals—and both the goals and the means are constrained by shared values. Thus, an "effective" approach may be rejected because it is anathema to a nation's values, and a more difficult strategy (from the perspective of efficacy) may be embraced because it accords with a nation's values. Modern democracies are largely foreclosed from embracing a repressive strategy: their domestic publics will rarely, if ever, embrace a strategy centered on killing civilians indiscriminately or resettling populations. The progressive strategy, in contrast, aligns with some of the highest values in the Western tradition: self-government and humanitarian action. Second, regardless of whether the progressive counterinsurgency strategy is the most effective approach to defeating insurgencies, it is central to modern warfare. Perhaps most importantly for my purposes, the U.S. government has formally adopted the progressive strategy: two presidents of different political parties have pursued it; the military has elevated it to the level of formal doctrine in the *Counterinsurgency Field Manual*; a generation of military officers has lived the strategy in Iraq and Afghanistan; and even civilian agencies like the State Department are reforming their structures and programs to improve their efficacy in counterinsurgency environments. Given the importance of progressive counterinsurgency to the actual and anticipated conduct of operations by the U.S. government, its consequences for law and legal operations are worthy of extended exploration.

## *The Logic of Insurgency and Counterinsurgency*

Understanding the relationship between law and counterinsurgency requires first grasping the basic logic of insurgency and counterinsurgency. An insurgency is an organized, protracted struggle designed to weaken and displace the authority and legitimacy of a government or occupying power.[6] Insurgency warfare is political warfare, with the insurgents seeking to gain political power and authority over a population. During this quest for power, insurgents rely on failures of the government—failure to preserve order, to accommodate diversity, to leave populations alone, to provide jobs and economic security, to embrace an alternative ideological vision. The government's failures create a rift between the people and the state, and as the gap widens, political obligation and order gradually unravel. Into this breach rushes the insurgency. Insurgents may have fewer resources than counterinsurgents, but as the *Counterinsurgency Field Manual* says, success in the early stages of insurgency only requires "sowing chaos and disorder anywhere; the government fails unless it maintains a degree of order everywhere."[7]

Insurgents rely on the population for new recruits, food, shelter, and logistical support. In gaining the support of the population, whether genuine or coerced, the insurgency denies that support to the government, reducing its intelligence-gathering capabilities, preventing the reestablishment of public services, and further eroding the bonds of political obligation. If successful in disrupting the government's ability to maintain political order and obligation, insurgents may develop a "counterstate" that provides security and essential services. Hezbollah in Lebanon is exemplary in providing social services and governance to the population in areas it controls, but it is by no means unique. The Taliban insurgency in Afghanistan maintains courts, shadow governors, tax assessors, and even an ombudsman for locals to report grievances against Taliban commanders. The creation of a counterstate solidifies the insurgency's support among the population, and it is the final step on its path to power.

In the face of the insurgency's challenge to its authority, the government has two options: force and reform. With force, the government seeks to eradicate the insurgency, to purge from its political community the rebels who would undermine it. With reform, the government recognizes that the insurgents have tapped into potentially legitimate grievances and that the broken social order can only be rebuilt by reforging the ties of political obligation with the aggrieved populations. At different stages in the insurgency, each strategy may prove successful: an incipient insurgency can be crushed before it gains a foothold with the population. A successful insurgent counterstate may necessitate constitutional reform, coupled with secession or the granting of local autonomy.

In the throes of insurgency, however, each strategy alone places the government in a position of peril. Force without reform has the potential to create a popular backlash and fuel the insurgency further, as military crackdowns alienate innocent bystanders. Even states that pursue force alone and with some degree of success pay a significant penalty: their repressive counterinsurgency tradition is decried as state-sponsored terrorism, and they are condemned as international pariahs, criminals against humanity. On the other hand, reform without force risks acquiescing to undesirable policies that a passive majority rejects. Unrelenting extremists do not compromise and may simply need to be killed or captured. Appeasement places power into the hands of the insurgents who can extort contemptible conditions from irresolute counterinsurgents.

The government's goal, then, is to reestablish order through a combination of force and reform, military power and political persuasion. All governments use both coercion and consent to maintain order, but in the throes of insurgency, progressive counterinsurgents argue that the balance must turn to consent. The reason is simple: the key to success in political warfare is the support of the people. Insurgents rely on them to survive. So to defeat the insurgency, counterinsurgents must therefore deny the insurgents their source of strength: the population. By separating the insurgents from the population, counterinsurgents disrupt the insurgency's intelligence networks, supplies, and freedom of movement, leaving them free for military targeting. Once the population is secure, the government can then rebuild its relationship with the population, thereby ensuring that the insurgency will not return to power. Not to be outdone, the insurgents will themselves compete for the population because they need its support in order to establish a counterstate. Each must therefore try to convince the population that it is a legitimate authority. If one side fails, the population will simply support the other side.

In winning popular support, progressive counterinsurgents apply a "full-spectrum" of programs: military, political, economic, and social. Militarily, they focus on clearing the insurgents from population centers, providing security to the population, and minimizing collateral damage to civilians. Politically, counterinsurgents undertake reforms to the government and the system of the rule of law, expanding the franchise, reconciling with former enemies, holding elections, rooting out corruption, and improving access to justice. Economically, counterinsurgents seek a stable environment that fosters reconstruction and development projects. Socially, counterinsurgents provide essential services, like water, sewage, and trash, and they respect local religious and cultural customs. Through operations in each of these arenas, progressive counterinsurgents seek to regain popular legitimacy and rebuild the social and political order.

## Law in the Age of Small Wars

Legal issues pervade full-spectrum counterinsurgency operations. In securing the population from the insurgents, counterinsurgents are confronted with subversives who wear no uniforms and move fluidly through the civilian population. Determining who exactly is a civilian and who is a combatant is challenging to say the least. Who can counterinsurgents target—and who should they target? How much collateral damage is allowed, how much is counterproductive? In counterinsurgency, reconciliation promises to reunify the political community, ending the insurgency by co-opting the insurgents. But reconciliation may preclude prosecuting war criminals and human rights violators. When should counterinsurgents think about reconciling with former enemies? How can truth commissions, war crimes prosecutions, and purges from political office be designed to accelerate the end of hostilities, while still respecting the demands of justice? Strengthening the rule of law is central to effective counterinsurgency strategy. But in many places, formal court systems are little used, displaced by traditional tribal processes. Should counterinsurgents recognize and legitimate these traditional approaches? Or should they focus on building national police forces and centralized courts?

Throughout this book, I argue that taking counterinsurgency seriously requires rethinking the conventional approach to legal questions during conflict and postconflict situations. Each of the book's three parts opens with a chapter outlining a crucial aspect of counterinsurgency theory and strategy: its approach to warfighting, its understanding of the transition from war to peace, and its theory of reconstruction. In these chapters, I show how counterinsurgency theory and strategy take an unconventional approach to those topics. Parts of these chapters summarize counterinsurgency's basic tenets, but I have also tried to contribute to counterinsurgency theory by integrating relevant ideas from political theory and political science, history, law, and social theory. Subsequent chapters in each part explore how counterinsurgency's insights and framework require rethinking corresponding legal issues.

Part I begins with the laws of war. The laws of war were designed on the assumption that the strategy for victory in warfare is to destroy the enemy— to kill or capture enemy forces. While this may have been true of conventional warfare, counterinsurgency rejects the kill-capture strategy and even suggests that it can be counterproductive. Instead, counterinsurgents follow a win-the-population strategy that focuses on protecting the population, establishing sound governance, building the rule of law, and stabilizing the economy.

This shift in military strategy creates a disconnect between the strategic foundations of the laws of war and counterinsurgency strategy. Addressing this disconnect involves revisiting the inherited approaches to many issues within the laws of war: the targeting of combatants, occupation law, detention policy, the use of nonlethal weapons, and compensation for civilian casualties. In each of these areas, chapter 2 shows, the result is not to eviscerate or weaken the humanitarian aims of the laws of war. Traditionally, states are said to comply with the laws of war out of reciprocal advantage: if both sides constrain themselves according to law, neither is at a military disadvantage. In small wars, however, reciprocity fails because insurgents do not follow the laws of war. But the insurgents' failures provide no license for the counterinsurgent. Rather, they redouble the counterinsurgent's commitment to law and humanitarian operations. Counterinsurgents must comply with the laws of war and with humanitarian principles in order to maintain their legitimacy and win over the population. Strategic self-interest thus provides the foundation for compliance with law in the age of small wars. And it suggests that lawyers and counterinsurgents alike should see military strategy and humanitarian goals as aligned, rather than in conflict.

In addition to rejecting the kill-capture strategy in favor of the win-the-population approach, counterinsurgency abandons conventional war's idealized model of crisp, clean transitions between war and peace, conflict and postconflict. This is the subject of part II. Counterinsurgency's transitions from war to peace are turbulent transitions. War moves to peace through fits and starts, evolving over a long period of time. Territories won by hard fighting can backslide from peace into war, and even into the hands of the insurgency. Different areas of the country see different levels of conflict; one province may be under the control of the insurgents, another held firmly by the government, a third mired in chaotic conflict. Perhaps most striking, traditionally postconflict operations take place not after the conflict but in its midst. Indeed, counterinsurgency holds that building the rule of law, establishing governance, and providing essential services are necessary to win over the population and are partly constitutive of success. The result is that any postconflict program must take into account the dynamics of conflict and must be integrated into the larger strategy for victory.

In turbulent transitions, then, legal programs become weapons of war that can win over the population, persuade the insurgency to lay down their arms, or punish insurgents for hostile recalcitrance. Chapter 4 explores how transitional justice programs—truth and reconciliation commissions, war crimes prosecutions, purges, and reparations—can contribute to ending an insurgency. Reconciliation is a central strategy of counterinsurgency, dividing compromising guerrillas and wayward locals from intractable enemies and ending the rebellion through negotiation rather than force. At the same time, however, reconciliation inevitably narrows the scope of transitional justice programs. Designing transitional justice during counterinsurgency therefore requires attention to the strategic context in which these programs operate—and necessitates crafting programs that can accelerate the end of conflict, while simultaneously meeting the population's need for justice.

In embracing turbulent transitions, part III argues that counterinsurgency takes a radically different approach to reconstruction from the popular peacebuilding and postconflict reconstruction narratives. Turbulent reconstruction sees warfighting and state-building as reinforcing. Effective military operations involve funding, logistical and transportation capacities, recruits, and supplies, each of which requires mobilizing and institutionalizing the community's resources. Mobilizing the population builds political and social obligation and order, thereby undermining the sources of insurgent support. Successful warfighting can therefore accelerate state-building, which, in turn, facilitates warfighting. However, mobilizing the population is impossible without understanding the population and tailoring social order to the population's needs and aspirations. Centralized, top-down approaches accommodate diversity poorly, rarely adapt to complex social dynamics, and often fail to incorporate popular participation in the design and implementation of policy. Counterinsurgency's strategy for reconstruction is therefore decidedly local. Its bottom-up approach, inspired more by sociology and anthropology than the standardized templates of postconflict reconstruction, involves mobilizing and empowering local communities along the full spectrum of social power: political, military, economic, social, and cultural affairs.

In light of the dynamic and local nature of reconstruction, the rule of law itself appears less as a bureaucratic system of coercive force and more as an ongoing work in progress, defined by local diversity and the nexus of warfighting and state-building. When it comes to building the rule of law, chapters 6 and 7 argue, counterinsurgents must focus less on developing centralized court systems and more on supporting institutions that work at the local level, including nonstate community dispute resolution processes. In training police forces, counterinsurgents must focus less on capturing insurgents and more on protecting the population through gendarmerie forces and community policing strategies. In designing the constitutional order, counterinsurgents must focus less on constraining government authority and more on mobilizing and unleashing community power.

## The Organic Approach

In following the laws of war, designing justice and reconciliation programs, and building the rule of law, I argue that counterinsurgents should follow an *organic* approach. To be organic, counterinsurgency strategy must embrace the mutual interdependence of every aspect of local life. Organic interdependence means more than just connections between different arenas of social life, like economics and politics. It involves *mutuality* between the parts: the individual elements cannot maintain themselves without each other. An organic counterinsurgency strategy has four features. First, it is focused on winning over the population and rebuilding political obligation, rather than simply killing and capturing insurgents, because people are the foundation of social and political order in any community. Second, it is full-spectrum, embracing every element of social life and power: military, political, economic, ideological, legal, and cultural. Third, it is evolutionary, constantly developing and growing, and seeking patiently to make incremental progress over a long period of time. And finally, it is bottom-up, based on the local context and conditions. The bottom-up approach recognizes that the local people are not merely passive recipients or teachable students but, rather, independent agents, whose actions are as important, if not more important, than those of a counterinsurgent. This approach mobilizes the population, rooting activities in their participation. And because the counterinsurgent becomes an active participant in the local community, it is grounded in the local culture. As a result of its contextual nature, an organic counterinsurgency strategy is constantly in flux, dynamically adapting to the turbulent environment.

The organic approach to law and legal issues follows these same characteristics and stands in stark contrast to the dominant approach to these issues during conflict and postconflict periods. Too often practitioners and commentators see the legal world as fixed, formal, hierarchical, and institutional. They see the law as doctrines codified in legal texts. Military strategy and legal permissibility are thus completely separate. They see justice as black and white. Because justice must be served, negotiation or reconciliation with enemies is abhorrent. And they see the rule of law as based on the command of the sovereign, enforced by centralized bureaucratic institutions like national police forces and court systems. The rule of law therefore looks much like a Western legal system, with adversarial procedures, judges in black robes, and columned courthouses. In sum, the dominant approach to legal questions in conflict and postconflict periods is based on an idealized image of a formalistic legal world.

Just as counterinsurgency rejects conventional warfare's strategies in favor of winning over the population, so too must counterinsurgency's law reject the conventional approach to legal issues. The organic approach holds that legal issues are embedded in society and integrated with strategy. The law grows and develops based on the conditions on the ground, varying by time and place. Law shapes popular sentiment, even as popular sentiment guides its development. Legal issues are defined not only by codified legal texts but also by their application, the people's reactions and responses, and the people's own forms of social organization. Under the organic approach, counterinsurgents must therefore align what is legal and what is popularly legitimate in determining who to target for airstrikes. Counterinsurgents must embrace locally driven forms of resolving disputes, even if those practices diverge from familiar court practices and procedures. And counterinsurgents must balance prosecutorial justice with the need to reconcile former insurgents and unify the population. Because it is crafted through grassroots consent and fortified by popular legitimacy, counterinsurgency's law depends less on an idealized vision of a stable, developed legal system and more on what the people will actually accept. Constantly changing and adapting to local circumstances, the organic approach enables the population to shape the rules and practices that govern them.

Legitimacy is at the heart of the organic approach. Legitimacy is "the perceived obligation to comply with the directives of an authority, irrespective of the personal gains or losses associated with doing so."[8] Illegitimate governments gain compliance with their actions only through force. In stable systems, an illegitimate government may have great longevity. But in the midst of insurgency, the population has the opportunity to reject the illegitimate government and can easily take up arms against it. In legitimate governments, by contrast, the population supports the political authority's actions and complies with them out of obligation. Because insurgents and counterinsurgents seek to win the population's support, both attempt to bolster their legitimacy while diminishing the legitimacy of the other.

The source of legitimacy can be either legal or sociological. An action is legally legitimate if it follows the procedures of the legal system. It does not matter if a person disagrees with an outcome or even if all of society disagrees with an outcome: the legal process is what gives the action legitimacy.[9] In contrast, an action is sociologically legitimate only when "the relevant public regards [the action] as justified, appropriate, or otherwise deserving of support."[10] To be sure, the legitimacy of the legal system itself rests on sociological legitimacy, but decisions arising from legal processes have power independent of agreement with the ultimate outcome. In other words, where legal legitimacy is supported by process, sociological legitimacy is supported by belief.

The crux of the organic approach derives from the relationships between law, legitimacy, and power. Following a legal process can result in a person perceiving an action to be legitimate even when she disagrees with the action as a substantive matter. Law therefore has the ability to legitimize the exercise of power. Whether government engages in the use of military force, regulation of behavior, adjudication of disputes, or channeling of dissent into politics, it is exercising power. Some members of the population will inevitably be dissatisfied with the substantive decisions of the government or its tribunals. Nonetheless, the government can gain the support of the population for its actions if it follows legal rules, procedures, and structures. This is the promise of legal legitimacy. All counterinsurgency operations involve exercising or expanding power over the population. Counterinsurgents use power when they seek to extend the writ of the government throughout the territory, to repair the bonds of political obligation between the aggrieved population and the government, to establish courts and resolve disputes, to reconcile with former enemies, and to destroy irreconcilable insurgents. Whether this exercise of power is effective or counterproductive turns largely on whether it is legitimate—and thus on its alignment with law. The power of law is that it legitimizes power.

Though legal legitimacy is necessary, it is not sufficient for understanding the counterinsurgent's use of power. In seeking to rebuild the bonds of political obligation, counterinsurgents must operate in accordance with both legal and sociological legitimacy because divergences from either can be exploited by the insurgents to undermine the government's authority. Actions that are sociologically legitimate but legally questionable may ultimately alienate the population. For example, providing development funds for popular infrastructure projects may be sociologically legitimate, but if funds are provided through informal dealings with corrupt leaders, rather than by transparent, fair processes, the counterinsurgent may be seen as corrupt and hypocritical. Likewise, actions that are "technically legal" but sociologically abhorrent will alienate the population despite their legality. Families who lose loved ones due to collateral damage will not likely be consoled by the fact that the use of force was proportional and therefore legal. Significantly, what is sociologically legitimate changes based on time, place, and context. Over time, building trust may expand the range of legitimate activities. Within a country, regional variation may create vast differences in legitimate behavior. Across contexts, legitimacy changes, such that breaking up crowds may be acceptable after an attack but unacceptable during a funeral procession. Despite so many variations, counterinsurgents must always operate in accordance with both legal and sociological legitimacy. Legality without legitimacy is no savior.

Counterinsurgency is attuned to legitimacy, legality, and popular perceptions because it is political warfare—war aimed at reconstructing social and political order. For the same reason, counterinsurgency emphasizes integrating all of the tools of government action—political, economic, social, cultural, and military—in order to gain victory. Law too can operate as one of the weapons in the counterinsurgent's arsenal. Law is not just a set of rules that evaluate actions and deem them legal or illegal. It is a set of interventions, those policies that society uses to structure the interactions and behaviors of its people. Establishing courts and the rule of law can be a tool for preventing disputes from spiraling out of control. Prosecuting specific insurgent groups can signal condemnation of groups with particular aims rather than all groups of disgruntled citizens. In political conflicts, law is inevitably an instrument of war.

During counterinsurgency, law therefore operates as both an asset and a vulnerability. It is an asset when used to maintain or increase legitimacy for the government; it is a vulnerability when it is violated because the violation can be exploited to undermine legitimacy. To harness law's power as an asset and protect against law's danger as a vulnerability is the counterinsurgent's task. Counterinsurgents cannot simply ignore legal processes or adhere only to the law's technical commands. The organic approach requires integrating law, legitimacy, and strategy.

In pursuing an organic approach, international counterinsurgents face greater challenges than their domestic counterparts. A purely domestic counterinsurgency features the government waging war against an insurgency. An international counterinsurgency involves a third-party actor—an international organization like the United Nations or a foreign country like the United States—either assisting a government with its counterinsurgency operations or itself waging war against a local insurgency. Third-party counterinsurgents are more likely to intervene in the strongest insurgencies because weak insurgents will have long since failed in their quest for power. Third-party counterinsurgents also suffer from a knowledge gap—a lack of local cultural and political knowledge and a dearth of intelligence networks to gain information about local dynamics. This knowledge gap is dangerously wide because the organic approach is rooted in understanding local dynamics. Third-party counterinsurgents face domestic political constraints in time, resources, and strategies that potentially hamstring their effectiveness.[11] And they are more likely to be of dubious legitimacy from the moment of their intervention simply because they are outsiders. Whether to intervene at all is a separate question from the role law plays in the midst of counterinsurgency.

But domestic or international, the counterinsurgent's mindset is similar when it pursues an organic approach based on popular legitimacy.

Perhaps the greatest challenge to the organic approach to counterinsurgency is that it assumes that the counterinsurgent is sympathetic and worthy of support. Yet not all counterinsurgency is desirable and not all insurgency is undesirable. Some counterinsurgents may be repressive regimes with little popular legitimacy, and some insurgents may legitimately seek political freedom. Despite this challenge, the strategies and tactics of the organic approach can be applied equally to insurgent and counterinsurgent. Because insurgents are political challengers with political aims, they too seek legitimacy and power—and can use law to further their ends. This is precisely why insurgent groups such as the Taliban often use legal operations like courts to further their goals. Indeed, when an insurgency gains control of a territory, it becomes, in effect, a counterinsurgent that seeks to defeat the government's opposition to its political authority. To be sure, insurgents may have greater difficulty than the government in implementing certain programs because they have comparatively fewer resources. But insurgents have long proven creative in finding supporters, and the disproportionate allocation of resources does not change the fact that the legal regime and strategy can be applied even-handedly to both insurgents and counterinsurgents.

The unique nature of the win-the-population counterinsurgency strategy also reduces this problem. Designed to increase legitimacy and popular support, the strategy suggests that all counterinsurgents pursue legitimate means as they consolidate power, regardless of whether they are authoritarian or democratic, ill-motivated or altruistically motivated. This strategy involves building the rule of law, expanding social and other essential services, and ensuring civilian security—and may even expand to negotiating a settlement, revising public policies, or rewriting the constitution. In these cases, even the authoritarian or ill-motivated counterinsurgent that follows a win-the-population strategy will be pursuing policies that the population sees as legitimate. The idea of an authoritarian state or imperial democracy consolidating its power over a homegrown, freedom-seeking insurgency may seem distasteful. But if the people welcome the counterinsurgent's governance and the counterinsurgent achieves success through, for example, expanding the electoral franchise, granting local autonomy to the insurgent territory, or fostering economic security, it becomes much harder to argue that the resolution of the insurgency is unjust or illegitimate. Indeed, the ill-intentioned counterinsurgent that pursues legitimate means to consolidate power starts looking better as it develops effective governance through popular legitimacy.

The heart of counterinsurgency strategy is the reconstruction of order and the rebuilding of obligation between the people and their government. The organic approach provides one path to success. Warfighters must follow the dictates of law and humanity in their attacks or cede legitimacy and, with it, popular support and obligation. Legal processes like war crimes prosecutions and truth commissions permit reconciliation and punishment, serving to accelerate the end of the insurgency—if supported by the people. The rule of law helps resolve disputes, govern behavior, and make rules for society, enabling stability and security in daily life. And the constitution provides for a nationwide order that, if designed well, can accommodate the diversity and complexity of local conditions while putting the nation on a path to a resilient and sustainable political order. In each of these areas, law is the link between the people and the political order. It enables them to fight and punish criminals and insurgents. It unites them as a community. And it empowers them to provide for their common future.

# PART ONE

## *Of Law and War*

# *I*

# *The Strategic Foundations of the Laws of War*

EVERY AGE HAS its own form of warfare and its own laws of war, based on the strategies of warfare dominant at the time. The positivists of the nineteenth century saw war as an extension of national policy and therefore conceived the laws of war in contractual terms. In the wake of the total wars of the twentieth century, international lawyers envisioned war as human tragedy, and in the process they reshaped the laws of war to protect civilians and innocent populations. In the face of today's challenges, in this age of small wars, the laws of war must continue to keep up with the realities of warfighting.[1]

The laws of war were created with an assumption that conventional war's strategy—kill or capture the enemy—was the route to victory. Despite tactical innovations such as the absence of uniforms and a networked enemy structure, the war on terror retains the same strategic mindset: to win, simply kill or capture all the terrorists. Counterinsurgency, however, rejects the kill-capture strategy. Instead, counterinsurgents follow a win-the-population strategy that is directed at building a stable and legitimate political order.[2] Winning the population involves much more than just killing and capturing enemy forces. It requires securing the population, providing essential services, building political and legal institutions, and fostering economic development. Though killing and capturing does take place, it is not the primary goal, and it may often be counterproductive, causing destruction that creates backlash among the population and fuels their support for the insurgency.[3] Counterinsurgency strategy is thus starkly different from the strategy that undergirds the laws of war and the debates on legal issues in the war on terror. At the same time, however, counterinsurgency is strikingly humanitarian. Instead of seeing war and law in conflict, with law placing a humanitarian constraint on destructive military operations, counterinsurgency rejects destructive operations, thereby aligning military strategy and humanitarian aims.

## Law in the Age of Conventional War

For over a century, the laws of war have assumed that the central strategy for victory in war is destroying the enemy.[4] This framework can be termed the "kill-capture" approach to victory because in a specific battle, destruction of the enemy is defined by killing or capturing the enemy's forces until the enemy is vanquished or gives up.[5] Not surprisingly, this approach was common to the military strategists of the era immediately preceding the codification of the laws of war. Frederick the Great argued that the objective of war was the "entire destruction of your enemies," and the Swiss theorist Antoine-Henri Jomini, whose contribution to military strategy was linking territorial conquest and victory, believed that "[t]he destruction of the enemy's field armies was the new military aim."[6]

The most famous modern strategist, Carl von Clausewitz, also envisioned a strategy for victory based on a kill-capture approach. For Clausewitz, the "overriding principle of war" was the "[d]estruction of the enemy forces," which can be accomplished by "death, injury, or any other means."[7] Clausewitz coined the term "center of gravity" to define the "hub of all power and movement, on which everything depends."[8] The center of gravity in war was the source of strength for the opponent, and it was the central objective against which force should be directed.[9] For Alexander the Great, Gustavus Adolphus, and Frederick the Great, Clausewitz argued, the center of gravity was the army, and therefore the central feature of warfare was battle against the army. That killing and capturing would define the battle was obvious, for the character of battles, he said, was "slaughter."[10]

Beyond the centrality of battle, Clausewitz also provided the groundwork for the total war theories of the twentieth century in which kill-capture expanded beyond soldiers to the broader population. Clausewitz argued that war involved the interplay of three actors: the people, the military, and the government.[11] The will and power of this trinity would determine the strength of each side. In the early twentieth century, strategists realized that a state's economic and military power were linked. That fact, coupled with development of devastating technologies and air power, refocused military strategy from the enemy's military to its population and government.[12] Total war required mobilization of the entire society and its resources.[13] Giulio Douhet, an Italian military strategist, perhaps put it best: total war required "smashing the material and moral resources of a people . . . until the final collapse of all social organization."[14]

Conventional war focused its attention on the destruction of the enemy—on killing and capturing enemy forces—and, in the age of total war, on destroying the population's will to support the national war machine. What even a brief history of the laws of war shows is that the central principles underlying the laws of war—military necessity, distinction, reciprocity, and inviolability—and the most important provisions of the Hague and Geneva Conventions reflect the assumption that the central feature of warfighting strategy is destroying the enemy, that is, killing and capturing the opponent.[15] As one scholar puts it, "The regulatory potential of the [laws of war] lay in the types of wars anticipated in Europe during the nineteenth century."[16] The centrality of the kill-capture strategy to warfighting has resulted in the laws of war taking two inextricably linked trajectories: their central goal is to limit destructive violence in order to protect humanity, but at the same time, they enable violence by recognizing that war is centered on killing and capturing.[17] In essence, the laws of war are a blueprint for the architecture of legitimate warfare, whose design assumes a kill-capture military strategy.[18]

The modern laws of war can be traced back to the Lieber Code, promulgated by Abraham Lincoln in 1863 as "Army General Orders No. 100."[19] With volunteers filling the ranks of the Civil War Army, ignorance about the laws and customs of war was widespread. The Code, written by Columbia professor Francis Lieber, was a way to professionalize the Army and spread both legal and warfighting principles.[20] The Code inspired similar codes over the next three decades and influenced the 1874 Brussels Declaration and Hague Law starting in 1899.[21]

Lieber's central contribution was the doctrine of military necessity as a limitation on violence, though necessity enabled violence as much as it curtailed it.[22] Under the Code, military necessity comprised "those measures which are indispensable for securing the ends of the war, and which are lawful according to the modern law and usages of war."[23] Military necessity did not allow cruelty, but it permitted expansive kill-capture operations, including

> all direct destruction of life and limb of armed enemies, and of other persons whose destruction is incidentally unavoidable. . . . it allows of the capturing of every armed enemy, and every enemy of importance to the hostile government, or of particular danger to the captor; it allows of all destruction of property and obstruction of the ways and channels of traffic, travel, or communication, and of all withholding of sustenance or means of life from the enemy.[24]

Military necessity even permitted starvation.[25] Lieber himself thought harsh and violent tactics would lead to shorter wars.[26]

Another significant early codification likewise incorporated the kill-capture nature of warfare. In the early 1860s Czar Alexander II of Russia called an international meeting in St. Petersburg to address the recent invention of exploding bullets. The 1868 St. Petersburg Declaration prohibited use of these projectiles but is notable for its description of the relationship between strategy and the law. The Declaration stated its goal as "fix[ing] the technical limits at which the necessities of war ought to yield to the requirements of humanity."[27] It then went further: "[T]he only legitimate object which States should endeavour to accomplish during war is to weaken the military forces of the enemy; [t]hat for this purpose it is sufficient to disable the greatest possible number of men."[28] The St. Petersburg Declaration's goals are notable for two elements. First, there is an acknowledgment, albeit implicit, that killing is privileged in many cases because it is a "necessity" of warfare. Weakening and disabling the enemy would not be banned in war. Second, the Declaration established the principle of unnecessary suffering, alluded to earlier in Lieber's view that necessity does not "admit of cruelty." The laws of war were thus a constraint inspired in opposition to the kill-capture strategy that undergirded warfare. In banning explosive projectiles, the Declaration at once embraced the strategy of destroying the enemy while pursuing the humanitarian goal that unnecessary suffering is eliminated.

In 1899 and 1907 the international community codified the laws of war during two conferences at The Hague.[29] A review of even a few provisions demonstrates the importance of the kill-capture approach. Article 1 of the Regulations appended to Hague Convention IV of 1907, for example, establishes one of the central principles in the laws of war, the principle of distinction between combatants and civilians.[30] As one commentator has noted, "[t]o allow attacks on persons other than combatants would violate the principle of necessity, because victory can be achieved by overcoming only the combatants of a country."[31] The principle therefore establishes that battle against combatants is the central feature of warfare and justifies killing and capturing the enemy.

Other provisions in the fourth Hague Convention's Regulations are similar. Under Article 20, prisoners of war must be repatriated to their home countries, indicating that a belligerent may hold captured enemy forces for the duration of hostilities.[32] Regulations announce that the means of warfare are not unlimited; that poison, actions that result in unnecessary suffering, and assaults on unarmed and surrendered persons are forbidden; and that armies shall not attack undefended towns, under the assumption that they can be occupied without bloodshed.[33] The common thread throughout the

Regulations is that warfare necessitates killing and capturing and that the laws of war can humanize that process, preventing extreme suffering.

Hague law also features the principles of symmetry and reciprocity.[34] Symmetry makes a rule self-enforcing because neither party gets a relative gain from the regulated practice.[35] For example, Hague Declaration 2 of 1899, banning the use of projectiles to spread asphyxiating gases, states that the Declaration is "only binding to the contracting Powers."[36] A related feature is reciprocity: if a belligerent violates the rule, the other side can retaliate in kind.[37] During World War I, when the German army used chlorine gas at the Second Battle of Ypres, their action was condemned by the British, who immediately began planning reprisals and themselves used poison gas at Loos.[38] Fundamentally, the hope of symmetry and reciprocity is that neither side will have an advantage in the battle by using more destructive means. As such, these rules are ultimately driven by the kill-capture imperative.

After the slaughter of World War II, nations saw war less as a matter of national interest and more as a "human tragedy," and they gathered to protect the victims of war.[39] The four Geneva Conventions of 1949 each protect people from the destructive violence that a kill-capture strategy requires. They protect wounded and sick in the field; wounded, sick, and shipwrecked at sea; prisoners of war; and civilians.[40] Yet even as the Geneva Conventions protect, they also enable violence. As the International Committee of the Red Cross (ICRC) commentary puts it, "it is only the soldier who is himself seeking to kill who may be killed."[41] The Geneva Conventions, inspired by humanitarian aims, thus also illustrate the core assumption that war's central feature and strategy is killing and capturing the enemy.

## War on Terror or Counterinsurgency?

Since September 11, 2001, and the wars in Afghanistan and Iraq, lawyers and scholars have worked to determine how the laws of war apply in the war on terror, given its unconventional nature.[42] The categories of international and internal armed conflict do not precisely apply to global terrorist networks, which are neither states that can be party to inter*national* conflict nor solely internal actors in one country.[43] The paradigms of crime and conflict are challenged by acts defined as crimes under law but having the scope of violence common to war.[44] Geographical limitations to a single battlefield are rendered meaningless by global actions.[45] The temporal boundary of war and peace is undermined because, "by its nature, the war on terrorism is unlikely ever to end."[46] The distinction between civilians and combatants is blurred by the obsolescence of pitched battles and the role of supporters and sympathizers.[47] As a result, the line between national security and domestic affairs is obscured, since greater intrusion into the lives of individuals is necessary to identify terrorists.[48] Notably, the war on terror's innovations share a common feature: they are developments in the tactics and operations of the opponents.[49]

These changes have sparked extensive debate as to the extent to which the laws of war apply in the war on terror. Commentators have taken a wide range of positions, and although each individual commentator has a nuanced position, there are three basic groups. The first group essentially argues that the laws of war do not apply in the war on terror. For simplicity, call this the "maximum latitude approach." In a 2002 memo, President George W. Bush linked the nature of the war to the legal regime structuring warfare: "Our Nation recognizes that this new paradigm—ushered in not by us but by terrorists—requires new thinking in the law of war.[50] For the Bush administration, the law of war was less relevant than this declaration perhaps suggested. Former U.S. Deputy Assistant Attorney General John Yoo believed the nation was at war with Al Qaeda, but he was imprecise as to whether that war was an international armed conflict, described in Common Article 2 of the Geneva Conventions, or a noninternational armed conflict, described in Common Article 3.[51] A Justice Department Memo from 2002, referred to frequently as the "Bybee Memo," declared that the war on terror fit neither category because international armed conflicts were limited to states, and noninternational armed conflicts had to occur within one state.[52] Thus, only customary international law applied. The new paradigm of a global war on terror, in then White House Counsel Alberto Gonzales's view, "renders obsolete Geneva's strict limitations ... and renders quaint some of its provisions."[53] As William Taft, another Bush administration legal adviser, announced, "Nothing in the law of war requires a country to charge enemy combatants with crimes, provide access to counsel absent such charges, or allow them to challenge their detention in court."[54]

The maximum latitude approach clearly expresses the kill-capture strategy. On this approach, the war on terror will continue until terrorists around the globe are captured or killed, thus ending the threat. As President Bush declared, "Our war on terror begins with al Qaeda, but it does not end there. It will not end until every terrorist group of global reach has been found, stopped and defeated."[55] Government must therefore "maximize its own ability to mobilize lethal force against terrorists."[56] That the laws of war do not explicitly cover the global nature of terrorism is, on this reading, fortunate, because it enables the kill-capture strategy to go forward unhindered.

The second group in the debate argues that the laws of war and criminal law are each adequate to handle contemporary global terrorism. Call this the "legal doctrine approach." Gabor Rona, a former legal adviser to the Red Cross, notes that "[h]umanitarian law is basically fine," and that "[t]here is little evidence that domestic and international laws and institutions of crime and punishment are not up to the task when terrorism and the War on Terror do not rise to the level of armed conflict."[57] If each package of laws is coherent and effective, then the only remaining question is determining which laws to apply.[58] One set of analysts suggests that terrorism must be treated as a crime because terrorists are not a state and therefore cannot be belligerents under the laws of war.[59] A second set understands the laws of war as applying in the war on terror; they argue that Al Qaeda and other terrorist groups can be understood as triggering either a noninternational armed conflict as described in Common Article 3 of the Geneva Conventions, or if they are working with a state, an international armed conflict under Common Article 2.[60] For this group, the laws of war as currently written are applicable, and there is nothing "quaint" or "obsolete" about Geneva. A final set have acknowledged that placing terrorism within Geneva is a challenge, but they have seen no need to revise the substantive laws; rather, they hope to clarify the threshold determination of which law applies.[61] At least some adherents to the legal doctrine approach have adopted their position partially because of fear of conceding ground to the maximum latitude approach. Recognizing any gaps or holes in the framework of relevant laws would enable exploitation and, ultimately, legal violations.[62] Others are concerned that a hybrid form of law, merging elements of the laws of war and criminal law, would be unprincipled and thus undermine human rights.[63]

Like the maximum latitude approach, the legal doctrine approach sees the kill-capture strategy as central to the war on terror. The difference is fear that the terrorists' tactical innovations will provide governments with the opportunity to undermine the laws of war's constraints. Adherents to this approach follow directly in the tradition of the laws of war—acknowledging the kill-capture nature of warfare and seeking to restrain war's horrors. Professor David Luban captures well the fear of the kill-capture approach. He worries that "the real aim of the war [on terror] is, quite simply, to kill or capture all of the terrorists—to keep on killing and killing, capturing and capturing, until they are all gone."[64] For Luban, the concern is that

> even if al Qaeda is destroyed or decapitated, other groups, with other leaders, will arise in its place. It follows, then, that the War on Terrorism will be a war that can only be abandoned, never concluded. The

War has no natural resting point, no moment of victory or finality. It
requires a mission of killing and capturing, in territories all over the
globe, that will go on in perpetuity.[65]

In a state of perpetual war, particularly one with the unconventional features of the war on terror, the threat to civil liberties and human rights is
considerable.

The third group of scholars acknowledges that the war on terror challenges the laws of war, but instead of finding them inapplicable, these scholars
seek to adapt the laws of war to fit contemporary conflict better. For short-
hand, call this group the "legal innovators." These scholars recognize that the
laws of war were designed for a different kind of warfare—the conventional
war model of massive armies waging war on distinct battlefields.[66] According
to the legal innovators, applying the laws of war to the war on terror and assuming a perfect fit is "anachronistic" because of developments "never even
imagined by the drafters of the Geneva Conventions."[67] Some in this group
go even further, historicizing the laws of war as responding to their particular
context. After all, they note, the laws of war have been revised every twenty-
five to thirty years since their first codification in the 1860s.[68] On that time-
line, since the last major revision—the Additional Protocols of 1977—another
thirty-five years have passed and perhaps a revision is due.

Scholars in this camp have focused on the failure of the crime and war
paradigms.[69] For the legal innovators, the goal is to develop a hybrid model of
law, between war and crime, that is better tailored to terrorists' tactics. Judge
Richard Posner's approach is paradigmatic. Judge Posner believes that the
threat of terrorism is different from traditional internal and external threats
such as criminals and foreign states.[70] Because terrorists fit neither the crime
nor war models, pragmatic judges and legislators must balance and evaluate
the effects a particular safety measure has on the values of security and liberty.[71] Although the conflict is not a conventional war, there is a strong enough
security interest to modify criminal law because the enemy leverages the scope
and destructive capacities of total war.[72]

Professor Bruce Ackerman has also rejected war and crime as appropriate
models, preferring instead the term "emergency" to describe terrorism's threat.
Terrorism is a "product of the free market in a world of high technology," and
even with peace and democracy around the world, fringe groups would still
have the capability to undertake acts of terrorism.[73] The war model is inaccurate because terrorism is not an existential threat and because war allows presidents to use rhetoric to "batter down judicial resistance to their extreme

efforts to strip suspects of their most fundamental rights."[74] The crime model is inaccurate because terrorism, unlike normal criminal operations, challenges the "effective sovereignty" of the state.[75] It does so only momentarily, since terrorists are not trying, on Ackerman's theory, to occupy or govern the state, only to destabilize it.[76] Professor Ackerman prescribes an Emergency Constitution—a statute that would provide for declaration of an emergency after a terrorist attack and would provide heightened security measures to protect against a second strike.[77] This statute would expire if not reauthorized frequently by escalating supermajorities.[78]

Many others have sought to find the appropriate balance between civil liberties and national security. Some focus on human rights law as inspiration for providing a baseline to apply in the context of terrorism; others advocate for a new category of "extra-state" hostilities. Looking to procedures as a way to address the balance between civil liberties and national security, commentators have suggested administrative analogies, establishing tribunals and devising statutory schemes. And one scholar notes that the absence of a clear hybrid model actually results in a flexible ad-hoc model that incorporates components of each approach.[79]

Although the legal innovators recognize that terrorism differs from both crime and conventional war, they often assume that the kill-capture strategy is the primary, or even only, way to increase security and defeat terrorism. Take Judge Posner: he assumes an unimpeded military could find, kill, and capture the terrorists, preventing terrorism and providing security. But he also acknowledges a conflicting value in constitutional rights and liberties. The law's role is to protect rights when the cost of protection outweighs the marginal security gains of a particular safety proposal. Professor Ackerman reaches a similar conclusion through different reasoning. Ackerman believes terrorists have no broad ideological or political agenda, so kill-capture is the only way to stop them. Yet kill-capture and liberty-protecting laws are in conflict. Instead of a balancing test, as Judge Posner suggests, Professor Ackerman advocates for a category of emergency that has a fixed set of provisions that balance security and liberty and would operate for a short period of time. The basic assumption in both cases is that the kill-capture strategy is the central feature of the war on terror and that law gets in its way.

In addition to assuming that the war on terror is defined by a kill-capture strategy, the balancing approach seems unsatisfying as a comprehensive way to think about law in the age of terrorism. The balancing approach merely tacks greater procedures onto the kill-capture approach. Moreover, when the legal innovators attempt to use a principled approach, the outcomes are often

vague or one-sided. Human rights advocates, for example, admit their approach is incompetent to address difficult cases of military necessity.[80] Finally,
the balancing approach also seems narrow in scope. It has a tendency to focus
on domestic law when the problem is global. It also focuses inordinately on
detention, interrogation, and similar issues.

What the legal debates on the war on terror have missed is the fact that,
between 2002 and 2008, military strategists have reconceived the contemporary national security framework from a war on terror to counterinsurgency.
The shift is significant because counterinsurgency rejects the kill-capture
strategy for victory, instead embracing a win-the-population strategy. The
importance of the shift to a counterinsurgency strategy has been noted with
sustained attention from popular commentators, with the most attention
paid to the publication of *The U.S. Army/Marine Corps Counterinsurgency
Field Manual* in 2007.[81] Prominent counterinsurgency strategist John Nagl
even appeared on Comedy Central's *The Daily Show with Jon Stewart* to discuss the *Field Manual.*[82]

There are stark differences between the terrorism and insurgency frameworks.[83] Terrorists are seen as unrepresentative and abnormal outliers in society. Insurgency is the manifestation of deeper, widespread issues in society.
Terrorism isolates terrorists from negotiation or constructive engagement. Insurgency is premised on winning hearts and minds. Terrorists' methods and
objectives are condemned. Insurgents' methods are condemned but their objectives might be reasonable if pursued through political means. Terrorism is
seen as either a law enforcement or a military problem, rooting out a few bad
apples. Insurgency is a social problem, requiring mobilization of all elements
of government power. Counterterrorism is tactical, focusing on catching particular terrorists. Counterinsurgency is strategic, seeking to undermine the
insurgent's strategy and envisioning capture as secondary.[84] In essence, terrorism is subordinate to insurgency. Terrorism is a particular tactic. Insurgency is the rejection of a political order.[85]

The shift from the war on terror framework to the counterinsurgency
framework proceeded roughly in three phases, as military strategists shifted
focus from tactical innovations to the strategic goal of political order. During
the first few years after September 11, national strategy envisioned the security
challenge as the war on terror and focused on killing and capturing terrorists.
In his address to Congress on September 20, 2001, President Bush announced
that the September 11 attacks were an "act of war" and declared that the United
States would eradicate terrorists anywhere around the globe. The United States
would "drive them from place to place, until there is no refuge or no rest."[86]

Between 2004 and 2006, however, there was significant flux in how to describe the global conflict. David Kilcullen, a leading counterinsurgency strategist, wrote in a wide-ranging article in 2004 that the "present conflict is actually a campaign to counter a globalised Islamist insurgency" and offered counterinsurgency as a superior alternative to counterterrorism.[87] Kilcullen sharply distinguished between insurgency and terrorism: insurgency is "a popular movement that seeks to change the *status quo* through violence and subversion, while terrorism is one of its key tactics."[88] In 2005 Stephen Hadley, the National Security Advisor, seemed to agree, writing in the *New York Times* that "military action is only one piece of the war on terrorism" and that while terrorists must be "hunted, captured or killed," "all of the tools of statecraft" would be necessary for victory.[89]

At the time, President Bush rejected the defense establishment's wavering and reiterated that the "war on terror" continued.[90] But by 2007 and 2008, a momentous shift had taken place.[91] In 2007 the *Counterinsurgency Field Manual* was published and became official U.S. Army and Marine Corps doctrine for operations in Iraq and Afghanistan. In Britain, the government decided to stop using the phrase "war on terror."[92] Army Lieutenant General William Boykin, serving as Deputy Undersecretary of Defense for Intelligence, commented: "If we look at is [*sic*] as terrorism, we have a tendency to think that the solution is to kill or capture all the terrorists. That's a never-ending process. . . . We'll never be successful, we'll never get there, if we think that's the primary solution, . . . [b]ut if we approach it from the perspective of an insurgency, we use the seven elements of national power [diplomacy, military, economy, finance, law enforcement, information, and intelligence]."[93] Other officials agreed. Secretary of State Condoleezza Rice stated that "[l]eading security experts are increasingly thinking about the war on terrorism as a kind of global counterinsurgency," and Secretary of Defense Robert Gates argued that "[w]hat is dubbed the war on terror is, in grim reality, a prolonged, world-wide irregular campaign—a struggle between the forces of violent extremism and moderation. . . . [O]ver the long term, we cannot kill or capture our way to victory."[94]

Perhaps most authoritatively, the National Defense Strategy of 2008 does not use the phrase "war on terror" once. Instead, the National Defense Strategy names the conflict the "Long War" and transforms the strategic imperative from kill-capture to broader, "full-spectrum" counterinsurgency operations. Instead of hunting, killing, and capturing terrorists, the conflict

is a prolonged irregular campaign, a violent struggle for legitimacy and influence over the population. The use of force plays a role, yet military efforts to capture or kill terrorists are likely to be subordinate to measures to promote local participation in government and economic programs to spur development, as well as efforts to understand and address the grievances that often lie at the heart of insurgencies. For these reasons, arguably the most important military component of the struggle against violent extremists is not the fighting we do ourselves, but how well we help prepare our partners to defend and govern themselves.[95]

The strategy, in essence, is not limited to kill-capture and is not even *primarily* kill-capture, as the war on terror framework implied. Rather, the "essential ingredients of long-term success include economic development, institution building, and the rule of law, as well as promoting internal reconciliation, good governance, providing basic services to the people, training and equipping indigenous military and police forces, strategic communications."[96] By December 2008 the Department of Defense had declared that irregular warfare, including counterinsurgency, was "as strategically important as traditional warfare."[97]

Counterinsurgency operations are not a new development of the twenty-first century, but they have never before seemed so central to the future of warfare. The national security establishment today believes counterinsurgency wars will be the likely wars of the future.[98] Secretary of Defense Gates has argued that enemies have realized they cannot challenge the military supremacy of the United States and therefore have turned to asymmetric insurgency. "[A]symmetric warfare," he notes, "will remain the mainstay of the contemporary battlefield for some time."[99] Secretary of State Rice agreed and projected that America will remain in this conflict "for many years."[100] And the *U.S. Government Counterinsurgency Guide* states forthrightly that "[i]nsurgency will be a large and growing element of the security challenges faced by the United States in the 21st century."[101] The American role may increasingly be indirect—"building the capacity of partner governments and their security forces"—but counterinsurgency operations will nonetheless take place.[102]

Outside the U.S. context, counterinsurgency operations are a significant feature in global politics. India alone faces multiple insurgencies, of which the most prominent is the Maoist rebellion. Thailand, Indonesia, Pakistan, and Yemen, among other places, also confront insurgent forces. Democratic revolts against authoritarian regimes in the Middle East are insurgencies that have been met with different counterinsurgency strategies: In Egypt, Hosni Mubarak took a reformist approach, changing the constitutional structure and eventually stepping down from office. In Libya, Muammar Qaddafi took a repressive approach, waging war against his own people, thus inviting an international intervention. In the longer term, the consequences of climate change may increase the frequency and power of insurgent movements. Population displacement as a result of flooding or famines can create conditions ripe for insurgents to exploit local suffering and mobilize people against their governments.[103]

If the military is correct that the likely wars of the future will be insurgencies, local and global, then applying the wrong strategy would be disastrous. Even if analysts are wrong about the future, the major U.S. government institutions are all taking counterinsurgency strategy seriously. Both Presidents George W. Bush and Barack Obama embraced counterinsurgency operations in Iraq, Afghanistan, and Pakistan. The U.S. military elevated counterinsurgency strategy to formal doctrine and instituted training programs for soldiers, airmen, and Marines based on the principles and practice of counterinsurgency. The military and State Department have sought to reorganize their internal structures to improve their ability to wage these conflicts. And a generation of military officers, aid workers, and diplomats have spent the defining years of their careers in the midst of counterinsurgency conflicts. For international and national security lawyers, relying on an outmoded notion of strategy for constructing a legal regime might lead to substantial disconnects between military operations and law that are over- or underconstraining, potentially ignored, or, if revised, are based on faulty premises. Rethinking the legal regime thus requires understanding the strategy with depth and precision.

## Counterinsurgency's Strategy for Victory

The significance of the shift from the war on terror to counterinsurgency lies in a shift in the strategy for victory: from kill-capture to win-the-population. Counterinsurgency's win-the-population approach differs from kill-capture in two central ways. First, although counterinsurgency has a place for killing and capturing enemies, kill-capture is not the primary focus. Because insurgents gain strength from the acquiescence of the population, the focus of counterinsurgency is building the population's trust, confidence, and cooperation with the government. Second, counterinsurgency is not limited to military operations. It includes political, legal, economic, and social reconstruction in order to develop a stable, orderly society, in which the population itself prevents the emergence or success of the insurgency. As David Galula once

wrote, "[V]ictory is won and pacification ends when most of the counterinsurgent forces can safely be withdrawn, leaving the population to take care of
itself with the help of a normal contingent of police and Army forces."[104]

Recall that an insurgency is a "protracted struggle conducted methodically, step by step, in order to attain specific intermediate objectives leading
finally to the overthrow of the existing order."[105] In the modern era, insurgency
often "follows state failure, and is not directed at taking over a functioning
body politic, but at dismembering or scavenging its carcass, or contesting an
'ungoverned space.'"[106] The central issue in an insurgency is political power
because "each side aims to get the people to accept its governance or authority
as legitimate."[107]

Insurgencies are social systems that grow organically in local society but
can link globally with other insurgencies.[108] Success in an insurgency depends
on the support, or at least the acquiescence, of the population.[109] To win support or submission, insurgents use disorder to undermine the counterinsurgent's power and legitimacy, and they mobilize support locally and globally.[110]
Among other things, insurgents advocate ideologies, pay individuals to conduct operations, employ violence and intimidation, and exploit local grievances such as communal or sectarian conflicts.[111] Insurgents may have fewer
resources than counterinsurgents, but success in the early stages of insurgency
only requires "sowing chaos and disorder anywhere; the government fails unless it maintains a degree of order everywhere."[112] If successful in disrupting
the counterinsurgents' ability to govern, some insurgents, like Hezbollah in
Lebanon, may develop a "counterstate" that provides security and essential
services.[113] The creation of a counterstate solidifies the insurgent's support
among the population when the government is impotent and the insurgents
can meet the population's needs.

A counterinsurgent's task differs considerably from a conventional warrior's because the enemy is embedded in the local community; focused on
developing popular support or submission; and committed to disrupting a
legitimate, stable political order. Counterinsurgency can be defined as the
"military, paramilitary, political, economic, psychological, and civic actions
taken by a government to defeat insurgency."[114] Success in counterinsurgency
operations "depends on the people taking charge of their own affairs and con-
senting to the government's rule."[115] Because insurgents derive their support
from the local population, only when the local population turns against the
insurgency and actively embraces the political order can the insurgency be
defeated. Counterinsurgents must therefore focus on rebuilding the bonds of
political obligation that unite a people and their government.

Even at this level of abstraction from operational details, it is immediately obvious that counterinsurgency is not centered on a kill-capture strategy. As the *Counterinsurgency Field Manual* states, "killing insurgents . . . by itself cannot defeat an insurgency."[116] As a starting point, it is impossible to kill every insurgent.[117] Insurgents are embedded in the population, indistinguishable from civilians. An insurgency is made up not only of those who engage in combat but also of active and passive supporters.[118] Seeking to kill or capture all insurgent supporters might require targeting much of the nation. Additionally, conducting kill-capture operations against insurgents—whether participants or supporters—may even be counterproductive. "[I]t risks generating popular resentment, creating martyrs that motivate new recruits, and producing cycles of revenge."[119] Because counterinsurgents need to rebuild political obligation, they must not alienate the population. Focusing solely or largely on enemy-centric kill-capture operations risks killing civilians, causing collateral damage, and engaging in repressive techniques that are likely to alienate the population.

Counterinsurgency thus follows a win-the-population strategy. The people, not the enemy, are the center of gravity in counterinsurgency.[120] They are the source of strength for both the insurgents and the counterinsurgents. The central causes of the conflict—for example, local grievances, poor governance, insecurity—are sociopolitical.[121] Addressing the root causes removes the population's reasons for actively or passively supporting the insurgency, and it will result in a withering insurgency. As a result, "all energies should be directed at gaining and maintaining control over the population and winning its support."[122] Traditional military operations—killing and capturing the enemy—are therefore not the central focus of a successful counterinsurgency strategy. Indeed, counterinsurgents need to prevent excessive damage and collateral civilian casualties in order to minimize the risk of backlash and negative feedback loops; and they also need to provide affirmative reasons for the population to support their political order. In other words, "[c]ounterinsurgency is armed social work, an attempt to redress basic social and political problems while being shot at."[123]

The foundations of progressive counterinsurgency theory are the feedback loops between the actions of the insurgent or counterinsurgent and the reactions of the population. Progressive actions lead to popular support, which reverberates to build counterinsurgent strength; repressive actions lead to popular alienation, fueling the insurgency. To establish positive feedback loops and build political obligation, counterinsurgents use the "full spectrum" of possible operations: securing the population; ensuring essential services;

establishing governance structures; developing the economy and infrastructure; and communicating with the population.[124]

Securing the population involves ensuring civil security and training host-nation security forces.[125] Ensuring civil security involves combat operations against insurgent fighters "who cannot be co-opted into operating inside the rule of law."[126] Operations are often small-scale and designed to avoid injuring innocent people both for humanitarian reasons and to win the population's support for the counterinsurgency.[127] Training host-nation security forces gives the population a stake in counterinsurgency and develops their capacity for providing security. Ensuring essential services guarantees that the population has the basic necessities of life: water, electricity, schools, transportation, medical care, and public sanitation.[128] The importance of essential services is not to be underestimated. One influential review showed a direct correlation between insurgent activity in the Baghdad neighborhood of Sadr City and poor provision of power and sanitation.[129] Infrastructure projects employ people, provide basic services, and place a wedge between insurgents and passive supporters.[130]

One of the "most important activities" is establishing governance structures because effective governance will address social problems better than externally provided services.[131] Developing governance includes establishing or strengthening local, regional, and national departments and agencies, creating a justice system, and working to secure fundamental human rights.[132] Ensuring fair and transparent political processes enables self-government and provides a nonviolent path for political expression. Guaranteeing a fair system of justice grants legitimacy to the state's more coercive actions. In some cases, these systems may not exist or function, and counterinsurgents will need to "establish legal procedures and systems to deal with captured insurgents and common criminals."[133] Economic and infrastructure development is also necessary to counterinsurgency because an effective economy gives the population a stake in society. Poor economic conditions provide an opportunity for insurgents' false promises to gain active and passive supporters.[134]

Finally, information operations are central to counterinsurgency and affect each of the prior operations. Every action is part of the information environment, particularly given the speed with which information travels on the Internet and through television.[135] Successful information operations require dialogue between soldiers and the population, a forum for dialogue with the opposition, and avenues for the population to voice its opinions.[136] Transparency is also central to establishing trust and legitimacy; thus, counterinsurgents must publicize treatment of detainees, allow for host-nation leaders and media to tour detention facilities, and even speak and eat with detainees.[137]

Effective information operations can neutralize insurgent propaganda and go a long way toward winning the population's support.[138]

As much as counterinsurgency stresses nonmilitary operations, it is vital to understand that killing and capturing still takes place. Counterinsurgency is war. The need to protect the population from violent insurgents requires not only a robust defense of the civilian population but also the careful and aggressive hunting of insurgents. The goal is to distinguish between reconcilables and irreconcilables. The reconcilables can be won over; the irreconcilables must be killed or captured.[139] The importance of the shift to a win-the-population strategy is not that it eviscerates the need to kill or capture, but rather that it substantially shifts the focus of military operations, the mindset and strategy of the military, and the default position from which the military begins. Destruction and killing is not undertaken lightly and when it does take place, the military is as concerned with its effects on the population as it is on the targets themselves.

Thus far, the discussion of counterinsurgency strategy has been focused on insurgency in one country. What is needed, however, is a strategy for countering *global* insurgency. After all, insurgency is not limited merely to Iraq or Afghanistan; some insurgents seek to transform the entire world by creating a Caliphate uniting the Muslim world and expanding the realm of Islam to all of human society.[140] Countering a global insurgency requires a global strategy. One possible strategy is a collective security approach that uses an international actor such as the UN Security Council as the global counterinsurgent.[141] The problem is that successful counterinsurgency requires considerable interagency cooperation—between political, military, police, administrative, economic, cultural, and other actors. No international organization has such power, nor is the emergence of such an actor likely. Another strategy, relying on one nation to act as the global counterinsurgent, would solve this problem, but that country would face a substantial legitimacy problem, and legitimacy is crucial to winning over the population in counterinsurgency operations.[142] In response to these challenges, David Kilcullen has argued that any strategy must be derived from the nature of the global insurgency itself. Global insurgency is not hierarchical or even networked, but organic and complex. Global insurgency is the set of transnational systems (such as propaganda, logistics, recruitment, and financing) and geographically defined insurgent systems that interact and collectively amount to the global counterstate that opposes the global order.[143] The power of the global counterstate derives not from the specific elements in any particular system but "from the links in the system— energy pathways that allow disparate groups to function in an aggregated fashion across intercontinental distances."[144]

This understanding of global insurgency as a system of systems that derives its strength from its interconnections leads directly to a strategy of disaggregation—a strategy of de-linking and dismantling the various parts of the system, preventing cooperation and connectedness. Disaggregating the global insurgency results in "a series of disparate local conflicts that are capable of being solved by nation-states and can be addressed at the regional or national level without interference from global enemies."[145] Disaggregation requires breaking linkages between regional or global actors and local actors; interdicting transmission of information, finance, materials, and persons between theaters; minimizing outputs like casualties and destruction; and denying sanctuary or ungoverned spaces. Within a particular theater, disaggregation looks like counterinsurgency as described earlier: conducting political, economic, and other operations, and tailoring action to local conditions. Disaggregation thus confronts the global nature of the threat not by applying a global solution but rather by preventing the globalization of insurgency.[146]

From the perspective of traditional warfare, counterinsurgency strategy is radically unconventional. The *Counterinsurgency Field Manual* has captured some of the counterintuitive elements of counterinsurgency as paradoxes. Five are worth noting. (1) "Sometimes, the more you protect your force, the less secure you may be." Traditional warfare encourages protection of one's forces and allows self-defense actions by military forces. In counterinsurgency, a protected military will lose contact with the people and have little understanding of their needs and conditions. Counterinsurgents must instead be embedded in the society—even if they assume greater risks. (2) "Sometimes, the more force is used, the less effective it is." In conventional war, total annihilation would guarantee victory because the enemy force was the center of gravity. Technology and economics thus worked together to develop ever more destructive weapons. In counterinsurgency, greater force means collateral damage and mistakes, which might result in the population losing faith in the counterinsurgent and instead supporting the insurgency. (3) "Sometimes doing nothing is the best reaction." Conventional war allowed for reprisals, retaliation, and even preemptive self-defense. But insurgents seek to provoke the counterinsurgent into overreacting and to exploit those errors in propaganda. The counterinsurgent thus may often determine that an otherwise permissible action may cause more harm than good. (4) "Some of the best weapons for counterinsurgents do not shoot." Counterinsurgency is not limited to or even primarily dominated by military means. "[T]he decisive battle is for the people's minds," which means that "dollars and ballots will have more important effects than bombs and bullets." Finally, (5) "the host nation doing something tolerably is normally better than us doing it well." Conventional strategy focuses on one's own military. Counterinsurgency suggests that building capacity in others is better than acting for oneself. Thus, whenever the host nation's forces can be embedded or included, they should be; and whenever they can undertake operations themselves, they should do so.[147]

These paradoxes demonstrate how different counterinsurgency is from conventional war. Counterinsurgency is defined by a win-the-population strategy for victory, not a kill-capture strategy for victory. It shifts the goals of war from destroying the enemy to protecting the population and building an orderly, functioning society. It expands the scope of operations for purely military operations to a broad set of operations including security, essential services, governance, economy, and information. And it holds that while security is essential, sustainable victory is dependent on more than military prowess.

## 2

# *The Laws of Counterinsurgency Warfare*

IN JULY 2009 General Stanley McChrystal, commander of U.S. and NATO forces in Afghanistan, issued a tactical directive governing the use of force by all U.S. and NATO forces. "[W]e will not win based on the number of Taliban we kill," he wrote. "This is different from conventional combat, and how we operate will determine the outcome more than traditional measures, like capture of terrain or attrition of enemy forces." General McChrystal stressed the importance of limiting civilian casualties and causing excessive damage and went so far as to curtail the use of air attacks and air support, except in cases of self-defense where no other options are available. McChrystal recognized in his directive that this policy was supported by both legal and moral considerations, but he underscored to the troops that the policy was grounded in operational concerns: "[L]oss of popular support will be decisive to either side in this struggle. The Taliban cannot militarily defeat us—but we can defeat ourselves."[1]

McChrystal's directive is perhaps most striking for its outright rejection of the kill-capture strategy in favor of counterinsurgency's win-the-population strategy. Equally important, however, is that the directive takes an organic approach, considering law and strategy together through the lens of popular legitimacy. The directive not only respects legal requirements but also goes beyond the legal constraints of the laws of war, establishing a higher standard for troops to use force. In doing so, it implicitly recognizes a disconnect between the laws of war and counterinsurgency strategy and explicitly roots military policy in the legitimacy of the local population.

The directive is but one example of how the shift from conventional war to counterinsurgency requires reassessing the laws of war in light of the win-the-population strategy. To be sure, not all the principles or doctrines in the laws of war need to be rethought, but counterinsurgents must understand where the laws of war are disconnected from counterinsurgency in order to identify divergences between legal limitations and popular legitimacy. In some cases, the laws of war have not gone far enough in enabling humanitarian operations. The internalization of the combatant's privilege, for example, has left civilians injured as a result of collateral damage with no legal recourse or remedy, when, in fact, civilian compensation would both provide humanitarian relief and strengthen the counterinsurgents' posture with the public. In other cases, the laws of war render necessary and beneficial operations illegal: occupation law prohibits political and social reform, but such reform may be indispensable to counterinsurgency. The use of nonlethal weapons, often illegal, would undoubtedly save lives and assist counterinsurgency.

Contrary to the conventional wisdom that law is opposed to strategy and acts primarily as a constraint on strategy, these examples show that law and strategy are dynamically connected and intertwined. Indeed, counterinsurgency strategy frequently aligns with the underlying goals of the laws of war because strategic self-interest pushes counterinsurgents to operate in accordance with the dictates of humanity. This organic relationship between law and strategy thus not only reveals areas of law that may require revision but also, more importantly, suggests ways in which law and strategy can work together to further their shared aims.

## The Law of Targeting: The Principles of Distinction and Proportionality

Perhaps the most important principle in international humanitarian law, the principle of distinction, holds that "parties to the conflict must at all times distinguish between civilians and combatants. Attacks may only be directed against combatants. Attacks must not be directed against civilians."[2] Distinction's importance cannot be underestimated. It has been called a "cardinal principle" of humanitarian law, the "single most important principle for the protection of the victims of armed conflict," and it is said that "[h]umanitarian law contains no stronger doctrine."[3] Despite its foundational status within humanitarian law, distinction actually grew out of a shift in military strategy. As the eighteenth-century Swiss philosopher and legal theorist Emmerich de Vattel noted,

> in former times, and especially in small States, as soon as war was declared every man became a soldier; the entire people took up arms

and carried on the war. Soon a choice was made, and armies were formed of picked men. . . . At the present day, the custom of having regular armies prevails almost everywhere.[4]

The shift to professional armies provided the necessary elements for distinction—a clear line of demarcation between those who fight and those who do not. Notably, the principle of distinction provides protections and restrictions on both combatants and civilians: the latter are protected from conflict but cannot engage in conflict; the former are protected from civilians attacking them and cannot attack civilians.[5]

The principle manifests itself throughout the laws of war. Additional Protocol I to the Geneva Conventions declares that parties to a conflict "shall at all times distinguish between the civilian population and combatants and between civilian objects and military objectives and accordingly shall direct their operations only against military objectives."[6] To expand on the definition, the laws of war describe what fits in each category. The Hague Conventions applied the laws of war to armies, militias, and volunteer corps as long as they had responsible command, wore a distinctive emblem, carried arms openly, and conducted operations in accordance with the laws of war.[7] The Geneva Conventions followed suit, providing the same criteria for distinguishing combatants and civilians, though in slightly different terms.[8] Given the conditions of struggle during decolonization, Additional Protocol I loosened these requirements somewhat, requiring only that combatants carry arms openly during engagements and preparations for launching an attack.[9] Civilians are defined as any persons who are not combatants.[10]

The "war on terror" has not changed the debate over the principle of distinction. Both prior to September 11 and since, the debate has turned on the fact that it is often difficult to tell whether a person is a civilian or combatant and whether an object is civil or military:[11] Is the civilian that takes up arms each day only to return home each night a civilian or combatant?[12] Is a television station spreading enemy propaganda a military object?[13] The laws of war address these challenges through two provisions. First, civilians are protected "unless and for such time as they take a *direct part in hostilities*."[14] Second, military objectives are those objects whose "destruction, capture or neutralization, in the circumstances ruling at the time, offers a *definite military advantage*."[15] Elsewhere, the Additional Protocols require consideration of the "*concrete and direct military advantage* expected."[16] Each provision has two prongs—the military character of the operations and a direct relationship between the operations and the actor or object—and each is subject to considerable debate.

The military/hostilities prong turns on what counts as "military" or "hostilities." One approach to interpreting these terms includes preparations for attacks and returning from attack, even though those are not, strictly speaking, military activities or hostilities.[17] A more extreme form of this argument even considers civilian support for the war effort as a military activity.[18] On this reading, "military" or "hostilities" includes anything that seeks "to adversely affect the enemy's pursuance of its military objective or goal."[19] Another approach, however, interprets the provision as requiring the use of force or "military activity" directed against the enemy.[20] Some narrow interpretations even exclude objects that are obviously military in nature. As one scholar has noted,

> [t]aken literally, the separate requirement that the attack must offer a definite military advantage means that even an attack on an objective of a military nature would not be lawful if its main purpose is to affect the morale of the civilian population and not to reduce the military strength of the enemy.[21]

Interpreting what constitutes "direct" participation is similarly challenging. One line of thought, expressed in the International Committee for the Red Cross (ICRC) Commentaries, reads the directness requirement strictly, seeking a "direct causal relationship between the activity engaged in and the harm done to the enemy at the time and the place where the activity takes place."[22] Direct causal relationships exist when acts are "intended to cause actual harm to the personnel and equipment of the armed forces."[23] The resultant view finds "a clear distinction between direct participation in hostilities and participation in the war effort."[24] The ICRC's recent interpretive guidance on the direct participation in hostilities thus declares that a specific act must have a "direct causal link" between the act and the harm that involves only one causal step between the action and the harm.[25] For example, those who build improvised explosive devices (IEDs) would fail to meet the ICRC's direct-participation-in-hostilities test because they do not cause the harm within one causal step, unlike the insurgent who plants the device.[26] The other line of thought is less restrictive, permitting as targets objects that "*indirectly but effectively* support and sustain the enemy's war-fighting capability."[27] This "American" approach follows Carl von Clausewitz's insight that war involves the total capacity of society.[28] For example, munitions factories are perhaps as important a source of military strength as the army itself.[29] Under this approach, status as a member of the warfighting apparatus is enough, making direct participants even out of those "who have laid down their arms."[30]

Understanding counterinsurgency strategy helps clarify what is problematic about these contending interpretations. Focusing narrowly on "hostilities" or "military advantage" is problematic in counterinsurgency. Insurgencies derive their strength from social dynamics in the population. Targeting only narrowly defined military objectives and/or hostile insurgent forces will not result in victory. Insurgents derive their support from the population, including food, shelter, intelligence, and logistical support. In the context of this war among the people, counterinsurgency operations require preventing insurgents from spreading propaganda and developing support within the population. In order to win over the population, the counterinsurgent must separate the insurgents from the population.

A brief illustration will be helpful. In April 1999 NATO forces bombed Radio Television Serbia (RTS), killing sixteen and injuring another sixteen.[31] The strike was questioned and criticized as not contributing to the military effort, and it was later reviewed by the International Criminal Tribunal for the Former Yugoslavia (ICTY) and European Court of Human Rights.[32] Although the ICTY found that the radio station was being used for military communications and was therefore an acceptable military target, it stated that stopping propaganda to undermine the government's support or demoralize the population was not sufficient to make the station a military target.[33] In the context of conventional war and a restrictive understanding of military targets, this approach perhaps seems natural. But in counterinsurgency, informational operations and the ability to communicate effectively with the population are central to the success or failure of the insurgency. A television or radio station is a much greater force multiplier for an insurgency than a few additional recruited combatants. Confronting these "nonmilitary" sources of power is therefore a key task of counterinsurgency.[34]

In addition, the "direct participation" prong is similarly problematic in counterinsurgencies. The directness prong focuses on how far removed a civilian's actions are from kill-capture military operations. This approach overvalues military operations. A civilian engaged in spreading propaganda may be highly effective in contributing to the defeat of the counterinsurgents, even though his actions are not intended to cause harm to physical forces. Requiring a narrowly tailored relationship between conventional military action and civilian participation thus prevents targeting many insurgent operations. The IED builder, excluded from targeting on the narrow ICRC construction, is a perfect example. However, if the military operations prong is interpreted more broadly to incorporate insurgent support systems, such as propaganda and other lines of support, then the directness approach becomes almost irrelevant.

Almost any action could be seen as directly related to the expansive reading of military advantage, because military advantage would be coextensive with counterinsurgency's broad scope. The focus on direct participation is also strategically overbroad. In one case during the Vietnam War, U.S. Marines discovered an old woman mining a road. The woman was not a Viet Cong partisan; rather, the Viet Cong had threatened to kill her granddaughter if she did not plant the mines.[35] The direct participation approach enables targeting the old woman, though a wise counterinsurgent would recognize that her actions were the result of her situation, not her commitment to insurgency, and therefore that targeting her would have little effect on reducing the insurgency itself.

From the perspective of counterinsurgency, Common Article 3 of the Geneva Conventions, which focuses on persons taking an "active part in hostilities," provides a less problematic approach.[36] Counterinsurgency distinguishes between active and passive support.[37] Active support consists of individuals or groups joining the insurgency, logistical and financial support, providers of intelligence, hosts of safe havens, medical assistance, transportation, and other operations on behalf of insurgents.[38] Passive support, while benefiting insurgents, is not material support. Passive supporters "allow insurgents to operate and do not provide information to counterinsurgents."[39] Passive support is acquiescence or tolerance.[40] Though it is by no means perfect, as in the case of the Vietnamese grandmother, this distinction is more tractable from the perspective of counterinsurgency. Instead of focusing on the distance an action has from military consequences, the active/passive distinction focuses on a difference in kind between actions. It separates those who are not actively supporting the insurgency—and therefore need to be protected under the win-the-population strategy—from those who may need to be confronted by traditional military means. Distinction is not jettisoned: passive participation would be fully protected, but active participation could potentially result in a loss of protection.

A counterinsurgency approach might therefore consider *taking an active part in the insurgency* as the appropriate interpretation of the principle of distinction. This approach, however, is subject to the criticism that it reduces, even undermines, the humanitarian ends of the laws of war. Focusing on active involvement in insurgency operations would mean that bankers, propagandists, even farmers and cooks could be targeted for kill-capture operations, regardless of whether they ever held a weapon. Allowing the targeting of those who indirectly participate in hostilities risks justifying the eradication of entire populations under the guise of counterinsurgency, especially given that these persons can simply be detained if they are a threat to security.[41]

Moreover, this approach seems misaligned with counterinsurgency's strategy of winning over the population. Counterinsurgency operations are not primarily focused on kill-capture operations, so even if the butcher and baker are active insurgents, it may not be in the strategic self-interest of the counterinsurgent to target them. Kill-capture operations can cause backlash and fuel the insurgency, rather than stamp it out. Particularly with the rise of instant communication and publicity, any kill-capture operation could easily be found to be unreasonable by domestic and international opinion, reducing the legitimacy of the counterinsurgent and its ability to win over the population. As one commentator notes, counterinsurgency "counsels greater restraint when confronting and targeting individuals."[42]

For this reinterpretation to even be plausible, then, counterinsurgents' discretion would have to be evaluated through a strengthened principle of proportionality. The relationship between distinction and proportionality is simple. Distinction asks whether or not the targeted object can be attacked under the laws of war. Civilians, for example, cannot be attacked. If the object can be attacked, proportionality asks whether the collateral or incidental damage from attacking the target is disproportionate to the gain from the attack.[43] If the damage is disproportionately high, then the attack must not take place—or else it will be deemed an excessive attack in violation of the Geneva Conventions.[44] Proportionality, therefore, involves the exercise of discretion by the attacking force.[45] Shifting the focus to proportionality in counterinsurgency operations does not require targeting all active supporters of the insurgency, and it may in fact prohibit targeting them if the attack's consequences would be disproportional to the gain.

Significantly, the conventional balancing test for proportionality also does not align with counterinsurgency—counterinsurgency suggests *greater* protection against excessive kill-capture operations. Under the conventional proportionality analysis, the military weighs two heterogeneous factors: the "concrete and direct" military benefits and the humanitarian costs.[46] In conventional warfare, in which kill-capture is the strategy for victory, the military and humanitarian goals are in direct opposition. Killing enemies and destroying facilities will always contribute to victory under the conventional approach. Not attacking to spare civilians was therefore a constraint against self-interest, enforceable through reciprocity. In counterinsurgency, this balancing act is different. Protecting the population is central to the counterinsurgent's strategy. Attacks resulting in collateral damage are not likely to gain popular support for the counterinsurgent. Even attacks that kill only insurgents may have the effect of sparking protests, creating the desire for vengeance by a family member or tribal relative, and fueling the insurgency further.[47] These indirect and often nonmilitary effects render the benefits of a military attack necessarily less certain and likely weaker than in the conventional model, which emphasizes the "concrete and direct military advantage anticipated."[48]

In counterinsurgency, the military side of the proportionality balancing test is thus handicapped by the fact that any attack may cause backlash.[49] As a result, counterinsurgency might interpret proportionality not as military benefits versus humanitarian costs but rather as a two-step cost-benefit analysis, in which humanitarian and strategic interests operate on both sides of the scale and incorporate direct and indirect effects. Step one asks how much military advantage is gained from an attack. This determination includes weighing the strategic or tactical disadvantages of civilian casualties. Military action itself is both a cost and a benefit when determining the extent of military advantage that will be gained from an attack. Step two of the proportionality analysis balances the military advantage against purely humanitarian, or moral, considerations. The likelihood of civilian casualties is, as a result, considered twice. Proportionality in counterinsurgency is thus likely to be far more humanitarian in its orientation than it was in conventional warfare.

Counterinsurgency's law of targeting thus suggests that the principle of distinction, as manifested in the direct participation standard, is often understood too narrowly, and the principle of proportionality is often understood too broadly. To be sure, a broader interpretation of distinction and a narrower interpretation of proportionality shifts the law of targeting from a clearer rule to a more discretionary standard. This shift provides the benefits of being better tailored to the varied contexts that arise in counterinsurgency warfare, but it has the risk of counterinsurgents' abusing their discretion. Despite these tradeoffs, the alignment of law and progressive counterinsurgency strategy can work to promote both humanitarian and strategic interests.

## Compensating Civilians

One of the central tenets of the laws of war, undergirded by the kill-capture strategy, is that soldiers are privileged combatants, afforded the right to attack, injure, and even kill the enemy without legal redress.[50] The laws of war, however, have gone further, recognizing more as a matter of pragmatics than principle that some civilians may in fact be harmed despite the protections afforded them by the principle of distinction. The pursuit of military objectives, necessary for destroying the enemy and winning the war, may result in harm to civilians. Recognizing this tragic reality, the laws of war provide that the collateral damage to civilians must not be disproportionate to the military advantage gained from an attack.[51] The result is that privilege extends not only to killing the enemy but also to killing and injuring civilians as long as it is a matter of collateral damage. Civilians harmed under collateral damage therefore have no legal recourse—they have no right to compensation or other remedies for their losses. The war-on-terror approach does not revise this situation. Concerned primarily with killing and capturing terrorists, that approach sees collateral damage as tragic, but necessary to eliminating the terrorist threat and attaining victory. Under this approach, civilians must simply realize they are, in the long run, being protected from terrorists.

Perhaps the best example of the military's limited responsibility to civilians harmed by collateral damage is its manifestation in the Foreign Claims Act (FCA). The FCA grants authority to create claims commissions to settle claims against the United States for damage or loss of property of a foreign country or person or for the injury or death of a foreign person caused by the U.S. military.[52] However, the FCA includes a "combat exclusion," which excludes any claim that arises "from action by an enemy or result directly or indirectly from an act of the armed forces of the United States in combat."[53] In essence, the FCA internalizes the law-of-war norm of the combatant's privilege, allowing compensation for torts and other injuries caused by the U.S. military only as long as those injuries occurred outside combat operations. A looser approach to compensating civilians who are injured is institutionalized through the payment of solatia—"nominal payments made immediately to a victim or the victim's family to express sympathy when local custom exists for such payments."[54] Even though solatia provide compensation, they send strong signals that these are not claims of responsibility or compensation for a particular loss.[55] Moreover, the practice is limited to countries that have a custom of solatia, which, according to the U.S. Army Regulations, consists of Micronesia, Japan, Korea, and Thailand.[56] In essence, compensation through both the FCA and solatia incorporates the central corollary of the laws of war's principles of privilege, distinction, and proportionality—that militaries have no responsibility to compensate civilians who are harmed, injured, or whose families are killed as a result of legitimate military operations.

In contrast to the kill-capture approach, counterinsurgency's win-the-population strategy suggests that compensating civilians who are harmed, injured, or killed even during legitimate military operations would be a smart tactic. Condolence payments have the benefit of expressing sympathy to victims and their families, providing humanitarian relief and aid to those who may no longer have the ability to earn a livelihood, and fostering good-will among the population.[57] Because counterinsurgents must convince the population that they are working in the population's interest, compensation through condolence payments can help the population distinguish the legit-imate, credible counterinsurgent. As a result, condolence payments have been called a "nonlethal weapons system" and have been heralded by com-mentators as an effective way to win the population in counterinsurgency operations.[58]

Indeed, the practice of compensation since the Vietnam War confirms the strategic value of compensation. The *Operational Law Handbook* notes that the combat exclusion "interferes with the principal goal of low intensity conflict/foreign internal defense: obtaining and maintaining the support of the local populace."[59] And in every conflict from Vietnam to Somalia, the U.S. Army has tried to get around the restrictive nature of the FCA's combat exclusion in order to pay condolences.[60] In Vietnam, the military got the government of South Vietnam to agree to pay claims; in Grenada, military personnel administered claims procedures but used State Department funds through USAID; in Panama, the United States provided funds to pay claims through a broader program of economic support for the government.[61] Indeed, the conflicts in Iraq and Afghanistan have been no exception—as of 2007, the military had provided $29 million in condolence payments.[62]

Although condolence payments are an effective weapon in counterinsur-gency's win-the-population strategy, recent practice in Iraq and Afghanistan and the laws of war themselves are severely disconnected from the win-the-population strategy. In Iraq and Afghanistan, condolence and solatia pay-ments were prohibited early in the conflict and were coupled with restrictive interpretations of the FCA. The U.S. Air Force procedures for the Iraq war stated that "[a]ll [FCA] claims arising within the . . . boundaries of Iraq during the period of the war, are automatically classified as combat activity claims, and therefore are prohibited."[63] With FCA claims absent, soldiers relied on condolence and solatia. Yet it was not until March 2004 that any condolence payments were made in Iraq and not until November 2005 that they were made in Afghanistan.[64] And solatia payments, amounting to a total of $1.9 million by 2007, were only made in Iraq from June 2003 to January 2005 and in Afghanistan since October 2005.[65] In addition, funding for condolence payments was limited. Condolences are paid out of a commander's emer-gency response program (CERP) funds, which are also a commander's main source for reconstruction and humanitarian relief projects.[66] Indeed, condolence payments amounted to only 8 percent of the expenditures from CERP funds in Iraq in 2005 and 5 percent in 2006.[67] In Afghanistan they amounted to 1 percent in 2006.[68] In some cases, the funding available for condolences would be used up, leaving commanders with limited or no resources from which to pay claims.[69] The strategic importance of condolence payments suggests that the restrictive interpretation of the FCA, the limited use of condolence payments early in the wars, and the limited funding available for condolence payments were all mistakes.

Even when implemented in Iraq and Afghanistan, the practice of condolence payments has not been as effective a "nonlethal weapon system" as those hopeful about its use might desire.[70] Because the condolence process is discretionary and decentralized to the level of particular commanders, the procedures and application have been inconsistent and largely ad hoc. Payments for similar injuries are inconsistent over time and places, claims are denied for no particular reason, and in many cases when an FCA claim is denied, the claimant is not referred to the condolence system.[71] The maximum payment for loss of life is $2,500, which prevents claims officers from adequately compensating in the most egregious cases or compensating when a family has lost its breadwinner.[72] Finally, because of the ad hoc nature of the program, particular units have established arbitrary interpretative rules, such as placing a three-month statute of limitations on payments and not paying condolences if another unit caused the harm, a particular problem given the migration of people because of violence and the high unit turnover.[73] Standardized rules are not unworkable, since the FCA allows for units to pay claims from damage caused by other units and places a two-year statute of limitations on claims.[74]

In addition to revising statutory and military practice with respect to condolences, the win-the-population strategy also suggests that the structure and principles of international law are in conflict with a robust condolence program. The laws of war, assuming the kill-capture strategy of victory, grant privilege to killing civilians as a matter of collateral damage during legitimate military operations. A win-the-population strategy would more clearly leave the question of remedy open. Some might go further, arguing a remedy is required. Under that approach, the counterinsurgent must try not to injure civilians and *must* also compensate those who are injured by military operations. The international community has suggested compensation for victims of war crimes and crimes against humanity, and Additional Protocol I to the Geneva Conventions requires parties to a conflict that violate the Conventions to pay compensation.[75] One commentator has even called for a "responsibility to pay."[76] Such a responsibility directly conflicts with the conventional kill-capture approach, which privileges killing civilians as a matter of collateral damage. Though it may at first seem aligned with counterinsurgency strategy, institutionalizing the "responsibility to pay" via direct compensation, however, could be unwise. Compensating a family during conflict may merely make them a target for insurgents who discover their wealth. Any proposal must at the minimum allow in-kind, communal, and other forms of compensation so as not to turn victims into targets.

## The Use of Nonlethal Weapons

Since their modern origins in the nineteenth century, the laws of war have prohibited some weapons and technologies in order to prevent unnecessary suffering. The laws assumed that military strategy and technological innovation worked in tandem to create weapons of ever greater destruction.[77] As true as the strategy-technology nexus may have seemed in the late nineteenth and early twentieth centuries, the history of military technology in the late twentieth century and the win-the-population strategy in counterinsurgency tell a different story. In recent years, military technology has focused on precision in order to reduce collateral damage and casualties. At the same time, counterinsurgency's win-the-population strategy suggests that the technologies of great destruction will be counterproductive. One of the promises of technological innovation is the creation of nonlethal weapons: weapons that incapacitate temporarily or that otherwise fall short of killing the enemy. Yet under the laws of war—inspired by the conventional kill-capture approach to war—many of these technological developments are severely limited, if not banned outright. The laws of war are thus not only disconnected from the strategy of counterinsurgency but also prevent means of warfare that are potentially humane.

In recent years, technological developments have promised the creation of nonlethal weapons (NLWs). These NLWs are "explicitly designed and primarily employed so as to incapacitate personnel or materiel, while minimizing fatalities, permanent injury to personnel, and undesired damage to property and the environment."[78] Nonlethal weapons come in many forms, including directed energy beams that can prevent people from moving forward, blunt projectiles like rubber bullets and beanbags, calmatives that make people relax or fall asleep, giant webs that trap people, tasers, malodorants that smell like excrement or rotting flesh and may cause vomiting, pepper spray, and antitraction spray that makes the ground more slippery than ice.[79] They can also include glare lasers that cause disorientation as well as acoustic and sonic weapons.[80] With such a broad variety of technologies, the term "nonlethal weapon" is somewhat misleading. Some nonlethal weapons, such as tasers, can cause death. (Though, of course, even "lethal" weapons, such as rifles, may merely leave a person injured.[81]) "Nonlethal" also suggests that the weapons are directed at personnel, but they could just as well be directed toward equipment and materiel.[82] Despite these terminological problems, the defining quality of NLWs is that they are "designed not to destroy or kill but to incapacitate."[83]

Perhaps surprisingly, the laws of war prohibit the use of many nonlethal weapons. The Convention on Certain Conventional Weapons' Protocol II on mines and booby-traps, for example, makes no distinction between lethal and nonlethal mines.[84] Under a straightforward reading of the Protocol, a mine that sprung a giant web and trapped personnel would be prohibited. Likewise, the Geneva Gas Protocol of 1925 prohibits "asphyxiating, poisonous or *other gases*, and . . . *all* analogous liquids."[85] Under this prohibition, an army could not deploy a sleeping gas. The Chemical Weapons Convention (CWC) bans chemicals that cause "temporary incapacitation" unless they are used in law enforcement or for other peaceful purposes.[86] More surprisingly, it prohibits the use of riot-control agents in military operations, even though it condones their use in domestic situations.[87] Finally, Additional Protocol I of the Geneva Conventions prohibits weapons that cause "superfluous injury or unnecessary suffering." The Red Cross's Superfluous Injury or Unnecessary Suffering (SIrUS) Project proposed to define the phrase according to whether the suffering causes

> specific disease, specific abnormal physiological state, specific abnormal psychological state, specific and permanent disability or specific disfigurement . . . field mortality of more than 25 percent or hospital mortality of more than 5 percent . . . Grade 3 wounds [large wounds] as measured by the Red Cross wound classification system . . . or effects for which there is no well-recognized and proven treatment.[88]

Some of these criteria, in particular the "specific abnormal physiological state" and "effects for which there is no well-recognized . . . treatment" criteria, would exclude nonlethal weapons that cause temporary effects such as disorientation or confusion.[89]

Counterinsurgency's win-the-population strategy challenges the conventional approach to the ban of nonlethal weapons—and indeed any blanket technological ban. Under the kill-capture strategy, the strategy-technology nexus would result in ever-more-dangerous weapons that needed to be banned for humanitarian reasons. But under counterinsurgency, one would expect less indiscriminate, more precise, and less dangerous weaponry. As one of the paradoxes of counterinsurgency asserts: "Sometimes, the more force is used, the less effective it is."[90] Indeed, the case for nonlethal weapons is that they create fewer fatalities and are particularly useful in situations when military targets are hidden within civilian populations.[91] Nonlethal weapons seem particularly appropriate in modern warfare, in which collateral damage is generally intolerable and can fuel insurgencies.[92] As one commentator has asked, "When we really want to stabilize or neutralize something, why incur greater wrath from the community by incinerating or by blowing something up if we don't have to do that?"[93] Nonlethal weapons also offer the opportunity to transform the use of air power, from dropping bombs that cause great collateral damage to spreading nonlethal substances.[94] In essence, counterinsurgency and weapons innovation point to the same goal. "Over time, old stereotypes which infer that killing or destroying the enemy is the only path to victory will be modified. . . . A new stereotype will emerge that recognizes that killing or destroying the enemy is not the only way to defeat him."[95] If a military seeks to use a win-the-population strategy, using NLWs to prevent collateral damage seems like a no-brainer.

Despite the value of NLWs to counterinsurgency operations, many believe allowing them is problematic, even dangerous.[96] Often NLWs *can* be lethal. In some cases, such as when the Russians pumped fentanyl into a Moscow theater to incapacitate hostages and hostage-takers, an NLW can be indiscriminately harmful. In Moscow, 127 hostages died.[97] Nonlethal weapons are also lethal for certain classes of people who are at higher risk—children, pregnant women, handicapped persons, persons with asthma. Such persons need to be monitored when engaged with pepper spray or anesthetics.[98] Although this concern is factually accurate, the lethality critique of NLWs suffers from the fallacy of using the wrong baseline of comparison. This criticism compares two situations: the use of NLWs with inherent risks, and no military action with certain safety. In reality, however, there is a third situation to consider: the use of lethal force with certain collateral damage. The right diagnosis of the problem requires determining whether in any given case the military would use conventional lethal forces, NLWs, or no force.

Take a case in which there are insurgents in a crowd of people. We must first ask whether a military would use a conventional lethal technology like a missile, would choose not to act against the insurgents at all, or, if available, would use an NLW. This creates three scenarios with three different baselines.

In scenario one, the military would choose lethal force over no action, but it would prefer NLWs to lethal force. In that case, the comparison is between certain collateral damage from bombing the crowd and the risk of lethality from NLWs. The skeptic of NLWs and the counterinsurgent would likely be aligned, preferring the mere risk of lethality to the certainty of collateral damage. Scenario two arises when the military would choose no action over lethal force and would prefer no action over NLWs. In counterinsurgency, this situation is not unlikely. As the paradox of counterinsurgency recommends, "sometimes doing nothing is the best reaction."[99] Militaries must take into account the adverse consequences of their operations—including the risks inherent in NLWs. In these cases as well, the counterinsurgent and humanitarian are in agreement and there will be no use of NLWs. The final scenario is one in which the military would pick no action over lethal force but would prefer NLWs to no action. The comparison is between the risk inherent in NLWs and the certain safety of no action. Here the counterinsurgent and the skeptical humanitarian are opposed.

Notice that clarifying the three baseline scenarios limits substantive disagreement to the cases in which the military would not use lethal weapons and prefers NLWs to inaction. A substantial number of cases are likely to fall outside of this category—and in those cases, the counterinsurgent and the skeptic of NLWs are in agreement. Additionally, it is not clear whether scenario one or scenario three will occur more frequently. In scenario one, lives are saved in the shift from certain casualties to risk from NLWs; in scenario three, lives are put at risk in the shift from no action to risk of NLWs. It is not clear which option—allowing or preventing NLWs—will save more lives. A counterinsurgency-inspired approach, however, would most likely enable the use of NLWs. Nonlethal weapons allow the saving of lives in scenario one, and scenario three has built into it the risks of NLWs—risks that a counterinsurgent must take into account as part of the proportionality analysis she undertakes.

Another criticism is that NLWs can be deliberately misused. There are many versions of this critique. One commentator has noted that "the only difference between a drug and a poison is the dose."[100] Some have argued that nations might use nonlethal weapons to incapacitate soldiers easily, and then kill them anyway.[101] Others believe NLWs could create a slippery slope leading to the redeployment of traditional chemical and biological weapons; malodorous weapons, for example, could be used to mask traditional chemical and biological weapons.[102] There is much truth in these concerns, but they too suffer from a baseline problem of comparison. It is true that NLWs may be misused, but the comparison is not necessarily between the misuse of NLWs and no action on the part of the misusing army. If a military that would mis-use NLWs is prevented from using them, it might instead use lethal force, misuse lethal force, misuse nonweapons, or ignore the ban on NLWs and still misuse them.[103] Given this problem, it is not obvious whether allowing NLWs as a general matter will cause greater unnecessary suffering than the alterna-tive. If the misusing state will misuse weaponry regardless of the legal struc-ture, the justification for prohibiting NLWs seems weak. The appropriate use of NLWs, even if only by well-intentioned counterinsurgents, will still alle-viate and prevent some death and injury.

Finally, some have argued that permitting NLWs will encourage policymak-ers to deploy troops more frequently.[104] Nonlethal weapons may lower the cost of civilian casualties and make it easier to wage war with less backlash. In this sense, NLWs reduce the collateral costs to the kill-capture approach. However, in a win-the-population approach to warfare, reducing civilian casualties is necessary but not sufficient. Reducing casualties can prevent fueling the insur-gency, but, in itself, it is unlikely to win over the population. What is needed is the slow and resource-intensive work of securing the population and providing services and governance. Deciding whether to go to war, in this context, would not likely turn solely on reduction of civilian casualties but rather substantially on the ability of the state to undertake serious win-the-population operations.

Despite the problems with the criticisms of NLWs, categorical supporters of NLWs are not completely free from criticism themselves. These supporters often argue that NLWs are superior because when compared to lethal force, nonlethal force is always more humane.[105] On this theory, blinding a person with a laser will always be superior to killing them. Indeed, they seem to believe that because death is permitted, anything less than death is per-mitted. Neither the laws of war nor counterinsurgency take this view. Rather, they acknowledge that unnecessary suffering and severe injuries can be so bad that they should be prevented. Under a win-the-population approach in counterinsurgency, nonlethal force may not be strategically desirable. In some cases, lethal force may be preferable. To take an extreme example, detaining and torturing insurgents captured in the midst of battle would be strategically problematic: torture creates backlash and fuels the insurgency by creating a grievance for local populations that are seeking protection and order, not ruthlessness and fear. Killing those insurgents in the midst of battle might, in that case, be preferable to the nonlethal option. In other cases, no action may be preferable to NLWs. When "doing nothing is the best reaction," the risk of adverse consequences of NLWs outweigh projected tactical advantage from NLWs. Under a win-the-population approach, the idea of preventing unnecessary suffering and superfluous injuries is thus centrally important because it prevents the creation of potential grievances.

The counterinsurgency approach to nonlethal weapons would therefore both support a significant restraint on unnecessary suffering and superfluous injury *and* also support the use of certain nonlethal weapons. But its support for both regimes would be contextual, focused on the actual effects in a particular case rather than on blanket rules. As in the case of the principle of distinction, it would suggest the strengthening of proportionality analysis. Likewise, it would recognize that in certain contexts, otherwise properly used NLWs might cause unnecessary suffering. The use of some NLWs in cities or villages might be reasonable, but in closed areas like caves or bunkers they might cause terrible suffering.[106] The right question in the debate on nonlethal weapons is thus not whether they should be permitted but how exactly to define unnecessary suffering and superfluous injuring in a manner that can accommodate the rich and varied contexts that animate counterinsurgency.[107]

## The Globalization of Detention

Insurgents who are not killed in an attack are often captured and detained. How should they be detained? And as importantly, where? The detention of terrorists and terrorist suspects has perhaps been the most hotly debated topic within the war on terror. The basic arguments, largely stemming from the need to balance national security with civil liberties, are well known. One camp believes preventive detention is necessary. They acknowledge that criminal prosecutions and the laws regarding capture and detention on the battlefield are often sufficient, but they also recognize that some cases fall between these regimes.[108] Prosecution risks disclosing intelligence sources and operations, evidentiary rules make it impossible to prosecute some terrorists who are captured in far-flung places, and, most importantly, prosecution is based on the principle that it is better for a guilty person to go free than for an innocent person to be deprived of liberty.[109] In the context of catastrophic terrorism, where the risks to so many are so high, society cannot allow terrorists to roam free.[110] Another camp believes that preventive detention is a threat to liberty and may even be counterproductive. Outside the battlefield context, criminal prosecution provides sufficient tools to ensure security and greater protections to personal liberty than a preventive detention system would.[111] Preventive detention may also limit the ability to make future arguments from human rights, enabling dictators to justify quashing dissidents and reducing support from others in the war on terror.[112]

To an extraordinary degree, the debate over detention policy has been shaped by the "enemy combatant" approach made famous by the Bush administration's war on terror and use of Guantanamo Bay as a detention facility. Under this approach, Al Qaeda and its affiliates are enemies in an armed conflict. The laws of war, therefore, license the United States to kill or capture these enemies and detain them, as it would detain enemies of a foreign state, for the duration of the hostilities.[113] This approach has two lasting effects: it has globalized detention and it has created a baseline status quo that has framed the debate.

Despite the flexibility that the enemy combatant approach provided, the Bush administration moved Al Qaeda members and terrorist suspects from Afghanistan and other countries to Guantanamo Bay under a theory that it was a legal black hole, free of the rules of the battlefield and free from the purview of American courts. Moving detainees to Guantanamo Bay can be interpreted as a global response to a global problem: If terrorism exists across boundaries and terrorists are independent entities, detention of terrorists could also be a borderless, global enterprise. Guantanamo Bay thus symbolizes the globalization of detention. Detentions that otherwise would have been subject to traditional geographic constraints and their associated legal regimes were now transformed, creating both the assumption and the practice that persons captured in one place in the global war could be moved to other places, detained, and potentially tried and convicted. Guantanamo and the enemy combatant approach have also shifted the baseline status from which debates on detention follow. Yet doing so does not adequately consider the purposes of detention and the role detention plays in an overall strategy.[114]

In addition to clarifying the purpose and strategy of a detention regime, the designers of a detention system must consider the scope of detention and the procedural safeguards provided after detention.[115] The scope of activities triggering detention could be as narrow as direct participation in hostilities or as broad as providing material support to terrorists.[116] Procedural safeguards that could be chosen include provision of counsel, access to information, limits on the fruit of interrogation, increased publicity, and institutions for review of decisions.[117] Focusing on the enemy combatant model threatens to assume a baseline of scope and process that may not be the optimal starting point, given the well-known status quo bias that afflicts decision making.[118]

The globalization of detention and the enemy combatant approach, driven by the war on terror framework, suffer from significant problems. The nature of contemporary threats is such that it is not obvious who the enemy combatant is because insurgents and terrorists deliberately blend into civilian populations. The result is a high likelihood of detaining innocent persons, particularly troubling given that the war on terror is potentially infinite in its duration.[119] An equally significant problem is that the globalization of detention has centered the detention debate on the Guantanamo Bay detainees. To be sure, Guantanamo is highly important, but there are other situations to address, such as newly captured insurgents held in facilities in Iraq and Afghanistan.[120] Indeed, courts are faced with the decision of whether detainees in Bagram Prison in Afghanistan have a constitutional right to challenge their detentions in U.S. courts.[121] From the perspective of designing a detention policy, simply assuming that the globalization of detention is the appropriate approach is dangerous. The contours of detention, like other legal regimes, are driven by policy choices that integrate political, legal, and strategic concerns. If the strategic foundations of the enemy combatant model of globalized detention are unsound, debate over the particular contours of detention policy might shift significantly.

The strategic shift from the global war on terror to global counterinsurgency provides a helpful critique of detention policy. At a strategic level, global counterinsurgency differs significantly from global counterterrorism. The latter approach, derived from the kill-capture strategy for victory, prescribes finding, killing, and capturing terrorists wherever they exist. It acknowledges the global and borderless nature of terrorism and responds in kind. Global counterinsurgency offers a different strategy: disaggregation. The insurgency framework envisions a global system of interconnections and linkages that provide strength and resilience to insurgent movements. Grievances, materials, and active and passive support in one location can migrate across borders and spark or fuel insurgency in other locations. A globalized counterterrorism strategy is therefore likely to be counterproductive. As David Kilcullen notes, "efforts to kill or capture insurgent leaders inject energy into the system by generating grievances and causing disparate groups to coalesce."[122] In contrast, the strategy of disaggregation suggests delinking parts of the system, creating a series of "disparate local conflicts that are capable of being solved by nation-states and can be addressed at the regional or national level."[123] Disaggregation thus has two components: At the global level, it suggests delinking conflict, grievances, and resources in order to contain insurgent operations to particular states or regions. Within each state or region, it suggests a robust counterinsurgency strategy of winning the population.

Disaggregation implies that the globalization of detention was and remains a misguided approach. In place of globalized detention, disaggregation suggests that detainees should be held and tried in the state in which they are captured. The benefits of disaggregating detention are substantial. The capture, detention, and prosecution of insurgents are potential grievances insurgents can use to attract new recruits or motivate existing insurgents. Transferring insurgents is likely to spread grievances across geographic jurisdictions and make receiving states focal points for the insurgency. Guantanamo is the best example. Detention policies in Afghanistan and Iraq spark little backlash or protest outside those countries when compared to Guantanamo, and a global insurgency analysis would predict that Guantanamo might inspire more terrorists than it holds. A disaggregation strategy has the potential to limit the spread of the grievances sparked by detention. Detaining and prosecuting insurgents in the territory in which they were captured decentralizes the grievances from the global counterinsurgent state and limits their ability to link to the global insurgency. Shifting the emphasis to particular states allows for the insurgency to be treated at a local, rather than global, level.

In addition to preventing the spread of insurgent grievances, disaggregating detention forces nations to develop their own legal structures for detention, thereby strengthening the rule of law around the world. On this theory, the best way for the United States to support counterinsurgency and state-building in Afghanistan, for example, is not to outsource Afghan detainees and legal problems to American prisons and courts but instead to help Afghans develop their own detention and legal systems to confront their particular challenges. Under a disaggregation strategy, countries that develop legitimate processes and the rule of law will win the support of their local populations and effectively grapple with dangers within their borders. Those that refuse to adopt legitimate legal regimes will face increased pressure from their constituents—and from insurgents.

The disaggregation strategy allows for a diverse range of detention policies via their tailoring to the particular conditions within a state. For example, in a state confronted with an active insurgency, such as Iraq or Afghanistan, detention policy might need to have a broad scope and limited procedural safeguards.[124] In a peaceful state without daily attacks from insurgents, such as the United States, detention policy might take on a narrower scope and offer greater procedural safeguards. The value of this diversity of policies across jurisdictions is both principled and strategic. It is principled because it affirms the rule of law and value of liberty rather than embracing a universal, global policy of expansive preventive detention. It is strategic because the win-the-population strategy in counterinsurgency requires developing legitimate governance structures, including legal and judicial institutions. Forcing the United States into a detention regime designed for the threats of Afghanistan does more harm than good to liberty at home. Forcing Afghanistan into American legal and constitutional structures does similar injury to the security and development of a distinctly Afghan government. Diversity enables both security and the rule of law.

Opponents of the disaggregation strategy raise important practical criticisms, though a correct understanding of global counterinsurgency strategy can meet each one. Some countries may not provide an expansive enough detention scheme to prevent against catastrophic attacks. A disaggregation approach places pressure and responsibility on the government to provide heightened security to its population, rather than transferring responsibility to a single state for all global detention operations. To the extent that a nation's detention policy falls short of the threat, global diplomatic forces and domestic political forces can pressure the undersecured state to change its approach. Additionally, some countries might torture individuals or engage in other human rights violations. Under the UN Convention against Torture, states must not transfer persons to another state "where there are substantial grounds for believing that he would be in danger of being subjected to torture."[125] The Convention poses no problem for a disaggregation strategy because it suggests keeping detainees where they are captured. And the state violating human rights may incite backlash, pushing it to change its policies. Finally, some countries might use detention policy as a method to clamp down on political opponents. Politically oppressive states could follow such policies regardless of disaggregation, but they will likely face a backlash because of the nature of grievances and feedback loops in insurgent systems. In each case, disaggregation strengthens the responsibility of states toward their citizens with respect to both security and liberty. If the state is incapable of providing either, it will face international pressure and may confront a heightened insurgency. At the same time, the focus on the state's responsibility to detain contains potential grievances at the national level, limiting their relevance and spread across geographical boundaries.

In each of these scenarios, effective detention relies both on the feedback effects inherent in counterinsurgency and the international community accepting a "managerial" role regarding detention issues.[126] The international community would ensure that each state has a clear understanding of what basic security and legal measures are appropriate and could assist states that have not met those measures but want to meet them. Moreover, networks of government officials, best practices, and technical assistance would help fortify national institutions.[127]

Pursuing the disaggregation strategy to detention requires designing detention policy for a variety of situations, from states with full-blown or active insurgencies to states with limited threats from insurgencies. Focusing on the particular state and its conditions involves considering the role detention plays in the state's overall strategy to address threats. A system of preventive detention can have four purposes at its core: incapacitating subjects who are deemed generally dangerous, deterring individuals from joining with radical groups, disrupting specific and ongoing plots or attacks, and enabling the gathering of helpful information.[128] Designing a detention system to incapacitate would focus on proxies for future dangerousness as a way to identify individuals who are generally dangerous.[129] Designing toward disrupting a particular plot would require a functional linkage between a person and a plot.[130] Note that the incapacity and disruption regimes are not necessarily coextensive: a financier may be generally dangerous and require incapacitation, but detaining a financier might not stop an ongoing plot. The financier could not be detained under a disruption regime. On the other hand, a courier may not be generally dangerous but might be transmitting information that will facilitate a particular plot.[131] The courier could not be detained under an incapacity regime. Additionally, detention with respect to a particular plot would imply a shorter duration of detention, since the threat would subside after the plot was disrupted.[132] Detention for purposes of gathering information provides a broad scope, suggesting potential detention of friends and relatives of a suspected person in order to interrogate them. At the same time, such a detention regime poses the considerable risk of alienating the population.[133] Finally, detention for deterrence seems like a blunt instrument, since prosecution or military action, depending on the context, would both seem to be sufficient deterrents.

By considering each of these purposes, detention policy can be tailored to both active and inactive insurgencies. In an active insurgency, such as in Iraq or Afghanistan, detention should seek to incapacitate and disrupt. Insurgencies are driven by violence and fear in the population, and the goal of the counterinsurgent is to secure the population and win over passive supporters of the insurgency. To that end, incapacitating active supporters of the insurgency, admittedly a broad category, would be an effective way to secure the population. Likewise, disrupting particular attacks would be necessary to protect the population. An information-based preventive detention policy might appear valuable, since it would provide helpful intelligence, but it would also alienate the population when mere questioning might suffice. Detention for incapacity and disruption in active insurgencies will inevitably sweep in many insurgents, but procedural safeguards should not be abandoned. Indeed, to win the population, the counterinsurgent must build legitimate legal institutions and not overdetain. One answer to this dilemma is a balancing approach that provides discretion to the counterinsurgents.[134] Another answer is a relatively expansive detention program that facilitates rehabilitation and reintegration. In Iraq, for example, many of the U.S. prisons rehabilitated active supporters of the insurgency who were not the most dangerous insurgents: the programs taught them to read and write, provided education in moderate Islam, and then released them.[135] This approach provides security to the population by removing active insurgents from society, and it rehabilitates those insurgents so they can reenter society in a peaceful and hopefully productive way.

In an area of inactive insurgency, such as the United States, where the threat is ongoing but not pervasive, a different approach is necessary. The justification for incapacitating potentially threatening persons seems weak given the resources of the state, the availability of surveillance, and the prospect of prosecution for material support of terrorism.[136] In contrast, preventive detention for disruption seems appropriate to provide security to the population. It also requires a nexus between an actor and a plot, a higher standard than general dangerousness, and a shorter duration. When the plot is disrupted, preventive detention would lapse and likely give way to a prosecution. The information and intelligence justification seems inappropriate in a state with an inactive insurgency. Detention for intelligence purposes has high costs to liberty and is largely unnecessary given surveillance capacity.

To be sure, the disaggregation approach will not work in all cases. In a failed state like Somalia, a captured terrorist cannot be turned over to a functioning government or prison system. In some cases, a state's assurances might be insufficient or diplomatic pressure might be inadequate to ensure human rights or security. In these cases, states should individually or cooperatively create backstops that protect against domestic failure.[137] These backstops could follow the globalized detention model, allowing foreign courts to hear cases of prisoners captured elsewhere, or they could follow a collective security model, with the creation of an international body to deal with the limited number of cases in which domestic institutions are insufficient.[138] But as much as possible, captured insurgents should remain where they were found.

The strategy of counterinsurgency and disaggregation cannot provide the details for how a detention policy should be designed. Policymakers will disagree as to the specifics of procedural mechanisms to be imposed, the scope of the threat and the potentially detainable population, and perhaps even the

purposes of detention. But counterinsurgency's global strategy of disaggregation does indicate that the globalization of detention—the transfer of insurgents across borders in search of a better forum for detention or prosecution—is
a misguided approach. It further suggests that the best approach would be to
encourage each state to detain its own suspects and develop its own detention
policies. Placing greater responsibilities on states helps minimize linkages and
weakens the focal points of a global insurgency.

## The Law of Occupation

In disaggregating global insurgencies to individual states, counterinsurgents
may find themselves, as the United States did, waging war against insurgents
in the context of a military occupation. In contrast to debates on targeting
and detention, the law of occupation has been comparatively ignored in
public discourse. To some extent, this is a function of the war on terror
framework, whose strategy of kill-capture is not obviously related to occupation and territorial administration. Killing and capturing small bands of
terrorists around the globe does not require overthrowing dozens of regimes
and building their governments. In contrast, insurgency is driven by grievances in social systems, and counterinsurgency's win-the-population strategy
requires security, basic services, and political, economic, and legal reforms
to address and minimize those grievances. With this framework, occupation
seems more relevant, if not central. Occupiers, like the United States in Iraq,
might seek to address insurgencies at their root—social and political structures—and in that process may need to reform state institutions. The law of
occupation governs these actions and has long expressed a tension between
a conservationist principle, in which the occupier maintains the ousted sovereign's institutions, and a reformist principle, in which the occupier can
change institutions for security, humanity, or, in its most recent form,
self-determination. Seeing contemporary conflict as insurgency and counterinsurgency rather than as a war on terror makes occupation law one of the
most important areas of the laws of war and rejects the conservationist
approach to occupation law.

Although occupation law has been applied infrequently between the occupations of Germany and Japan and the occupation of Iraq in 2003, it technically applies to a broad set of cases.[139] Under Article 42 of the Hague
Regulations of 1907, "[t]erritory is considered occupied when it is actually
placed under the authority of the hostile army. The occupation extends only
to the territory where such authority has been established and can be

exercised."[140] In fact, the scope of Article 42 is so broad that occupation can occur during the conflict if a territory is under foreign control for even a few hours.[141]

The fundamental, pervasive characteristic of occupation law is a tension between conservation and reform.[142] The conservationist principle arose out of the nature of conventional warfare. The Franco-Prussian War, considered the inspiration for occupation law, provides an example.[143] After the war, Prussia occupied French territory until the peace treaty, under which some of the land was ceded to Prussia. As a model for occupation, the Franco-Prussian War had paradigmatic features of conventional warfare: war was fought to achieve limited national goals rather than regime change or expansive conquest, and it was fought between professional armies with little interest in involving ordinary civilians.[144] The goal of occupation was to maintain the status quo prior to the war, until the peace treaty was signed and the temporarily ousted sovereign could retake control.[145]

Occupation law, on this model, is not focused on territorial administration or long-term peacemaking.[146] It does not provide the occupant with "general legislative competence," and it is "not intended to provide a general framework for reconstruction and law reform."[147] Any "extensive forcible changes are unlikely to be lawful."[148] The occupant cannot change internal borders or create new constitutional or government structures because changes in political institutions could have consequences beyond the occupation and therefore undermine the ousted sovereign's authority.[149] Indeed, the ICRC Commentary to Article 47 of the Fourth Geneva Convention notes that occupier changes during World War II were illegal under Article 43 of the Hague Regulations—even with the cooperation of portions of the population.[150] The occupier is merely a "de facto administrator."[151]

The Hague Regulations are the clearest example of the conservationist principle. Article 43 states that

> [t]he authority of the legitimate power having in fact passed into the hands of the occupant, the latter shall take all the measures in his power to restore, and ensure, as far as possible, public order and safety, *while respecting, unless absolutely prevented, the laws in force in the country.*[152]

Even though it allows some reformation of the laws, setting the default rule as respecting the laws in force expresses the conservationist principle underlying occupation law.[153] The Hague Regulations also express this conservationist vision elsewhere. For example, if the occupier collects taxes, it must do so "in accordance with the rules of assessment and incidence in force."[154]

The conflicting principle in the law of occupation is that of reform: the occupier's power and authority to change the status quo in the territory. The impetus for reform can be grouped into three categories: security, humanity, and self-determination. The security imperative was built into the Hague Regulations and has remained part of occupation law since. Article 43 allows the occupier to change the "laws in force in the country" in order to ensure "public order and safety." Article 49 notes that any levy of money "shall only be for the needs of the army or of the administration of the territory in question."[155] The Fourth Geneva Convention also expresses this principle, allowing the occupant to take "necessary" measures of "control and security in regard to protected persons," to transfer or evacuate persons for security reasons, and to force the population to work if needed for the occupier's army.[156]

At the same time, the Fourth Geneva Convention added a humanitarian justification for reforming the laws in force. With that shift, Geneva law transformed the occupier from a disinterested administrator to an administrator with many duties.[157] Article 47 makes the shift, asserting that persons must not be deprived of "the benefits of the present Convention by any change introduced, as the result of the occupation."[158] The ICRC Commentary demonstrates the tension this change wrought. On the one hand, Hague Article 43 prohibits "changes in constitutional forms or in the form of government, the establishment of new military or political organizations, the dissolution of the State, or the formation of new political entities," even if the occupier tries to get the cooperation or assent of part of the population.[159] On the other hand, some changes to political institutions "might conceivably be necessary," because under Article 64 the occupier must "fulfill its obligations under the [Fourth] convention."[160]

Geneva's expansive rights enable this reformist project. Some require little reform: Occupation law prevents forcing the population to divulge information about the enemy's army or defenses or to serve in the occupier's armed forces, it prohibits requiring allegiance to the occupier, and it forbids pillage.[161] Others may require considerable reform: protecting "family honour and rights, the lives of persons," private property, and religious beliefs may require shifting a state's balance of church and state or reforming a planned economy.[162] The occupier must also ensure food and medical supplies; maintain public health, hygiene, and hospital functioning; and permit religious practice and ministry.[163] It is quite possible that fulfilling these obligations would require not disinterested stewardship or administration but, rather, the overthrow and reformation of the country's laws.

United Nations Security Council Resolution 1483, which provided the legal framework for the United States–led occupation of Iraq, introduced self-determination as another justification for reform. Under the conservationist approach, an occupier was unable to promote representative government or facilitate a process of self-determination, as it would directly contradict Hague Article 43, even with Geneva's humanitarian reform principle. But since the Geneva Conventions, many contemporary instruments in international law have enhanced the right to self-determination.[164] By incorporating self-determination, one commentator has argued, Resolution 1483 "invented a new model of multilateral occupation."[165]

Resolution 1483 recognizes the United States and United Kingdom as occupying powers and grants authority that is in tension with the conservationist approach.[166] Paragraph 4 calls upon coalition authority "to promote the welfare of the Iraqi people through the effective administration of the territory, including . . . *the creation of conditions in which the Iraqi people can freely determine their own political future.*"[167] Paragraph 8 expands on this requirement, authorizing the Special Representative for Iraq to coordinate with the coalition authority to "restore and establish *national and local institutions for representative governance*," to facilitate "economic reconstruction and *the conditions for sustainable development*," and to promote "legal and judicial reform."[168] At the same time as the Resolution authorizes radical transformation, it calls upon the authority to "comply fully with their obligations under international law including in particular the Geneva Conventions of 1949 and the Hague Regulations of 1907."[169] Yet the reforms allowed under Resolution 1483 would violate either of these regimes. Each of these reforms could "take root and have enduring consequences."[170]

Resolution 1483's approach can be justified on a variety of theories. Under the traditional doctrine of debellatio, when the institutions of state have totally disintegrated, occupation transfers sovereignty. Some commentators have adapted this principle to popular sovereignty and asserted that debellatio could justify reform of institutions along the lines of self-determination and representation.[171] Another approach is to understand Resolution 1483 as providing a "carve out" from Hague and Geneva; under this approach, the Security Council can derogate from occupation law, at least as regards nonperemptory norms.[172] Finally, Resolution 1483 could constitute a description of the contemporary state of occupation law: affirming popular sovereignty, requiring the occupant to promote human rights and representative political institutions, and using public resources to those ends.[173]

The conflict between conservation and reform illustrates an important shift in occupation law, one that has significance for thinking about contemporary insurgency. Under the kill-capture model of conventional warfare, the conservationist approach to occupation law made perfect sense. The occupier's army, having defeated the enemy's army in battle, needed to wait until the resolution of the peace treaty before departing the territory. As such, occupation was temporary and primarily directed at protecting the army as it waited for resolution.[174]

Strikingly, the war-on-terror approach aligns with the traditional, conservationist approach to occupation law, inasmuch as it finds occupation law relevant at all. First, if the goal in the war on terror is to kill and capture the terrorists, then it is not obvious why occupation is relevant at all. In a globalized conflict between small bands of terrorists who are often not members of a state, occupying territory seems like a foolish strategy. It would take up considerable resources in large geographic areas, when a better approach would be to target specific groups in particular areas in many countries. Second, even if a nation following the war-on-terror approach were to occupy another state, the conservationist approach seems more than appropriate. Massive reforms to the political, legal, and economic structures of the state are unnecessary. At most, the occupier needs to change laws that would assist in the targeting or capture of terrorists. To that extent, the Hague approach of allowing changes for purposes of ensuring security would be sufficient. If the goal is kill-capture, there is no reason to democratize the state, establish a market economy, build the rule of law, or do any of the other things associated with the reformist principle that Resolution 1483 authorizes.

In contrast to the conventional and war-on-terror approaches, seeing contemporary conflict as insurgency not only emphasizes the importance of occupation law but also rejects the conservationist impulse within occupation law. Counterinsurgency requires expanding the focus of legal debates from detention, torture, and targeting, on which the war-on-terror approach has led to considerable debate, to other fields such as occupation law. The win-the-population strategy requires securing the population; guaranteeing basic services; and reforming political, economic, cultural, and legal institutions. It may therefore be more important to focus on the areas of law that touch on these broader set of concerns, and the law of occupation is one, if not the, central part of the laws of war that treats win-the-population operations. Shifting to counterinsurgency thus requires thinking more seriously and debating more vigorously the contours of occupation law.

Additionally, thinking in terms of counterinsurgency suggests rejecting the conservationist vision of occupation law. Under the kill-capture approach, the background conditions of the social structure are relatively innocuous and hence largely irrelevant, except inasmuch as they prevent the occupying army from securing its own forces or moving around the territory in search of terrorists to destroy. Unlike conventional war and the war on terror, the counterinsurgency framework assumes that part of the problem—the root cause of the insurgency—is related to the status quo in the social system. The status quo has embedded within it certain grievances that can be political, economic, cultural, or religious, among other things, and they fuel the insurgency, creating active supporters who seek to disrupt or forestall the social structure. The status quo is not a neutral position, disconnected from the causes of armed conflict or the strategy for success. Counterinsurgency's win-the-population approach is centered on addressing the grievances head-on, and that may require considerable transformation of state institutions. The reformist vision of occupation better fits the underlying causes of insurgency and the win-the-population strategy of counterinsurgency.

To some extent, the law of occupation as codified by Hague and Geneva goes far in aligning with the win-the-population strategy, but it does not go far enough. Counterinsurgents may need to reform constitutional, political, economic, infrastructural, and legal institutions within the occupied state. Under Hague and Geneva, such changes will most likely result in violations of international law. One commentary, channeling the conservationist ideal, even argues that the occupier has a responsibility to maintain the infrastructure as it was before the conflict: "The construction of a new hospital or the expansion of the road system would likely fall outside the [occupying power's] mandate as administrator."[175] Assistance, under this interpretation, "should not contribute to projects that alter permanently and in a significant manner the social and physical infrastructure of Iraq before the re-establishment of legitimate competent authorities."[176] But in counterinsurgency, operations with long-term effects are absolutely necessary. Take the example of expanding the road system. After a study of road building in Kunar province, Afghanistan, in which he identified sixteen ways in which road building had assisted the win-the-population strategy, David Kilcullen concluded that road building is "a tool for projecting military force, extending governance and the rule of law, enhancing political communication, and bringing economic development, health, and education to the population."[177] The conservationist approach, even with the limited reforms allowed by Hague and Geneva guaranteeing security and the population's humanitarian rights, simply does not go far enough. In contrast, under the Resolution 1483 approach, road building or constitutional and legal reform would be allowed or even mandated.

Embracing the reformist approach to occupation would provide greater legitimacy for reforms in occupation settings, a necessary element of the counterinsurgent's need to win over the trust of the population. Under a robust reformist approach, for example, the questions surrounding the legitimacy and legality of the Coalition Provisional Authority's (CPA) actions would have been mitigated if not eliminated.[178] At the same time, the reformist approach need not imply neocolonialism or de facto annexation. A reform-oriented occupation law could require occupiers to make changes in accordance with principles of organic, democratic self-governance. Indeed, Resolution 1483 required a self-determination approach to building representative institutions, a process that is a far cry from de facto annexation or colonialism—and one that aligns with counterinsurgency's principle that "the host nation doing something tolerably is normally better than us doing it well."[179] Shifting from conservation to reform therefore not only follows the evolution of occupation law over the century from the Hague Regulations to Iraq but also better addresses the causes of insurgency and strategy of counterinsurgents.

## *From Reciprocity to Exemplarism*

As disconnected from counterinsurgency strategy as the laws of war often are, counterinsurgents have no recourse to cruelty or lawlessness. Driven by the need for popular support, counterinsurgents should follow the dictates of law and humanity whether targeting insurgents, compensating civilians, detaining prisoners, or occupying territory. The counterinsurgent's conduct should always be designed to win over the population.

In recent years, however, many have argued that counterinsurgents can ignore the laws of war altogether because the laws of war are based on the concept of reciprocity between states, and terrorists do not comply with the law. As Ruth Wedgwood has said, "To claim the protection of the law, a side must generally conduct its own military operations in accordance with the laws of war."[180] Others have argued that the United States has no duty to follow the laws of war because reciprocity is absent. John Yoo is probably the most prominent advocate for this view. "The primary enforcer of the laws of war has been reciprocal treatment: We obey the Geneva Conventions because our opponent does the same with American POWs. That is impossible with al Qaeda."[181] Eric Posner has argued that the laws of war are premised on self-interest through reciprocity. On his theory, the laws of war come into being when parties find a way to reduce costs and destruction while not providing significant advantage to any of the other parties.[182] Posner argues that the Bush administration's claim that Common Article 3 did not apply to the war on terror was based on a reciprocity justification. The United States had nothing to gain from adhering to the rules because Al Qaeda would not follow them regardless of what the United States did.[183] Other commentators are deeply troubled about the end of reciprocity. Some argue that reciprocity would require giving the combatant's privilege to both sides; others that the absence of reciprocity and the resultant violation of law by both sides might lead to the degradation of the laws themselves; and still others think it is simply unsustainable to have law without reciprocity.[184] As one scholar puts it, "the regulation of asymmetric warfare requires a different structure of incentives to have any effect on the parties."[185]

The principle of reciprocity is defined as "the relationship between two or more States according each other identical or equivalent treatment."[186] Reciprocity enables cooperation between parties in the context of a world system in which states are unwilling to act unilaterally.[187] By cooperating with equivalent terms, states constrain their actions and the actions of others, without losing any advantage, while at the same time channeling energies into other fields or arenas. Reciprocity also has the benefit of making international law enforceable.[188] Given that there is no global sovereign to punish those who violate international law, reciprocity makes international law self-enforcing. Consider a situation in which two parties make an agreement, for example, not to use exploding bullets in a conventional war. They are both better off if they cooperate than if they both defect because their soldiers will not go through the suffering that accompanies that destructive technology. If one side follows the ban and the other side defects, the defector benefits because it may incapacitate soldiers faster. Defecting seems rational. But if the two sides know that they will face each other in battle multiple times, cooperation then becomes rational. A party could defect in the short term, gaining high benefits, but would face considerable future costs as the other party decides it too must defect. Both sides would then face horribly destructive costs. Instead, if both parties cooperate, each benefits in the short and long term.[189] Thus, the potential for future defection by the other party provides a check on a party's actions and enforces cooperative action. Through this mechanism, the principle of reciprocity provides international affairs with a way to enable cooperative action when defection may be more profitable in the short run.

The challenge arises with terrorists and insurgents. Terrorists and insurgents are perennial defectors, rendering the enforcement element of reciprocity meaningless and leading Wedgwood, Yoo, and others to question the relevance of reciprocity and the laws of war as a whole. In response to these criticisms, commentators have pursued two tracks. One response is that the laws of war are not really based on reciprocity but rather on humanitarian principles.[190] The humanitarian approach concedes that there is no interest-based argument for following the laws of war in asymmetric situations. In cases when reciprocity fails, the needs of humanity are a backstop justification for compliance. The other response is that reciprocity may still provide a justification for adherence to the laws of war despite the asymmetry of compliance between state and nonstate actors. As a matter of "specific" reciprocity, it is unlikely terrorists will comply with the laws of war; however, with defection by the United States, terrorists might act even more ruthlessly than they would have otherwise. The "diffuse" reciprocity argument warns that violating the laws of war will undermine humanitarian norms generally, which may be harmful in the long run. And the "indirect" reciprocity argument cautions that U.S. personnel and POWs might be treated poorly in future conflicts given the actions of the United States in this conflict.[191] Thus reciprocity still works and the United States should continue to follow the laws of war.

The trouble with these approaches is that they fail to account for the strategic self-interest at work in counterinsurgency. Reciprocity in the laws of war is based on two premises that are inapplicable in counterinsurgency. First, the opponents are each better off using violence to destroy the enemy, but each side can reduce its costs if both limit certain tactics. Second, if one side defects, the other side is at a disadvantage. Counterinsurgency's win-the-population strategy for victory rejects these propositions. The counterinsurgent is not better off using destructive violence to kill and capture the enemy; rather, the counterinsurgent must win the population by securing the population, ensuring essential services, establishing governance structures, developing the economy and infrastructure, and communicating with the population. These operations require limitations on destructive violence. The reason for the counterinsurgent to limit its actions is not out of reciprocity with the enemy to reduce mutual costs but pure unilateral advantage. What is important is that the win-the-population strategy does not turn on the operations of the insurgent enemy: whether the insurgent is ruthless and vicious or lawful and humanitarian is irrelevant to the counterinsurgent's strategy.

As importantly, the fact of asymmetry—of the insurgency's defection from the laws of war—is irrelevant to the counterinsurgent's strategy. It may even be helpful to the counterinsurgent's operations. Because the goal is to win over the population, a counterinsurgent that follows the laws of war may be at an even greater advantage in the context of an insurgency that is ruthless and vicious than in the context of a lawful and humane insurgency. A ruthless insurgent will alienate the population, creating fear and terror. A humane and lawful counterinsurgent, in contrast, gains legitimacy and the support of a population that seeks a stable, orderly society, free of violence and fear. The counterinsurgent seeks legitimacy, which is assisted by its adherence to law and humanity *and* by the insurgent's disregard for law and humanity. In essence, asymmetry does not undermine an interest-based justification for adherence to law but rather supports and deepens it.[192] Instead of interest based on cooperative reciprocity, interest is driven by unilateral advantage. As a result, the counterinsurgency approach rejects the basic tension between humanity and military efficacy and replaces it with the idea that humanity is needed for military success.[193] The reciprocity approach is thus grounded on strategic assumptions about cooperation, compliance, and interest that are inapplicable given the strategic realities of counterinsurgency operations.

Counterinsurgency suggests a different principle: exemplarism.[194] Exemplarism is an inherently asymmetric approach. It holds that a party can be bound to law regardless of the actions of other parties. In doing so, the exemplarist state gains in prestige, legitimacy, and power. Unlike "indirect" reciprocity, exemplarism does not premise adherence to law on the future threat of direct equivalent retaliation by a third party. And unlike "diffuse" reciprocity, it does not premise adherence to law based on the future threat of equivalent retaliation by the reduction of a community norm. Importantly, exemplarism is also not based on moral or professional ideals of martial virtue or national self-respect.[195] Instead, exemplarism is based on the strategic self-interest of the party. In essence, exemplary conduct leads to victory.

The self-interested justification for rules in armed conflict provides a nonhumanitarian and nonreciprocity justification for following those rules.[196] Military manuals and codes of conduct were some of the earliest restraints on combat and had no reciprocal element.[197] Manuals provided greater internal discipline and war-readiness and would sometimes limit damage caused "to facilitate the return to normality after the end of hostilities."[198] The impetus and success of these measures was tied to their strategic advantage, not humanity or reciprocity. Over time, it is worth noting, some of the principles established in manuals have even become customary law, such as the requirement that superior officers authorize any belligerent reprisals.[199] Exemplarism also provides a new justification for certain norms, to date justified under humanitarian aims. For example, Article 54 of Additional Protocol I bans destroying objects needed by the population, even if destruction would also harm the enemy.[200] The traditional justification is humanitarian, not reciprocal.[201] An exemplarist approach provides a self-interested justification for these rules: harming the population fuels insurgency and spreads the conflict.

Instituting the exemplarist principle into law ensures that the feedback effects it relies upon will apply to both well- and ill-intentioned counterinsurgents. Some states may seek to characterize freedom fighters, political opponents, or disgruntled members of the population as insurgents in order to quash them. Indeed, many nations have used the Bush administration's war on terror theories to clamp down on domestic opposition.[202] Moreover, we cannot assume that all insurgencies need to be overcome. Some may rightfully seek political freedom or independence. Under exemplarism, well-intentioned counterinsurgents will act in accordance with strategic necessity and law, thus retaining their efficacy and adding legitimacy to their operations. At the same time, ill-intentioned counterinsurgents—the dictator seeking to crush domestic political opposition by calling it an insurgency or terrorist group—will be seen as violating the law. The law therefore serves as a baseline for evaluating conduct and as a tool of warfare itself.[203] Legal violations will fuel grievances, spur on insurgency, and undermine international support; legal compliance will help win the population, build international support, and undermine insurgent propaganda. This enforcement mechanism is not based on the reciprocal threat of retaliation. Rather, the exemplarist model creates a standard of conduct based on the strategic foundation of win-the-population. Because victory is tied to the counterinsurgent's behavior, rather than its relation to the enemy, a legal structure that sets a standard for that behavior—even as it enables operations—is internally enforcing. Legitimacy and success build on themselves more than on the destruction of the opponent. Hence the ill-intentioned counterinsurgent will confront a downward legitimacy spiral, with exemplarist laws working against it, and the well-intentioned counterinsurgent will see an upward legitimacy spiral, with the law assisting its operations.

One example of how the exemplarist principle would manifest is in removing any thresholds for applying humanitarian norms that are conditioned on the nonstate opponent. As one commentator has noted, the applicability of norms in international armed conflict is currently "conditioned on reciprocity of obligations."[204] This is not true of internal armed conflict, since Common Article 3 does not have a reciprocity-based threshold for applicability. But

Additional Protocol II to the Geneva Conventions, which is intended to apply in conflicts between the armed forces of a contracting party and "dissident armed forces," reintroduced this threshold. It requires that the insurgent forces are "under responsible command, exercise such control over a part of [the country's] territory as to enable them to carry out sustained and concerted military operations and to implement this Protocol."[205] Through the requirements of territory and command, the Protocol attempts to ensure equality of the parties as a foundation for reciprocity: the implementation of the Protocol by the insurgents.[206] An exemplarist would reject this condition as driven by the wrong strategic model. Because counterinsurgency does not rely on reciprocity but unilateral self-interest, it is unnecessary to have threshold requirements of rough equality between the insurgents and the state or for the insurgents to follow the humanitarian norms themselves. An exemplarist approach would apply the relevant provisions to the counterinsurgent state regardless of the insurgent's conduct or degree of organization and territorial control.

The objection to this position is familiar from the debates over Additional Protocol I to the Conventions: reducing the formal requirements for privileged combatants would legitimize and grant rights to terrorists, resulting in a perverse incentive that would encourage terrorism by reducing its costs.[207] While it is true that the costs of insurgency would be reduced, this argument may be misplaced. It is not clear that Additional Protocol I's loosening of threshold rules has resulted in more terrorism or insurgencies. Even assuming that there has been an uptick in the incidence of terrorist attacks or insurgencies, it is not clear that the legal change drove that change. More likely, the extraordinary asymmetry of power has forced those who fight against superpowers to take up unconventional means.[208] In addition, changing one set of rules does not require changing all of the rules. It is possible to decouple the legal obligations of counterinsurgents from the tactics used by insurgents. The law could obligate counterinsurgents even as it simultaneously rejects providing privilege or legitimacy to insurgent tactics such as targeting civilians.[209] It does not follow, for example, that insurgents who place tanks in mosques to protect themselves from attack need to be privileged; rather, that practice can be justly condemned even as law binds the counterinsurgent.

Instead of replacing reciprocity with humanity, exemplarism retains self-interest as a justification for following the laws of war. It also illustrates a self-interested, strategically sound response to the war-on-terror theorists who assert that states have no obligation to follow the laws of war.

## Strategy and the Structure of the Laws of War

Under the exemplarist principle of strategic self-interest, the counterinsurgent's strategic incentives are aligned with humanitarian goals. Given that counterinsurgency's feedback effects provide incentives to follow humanitarian ends, it might seem that the disconnect between the laws of war and counterinsurgency strategy is largely inconsequential. Counterinsurgency-inspired rules could simply apply as policy, rather than law. However appealing this approach may seem, policy alone is insufficient. Leaving counterinsurgency-inspired rules to policy will prevent some practices in which strategy and humanitarian ends are aligned. For example, policy cannot change the ban on nonlethal weapons or formally legalize the reformist approach to the law of occupation. In those cases, the law actually prevents beneficial operations and would need to be revised.

In other areas, such as targeting, policy itself might be sufficient. In fact, the McChrystal directive on air strikes shows that the U.S. military has already started implementing an interpretation of proportionality similar to that considered here. But if policy is sufficient in certain cases, some might think that the laws are perfectly suitable as they are—and that there is little payoff to having identified the disconnect between counterinsurgency strategy and the laws of war. Others might instead suggest that because policy is sufficient, the laws of war are completely unnecessary, and that we can rely *solely* upon policy and the feedback effects inherent in exemplarism to align military operations with humanitarian values. Both of these conclusions would be unwise because they both ultimately rely upon a narrow and myopic view of the role law plays in society—that of a hard-and-fast constraint on behavior, and one that is usually enforced through punishment. But even when the law does not provide a firm constraint on behavior and even when the invisible incentive of self-interest rightly understood exists, law can nonetheless help foster desirable conduct—and this help alone is enough to justify revising the laws of war.

As a starting point, some actors will not always follow the progressive counterinsurgency strategy and its humanitarian goals. Occasional violations would certainly be punished by the feedback mechanisms that shape legitimacy during counterinsurgency operations, but the law can magnify, deepen, and accelerate those effects. By pointing to a violation of law, the local population, NGOs, the counterinsurgent's domestic population, and other actors can raise the salience of violations and gain greater traction in holding the counterinsurgent accountable. The law thus provides greater incentives for following wise policy. Moreover, when states reject the progressive strategy altogether by choosing to repress the population, the law of war helps shame the repressive state and reduces the cost for other countries to take action—such as instituting sanctions, intervening in a no-fly zone, or undertaking military operations—against the repressive state. The law thus raises the costs of violating the strategy. The result is that instituting the progressive counterinsurgency strategy into law can help channel the actions of states toward progressive actions and away from repressive actions. To be sure, law itself cannot guarantee that states will act in accordance with the progressive strategy, but it can make it more costly for states to deviate from it.

Moreover, international law can act as a precommitment mechanism to help counterinsurgents pursue sound strategy. In Homer's *Odyssey*, Ulysses seeks to hear the Sirens' song without being tempted to join them. He asks his crewmates to bind him to the mast of their ship so that he can hear the Sirens' song but cannot pursue them. Like the ropes that tied Ulysses, law can act as a mechanism to commit a state to a desired strategy when, at some later time, it may be tempted to deviate from that approach.[210] In the wake of a horrible insurgent attack or as the war progresses, third-party counterinsurgents may be pressured by domestic political constituencies to deviate from counterinsurgency, as anger, passion, and frustration triumph over reasoned judgment. A law that aligns with wise strategy can provide support to actors who seek to repel such pressures. Indeed, one of the most important stories of the legal debates on detention and interrogation practices during the Bush administration is the military, FBI, and lawyers' pushback against the administration's most extreme suggestions.[211] The institutionalization of wise policy into law and the respect for law in professional culture provided a check on expedient but counterproductive actions.

Law also provides other important benefits. It can act as a blueprint or focal point for action, providing guidance to actors looking for help in devising policy. For example, the U.S. military looked to the Fourth Geneva Convention in justifying a security internment regime in postoccupation Iraq, even though the terms of occupation law no longer applied.[212] There, the law served as a starting point for policy. This function may be particularly important for an insurgent counterstate seeking to gain international legitimacy. The American Revolutionaries, for example, drew upon international law in developing the Declaration of Independence, in hopes of winning over the opinions of all mankind to their cause.[213] In addition, the law can accelerate the development and spread of social norms and behaviors, socializing states into acting in more humanitarian ways.[214] Finally, law can provide an important psychological benefit to soldiers themselves. Engaged in the morally fraught enterprise of warfare, law enables soldiers to justify their actions. The ethos of the warrior depends in great measure upon the legitimacy—and therefore the legality—of his actions.

Given the important benefits of law, the central question is how to best revise the laws of war. Although counterinsurgencies are the likely wars of the future, conventional warfare is by no means extinct. Fear of conventional state-on-state violence is pervasive: sources of tension include Russia and Ukraine's gas disputes, India and Pakistan's border and terrorism issues, and China and Taiwan's ongoing cold war. In cases of conventional war, the traditional rules of warfare might be more suitable than ones centered on counterinsurgency. The challenge is to fashion laws of war that can satisfy two different strategic realities: the kill-capture approach to conventional warfare and the win-the-population approach to counterinsurgency warfare.

In some cases, revising the laws of war to accord with the win-the-population strategy of counterinsurgency will have little or no negative effect in conventional wars. For example, the ban on nonlethal weapons originated in agreements that were deliberatively all-inclusive, fearing the worst of technology based on the kill-capture strategy. Technological innovation, spurred on by the strategic imperatives of counterinsurgency, now produces nonlethal weapons. Rolling back the blanket technology bans in favor of a regime that differentiates between types of nonlethal weapons would align with counterinsurgency and cause little trouble for conventional war. For the same reasons as in counterinsurgency, the use of nonlethal weapons in conventional warfare is unlikely to cause more humanitarian suffering, and it may even lead to less suffering. In such cases, where the legal implications of both strategic models coincide, revision is thus unproblematic. In other cases, however, the legal implications of the two strategic models may collide, and revision becomes more difficult. Take the principles of distinction and proportionality. The clear tradeoff in shifting emphasis from distinction's rigid rules to proportionality's discretionary standard may, on balance, be beneficial in counterinsurgency, given the systemic nature of insurgency, the need to win over the population, and the feedback effects involved. But in conventional warfare, weighing the tradeoffs may cut more strongly in favor of relying more on distinction and a narrow reading of direct participation to prevent widespread attacking of civilians. Although the tradeoffs may still lead to preferring the counterinsurgency-inspired regime in conventional warfare, the precise contours of the tradeoffs are more questionable in this context. Universalizing one rule could potentially result in a regime that poorly fits the reality of the alternative form of warfare—conventional or counterinsurgency.

Lawmakers are therefore faced with multiple options. Taking a retail approach, lawyers could consider revisions for each doctrine, rather than the laws of war as a whole. One approach would be to reinterpret existing laws in line with counterinsurgency strategy. For example, the principle of proportionality can be reinterpreted without injury to require militaries to consider civilian casualties when calculating military advantage. Another approach would be to allow some laws to be revised through resurrecting doctrines and policies that have long remained dormant. For example, a revival of the principle of debellatio could address some occupations. Moving beyond doctrine-by-doctrine revisions, a more extreme measure would be to devise two laws of war: a conventional law of war and a law for counterinsurgency war. This solution is perhaps the most fraught with challenges: First, how would one decide which regime applied? In the late nineteenth and early twentieth centuries, scholars debated the right of a participating or foreign state to recognize belligerency or insurgency and the duties that went with recognizing each legal regime.[215] That kind of dualist system for the laws of war would have to establish criteria including who decides which regime applies and what happens in cases of conflicting judgments.[216] Additionally, it is not obvious that only two laws of war would be needed. In recent years some have suggested that the laws of war add to international and noninternational conflict a category of extrastate or transnational armed conflict.[217] The proliferation of legal regimes would require numerous threshold determinations for applicability and result in considerable conflict over applicable regimes. Another option would be to devise legal regimes for the broader categories of symmetric and asymmetric warfare. Symmetric conflicts are those between similar actors: states or nonstates. Asymmetric conflicts pit a state against a nonstate, the international community against a state, or the international community against a nonstate. Frequently, though certainly not always, asymmetric conflicts are driven by changes to governance—democracy promotion, humanitarian protections, or the spread of the rule of law—and they therefore generally embrace the win-the-population strategy that is central to counterinsurgency. Given these aims, it may be possible to hold asymmetrically powerful actors, like counterinsurgents or United Nations peacekeeping forces, to the exemplarist standard. The category will not be perfect in its overlap with the win-the-population strategy, but every categorization will be somewhat over- and underinclusive. Asymmetry may be sufficiently close, however, to create a workable category that limits the need for a proliferation of legal regimes. In any event, however, as a practical matter it seems unlikely that the world will come together to write a new Geneva Convention for counterinsurgency operations or asymmetric warfare, particularly as many nations might see revisions to the laws of war as merely an expedient tactic by the United States to improve its ability to wage war.

Revision of the laws of war to better fit the realities of counterinsurgency is, of course, not simply an attempt to justify current U.S. military preferences. As an initial matter, the core interest in counterinsurgency is not a United States–defined interest—it is developing a sustainable order. Although sustainable order around the world is surely in the broad interest of the United States, it is also in the interest of the peoples of the world and the people affected by the conflict itself. The chaos of war has long been recognized as inferior to a secure peace. Additionally, under a counterinsurgency-inspired legal system, the United States has no claim to universal success. United States–backed insurgents could be defeated by United States–opposed counterinsurgents; likewise, United States–backed counterinsurgents (or the United States as a counterinsurgent) could be condemned for violating the laws of war. Indeed, institutionalizing counterinsurgency's principles into law will encourage and facilitate U.S. compliance when it engages in counterinsurgency operations.

As importantly, a counterinsurgency-inspired law of war is not completely unfavorable to insurgents—who could as easily be freedom fighters as well as potential tyrants. Insurgents surely suffer under the laws of counterinsurgency when they engage in terrorism to create chaos and destabilize the government. But this seems wholly appropriate, as the law should seek to channel reformers to peaceful action. Peaceful insurgents benefit from the laws of war when the counterinsurgent government oppresses them; the repressive authority invites global condemnation and perhaps even intervention. At the later stages of a violent insurgency—when the insurgents gain control over territory and develop a counterstate—the laws then begin to work in the insurgents' favor as well. In effect, the insurgents become the counterinsurgents. As a matter of strategy, the insurgents recognize this fact, which is why Hezbollah provides so many social services to its constituents and the Tamil Tigers operated a three-tiered court system and offered legal services to the poor. Closer to the laws of war, this is (in part) why the Taliban at one point issued directives not to kill civilians.[218]

The fact that the laws of counterinsurgency warfare can apply equally to all actors indicates a broader fact about the relationship between law and strategy. However changes are made to adapt to the realities of counterinsurgency, they should be shaped by the organic relationship between law and strategy. The examples of targeting, occupation law, nonlethal weapons, detention, and exemplarism all show that law and strategy are inextricably intertwined.[219] Law does more than constrain actors; it provides pathways for action. Because it is at once enabling and constraining, law can shape strategy. The change in laws wrought by the French Revolution allowed the *levée en masse*, providing Napoleon the army needed to dominate Europe.[220] Yet, at the same time, the laws created are dependent on strategy. Czarist Russia, for example, sought bans on new technologies at the Hague Conference of 1899 because it knew it could not compete with other industrializing nations. The upstart American delegates, aware of their growing economic prowess and accompanying military might, counseled against such bans.[221] Their legal positions were shaped by their strategic posture. As Professor Phillip Bobbitt writes, "The legal and strategic choices a society confronts are often only recombinations of choices confronted and resolved in the past, now remade in a present condition of necessity and uncertainty."[222]

The laws of war, in this story, are not simply a humanitarian constraint on the horrors of war, though they do serve that function. Rather, the laws of war are an organic expression of the political values of the community they govern.[223] They construct and legitimize military activities including violence, channeling them into certain avenues and condemning others. The laws of war therefore favor certain strategies and foreclose others: they can facilitate progressive counterinsurgency operations while punishing repressive counterinsurgency operations. They can accelerate and magnify feedback loops and increase costs to noncompliance. The legal construction of warfare is thus ultimately shaped by strategy—by the characterization of the conflict, the definition of goals, and the plans and operations that will lead to victory. In fact, the goals of a strategic doctrine are not so dissimilar from many of the goals of law. Strategic doctrine seeks to influence others, to provide guidance to lower-level officials, to inform the public, and to establish neutral and general principles for action across a necessarily varied and contextual set of cases.[224]

To put it another way, the laws of war may have the function of increasing humanitarian aims, but their bounds are defined by the necessity of compliance by states in an anarchic society.[225] Whether a state agrees to the laws of war and complies with them will depend on the nature of warfare and the strategy adopted. The law, on this approach, can place duties or constraints upon states as long as those duties or constraints are in accordance with strategy. A correct understanding of strategy is therefore essential for shaping the substance of the laws of war.[226] It provides the framework within which legal obligations can be crafted. A misinterpretation of strategy may result in imposing legal obligations that will be ignored, in omitting legal obligations that could create new norms and encourage humane behavior, or in failing to address entire areas of law. The law is always evolving, growing organically as new circumstances arise. Those changes do not necessarily mean that law is merely at the mercy of expedient politicians, but rather that law must keep up with changes in society. So too with changes in strategy.

# PART TWO

*From War to Peace*

# 3

# *Turbulent Transitions*

FOR CENTURIES, INTERNATIONAL law understood war and peace as separate, as independent legal systems that triggered particular rights and responsibilities of states. Though there were challenges and exceptions to this rigid distinction, the formalistic separation of war and peace lasted well into the twentieth century. Important legal questions have likewise been dominated by an assumption that there is a separation between war and peace. When the war is over, transitional justice can begin, the rule of law can be rebuilt, and postconflict reconstruction efforts can take place.

Despite the inherited assumption that transitions involve a clean break between war and peace, contemporary conflict does not end neatly in a single moment. Counterinsurgency can persist for years, progressing slowly, province by province, with conflict and peacetime operations precariously coexisting. Peacekeeping operations, despite their deceptively pacific name, often require warfighting. And even in cases when a ceasefire has been declared, conflict is not at an end but often remains an ever-present risk. In modern transitions, the distinction between war and peace is at best rare and at worst a myth. Peace spirals into war. War moves by fits and starts toward peace. Military operations coexist with "postconflict" state-building programs. Conflict may be present in some areas but not others. Counterinsurgency thus rejects the dichotomy between war and peace, between conflict and postconflict. Instead it holds that contemporary transitions are turbulent transitions.

Counterinsurgency's embrace of turbulent transitions requires a revolution in thinking about supposedly "postconflict" issues. As radical as the shift from a kill-capture to a win-the-population strategy is for military operations, perhaps more extraordinary is counterinsurgency's tenet that civil affairs operations are as important to victory as military operations. The counterinsurgent focuses on building the rule of law, justice, and reconciliation, developing legitimate and effective governance, humanitarian aid, and economic development.

These civil affairs operations do not take place in a peaceful, postconflict world in which enemies are vanquished and stability is assumed. They take place in the midst of battle because the war itself is about the consolidation of political order. Counterinsurgents must build the rule of law even as they attack guerrilla forces; they must promote economic development even as they interdict illicit trade that funds insurgent activities; and they must create political institutions even as they infiltrate and subvert enemy organizations.

This shift requires a transformed mindset. The warrior must become the humanitarian, the state-builder, the lawgiver. Likewise, the humanitarian, state-builder, and lawgiver must understand the dynamics and strategies of war. In counterinsurgency, political and military affairs are fused. Understanding turbulent transitions is thus essential to designing and implementing successful civil affairs programs from rule-of-law operations to justice and reconciliation to new constitutions.

## The War/Peace Distinction

To some extent, it is not surprising that legal thinkers, aid workers, and warriors have assumed a clear split between war and peace. After all, the modern separation between war and peace has persisted for over three hundred years, beginning with the Dutch political philosopher Hugo Grotius's famous work *Ius Bellum et Pacis*. One of Grotius's major innovations was arguing that "war ought not to be seen in terms of specific *acts*, but instead as a legal condition in which specific acts take place."[1] Under this view, countries were in a declared state of war or they were not. Whether particular acts of war took place was irrelevant because "war" was a formal, legalistic category. Grotius's argument ushered in a major change in the international system. Medieval law had envisioned a permanent peace within Christendom that was merely punctuated by individual or collective aggressive acts. Grotius revolutionized that notion, such that he could favorably quote Cicero's statement that "between war and peace there is no middle."[2] Either one was at war, or one wasn't.

By the nineteenth century, the distinction between war and peace was universally accepted.[3] For example, in 1902 Lord MacNaughten declared from the bench, "I think the learned counsel for the respondent was right in saying that the law recognizes a state of peace and a state of war, but it knows nothing of an intermediate state which is neither one thing nor the other—neither peace nor war."[4] In practice, clarity was essential to determine precisely when the laws of war and the obligations of neutrality applied. The Boer War, for example, began at 5:00 P.M. on October 11, 1899; and when

Serbia declared war on Bulgaria in 1885, it was clear to note that war began at 6:00 A.M. on November 14.[5] This precise formalism applied just as well to the conclusion of wars, so "states should know precisely when their various belligerent activities would cease to be lawful."[6] The seriousness of the distinction is perhaps best seen in one textbook's indexed reference to "Peace" as "Peace: see Termination of War."[7]

After World War II, the international legal regime changed substantially. The United Nations Charter replaced the ancient category of war with the broader category of "the use of force" in Article 2(4), which required all members of the United Nations to "refrain . . . from the threat or use of force" against other states.[8] Banning the use of force did more than ban "war"; it also banned measures short of war, including support for insurgents or full-on participation in a civil war.[9] The Geneva Conventions likewise jettisoned "war" terminology in favor of "armed conflict." It created two regimes—international armed conflict and noninternational armed conflict—in addition to peace.[10] Importantly, the Conventions did not require formal recognition of an armed conflict by both parties, only the actual existence of an armed conflict.

These postwar revisions decidedly reformed Grotius's international system, but the postwar institution-builders could not totally overthrow the Dutch philosopher's regime. Even under the Geneva Conventions' framework of armed conflict, it is still necessary to determine where the line is between armed conflict and other activities, such as civilian police operations. Although Common Article 3 of the Geneva Conventions did not define "armed conflict," the Commentaries to the Conventions suggested "convenient criteria" to clarify the term. An armed conflict would exist in situations when:

- the insurgents against a government have "an organized military force, an authority responsible for its acts, acting within a determinate territory" and respect for the Conventions;
- the government would use regular military forces against insurgents who were organized as military and possessed territory;
- the government recognized a situation of belligerency or the UN recognized a threat to international peace; or
- the insurgents have the characteristics of a state, including de facto authority over a territory, willingness to follow the laws of war, and agreement to be bound by the Convention.[11]

Additional Protocol II to the Geneva Conventions, which expanded protections in noninternational armed conflicts, defined armed conflicts as between armed forces of the state and "dissident armed forces or other organized armed groups" who were "under responsible command," had control over territory, and were able to implement the Protocol.[12] It excluded "internal disturbances and tensions, such as riots, isolated and sporadic acts of violence and other acts of a similar nature."[13] In effect, both the Geneva Conventions and Additional Protocol II established a threshold for when "conflict" exists. Grotius's hand remained, shaping the conflict/peace distinction, just as it had created the war/peace distinction.

Since World War II, commentators have, on occasion, questioned the war/peace distinction. The early critics asked whether the Cold War was a time of conflict or peace. Clearly there was animosity, even hostility, between the Soviet Union and the United States. Clearly the tension was fundamental, reaching to basic questions of the state and ideology. And yet neither side wanted to declare and wage war. The prominent international law professor Phillip Jessup thus asked whether international law should recognize a status between war and peace, and answered that it should be called "intermediacy."[14] In doing so, Jessup actually followed a few scholars of the same period who had challenged the war/peace distinction when looking back at the armed conflicts, insurgencies, and civil wars of the preceding half-century.[15] Georg Schwarzenberger had written in 1943 that there was a *status mixtus* between war and peace that characterized insurgencies and many other armed conflicts short of war. In fact, Schwarzenberger went so far as to say that "within any system of power politics, there cannot exist any intrinsic difference between peace and war," because power was needed to maintain peace just as it was to win a war.[16] A decade later, when World War II had ended and the Cold War had emerged, Jessup's suggestion was picked up by Yale professor Myres McDougal, who asserted that a dichotomy or even trichotomy was insufficient. Instead, he argued, there was a continuum between war and peace.[17] But by the end of the Cold War the willingness to see a middle ground or continuum between war and peace was at an end. As another Yale professor, Michael Reisman, wrote in 1990, "[s]ome of the traditional norms and practices of international law that were suppressed during the Cold War can now be revived. As between the two blocs, the distinction between war and peace, each with its own legal regime, will be reinstated."[18]

In the 1990s, peacekeeping operations again raised questions about the distinction between war and peace. Peacekeeping, as the U.S. military defined it, was "undertaken with the consent of all major belligerents, designed to monitor and facilitate implementation of an existing truce and support diplomatic efforts to reach a long-term political settlement."[19] But were soldiers really just keeping the peace? Somalia, for example, "began as a humanitarian-aid effort, evolved into a peacekeeping mission, and then deteriorated into a legally indeterminate conflict."[20] Indeed, some argued that the distinction between peacekeeping, peacemaking, and combat is almost impossible to make—they exist "in a murky twilight zone between war and peace."[21] Among lawyers, much of the debate centered on whether the Constitution's requirement of a congressional declaration of war was applicable in these situations.[22] Some scholars argued that peacekeeping operations and covert actions were authorized by the Constitution, and others thought that peacekeeping and peace enforcement operations were distinct from warfare because they do "not involve U.S. troops in hostilities or situations in which hostilities are imminent."[23] The central issue in the 1990s was that a military intervention to "stop the killing while promoting a genuine resolution of the underlying conflict" was "not exactly 'war fighting,' but it is clearly not 'peace-keeping' either."[24]

Terrorism and the war in Iraq have prompted another set of commentators to note the breakdown of the conventional war/peace distinction. One group has wondered how to characterize terrorism, because it fits poorly into the wartime categories of international and noninternational armed conflict and the peacetime category of ordinary crime.[25] As Noah Feldman has written, "terrorist attacks on the United States, planned from without, cannot definitively be categorized as either war or crime. They are crime from the perspective of provenance, war from the perspective of intentionality, probably crime from the perspective of identity, and very possibly war from the perspective of scale."[26] In light of this challenge some have called for a new category of "extrastate" hostilities or a hybrid category between internal and international armed conflict called "transnational armed conflict," and others have taken inspiration from Grotius and the Swiss jurist Jean-Jacques Burlamaqui and sought to revive the category of "imperfect war."[27] A second group has seen the occupation of Iraq as an opportunity to reinvigorate the *jus post bellum*, the moral theory of justice after war. They challenge the widespread belief that the rules for using force and notions of postconflict peacemaking are separate because the reasons for going to war are often linked to the nature of the postintervention regime. As a result, war and peace are linked, not divided.[28] For the most part, however, these commentators have defined *jus post bellum* as "seek[ing] to regulate the ending of wars, and to ease the transition from war back to peace" either through postconflict reconstruction, a "responsibility to rebuild," the promotion of human rights, or criminal accountability for crimes.[29] And they seek to define a triggering moment for the *jus post bellum* to apply—either the actual end of hostilities or a Security Council resolution.[30]

The result of only a limited rethinking of the war/peace distinction is that the essential works of winning over the population—the civil affairs operations of building the rule of law, reconstruction, and transitional justice—have remained trapped in the outmoded assumption that there is a division between war and peace, between the conflict phase and the postconflict phase. To some extent, this mindset is rooted in the very origins of these modern disciplines. Reconstruction, transitional justice, and rule of law issues emerged in the wake of World War II's totalizing war, and that experience has remained seared in the memory of participants as the archetype of successful transition. Analogies to the Marshall Plan have been made in describing the reconstruction needs of Bosnia, Rwanda, Iraq, and Afghanistan, and the Nuremberg tribunals loom large over modern war crimes trials and transitional justice programs in Yugoslavia, Rwanda, and Iraq.[31] The model for successful action is one in which the conflict had ended—and ended decisively.[32]

And so the contemporary debates sidestep the simultaneous existence of war and peace. Debates about how best to build the rule of law, for example, are rife with commentators who focus on "postwar" needs.[33] They assume that they are tasked with "establishing the rule of law *after* violent internal conflict."[34] Other commentators note that building the rule of law is difficult "[i]n societies that have been wracked by violent conflict" or in "the aftermath of a military intervention."[35] Indeed, the titles of articles in this field demonstrate that their parameters are defined by the phase after conflict. For example, scholars write on *Post-Conflict Rule of Law Building* and *United Nations Reform and Supporting the Rule of Law in Post-Conflict Societies.*[36]

Discussions about transitional justice are no different. Jon Elster defines transitional justice as "made up of the processes of trials, purges, and reparations that take place *after* the transition from one political regime to another."[37] Ruti Teitel begins her work on transitional justice by noting that "societies around the world . . . have overthrown military dictatorships and totalitarian regimes for freedom and democracy" and she asks, "[t]o what extent does bringing the *ancien regime* to trial imply an inherent conflict between predecessor and successor visions of justice?"[38] Her vision of transitions is one of a clean break—of overthrown and successor regimes. Indeed, at one point she notes that "[w]ars, revolutions, and repressive rule represent *gaps* in the life of the state that threaten its historical continuity."[39] Louise Arbour, who served variously as UN High Commissioner for Human Rights, a justice on the Canadian Supreme Court, and chief prosecutor for the International Criminal Tribunals for the former Yugoslavia and Rwanda, likewise assumes the conflict is over when transitional justice begins. She notes that transitional justice addresses "crimes and abuses committed during the conflict that led to the transition" and "human rights violations that pre-dated the conflict and caused or contributed to it."[40] Many scholars in this area explicitly recognize the importance of debates about the Nuremberg Trials in their work, despite the differences between World War II and contemporary conflicts.[41]

The area where the assumption of separation between war and peace is most clear is ironically the area that comes closest to taking seriously the possibility that conflict might persist—the field of postconflict reconstruction. The very name of the field itself has built into it the assumption that the main thrust of the conflict has ended, and scholarly symposia on the topic similarly reflect the war/peace dichotomy, announcing topics such as "When the Fighting Stops: Roles and Responsibilities in Post-Conflict Reconstruction" and "State Reconstruction after Civil Conflict."[42] Most commentators define the tasks of postconflict reconstruction as involving state-building or nation-building: "[A]ddressing crimes committed during the conflict, reestablishing a functioning government, and healing residual animosities and divisions within the society. In addition to post-conflict issues, these societies must also address problems such as poverty, corruption, and the lack of a legal infrastructure—problems that confront other underdeveloped countries."[43] The assumption is simply that reconstruction takes place after the conflict, and can therefore focus on the components of state- or nation-building.[44] Indeed, one prominent framework for postconflict reconstruction begins by defining its scope as the "tasks between the cessation of violent conflict and the return to normalization."[45] In essence, the field of postconflict reconstruction "refers to that which is needed to help reconstruct weak or failing states primarily after civil wars."[46]

To be sure, some commentators have recognized that conflict might reemerge or that it may not have fully subsided, but they nonetheless continue to express a distinction between conflict and postconflict. Simon Chesterman, for example, notes that "half of all countries that emerge from war lapse back into it within five years."[47] And the Center for Strategic and International Studies (CSIS) and U.S. Army Post-Conflict Reconstruction Framework recognizes that "reconstruction often takes place at various times during and after conflict."[48] This recognition of the possibility of conflict has led scholars and practitioners to one of two responses. The first, and dominant,

approach is to make security an essential component of postconflict reconstruction operations.[49] However, the security approach is dominated by the
model of *peacetime* security. Commentators focus on civilian police capacity;
reducing crime; and demobilization, disarmament, and reintegration of belligerents. These issues are certainly important, but they indicate a belief that
in the *postconflict* phase, the nature of security must be that of peacetime, not
wartime. The second approach is to recognize that conflict and reconstruction may occur at the same time within a country but that they should be
geographically distinguished so that postconflict reconstruction only happens in the places where the conflict has actually ended. In other words, this
approach disaggregates the country into many areas, some of which can be
categorized as war and others as peace. As John Hamre and Gordon Sullivan
put it, "the term postconflict applies to those areas where conflict has indeed
subsided, but not necessarily to all parts of a nation's territory."[50] These approaches thus assume that reconstruction programs only take place in the
postconflict or peaceful sectors; they do not consider military operations or
the overarching strategy for military victory as part of their field.

## Challenging the War/Peace Distinction

Contemporary conflict makes the war/peace distinction look deeply problematic. Many states are not so fortunate as to be totally at peace. Rather they
wage war internally, even as they try to create or consolidate the authority and
legitimacy of the central government. The armed conflict in Colombia has
persisted from the mid-1960s until the present, with no peace agreement or
decisive resolution. India has faced a Maoist insurgency since an uprising in
1967. More than six thousand people have been killed during the conflict, including more than one thousand in 2009.[51] In Southern Thailand, insurgents
have challenged the government periodically since the 1902 annexation of
Patani, a largely Malay and Muslim region. Uprisings occurred from the 1940s
through the 1980s and, despite a respite in the 1990s, violence has returned,
with more than three thousand killed between 2004 and 2008.[52] Since 1969,
the Philippines has waged war against an insurgency in the south of the country.[53] Somalia has effectively been without a central government since 1991,
with civil war, piracy, insurgency, terrorism, and an Ethiopian occupation
existing side-by-side with efforts to develop local political authorities and rec-
reate a central government. In Iraq since 2003 and Afghanistan since 2001,
military force has been necessary to guarantee security, even as a civil government seeks to return life to normalcy. Pakistan faces insurgents in the Northwest

Frontier Provinces and rebellion in Baluchistan. Nepal waged war against Maoists for years, until the Maoists eventually gained power. Conflict is widespread around the world—in seemingly stable states, and in states trying to consolidate government authority. Are these states at war or at peace?

The challenge to the war/peace dichotomy does not end with ongoing, enduring conflicts. Indeed, in many cases the transition from full-fledged war to progressively more stable, peaceful societies is one that is turbulent and gradual. Peace must be won during war; and in some cases, a seemingly stable peace may be better interpreted as a break from war.

Situations of insurgency and counterinsurgency are perhaps the best place to understand turbulent transitions because both insurgents and counterinsurgents must engage in traditionally "postconflict" operations of building the rule of law, establishing legitimate governance, and providing essential services in order to win over the population. Recall that an insurgency is "an organized, protracted politico-military struggle designed to weaken the control and legitimacy of an established government, occupying power, or other political authority while increasing insurgent control."[54] Insurgencies are focused on political power, challenging the legitimacy of the state through the creation of a counterstate, and they are social systems, deriving their support and energy from the active or passive support of the local population.[55] Insurgents therefore seek to drive a wedge between the people and the government by exploiting and creating popular grievances that undermine popular support for the government and by fomenting backlash when counterinsurgents overreact or make mistakes. Populations targeted by insurgencies are often vulnerable because they already have political, social, economic, religious, or cultural dissatisfaction with the regime.[56]

To win over the population, insurgents often develop governance and administrative institutions. At their peak, the Tamil Tigers in Sri Lanka had a police force of 3,000, property taxes, a law college, free legal representation for the poor, a penal code, and a hierarchical system of courts.[57] Rebels during the French counterinsurgency in Algeria were organized into military, justice, and tax divisions, and they conducted dispute resolution for villagers rather than forcing them to visit larger cities.[58] And Hamas and Hezbollah famously provide mutual aid and social services to the local population.[59] Insurgents thus engage in more than terrorism and warfighting: they try to provide justice and governance for the local population.

Counterinsurgents also seek to rebuild the political bonds of a society, winning over the reconcilable supporters of the insurgency and killing or capturing the irreconcilable supporters of the insurgency. Converting insurgents into supporters of the government may be more likely than it might initially seem. Insurgencies are often supported by "accidental guerrillas"—those who are allied with the insurgency not because they believe in the cause but because they have some other grievance against the government. The accidental guerrilla process is simple: extremists such as Al Qaeda move into a remote, ungoverned, or conflict-ridden area and try to build relationships locally, though they are often rebuffed at first. Over time, they spark violence and get national or international attention, prompting an external intervention (often repressive) in the region by a domestic or foreign government. During the intervention, the local dynamic shifts. The intervention creates a backlash among the local people, who now align with the radical extremists to defeat the external intervention. These accidental guerrillas fight with extremists "not because they support the . . . ideology but because they oppose outside interference" or are simply alienated by heavy-handed tactics.[60] In other words, local people fight because of their independent grievances. Their war is local, perhaps even parochial; it is not ideological. Backlash is thus central to modern insurgent tactics. Insurgents seek to "provoke overreaction from counterinsurgent forces" in order to discredit them.[61] Any of the counterinsurgent's human rights or legal violations are exploited and used to illustrate hypocrisy.[62] In this context, the counterinsurgent must recognize that any action can influence the shape of the conflict, and that all operations must be designed in order to build popular support.

Because insurgency is ultimately a political challenge, counterinsurgency involves shoring up the power and legitimacy of the government. As a result, victories in traditional military battles cannot end the conflict. The war ends not because the military has defeated the enemy but because the government has created peace by winning over the population and reestablishing political order and stability. As David Kilcullen has noted, "a government that is losing to an insurgency is not being outfought, it is being outgoverned."[63]

To win the population's allegiance through governance, counterinsurgents pursue civil affairs operations—securing the population, ensuring essential services, establishing governance structures, developing the economy and infrastructure, and communicating with the population.[64] Counterinsurgents believe the most helpful actions are "local politics, civic action, and beat-cop behaviors."[65] The job is not "the job of a diplomat, a development worker, or a soldier: it was the job of a 1920s Chicago ward politician."[66] It is for this reason that counterinsurgents focus so much on interagency cooperation—with nongovernmental organizations (NGOs), civilian partners, and local populations. Without those actors' cooperation and support, a counterinsurgency cannot succeed. As one strategist has put it, "civil affairs is a central counterinsurgency activity, not an afterthought. It is how you restructure the environment to displace the enemy from it."[67]

As a result of the insurgents' ability to exploit grievances and heavy-handed tactics, modern counterinsurgency strategy holds that "[l]egitimacy is the main objective."[68] Actions, programs, or institutions that the population deems as illegitimate will be fuel for insurgents. Significantly, legitimacy is contextual. Not only are all counterinsurgencies unique but there may be differences at a granular level, even between villages in the same district.[69] As one of the *Field Manual's* paradoxes states, "[w]hat works in this province, may not work in the next." When counterinsurgents' visions of legitimacy clash with those of the local population, the local population's views are more important.[70]

The result of backlash effects, the importance of legitimacy, and the need for civil as well as military affairs is that counterinsurgency must proceed in phases over a long period of time. Counterinsurgency thus follows a "clear-hold-build" framework. First, counterinsurgents ensure basic security by clearing the insurgents from an area, a process that is often military in nature. Then they hold that area while building up the local institutions of society that enable the indigenous people to hold the area themselves.[71] This process does not occur at the same pace across a country or even a province. Baghdad may be as violent as Basra is peaceful. And these phases cannot be neatly divided into conflict and postconflict because insurgents will try to infiltrate or retake areas that have been made peaceful. Tomorrow Basra may be violent and Baghdad peaceful. At any point, these phases may lurch forward into relative normalcy and stability or stumble backward into renewed chaos.

Counterinsurgency is perhaps the best example of the coexistence of violent conflict amounting to warfare with the "peacetime" operations of reconstruction, building the rule of law, and transitional justice and reconciliation. It is not only the case that conflict exists alongside these operations, but that these operations are a necessary and even *constitutive* element of gaining victory in the conflict. A purely military strategy is anathema to counterinsurgency, and a purely civil affairs strategy is ineffectual in counterinsurgency. The two elements are each necessary to win the population, defeat the insurgency, and establish a stable, orderly society.

Counterinsurgency's challenge to the traditional conflict/postconflict dichotomy is not unique. The United Nations' long history of peace operations provides another example of the difficulty in finding a clear line between peace and war, conflict and postconflict. Defining precisely what constitutes peacekeeping operations is difficult; the British Army's field manual on peace-keeping, for example, provides thirteen different definitions.[72] But at its heart, peacekeeping was intended to operate after a ceasefire and political settlement in order to prevent backsliding into conflict.[73]

Almost since it began peacekeeping operations, the United Nations has found it difficult to define precisely how much force can and should be used. Peacekeepers were allowed to use force in self-defense, but the scope of self-defense proved to be "infinitely malleable."[74] At times, self-defense incor-porated the peacekeepers' "freedom of movement" as impartial and neutral parties, and it even expanded to include the "defense of the mission."[75] As an example, consider UN peacekeeping operations in the Congo from 1960 to 1964. Though its mandate began with a narrow scope for using force, the UN Operation in the Congo (ONUC) needed to gain freedom of movement throughout the Congo in order to stabilize the country and maintain peace. In the process, ONUC's mission changed and expanded from restoring public order, which included patrols and disarming civilians and militias, to preventing an intertribal conflict and civil war. To gain freedom of movement the peacekeepers deployed throughout the country, only to face attacks, re-quiring them to fight back. One area, Katanga province, which was partially backed by foreign mercenaries, refused UN troop entry. Seeking freedom of movement and mandated to take action to remove foreign military persons, ONUC expanded into Katanga, and upon meeting resistance, used force to remove its government as part of a strategic approach to defending them-selves. The Congo experience demonstrated that self-defense was extremely flexible and could be used to justify even the most conventional of military operations.[76] As one commentator notes, UN actions were "indistinguishable from a standard military campaign" even though they continually stated they were engaged only in peacekeeping operations.[77]

The challenges only grew more complex after the Cold War ended. In a 1992 report, *An Agenda for Peace*, Secretary-General Boutros Boutros-Ghali identi-fied the United Nations' peace operations goals as involving both peacekeeping and peacebuilding.[78] Peacemaking and peacekeeping, he noted, were needed "to halt conflicts and preserve peace once it is attained."[79] Peacebuilding involved "rebuilding the institutions and infrastructures of nations torn by civil war and strife; and building bonds of peaceful mutual benefit among nations formerly at war."[80] Some commentators called this the second generation of peacekeeping, others "expanded peacekeeping," and still others called it "peace enforcement."[81] Whatever the name, these operations would involve "political, societal, eco-nomic, humanitarian, electoral, diplomatic, and military initiatives."[82]

United Nations operations in the Balkans are illustrative of the challenges of peacekeeping and peacebuilding. Unlike traditional peacekeeping, which had been limited to minimal involvement in cases such as the Israel-Egypt border, these peace-enforcement operations eroded the central principles of peacekeeping. Consent was often questionable and, as a result, peace was not always present in reality.[83] The Balkan force, for example, was tasked with an "interim arrangement to *create* the conditions of peace and security required for the negotiation of an overall settlement to the Yugoslav crisis."[84] Moreover, the United Nations' mandate was expanded to include providing and protecting humanitarian aid, something that required significant military support. Protecting aid required troops at storage and distribution sites and convoys to transport aid, in addition to military protection for civilian aid workers.[85] Moreover, in a context where the belligerents were dispersed throughout the society, rather than on two sides of a border region, peacekeepers found themselves in greater danger and with less chance of popular acknowledgment of their neutrality and impartiality.[86] When the peacekeepers used force even in defense of humanitarian aid or protecting civilians, they faced retaliation and, in some cases, peacekeepers were even taken hostage.[87] Soldiers on the ground recognized that they were not merely peacekeepers, but were rather being asked to restore the monopoly of violence in Balkan societies; British commanders even argued that the most effective techniques were not the new doctrines crafted for peacekeeping, but rather those they had used in counterinsurgency operations.[88] In sum, UN Forces had pushed themselves into the midst of an ongoing, complex conflict with the goal of providing humanitarian aid and creating peace. Yet somehow the entire operation was justified as simply "peacekeeping."

In 2000, after a decade of debate, a UN review panel released a wide-ranging report that emphasized the turbulent nature of peacekeeping operations.[89] The Brahimi Report recognized that peacekeeping had evolved from "a traditional, primarily military model of observing ceasefires and force separations after inter-State wars, to incorporate a complex model of many elements, military and civilian, working together to build peace in the dangerous aftermath of civil wars."[90] Modern peacekeeping involved cases where one side had not resulted in outright victory, but rather in which conflict was ongoing: "United Nations operations thus do not deploy into *post-conflict* situations so much as they deploy *to create* such situations."[91] The hope was that UN operations could create peace and then pursue peacebuilding activities.[92] Moreover, the report noted that in intrastate conflicts consent is

often manipulated or uncertain. Some parties consent to create time to prepare another offensive; other parties provide consent, but the rank-and-file
belligerents are under loose control and continue to fight on.[93] The report
also recognized the difficulties with strict impartiality or neutrality because
some parties may violate agreements, becoming clear aggressors. The report
even regretted the United Nations' failure to realize and act on this fact: "No
failure did more to damage the standing and credibility of United Nations
peacekeeping in the 1990s than its reluctance to distinguish victim from
aggressor."[94] In the end, the Brahimi Report thought it would be possible to
engage in more robust peace operations and it recommended "bigger forces,
better equipped and more costly, but able to pose a credible deterrent threat,
in contrast to the symbolic and non-threatening presence that characterizes
traditional peacekeeping."[95]

A core component of the conflict/postconflict distinction is the creation
of peace agreements that allow the enemy to reintegrate into the society.
Once the war is over, former enemies must reunify the country. As a result,
peace processes often face the challenge of "spoilers"—those who will return
to war in order to win outright or gain more in the negotiations.[96] Spoiler
problems operate across different types of conflict: reconciling with insurgents, peacekeeping and peace operations, and civil wars. In spoiler situations,
an agreement brings peace, but it is really peace with the risk of a return to
war. The "postconflict" world is thus perilously maintained.

To see the problem of spoilers in concrete terms, consider the conflict in
Angola in the early 1990s. In May 1991 the Angolan government and the
UNITA faction signed a peace agreement that provided for a transition period of demobilization that would culminate in elections. By late summer of
1992, it became clear that Jonas Savimbi, the president of UNITA, would be
unwilling to accept defeat in the elections. During the transition period,
UNITA had stored weapons for easy access, stationed soldiers around the
country, and grew ready to take control of the country quickly. Despite
peaceful elections that were certified by the United Nations as without intimidation or fraud, when the government's party received more votes than
UNITA in the preliminary results, Savimbi declared widespread fraud, with-
drew his generals from unified command of the Angolan army, refused to
discuss the situation with foreign diplomats, and eventually launched attacks
around the country. One year later, when Savimbi finally returned to negotiations, over 300,000 Angolans had been killed.[97]

Spoiler problems provide an important case for those interested in war to
peace transitions. Foremost, they are situations in which the failure to attend

to the risk of conflict, despite the existence of a formal peace and an actual ceasefire, can be disastrous. In the case of Savimbi, it may be better to interpret the transition period as either an agreement conditional on his victory or an opportunity for him to reorganize and rebuild his strength in order to prepare for his next offensive. Seeing spoiler problems as an example of turbulent transitions involves thinking about the transitional and immediate postconflict period as one defined not just by an emerging peace but also by the possibility of an imminent return to war.

Additionally, the strategies for managing spoiler situations are similar to the strategies employed against enemies in other kinds of conflict, including counterinsurgency. The primary strategies for managing spoilers are inducement, or giving the spoiler what it wants; socialization, or changing the spoiler's behavior to meet a set of norms by those who commit to peace; and coercion, punishing the spoiler.[98] Though they are conventionally understood in the context of diplomatic negotiations, the same elements apply to gaining victory in counterinsurgency, in which conflict and rebuilding are more closely linked. Inducement is merely a form of addressing the grievances of the local population; without grievances, they have no need to fight and will support the government. Socialization for spoilers requires getting them to follow certain values, such as becoming a political party; socialization in insurgencies similarly could involve winning over reconcilable supporters and including them in the local government. Coercion may mean threats in negotiation, but it may also mean the pure application of force. Of course, coercion is frequently used in insurgencies to kill or capture irreconcilable enemies. The fact that the strategies for addressing spoilers are so similar to those of addressing insurgents illustrates that turbulent transitions are ultimately about who will control the political order of the state.

## *The Dynamics of Turbulent Transitions*

Counterinsurgencies, peace operations, and spoiler problems all demonstrate that the war-peace dichotomy is a poor assumption upon which to build an understanding of transitional policies. Civil affairs—building governance, providing humanitarian aid, and reconciling factions—operate in the midst of war, not simply in its shadow. Taking seriously the presence and importance of conflict requires distilling some of the major dynamics of conflict. These dynamics form the foundation for rethinking civilian operations during counterinsurgency operations and, indeed, all turbulent transitions.

## Backsliding

The most obvious implication is that in conflict-ridden transitions, back-sliding is possible—a peaceful area could become wartorn, and a wartorn area could be won by the enemy. Insurgents may retreat briefly to rebuild their capacities, providing short-term victory to the counterinsurgents. But they may return in full force, particularly if the counterinsurgents reduce their commitment to supposedly peaceful areas. The Congo's peace operations provide a broader example, in which civil war was restarted after the United Nations left Katanga. And spoiler problems illustrate the clearest and least obvious case of backsliding. Even when peace seems present and achievable, it cannot be taken for granted, as Angola's history shows. As a result of the possibility of backsliding, civil affairs operations must take into account the strategic and tactical consequences of its programs. Programs may help consolidate gains or may contribute to backsliding. Any action that takes place in a conflict zone therefore has strategic implications.

## Segmentation and Fragmentation of Territorial Control

The ongoing existence of conflict implies that control over territory will be segmented and fragmented. The segmentation of territory means that different portions of the territory may be in control of different parties. The fragmentation of territory means that some portions of the territory may have overlapping control between two or more parties—that is, they may be in the midst of a struggle for control. In segmented areas, violence is easier to minimize because the party in control can protect civilians and get the support of the population against outliers who seek to disrupt control. Civilian collaboration with the local authorities is thus a consequence of control, not a cause. In fragmented areas, it is unclear who is in control and who will be in control in the future. Collaborators are less likely to flock to one side or the other because they fear the consequences if they choose the eventual loser.[99] Building trust and support among individual civilians is therefore vital to gaining the necessary support and information needed to eliminate the opponent.

The segmentation and fragmentation of territorial control suggests that it is unwise to assume that military or civil operations need to be national in scope. Because different portions of the country may be in different stages of conflict—some totally at peace, some in the midst of war, and many in between—programs can differ based on the status of the conflict in a particular geography. Policies in totally peaceful, consolidated areas should differ from those where war is at its most chaotic and from areas where the opponent controls the territory. Targeting programs and policies to particular geographies may be more successful because, as counterinsurgents like to say, what works in one province may not work in the next.


## Organic Evolution

The indeterminate boundary between conflict and peace also implies that transitions are more likely to follow an evolutionary path, growing organically out of the conditions of the country and the conflict, rather than a single moment of transition in which the society is established from a blank slate. In other words, it may be misguided to focus on a "constitutional moment" or to see the political system as analogous to a social contract.[100] These staples of liberal political theory assume that a society can come together at one time and agree upon a set of principles or rules for their governance. In conflict-ridden transitions, however, constitutional moments may be mirages, providing the appearance of settled political structures without the substance. Because there is no clear moment when the violence ends and the war is won, it is unlikely that the whole people will be able to create a government under the social contract model—or that such government will be effective. Certain areas of the territory may remain under insurgent or spoiler control; other areas may be rife with conflict. Some areas may become peaceful relatively quickly, requiring government and reconstruction; other areas may remain ungoverned for extended periods of time, perhaps even indefinitely. In some cases, states may simply have to embrace durable disorder.[101] It may therefore be more helpful to see transitions as evolving from the conditions on the ground—slowly, over time, and variable based on each particular locality.[102]

The organic evolution approach also helps focus on the fact that the conflict itself changes the nature and extent of the grievances and identities. The accidental guerrilla syndrome in insurgencies is the clearest example. The intervention of outside actors alienates the local people who were initially opposed to insurgent extremists, and the local people then ally with the extremists. Indiscriminate violence and heavy-handed tactics may further alienate the population against the counterinsurgents, even if the counterinsurgents have the interests of the people in mind. The most recent studies on civil wars concur, noting that polarization is endogenous to the conflict.[103] In many cases, polarization is not simply predetermined by census-measuring statistics such as Sunni versus Shia or Catholics versus Protestants. In many cases there are clan-based conflicts, blood feuds, tribal rivalries, and other cleavages that are overlaid with the population's general tendency to "avoid risky commitments."[104] The major parties in the civil war thus seek to unite these disparate and often conflicting groups around their single cleavage. The war itself may therefore harden identities even as it places stresses on local cleavages.[105] Moreover, war may even create entirely new identities. In Afghanistan, for example, those who lived in the Panjshir valley had no distinct political identity, but when the valley was consumed by war and required military action, the Panjshiri grew an ethnic identity.[106] In conflict-ridden transitions, then, identities and commitments within the population may change, creating new unified groups, exposing preexisting cleavages, and hardening identities. In this dynamic environment, it may be more helpful to understand the particular changes and commitments of the people as they change instead of developing inflexible or permanent institutions.

## Popular Support and Backlash

It is intuitive and obvious that building institutions—whether the rule of law, constitutional government, or administrative and civil capacity—will be difficult if the institutions do not have popular support and legitimacy. Seeing transitions as involving conflict, however, implies that considering "popular support" is not sufficient. The more precise question is *whose* support is needed. In insurgencies driven by the accidental guerrilla syndrome, the "population" could include the irreconcilable extremists, the accidental guerillas who are not committed to extremism, the passive supporters of the insurgency, or the opponents of the insurgency. In civil wars, the "population" may include high-level political actors who operate on the level of ideology, the mid-level political actors like local leaders or mid-level supporters, or the micro-level populations who are divided by factions, tribe, family, and location.[107]

Building popular support for institutions requires taking into account these breakdowns and cleavages or else suffering from popular backlash that can fuel the conflict. Military operations or civil affairs programs will inevitably appeal to some groups and not to others, based on a variety of ideological, political, social, and local cleavages. Any action taken, therefore, can build support with some populations even as it alienates other populations. Alienated populations—in particular their leaders or the extremists—may use these actions as propaganda to consolidate their power base and popular support. Polarization and radicalization in the population can be a result of the conflict itself, and actions that alienate segments or the totality of the population provide a lightning rod around which segments can cohere. To be sure, backlash effects are present in genuinely postconflict situations as well. But in cases of ongoing conflict or the risk of conflict, the stakes are much higher: unlike peacetime situations, groups are already seeking to overthrow the regime using violence. As a result, the ongoing conflict lowers the barrier to participating in violence. Backlash thus has the potential to push people toward active or passive support for the warfighting parties.

## The Myth of Impartiality

In conflict-ridden transitions, impartiality, neutrality, and merely technical assistance are impossible. Any action taken will support one side and harm another side. Counterinsurgency is again the best example of this phenomenon. Because insurgencies are social systems that seek to accomplish political and social goals, they rely upon all elements of social power—not just military power. When they can, insurgents therefore establish dispute-resolution processes and facilitate increasing local livelihoods, and they provide for governance and humanitarian aid to victims of natural disasters or military attack. The counterinsurgent is no different. Reconstruction, civilian security, economic development programs, and even humanitarian aid are leverage to win the population's support and to identify and develop collaborators who can assist in preventing further conflict. They are essential mechanisms for denying popular support to the insurgency and are therefore seen as necessary to successful operations. Because civilians are targeted in these activities, "[n]o one is allowed to remain neutral and watch the events in a detached way."[108]

As a result, these activities—even when practiced by NGOs and other humanitarians or nonmilitary groups—are partisan activities. When they take place as an adjunct to the counterinsurgent's military operations, aid and assistance activities contribute to the creation of a stable political and social order under the counterinsurgent's provision of security. They thus reinforce the counterinsurgent's order. When they take place in insurgent-held territory, humanitarian and other aid free up resources for the insurgents to spend on other activities, including military and governance operations.[109] They also provide a basic level of support to the population, thus reducing the population's grievance with an insurgent authority that does not or cannot provide for it. As a result, as David Kilcullen has said, "there is no such thing as impartial humanitarian assistance or civil affairs in counterinsurgency. Every time you help someone, you hurt someone else."[110] To be sure, this does not mean that humanitarian aid in insurgent territories is never appropriate. It only means that it must be understood as contributing to the dynamics of the conflict. Aid may be necessary as a matter of morality, to prevent unconscionable human suffering. But it cannot be ignored as playing an active role in the dynamics of the conflict.

TOGETHER, THESE CORE dynamics define turbulent transitions from war to peace. They see civil affairs and military operations as coexisting in time and place and evolving through their interactions. They embrace the shattering of the state into areas of contested and singular control. They recognize hard-won stability as only a limited success, precariously held unless consolidated over time. And they root victory in the will and support of the population. In so doing, turbulent transitions erase the distinction between war and peace, between conflict and postconflict. Instead, they recognize the overlap of war and peace and the interplay between warfighting and peacebuilding.

# 4

## Transitional Justice as Lawfare

IN EARLY 2010 journalists and human rights advocates discovered that Afghanistan had quietly passed a justice and reconciliation law, providing amnesty for war crimes and human rights violations that took place before the fall of the Taliban in 2001. With righteous fury, they condemned the law as establishing a culture of impunity, as a giveaway to warlords, and as a sanction to commit horrific human rights violations. As importantly, they chastised the Afghan government for its surreptitious process—its failure to engage in serious public debate and its willingness to pass the law without fanfare or publicity.[1] They argued that transitional justice—programs that address past violations of human rights and humanitarian law like war crimes prosecutions, truth and reconciliation commissions, purges from office, and reparations—requires transparency and accountability, not amnesty.[2] While controversy brewed over the government's law, U.S. Marines began military operations to retake the Taliban stronghold of Marjah in Helmand province. In the subsequent months, they would be caught in the midst of improvised explosive devices, small firefights, and unexpected battles. The war continued even as the traditionally *post*conflict activity of transitional justice proceeded.

Three years earlier in Iraq, Sunni tribal leaders who had cooperated with Al Qaeda turned on their terrorist allies. In what would be called "the Awakening," the Sunni tribes worked with coalition troops to eradicate Al Qaeda forces, contributing to the substantial decrease in violence in Iraq in 2007 and 2008. They even reconciled with the government, integrating into the Iraqi army and taking positions in the Ministry of the Interior. However, many involved in the Awakening had outstanding arrest warrants from their time as insurgents, and in 2008, Iraqi Security Forces began arresting members of the Awakening. The tribes worried that the government had forsaken them, and the possibility of a return to insurgency grew stronger. To preserve peace, the government chose not to execute the valid warrants.[3] Effective counterinsurgency required reconciliation. Justice stepped aside.

Reconciliation is a central strategy of counterinsurgency, promising to end the insurgency by co-opting the insurgents. With reconciliation, the government brings back into the political community the discontents who had rebelled against it. Through a balance of shared interest, compromise, punishment, and rehabilitation, the insurgents agree to lay down their arms and bring the war to an end. At the same time, the scope of reconciliation expands or contracts the possibility of transitional justice. Broad reconciliation, for example, means limited war crimes prosecutions. Narrow reconciliation, by contrast, enables expansive justice for criminals. Reconciliation and transitional justice are thus intimately connected.

Operating in the midst of conflict, rather than in its aftermath, transitional justice and reconciliation programs can influence and shape the conflict. Prosecuting insurgent supporters may make peace difficult as accidental guerrillas and reconcilable insurgents fight on, seeing no way to defect. Widespread amnesties may alienate the population from the government, as former war criminals and human rights violators are rewarded with positions of power. During counterinsurgency, then, transitional justice becomes a form of lawfare—the practice of using law as an instrument or tactic for accomplishing strategic objectives. Will reconciliation reduce the fighting? Will lenient justice programs alienate loyal supporters of the government and spark more insurgents? Can transitional justice programs be designed to win the population and end the insurgency?

Counterinsurgency requires rethinking the themes, frameworks, and mechanisms of transitional justice to understand how they operate in conflict-ridden transitions. As an instrument of lawfare, transitional justice is as concerned with military strategy as it is with human rights. It requires warriors to see transitional justice programs as strategic and tactical tools that shape the battlefield and can help bring an end to conflict—or spur it on. It requires human rights advocates to consider the strategic implications of justice and reconciliation programs, jettisoning the assumption that peace and stability have arrived. And it requires both warriors and advocates to work together, to embrace the interactions and intersections of counterinsurgency strategy and transitional justice. There are no simple solutions to designing transitional justice programs in the midst of conflict, but understanding the tradeoffs and opportunities can help strategists and activists alike develop policies that better integrate tactics, morality, and law.

## *Just Lawfare*

In recent years, many commentators have decried the phenomenon of lawfare, the "strategy of using . . . law as a substitute for traditional military means to achieve an operational objective."[4] Critics of lawfare focus on international groups and adversaries. They criticize nongovernmental organizations for bringing lawsuits—habeas corpus for detainees, stays of execution, and civil liability for governments that use torture—and they criticize adversaries for trying to get the military to violate the laws of war.[5] For example, insurgents might illegally put a tank in a mosque, seeking to provoke the military to attack the mosque and face popular backlash.[6]

This negative vision of lawfare is based on an incomplete understanding of law. It sees law primarily in its formal capacity, as a clear set of structures that operate as a constraint on behavior. Law is meant to be totally independent of warfare, not a tool or tactic of warfare. And yet, lawsuits for prosecuting financiers of terrorism are a weapon to take down enemies' fiscal and material capacity, and establishing a legitimate rule of law is a strategic operation that reduces popular support for the insurgency.[7] Law can indeed be a weapon of war, an affirmative tool for advancing strategic and tactical interests during conflict. Lawfare, in other words, "is a continuation of warfare by political or legal means."[8]

This symmetrical understanding of lawfare—of law as a weapon that either side can use—fits naturally with counterinsurgency. Counterinsurgency is political war, war aimed at achieving political and social goals. Counterinsurgents are not limited simply to military means but rather can use all the tools that build order in society—economic, political, military, cultural, and legal. Justice programs institutionalize and legitimize the state's power, in the process reducing strife.[9] And the laws themselves influence people's beliefs and behaviors. Lawfare requires both sides to integrate law and strategy. Armies must not kill civilians, for those deaths can be used as both emotional and legal propaganda. Insurgents and counterinsurgents alike must try to establish legal systems to legitimize their authority in a territory. Violations of law by either the insurgents or the government reduce the likelihood of that side winning over the population. In counterinsurgency, it is no stretch to see transitional justice programs as weapons of war, instruments of lawfare that can be designed to reduce or even eliminate the insurgency.

Yet the field of transitional justice has been dominated, even defined, by the assumption that it is a postconflict process, coming after a repressive or conflict-torn past in a now-peaceful, stable present. Most transitional justice advocates focus on transitions to liberal democracy—in Eastern Europe after the fall of the Soviet Union, in Latin America in the 1980s and 1990s, and in South Africa after apartheid.[10] These "paradigmatic transitions" feature a shift from nondemocratic regimes to democracy, bringing with that transition governmental legitimacy, the rule of law, acknowledgement of human rights violations, and transformed institutions.[11] This aspect of transitional justice— dealing with a former regime—is as old as the field itself, which began at least with the ancient Greeks, who twice engaged in transitional justice after democracies overthrew oligarchies in Athens.[12] In those situations where a territory has been mired in war, transitional justice has remained in the shadows of World War II. In particular, the Nuremberg Tribunal has loomed large over modern war crimes trials in Yugoslavia, Rwanda, and Iraq.[13] But other issues of transition are equally dominated by that model: the Marshall Plan is frequently referenced as the archetype for reconstruction, and de-nazification was a prominent analogy for the 2003 de-Ba'athification of Iraq.[14] As a result, prevailing accounts of transitional justice have been developed with a kind of transition in mind that is disconnected from the turbulent realities of counterinsurgency.[15] As the coexistence of military operations and transitional justice programs in both Iraq and Afghanistan show, transitional justice operates in the midst of conflict, not just in its wake.[16]

Understanding how transitional justice can be a tool of lawfare requires reconsidering the goals of transitional justice programs. The standard list of goals for transitional justice programs can be grouped as vengeance/retribution, reparations, deterrence, communication, rehabilitation, building the rule of law and democracy, and reconciliation.[17] Vengeance and retribution channel moral ideals of what people deserve based on their actions; criminals should be punished for their behaviors, whether through a war crimes trial or purging from office.[18] Reparations-based justifications for transitional justice focus on the relationship between the victim and the perpetrator.[19] The hope is that compensating the victims for their suffering and loss may facilitate individual and social healing and, at the same time, that the perpetrator's compensation to the victim will restore balance in their relationship and serve as a lesson or punishment for the perpetrator. Reparations, however, can rarely compensate for extraordinary losses and may be better seen as symbolic actions, particularly as compensation may be impossible in cases of heinous crimes. Another possible goal of transitional justice is deterrence, as the threat of prosecution for war crimes provides an incentive for potential war criminals not to undertake heinous acts.[20] Many see transitional justice as having a communicative purpose—as establishing the truth and asserting the moral norms of a community. Focusing on truth can help determine what happened to the disappeared, reverse the silence and secrecy of past regimes, provide psychological closure for victims who were living with doubts and uncertainty, and even foster forgiveness.[21] Declarations of the truth can also educate the public as to what happened and help establish new moral norms on what actions the society condemns. At the same time, however, the communicative power of transitional justice may "create scapegoats and feelings of bitterness."[22] Rehabilitation involves "healing individuals and society after the trauma of mass atrocity."[23] Transitional justice is also often justified as necessary to establish liberal democracy and the rule of law.[24] In postconflict settings, trials can help create a legitimate legal system in the eyes of the population, and in postauthoritarian states, trials for serious offenses may help distinguish the new legal system from the old.[25] In addition, some argue that transitional justice protects democratic values and therefore assists the transition to democracy.[26]

Finally, some commentators believe that transitional justice should focus on reconciliation. In many transitions, the key is to "get opposing factions who have committed atrocities against each other and against an innocent civilian population to come to a peaceful settlement."[27] Those who focus on reconciliation more often than not argue against strong transitional justice processes in order to minimize division within society.[28] Amnesties can facilitate reconciliation between factions and democracy itself is based on reconciliation, not retribution.[29] Some, however, argue that accountability is central to reconciliation because "one cannot be reconciled if there is a feeling of injustice."[30] At the core of the debate is whether stability and reconciliation are the consequences of reestablishing justice and law or the conditions for it.[31]

Seeing transitional justice as lawfare shifts attention from these varied goals to a more pragmatic one: success in the conflict. Focusing on transitions from authoritarianism to democracy, scholars have written that transitional justice processes should be evaluated with respect not just to moral concerns but to their ability to facilitate or forestall the transition to democracy.[32] Similarly, then, an overarching concern in turbulent transitions from war to peace is how transitional justice processes will influence the course of the conflict. As counterinsurgency strategy describes, political, social, economic, and cultural action influence the course of the war.[33] Even something as simple as building roads can be an effective weapon of war, creating support among the population for the counterinsurgent and turning wavering citizens against the insurgency.[34] Because trials, truth commissions, reparations, and purges will have an effect on the conflict, they must be seen as part of the overall strategy to end the conflict, and they must be evaluated on their ability to help end the insurgency.

Traditionally, pragmatists focused on reconciliation as a way to end the conflict, but as a tool of lawfare, transitional justice programs must also embrace reconciliation's opponent—division. The debate on transitional justice has long sought to avoid divisiveness. Bruce Ackerman, writing during the post–Cold War transitions, argued against transitional justice mechanisms because they were too divisive. "Constitutional creation unites; corrective justice divides," he wrote. "[I]f backward-looking faultfinding spirals out of control, the bitter divisions that ensue may divert the community from its main task, which is to prevent the recurrence of an arbitrary dictatorship by building a solid constitutional foundation for the future."[35] Samuel Huntington concurred in his worry about divisiveness, concluding that the "least unsatisfactory course may well be: do not prosecute, do not punish, do not forgive, and above all, do not forget."[36] On the defensive, some argued not only that justice was not divisive but also that it was necessary for political stability, democracy, and reconciliation.[37] But the basic assumption of both skeptics and advocates of justice is that divisive actions are to be avoided.

During conflict, transitional justice embraces a certain kind of division. Success in the conflict may come not only from reconciling with the enemy but also from outright victory over the enemy. For example, counterinsurgents may want to create and exploit a cleavage between foreign radical insurgents and the local accidental guerrillas who do not share the extreme ideology of the foreign insurgents. The strategic use of transitional justice to facilitate division may enable the government to identify the extreme insurgents, who need to be killed or captured, and the reconcilable local insurgents, who may have legitimate grievances and can be reintegrated into society. Moreover, divisions need not be limited to the cleavages within the enemy: the government may want to create or exploit a division between the enemy and the civilian populations. They can signal the differences between the enemy and the population—their divergent moral compasses, goals, and aspirations—and they can condemn the enemy and expose their atrocities in order to solidify the population's dislike of the insurgency. To put it simply, during times of conflict, reconciliation is not a universal good. Division may be just as important.

Because it is pragmatic, transitional justice as lawfare does not take a one-sided position in the most pervasive debate in transitional justice: the conflict between politics and justice. This theme appears in many forms, such as peace versus justice, forgiveness versus vengeance, truth versus justice, reconciliation versus punishment, political precautions versus liberal commitments, or pragmatism versus legalism.[38] On the one side of the debate are those who believe that justice must be served: criminals must be punished for their actions. Many advocates of this approach hold that international law requires a state to prosecute the human rights violations and atrocities of a former regime.[39] Although they recognize that there may be an actual threat to reconciliation and peace, some believe in the dictum, "Let justice be done though the heavens fall."[40] Others think states should prosecute even if there are risks because in many cases such risks are overstated.[41] Alternatives to prosecutions, such as truth commissions, are "no substitute for enforcement of criminal law through prosecutions."[42] In other words, "justice [can] not be seen to yield to politics."[43] Some are willing to loosen the demands of justice, but only grudgingly, because they see amnesties, for example, as a "devil's bargain with necessity."[44] They take the default position that justice should be done "if at all feasible."[45]

On the other side of the debate are those who focus on the political nature of transitions and recognize that a spirited pursuit of justice may prevent the creation of peace or destabilize the transition to democracy.[46] Advocates of this position believe those who focus on justice go too far in "assuming that prosecutions are possible in the wake of human rights disasters."[47] Nations may not have "the power, popular support, legal tools, or conditions necessary to prosecute effectively."[48] Even if nations have the capacity to prosecute, prosecution might be counterproductive. In negotiated transitions, leaders who foresee potential prosecution might be less likely to negotiate, resulting in neither justice nor peace.[49] Indeed, many transitions in the post–Cold War era shifted toward a model of truth commissions in lieu of prosecutions in order to focus on collective peace and reconciliation rather than individual justice.[50] The second-best solution, the argument goes, may be preferable to no solution at all. Beyond these political constraints on pursuing justice, some argue that the case against justice is even more profound because vengeance through justice may not bring relief to victims and instead just continue and prolong their horror.[51]

Seeing transitional justice as lawfare does not provide a simple answer to the politics versus justice debate. If anything it entrenches the debate because the effects of transitional justice during conflict are complex and unclear. During insurgencies, the support of the population is the deciding factor for success. But popular support does not overlay perfectly with either politics or justice; rather, political and justice programs can each result in either popular support or backlash. Consider politics. Under counterinsurgency theory, the

population of insurgents can be divided into irreconcilables and reconcilables.[52] The task for counterinsurgents is to kill or capture the irreconcilables
and to win over the reconcilables such that they support the counterinsurgents' government instead of the insurgency. If the government negotiates
with one insurgent faction's leader and gains his support, the government may
create stability. Likewise, providing amnesties or inducements to the reconcilables of one insurgent group may result in defections, reducing the strength of
the insurgency. But both processes may also create popular backlash among
loyal supporters of the government, who see a culture of impunity and a government led by or involving former war criminals. They may withhold support from the government or even begin to support other rebel factions.
Political actions can thus cut in both directions.

Justice processes have similarly complex and unclear effects. On the one
hand, prosecutions and purges and other transitional processes could deter
potential insurgents from joining the conflict and can galvanize the population by spreading a moral norm and expectation throughout society. On the
other hand, if an insurgent is already waging active war against the state, then
the threat of prosecution or purges may make the insurgent less likely to reconcile for fear of future prosecution or inability to get a job. Those insurgents
who want to return home because they miss their family and friends, are
weary of war, or no longer see economic justifications for fighting may continue on.[53] If insurgencies are overlain with class, ethnic, or other identity-
based divisions, prosecutions and purges might also entrench those conflicts
and make reconciliation of any kind more difficult.

Turbulent transitions, therefore, support the idea that a blanket trump for
politics or justice is unworkable and reinforce that the core question is how to
navigate between politics and justice. Many simply assume that the right approach is a default rule in favor of justice, with exceptions carved out for political necessities. In turbulent transitions, both politics and justice have
unclear effects, suggesting that a single approach to navigating between politics and justice may be inappropriate. In other words, there may be many ways
to bridge politics and justice, and in some cases, the default rule in favor of
transitional justice may have negative consequences.

In pursuing these paths through politics and justice, transitional justice
programs must never be fabricated. If court proceedings become show trials
and truth commissions become organs of state propaganda, they cease to be
just—and cease to be effective. As artificial legal processes, their legitimacy is
minimal, or even nonexistent, as the procedures and protections that law provides are ignored or evaded. Counterinsurgents will therefore fail to win the

population over and their actions may even be counterproductive, creating backlash from a population that sees an increasingly desperate and illegitimate government.

Instead, the pragmatic approach recognizes that the choices made in designing justice programs for lawfare are simply discretionary policy choices, akin to those that legal actors face every day. Criminal prosecutors, for example, exercise extraordinary discretion in determining who to prosecute, as they are constrained by limited resources and policy priorities.[54] These same considerations operate in transitional prosecutions. Resources during wartime are limited and there are significant tradeoffs between funding legal operations and funding military or other civil affairs operations. Discretion and judgment enable leaders to make those tradeoffs. As importantly, transitional prosecutions also require policy-based discretion. For example, what counts as wrongdoing? Is conspiracy enough or should prosecutions be limited to crimes themselves?[55] Who should count as a wrongdoer—those who issued orders, executed orders, the intermediaries between them, those who facilitated those actions?[56] In the real world, these questions are driven as much by public policy and practical considerations as by moral theories of justice. The pragmatic approach recognizes the inevitability of discretion, and it focuses that discretion on the goal of waging effective lawfare. During turbulent times, transitional justice can be a form of lawfare, but only when it aligns legal and popular legitimacy with strategic gains.

## *Frameworks for Turbulent Transitional Justice*

Turbulent transitional justice—transitional justice designed for turbulent times and geared toward lawfare—must be inspired by and geared toward the dynamics of conflict.[57] Three frameworks help guide transitional justice during times of war. *Minimalist transitional justice* seeks to ensure transitional justice at the lowest cost to political concerns by pursuing either shallow or narrow policies, rather than intense policies. *Targeted transitional justice* uses transitional justice processes when strategically beneficial, targeting particular individuals or geographic areas, thereby sacrificing both scope and nationality. *Evolutionary transitional justice* applies varying transitional justice processes at different points in time, undermining the assumption of finality. Particular principles drive each framework, thereby helping clarify possible paths between politics and justice. These three frameworks provide the foundation for designing transitional justice programs during counterinsurgency. They are not mutually exclusive "models" that are or should be applied independently of each other. Quite the contrary. Each framework can be used in conjunction with the others or could be used separately, and different frameworks can apply to different mechanisms of transitional justice.

## Minimalist Transitional Justice

Perhaps the central feature of turbulent transitions is their complexity. The need to gain popular support and prevent popular backlash, coupled with the myth of impartiality, suggests caution in undertaking any endeavor during conflict. Any program can have complex and difficult to foresee second- and third-order effects that may be helpful or ultimately prove counterproductive.[58] Given the difficulty of anticipating consequences, a Hippocratic principle of "first do no harm" may be appropriate in these situations. On this theory, preventing backlash is preferable to taking the risk of alienating the population and fueling the insurgency. This approach to transitional justice can be called "minimalist transitional justice."

Minimalist transitional justice balances politics and justice at a particular moment by doing as little as possible. In this sense, it is similar to Cass Sunstein's theory of minimalist constitutional interpretation. Sunstein's minimalism is the "phenomenon of saying no more than necessary to justify an outcome, and leaving as much as possible undecided."[59] With turbulent transitional justice, the desired outcome is justice with an end to the conflict. Minimalism pursues some justice, but the least amount of justice, in order to guarantee the outcome of both peace and justice. Importantly, minimalist transitional justice is driven by justice, not by strategy; it holds that transitional justice is important as a principled matter, but it is cautious as to its applicability for fear of doing too much and causing backlash. As a result, it sacrifices the *intensity* of traditional transitional justice. Minimalism's central fault therefore is that it hesitates to act, potentially missing strategic and moral opportunities—and therefore risks underestimating the population's desire for accountability.

Similar to Sunstein's minimalism, minimalist transitional justice manifests in *shallow* and *narrow* species.[60] Shallow decisions, for Sunstein, are those that "avoid issues of basic principle" and allow "people who disagree on the deepest issues to converge" in acceptance of the outcome of a case.[61] Translating the principle into transitional justice, a shallow program would engage in symbolic or comparatively unsubstantial programs, such as reparations in the form of apologies, rather than deep programming, such as reparations in the form of monetary payments from perpetrator to victim. Shallow transitional justice provides a comprehensive program in terms of applicability, but a program that is weak in substantive accountability.

Narrow decisions, Sunstein argues, seek to do little more than confront the instant case. Minimalists, he writes, "do not decide other cases too, except to the extent that one decision necessarily bears on other cases."[62] Narrow transitional justice programs are also limited in focus, but they limit their focus on a specific class of crimes. Instead of seeking to address all crimes, narrow transitional justice zooms in on the worst crimes, leaving others undecided.

## Targeted Transitional Justice

When coupled with the goal of preventing backsliding and the phenomenon of territory segmenting during conflict, the principle of popular support could suggest a more ambitious program for transitional justice than minimalism. Instead, it could suggest tailoring transitional justice programs pragmatically toward specific people who need to be won over or toward specific geographies in which transitional justice can be pursued most freely. This is targeted transitional justice.

Targeted transitional justice balances politics and justice at a particular moment, just as its minimalist relative does, but it is inspired by a strategic principle rather than a moral principle. As a result, it applies transitional justice pragmatically. Specific people or places are targeted depending on the administrability and strategic possibilities of the program, rather than on their degree of moral culpability. Targeted transitional justice uses transitional justice programs the same way as a military uses a platoon or airpower—as a means for gaining success in the conflict. As a result, it sacrifices the *scope* of traditional transitional justice, focusing not on the whole population but only on areas that present strategically valuable opportunities. Two features are important: first, targeted transitional justice is planned, not haphazard; second, and consequently, it relies on discretion and policy choices, and may seem unfair as a result.[63] This is, in turn, the main risk of targeted transitional justice—policy choices might be perceived as haphazard or deliberately unfair, sparking backlash and fueling discontent.

Consider first who to target for prosecution, purges, or other punishments. This issue involves two components: who to target and what to target them with. Both decisions can be made strategically. As described earlier, counterinsurgency theory distinguishes between two sets of insurgents: irreconcilables and reconcilables. The irreconcilables will not be turned from the insurgency because they are dedicated followers of the ideology or cause. The reconcilables might turn away from insurgency. Their motivations for fighting are weaker, ranging perhaps from money to nonideological grievances to following the crowd. Targeted transitional justice suggests identifying particular groups for a transitional justice process—such as irreconcilables. For example, strong measures against irreconcilables might have moral benefits in addition to communicating norms and separating the radicals from the moderates. For reconcilables, targeted transitional justice might suggest inducements and amnesties for the rank and file, in order to encourage their defection from the insurgency.[64] In addition to targeting certain groups or individuals, the programs with which they are targeted can differ. This *graduated* program would tailor remedies to the targeted groups.

Distinguishing who to target and what to target them with is not enough. It is necessary for the reconcilables to know they will be treated differently from irreconcilables. To that end, the counterinsurgent may want to declare openly and reiterate frequently the standards of conduct or the types of persons who they target. For example, in accidental guerrilla situations, a counterinsurgent might declare that it will fully prosecute all foreign insurgents for their actions. Such a policy would signal a cleavage between two categories of insurgents, helping distinguish between indigenous warriors, who would be recognized as having potentially valid claims, and interlopers, whose motives are presumed illegitimate. Clear rules in targeting help prevent the claim that the programs are haphazard or unfair.

In addition to addressing certain persons or populations, targeted transitional justice embraces the segmentation of territory and suggests applying divergent transitional justice mechanisms in different parts of a territory, depending on their level of conflict. In doing so, *segmented transitional justice* loosens traditional transitional justice's assumption of nationality. In areas that are safe, more expansive justice processes can progress. In some areas deep in conflict, no transitional processes may be administrable. Targeted transitional justice rejects the idea that programs need to be based on national-level justice and reconciliation; they can instead be tailored to smaller political units, particularly if strategically beneficial or if some areas have progressed toward peace faster than others. To be sure, applying different transitional justice processes in different areas in the country may not always be optimal. Administrability concerns will arise. A single national program will often be cheaper and easier to administer, compared to many local programs, though even this will not always be the case. In Rwanda, for example, an overcrowded prison population and court backlog lead to decentralizing the justice process.[65] Second, transborder incidents will be more difficult to address in a decentralized system. Third, there will be variability across different regions, potentially raising charges of unfairness or arbitrariness. Each of these concerns are important, but they must be considered in light of the particular circumstances. In a country with well-defined regions and considerable regional variation, for example, the benefits of diversity may be greater than the costs.

## Evolutionary Transitional Justice

Turbulent transitions' shattering of geography is as important as its rejection of the distinction between war and peace.[66] In turbulent transitions, there are no clean breaks. Conflict persists as reform and reconciliation create peace over a long period of time or as coercion dominates holdouts and quashes an insurgency. This principle, of organic evolution from war to peace, suggests that transitional justice not be seen as a short-term project that operates at a specified historic moment but rather as a long-term project operating across time. This approach can be called evolutionary transitional justice.

Evolutionary transitional justice, unlike both minimalist and targeted approaches, balances politics and justice across time, rather than in one particular moment. It recognizes that both politics and justice can be accommodated, just in different degrees at different times. In other words, it sacrifices the *finality* of traditional transitional justice; it sees programs as ordinary and continuous, able to be made and remade as necessary. Transitional justice processes can therefore be ongoing over long periods of time or they can operate for a limited time before expiring and being revised. It is important to note that evolutionary transitional justice identifies and resolves a potential problem with traditional transitional justice. Waiting until the end of conflict effectively means that politics decisively and completely dominates justice during the conflict. After the conflict, justice may dominate politics or a balance might be struck. Evolutionary transitional justice evades this unstated presumption in favor of politics during war, seeking instead to balance politics and justice both during and after the conflict. Evolutionary transitional justice's central fault is that present intentions can be realized only by future personalities who may not share the views of their forebears; that intertemporal disconnect may result in either too much or too little justice as measured across the entire time frame.

The possibilities within evolutionary transitional justice are expansive. On the macro level, evolutionary transitional justice can pursue a dynamic strategy, applying targeted or minimalist transitional justice during early phases in the conflict and pursuing more expansive transitional justice in the future. One approach would be to use *delay rules*, which prevent all transitional justice or particular mechanisms and punishments until a certain amount of time has passed.[67] Delay rules are explicit, pursued through declared law or policy, but the delaying strategy can be implemented implicitly if social conditions are right: the government can rely on social norms to change over time and the public to eventually desire greater accountability. Moreover, intertemporal policies can apply in both directions: justice can be pursued vigorously during the conflict, with amnesties to follow far in the future; or amnesty can be pursued during the conflict, with justice to follow far in the future. Evolutionary transitional justice is thus neutral to the direction of justice. Note also that the dynamic strategy is not unidirectional over time; evolutionary transitional justice adapts to the conditions on the ground, such that the programming grows with the conflict. If the conflict turns for better or worse, transitional justice programs can adapt, and then readapt later as the conflict turns once again. Finally, the dynamic strategy is compatible with minimalist and targeted transitional justice programs; those strategies can be pursued in one phase, only to be expanded, contracted, or replaced later in the conflict.

On a micro level—within a short period during a conflict—evolutionary transitional justice underscores the fleeting, temporary nature of transitional justice policy. Transitional justice is not eternal and need not strive for the permanence that some ascribe to constitutions; rather it is as revisable as circumstances require.[68] Among the many possibilities are *limited time offers*, in which insurgents are provided with amnesty or other inducements that incorporate rehabilitation and reintegration and expire if not taken. Such policies might be particularly useful when the conflict is at a tipping point, in order to convince pessimistic insurgents to switch sides, or when a fracture that can be exploited emerges within the enemy. In addition to limited time offers, the government can pursue *ratcheted transitional justice*. The government would provide a standing offer; but upon victory during a particular campaign, it would provide harsher transitional justice terms to the holdouts. In calibrating the magnitude of the punishment to the phase of the campaign, the counterinsurgent can accelerate its initial successes and harshly punish those who fight until the end, thereby encouraging early defection.

Finally, evolutionary transitional justice's erosion of the temporal boundaries on transitional justice suggests that transitional justice need not be a backward-looking process or a backward-looking process with forward-looking effects. Rather, in a long conflict, *ongoing transitional justice* is defined at any given moment by present possibilities. In other words, processes like truth commissions could operate throughout the conflict in real time. Standing transitional justice processes would act as a much stronger deterrent because the conflict and, with it, the risk of crime persists. The reduction of time between the act and the possible punishment increases the likelihood of punishment and thereby enhances the deterrent effect of the process.

## Trials and Amnesties

In recent years, there has been a divide between "international retributionists" and "national pragmatists" over international law's position on amnesties, and due to changes in international criminal law and international human rights law, the international retributionists have the upper hand.[69] As a result, prosecutions have gained steam, displacing the flexibility political actors had in choosing between amnesties and trials.

Two transformations have led to the prominence of international retributionists over national pragmatists.[70] The first is the transformation of international criminal law. With the creation of the international tribunals for Yugoslavia and Rwanda in the 1990s and the institutionalization of tribunals through the International Criminal Court, international criminal law has increasingly entrenched processes for criminal prosecutions. Moreover, the institutionalization of international criminal law also reduces the perceived politicization of transitional justice prosecutions by providing a continuous legal regime under which perpetrators can be prosecuted.[71] With the rise of international criminal law has come increased pressure on amnesties. The Rome Statute, which created the ICC, demands "an end to impunity,"[72] and scholars have challenged the practice as letting murderers get off without punishment.[73] Amnesties are increasingly seen as allowing perpetrators to go free, without even providing the benefits of reconciliation.[74]

The second transformation has been in international human rights law, in which courts, particularly the Inter-American Court of Human Rights (IACtHR) have established a duty to prosecute human rights violations that cannot be derogated by domestic statute.[75] In the landmark Velásquez Rodríguez Case, the IACtHR held that "States must prevent, investigate and punish any violation of the rights recognized by the [American] Convention [on Human Rights] and, moreover, if possible attempt to restore the right violated and provide compensation as warranted for damages resulting from the violation."[76] Over time, the IACtHR began to use this duty to prosecute to challenge amnesties.[77] The Barrios Altos Case in 2001 saw the court declare that

> all amnesty provisions, provisions on prescription and the establishment of measures designed to eliminate responsibility are inadmissible, because they are intended to prevent the investigation and punishment of those responsible for serious human rights violations such as torture, extrajudicial, summary or arbitrary execution and forced disappearance, all of them prohibited because they violate non-derogable rights recognized by international human rights law.[78]

As Lisa Laplante argues, Barrios Altos applies to all amnesties—not just self-amnesties by authoritarian regimes, as was at issue in that case.[79] Whatever doubt remained was removed by the 2005 Case of the Mapiripán Massacre, in which the court declared that "no domestic legal provision of law can impede compliance by a State with the obligation to investigate and punish those responsible for human rights violations."[80] In sum, these and related cases established a number of rights for victims, including the right to truth, the right to a remedy, and the duty to prosecute.[81] As a result, "the choice of amnesty no longer depended solely on internal political considerations and 'elite preferences' because legal rules now tied the hands of politicians in regime changes."[82]

Significantly, the impetus to declare amnesties in violation of international law has not been unique to the Americas. The International Criminal Tribunal for the Former Yugoslavia (ICTY) found amnesties to be a violation of international law.[83] And in the wake of the Rwandan genocide, some advocates for transitional justice went further than just amnesties, declaring that "to allow any deviation from norms of fair trial and of humane detention, or to apply the death penalty in any case, would delegitimize the process of accountability in Rwanda."[84]

In the context of turbulent transitions, entrenching prosecutions through international criminal and human rights law is problematic. A blanket rule constrains the flexibility of political actors to devise a set of policies that are most likely to bring an end to the conflict. Widespread accountability procedures may create substantial backlash and reduce popular support for the government, and mandatory prosecutions might be seen as unfair and undesirable. For example, Mozambique in the early 1990s ended a horrific civil war that affected virtually everyone in the country. Instead of pursuing prosecutions or even a truth commission, Mozambique put the entire conflict behind it, preferring never to speak of it again. Mozambiquers believed that prosecutions, truth commissions, or other approaches would have prevented reconciliation.[85] Additionally, resource constraints and priority-setting might suggest focusing more attention on warfighting operations or developing governance capacity than on broad transitional justice programs. Finally, a blanket prosecution strategy might risk the tactical gains in the conflict that could arise from targeted prosecutions that seek to divide the enemy. Narrower or targeted prosecutions might have a greater overall effect on the population's support.

The opposite approach—the absence of accountability—has also recently manifested itself, most notably in Afghanistan. After the U.S. intervention to topple the Taliban regime in 2001, the United States and the international community supported incorporating leaders of armed factions into the government—even if they were suspected of serious crimes and human rights violations.[86] As one of the members of the Afghan Independent Human Rights Commission (AIHRC) put it, "[t]he policy of 'peace first, justice later' encouraged more violence by the local warlords and promoted a state of impunity."[87] By 2005, Afghans were frustrated, so much so that the AIHRC's report, *A Call for Justice*, noted that 69 percent of Afghans identified themselves or immediate family members as victims of a human rights violation in the previous twenty years, and that 41 percent believed the international community had supported war criminals—a greater number than believed the international community had tried to limit the power of war criminals.[88] Although data on the relationship between impunity and trust and support in government is not available, the principle of popular support suggests that the retention of warlords and war criminals has likely delegitimized the government and the international community in the eyes of Afghans.

Notably, Afghanistan's lack of accountability was not coupled with a comprehensive reconciliation plan. In fact, from 2001 to 2008, international organizations did not seriously pursue reconciliation with members of the former Taliban regime.[89] In 2001–2002, most Taliban stayed in Afghanistan, using traditional reconciliation mechanisms to reintegrate into their communities.[90] Left in an uncertain state by international forces and the Afghan administration, the governments of the southern provinces harassed many of the reintegrated Taliban, who either fled to Pakistan or went underground.[91] Only later—in 2005—did they launch the insurgency.[92] In the meantime, reconciliation efforts have been minor. They have not been pursued for mid- or senior-level Taliban commanders, and of the 142 most important Taliban leaders on the United Nations' sanction list, only 12 had been reconciled as of 2009, with most of them using informal channels.[93] The absence of account-ability procedures and a comprehensive reconciliation plan resulted in both reduced confidence in government and a rekindling of the insurgency.

Given the problems with a legal requirement for justice, a political policy of impunity, or neither, the three frameworks of turbulent transitional justice provide insight into navigating the space between prosecutions and amnesty. The minimalist approach suggests identifying shallow or narrow processes for transitional justice; that is, accountability with minimal punishment (shallow) or accountability for only the worst crimes (narrow). The best example of minimalist transitional justice is the Colombian Peace and Justice Law, which established a disarmament, demobilization, and reintegration program (DDR) in the midst of a long-standing insurgency.

Although pervasive violence and instability began with the 1948 killing of a presidential candidate, the Colombian insurgency took shape with the growth of revolutionary guerrilla groups in the 1960s and expanded to incor-porate the growing counterrevolutionary paramilitary groups in the 1980s.[94] After decades of fighting and failed attempts at negotiation, in 2002 the para-military groups, united under one banner, announced a ceasefire in order to begin peace negotiations with the government.[95] A 2002 law established a process for demobilization: paramilitary groups first provide a list of people and equipment that will be demobilized; members then provide information to the prosecutors, who determine whether to pursue criminal charges; finally, members are pardoned for minor crimes or held if suspected of serious crimes.[96] Those pending serious charges are supposed to get a special, more lenient, criminal process designed precisely for demobilization and intended to get around the ban on amnesties for committing human rights violations.[97]

The Justice and Peace Law provided this special process. Introduced first in 2003, it was debated, withdrawn, reintroduced, and debated over two years. By March 2005, there were eight congressional proposals in addition to the presidential initiative, which was finally passed in July 2005.[98] Despite the ongoing political debate and negotiations with the paramilitary leaders, de-mobilization began in 2003, with over 22,000 demobilized by February 2006.[99] Under the Justice and Peace Law, the special process required demo-bilized paramilitaries to spend a five-to-eight-year term in prison; to partici-pate in resocialization programs through work, study, and teaching; to assist in the demobilization of members of their former armed group; and to be on probation for one-half the length of their prison term, the violation of which would result in revocation of the alternative punishment altogether.[100]

The DDR program was undertaken before peace was firmly established as an incentive to encourage guerrillas to stop fighting, and as such is an exemplary case of minimalist transitional justice.[101] The Justice and Peace Law involved narrow punishment, providing amnesties for all but the most serious violations of human rights. And it also provided shallow punishment: serious violators faced a limited punishment program consisting of a short prison term, rehabilitation, and cooperation with the authorities to encourage further demobilization.

As is to be expected with minimalist transitional justice programs, the law was challenged as not going far enough. The challengers argued that reduced sentences were merely a form of veiled amnesty, constraints on investigations such as time limits prevented the accommodation of justice, and victim participation was limited.[102] Truth was undermined as there was no incentive to confess; the focus was on individuals rather than collective entities, such as paramilitary structures; and the national reconciliation and reparations commission was not actually a truth commission.[103] They also thought the reparations processes were insufficient because they used illicit goods to fund reparations and did not require judicial determinations to establish claims.[104]

Despite these wide-ranging arguments, the Colombian Constitutional Court took a balancing approach to evaluating the law, declaring that there was a "right to peace" that was on par with the right to justice.[105] In the end, the court largely upheld the Justice and Peace Law because the law reasonably balanced the competing demands of peace and justice.[106] The Colombian court's decision represents a slight pushback against the march toward a universal requirement for prosecutions, and it provides one example of how a minimalist criminal accountability system can be structured.

Under a system of targeted transitional justice, prosecutions, trials, and amnesties would be directed at particular populations in order to create cleavages in the enemy, induce some to defect, or build popular support against a cadre of extremists. Recall that targeted transitional justice can be designed either geographically—applying transitional justice mechanisms in some places but not others—or individually, focusing on particular classes of people to receive transitional justice processes.

Though it did not take place during the conflict, Rwanda provides a good example of the decentralization approach. Rwanda started using *gacaca*—a traditional dispute-resolution mechanism involving local elders who meet to resolve civil disputes in the community—to relieve the ballooning prison population after the genocide.[107] Adapted to transitional justice, the gacaca involved popular participation moderated by community leaders to address crimes including genocide.[108] In the first phase of a gacaca, the community would create a record of the genocide and determine who to charge with crimes, including identifying the category of crimes for which each individual was allegedly responsible. During the second phase, the gacaca courts, a panel of judges elected from the community, would conduct a public trial that depended largely on popular participation.[109] To be sure, not all of the Rwandan genocide was local, so many mass killings and killings of those who had fled their villages could not easily be addressed through gacaca.[110] But despite this and other problems, the gacaca process illustrates one way in which geographical divergences can be incorporated into the transitional justice process.[111]

More complex is targeting classes of people. As a starting point, targeted programs need to identify people and remedies based on the dynamics of the conflict. Consider two factors particular to the Afghan conflict that shape transitional justice programs. First, the insurgency in Afghanistan involves individuals not as members in an organization but as members of a "network with which he shares beliefs, values, fraternal bonds, and, through patronage links, economic interests."[112] As a result, reconciliation approaches that are premised on the individual and assume the individual can defect from the insurgency will be difficult to implement because individuals rely on the solidarity of their networks and because a reconciling individual would likely be targeted upon returning back to his home area.[113] Group- or area-based reconciliation that engages either the entire network or all the insurgents in a particular region will likely be more effective even though it is more politically complex.[114] Second, many insurgents in Afghanistan are motivated by the need for individual and collective security, the need for economic sustenance, and grievances against government security forces. Indeed, scholars have argued that most radical groups maintain their strength, in substantial part, by providing social and aid services to members, as if they were part of a "club."[115] Although every situation may not have these same dynamics, the broader lesson is that targeted programs need to be grounded in the dynamics, sources, and structures of the insurgency. Targeted reconciliation programs must "address the range of factors that motivate participation."[116]

In addition, two more general types of targeted programs warrant discussion: graduated amnesties and tactical prosecutions. Graduated amnesties are programs that provide varying degrees of amnesty to different segments of the enemy population in order to induce their defection while protecting against recidivism. The idea is simple: Depending on the degree of the defector's involvement in the insurgency, amnesty will be coupled with an increasing degree of remedial requirements, such as interrogation, rehabilitation programs, and so on. Graduated amnesties require decisions on two different tracks: identifying the targeted population and determining the remedy that enables amnesty. Two examples will demonstrate a few of the possible configurations.

One of the best examples of a graduated amnesty program to encourage enemy defections was the U.S.-designed Chieu Hoi (Open Arms) program during the Vietnam War. Chieu Hoi provided "ralliers" with vocational training, qualification for jobs, political indoctrination, and occasionally jobs in the army or the Chieu Hoi program itself.[117] During the war, studies showed that most of the ralliers were low-ranking participants who defected for personal, not political, reasons.[118] Participating in the war was a personal hardship, creating economic challenges for families and resulting in homesickness and a fear of dying.[119] At the same time, potential ralliers were often deterred by fear of mistreatment by the Vietnamese government and U.S. forces, the difficulty of getting away from their superiors, fear of reprisals to their families, and ignorance of the local terrain.[120] Over time, analysts found ways to make the program more successful, including hiring ralliers to work for Chieu Hoi because they had a better sense of local politics and persuasive arguments, and working with families of Viet Cong to convince the guerrillas they would be treated well if they defected.[121]

One analyst's suggestions are worth particular consideration. In 1966 Lucian Pye of MIT and the RAND Corporation suggested targeting the Chieu Hoi program toward different groups: refugees, marginal or low-level Viet Cong, activists, and prisoners.[122] The challenge, he argued, was to use clemency to win defectors while not alienating loyalists—a variation on the politics versus justice and popular support versus backlash themes—and the prescription was a more narrowly tailored regime of remedies for each class of defector.[123] Refugees were included for administrative convenience and as a way to enable low-level defectors who did not want to admit to their role in the Viet Cong to have an excuse for joining the government.[124] Ralliers, the low-level Viet Cong who had been forced into service or were untrained, would be interrogated for information and then sent back to their normal lives.[125] Activists, the Viet Cong who enjoyed the pace or culture of the warfighting machine, would be subject to interrogation and political indoctrination before being offered a chance to work in rural pacification, counterguerrilla operations, or civil administration (including the Chieu Hoi program).[126] Finally, the most committed Viet Cong, those who refused to defect but were captured against their will, would be prisoners of war, but they could potentially participate in a stringent review process that would enable them to enter the Chieu Hoi program.[127]

Although there were challenges to implementing Chieu Hoi, the program shows the possibilities of a targeted and graduated structure to encourage defectors.[128] Analysts deemed the program successful: between 1963 to 1971 194,000 Viet Cong defected at what was considered a cost-effective amount of $350 per capita.[129]

A more recent example of a graduated amnesty program is the rehabilitation programs implemented in Iraq during 2008. At Camps Bucca and Cropper, the military began to divide prisoners into irreconcilables and reconcilables. Many of the reconcilable prisoners in Camp Bucca were put through rehabilitation programs including moderate religious teaching, literacy programs, and skill building projects, so they could reenter society fully reconciled and with fewer temptations to return to active warfighting.[130] Moreover, the army realized that reconcilable insurgents need not be punished only by formal legal means such as rehabilitation and release. Instead, community-based solutions could both punish wrongdoers and prevent recidivism. In Anbar province, for example, soldiers worked with tribal sheiks to identify suspected insurgents within their tribe. The sheik would ensure that the insurgent was monitored by the tribe to prevent future insurgent activity and, in extreme cases, could use tribal justice and dispute mechanisms to address criminal actions.[131] The result was a system that provided ongoing monitoring—akin to tribal probation—as the remedy attached to what was effectively amnesty for insurgent activity.

In addition to these examples, there are other possible tools for those designing remedies for graduated amnesties. One promising mechanism that gets less attention than deserved is the use of loyalty oaths.[132] Psychologists have shown that persons who have taken an oath or pledge are more likely to behave in accordance with that oath than those who have not.[133] To be fair, these experiments operate in antiseptic environments, without the threats and fear that animate conflict zones. But if they prove effective in preventing even occasional actions by passive supporters, that may be enough to make them useful tools.[134]

The corollary to the graduated amnesty is the tactical prosecution, the targeting of a class of criminals with prosecution in order to create or exploit a cleavage in the population. The design of a tactical prosecution would immediately be suspect, because it focuses prosecution on a limited set of actors. But as a matter of policy discretion, akin to prosecutorial discretion in ordinary justice, it can be made credible by rationally determining a class of persons to target. For example, in Afghanistan, the government could establish a policy of prosecuting all foreign-born insurgents. The class has a reasonable and fair basis, as foreign insurgents can be interpreted as participating in an internal struggle for political power and are understood by the population as outsiders. The result of a prosecution program targeted at foreign insurgents would be to demonstrate to domestic insurgents that they will, correlatively, be treated more leniently (which could be strengthened by announcing a graduated amnesty program simultaneously). The policy would also signal to the population that there is a difference in supporting domestic insurgents and foreign insurgents, a signal that could ease the process of internal reconciliation.

The evolutionary framework provides evident lessons for designing trials and amnesties. A dynamic strategy would enable the use of delay rules. A government could establish a policy of not prosecuting insurgents for a period of years, after which a truth or prosecution program could be established; it could also prosecute immediately and suggest that, after a period of years, the guilty would have their case reconsidered and become eligible for pardon. In either case, the result would be to signal flexibility, thereby reducing the stakes of the politics-versus-justice conflict. The opportunity for revision in the future would enable those seeking justice or reconciliation to see an opposing policy as only temporary. Alternatively, an evolutionary approach suggests that a government could pursue whatever policy at the time, knowing that, over time, social norms and beliefs will change, enabling the people to reopen the question of justice at some point in the future. On the micro level, within a short period during the conflict, limited-time offers of amnesty and ratcheted prosecutions and punishments could be useful for incentivizing defections at tipping points, accelerating the defeat of the insurgency, and punishing holdouts.

In recent years, commentators have argued not only that a no-amnesty norm has emerged for new cases of transitional justice, like in Colombia, but also that amnesties established decades ago are now subject to revision or revocation. They argue that this signifies a "new normative milieu" for transitional justice.[135] The central example provided is Argentina, where advocates have developed "legislative and judicial strategies for declaring amnesty laws null and void."[136] They also cite Chile and Uruguay as places where efforts are ongoing to follow in Argentina's footsteps.[137]

An evolutionary approach to understanding amnesties and trials suggests that reading these developments as signifying a new equilibrium in the debate between politics and justice is mistaken. The evolutionary approach instead interprets these events as a natural growth and healing that takes place over time. Years after the initial amnesties, which were established for political reasons of reconciliation and power, the political situation simply changed.

Take Latin America, for example. In 1992 the Inter-American Commission on Human Rights found that Argentina and Uruguay's amnesty laws violated their human rights obligations, but the political climate was such that amnesties continued as a necessary element of policy.[138] By 2001, when the Barrios Altos decision was handed down addressing Peru's 1995 amnesty law, and by 2005 when Argentina's law was declared unconstitutional, the political situations in each country had changed.[139] In Peru, the Fujimori regime had collapsed and in Argentina over a decade had passed.[140] As James Cavallaro and Stephanie Brewer have argued, "the positive impact of the [Inter-American] Court's amnesty law jurisprudence stems largely from the fact that the political landscape of the Southern Cone had shifted dramatically since the time of the Commission's first amnesty law cases."[141] To be sure, there were many factors that led to these political changes, but the "growing distance between current and former governments" helped establish a context in which reversal of the amnesty was possible.[142]

Returning to Colombia's Justice and Peace Law with this in mind suggests that the Colombian Court could have taken into account that transitional justice blends politics and justice over time. With an evolutionary mindset, it is easy to see the government providing a very limited DDR program in the midst of the conflict in order to evaluate its success in conjunction with military and other operations. Over time the government could expand or contract the justice, truth, and reparations provisions depending on the progress of the conflict. A court with this mindset would have been far more deferential to the government's initial program than the Colombian Court was. But at the same time, it would have limited its deference to a particular time period, after which the government would have to argue for continued deference.[143] That approach would recognize that the evolutionary transitional justice project of balancing politics and justice is an ongoing one, requiring revision over time, rather than a fixed, once-and-for-all approach.

## Purges and Lustration

Another area in which the war-peace dichotomy can potentially drive overexpansive justice is the use of purges or lustration to eliminate members of the old regime from administrative and military posts.[144] The impetus for purges is simple: the old regime was filled with persons who committed crimes or are otherwise compromised. Retaining them would amount to governance by the old regime, just under a new name.[145] Purges are thus often justified under backward- and forward-looking theories: they not only punish wrongdoers who participated in the old regime but also help establish that the new regime will be built with morally straight personnel.[146] At the same time, however, purges are in tension with the goal of reconstruction, as members of the old regime may have more expertise and experience—or be the only ones in the country with expertise and experience—in managing and operating a bureaucracy.[147] And they may be in tension with political goals, as purged individuals might be part of a political group whose power is necessary to maintaining peace.

In recent years, some have mounted a strong case for purges. Foremost are those who see the denazification process after World War II as a failure because it did too little. In its first phase, denazification focused only on high officials; in the second phase it cast a wider net and categorized persons as "major offenders" or "followers."[148] Because most people were identified as followers and the sanction for followers was limited to a fine (only a few were actually excluded from office), denazification did not go far enough in purging German government.[149] Others make an affirmative case for purges, likening them to requiring a security clearance for government employees to ensure their trustworthiness.[150] And some even argue that purges can be supported as redistributive justice, enabling others to participate in government.[151]

In turbulent transitions, designing a policy of purges seems more difficult than in peacetime conditions. First, it may be extraordinarily difficult to determine who exactly should be purged because there may not be an "old regime." Take Afghanistan, for instance. Many Afghans see their country's conflict as continuous since at least the Soviet invasion, if not the overthrow of the Shah government before that.[152] In this complex conflict, it is unclear who should be purged from the government or military. Taliban overlap with tribal leaders, tribal leaders with warlords, former government officials with leaders of armed groups, persons in armed groups with Al Qaeda or with freedom fighters supported by the United States. Shifting alliances, overlapping identities, and the extremely long period of conflict make it difficult to determine what the "old regime" was and who should be excluded from it.

Second, the political arguments for limiting purges to a small segment are magnified in conflict transitions. In the war-peace situation, a reconstructing government needs personnel to staff its operations, but there is presumed to be relatively little risk of the old regime returning to power or of the war restarting. In turbulent transitions, conflict is ongoing or the risk of conflict returning is high. As a result, excluding a large segment of talented and experienced soldiers and bureaucrats from service in the government may result in alienating them and pushing them into the hands of an insurgency. Indeed, insurgents are likely to exploit the unemployed's grievances with the government.

No situation better exemplifies the complexities in the politics of purging than the disbanding of the military and the de-Ba'athification policy in Iraq in 2003. The disintegration of the Iraqi military demonstrates the risk of increased violence in turbulent transitions. Although President Bush and Secretary Rumsfeld initially planned to retain the Iraqi army, the U.S. military's lack of capacity to hold Iraqi soldiers pushed the Iraqis to demobilize and return to their homes.[153] Coalition Provisional Authority (CPA) head Paul Bremer, as his second order, formally dissolved all armed forces and security units.[154] One of the problems of the disbanding of the Iraqi army was that roughly 230,000 officers and noncommissioned officers were unemployed, had weapons training, and retained substantial networks across the country.[155] Although it is unclear how many of these former soldiers joined the insurgency, their financial troubles sparked by unemployment may have fueled early support for the insurgency.[156] Given this result, the better approach, some commentators have suggested, would have been to "put all army personnel on inactive status, continue to pay them, and recall individuals incrementally and selectively."[157] An even more serious error, they note, was failing to create a new force quickly, including members of the old army. In so failing, "the CPA's early plans regarding the size, composition, and external orientation of the new Iraqi army failed to anticipate the mounting threat of insurgency and eventual civil war."[158]

Where disbanding the military demonstrates the potential for purges to facilitate conflict, de-Ba'athification, the policy of excluding the top four tiers of members of Saddam Hussein's Ba'ath Party from positions in government, illustrates the political complexities of purges. De-Ba'athification was consciously modeled on the denazification of postwar Germany, though it was scaled back to effect only .1 percent of the population (as compared to 2.5 percent of the U.S. zone in postwar Germany).[159] For much of 2003, the Coalition Provisional Authority was consistently pushed to expand its de-Ba'athification program, as it had taken a cautious approach to avoid overpurging.[160] In September, the Iraqis took control of the process, voiding all exceptions granted to Ba'athists within the top four tiers of the party and expanding the ban to include media and civil society institutions.[161] By the winter, Bremer was worried the policy was being taken much too far, particularly given that the risk of a Ba'athist return to power was minimal now that Saddam had been captured.[162] Moreover, Ahmed Chalabi, head of the de-Ba'athification commission, was thought by some to be using de-Ba'athification to further his political ambitions.[163] The politicization of de-Ba'athification came to a head over 12,000 teachers who had been dismissed from service. Although there was no actual shortage of teachers in Iraq, Bremer still argued for reinstating many of the Ba'athist teachers.[164] The reason was primarily political: Sunni leaders pressured Bremer to reinstate these teachers, many of whom were important figures in their communities, and Bremer wanted to limit the bitterness and anger of Sunnis to ensure they remained part of the political process.[165] In doing so, Bremer was walking a thin line between preventing the alienation of the Sunnis and alienating the Shia and Kurds by appearing to retreat on de-Ba'athification.[166] In effect, the policy of de-Ba'athification was driven primarily by political concerns, including the initial need to signal a commitment to establishing a new kind of regime in Iraq; the likelihood of Ba'athists returning to power, which decreased substantially after Saddam was captured; and the need to balance reconciliation with the Sunnis with vengeance for the Shia and Kurds.

As with trials and amnesties, the three frameworks for turbulent transitional justice can provide some help in navigating the political challenges of purges during conflict. Minimalism suggests narrow and shallow purges. A narrow purge would exclude only a very small group from continuing to serve in the government or military. The plan for Iraq, including only .1 percent of the Ba'athists, could be seen as a narrow minimalist purge; however, it is also possible to envision an even narrower process, which would only exclude leaders of the government or junta. A shallow purge would involve everyone who participated in the insurgency, but it would place a weak requirement on them, such as a loyalty oath, before they could participate in government or the armed forces. It is worth noting that loyalty oaths themselves need not always operate as shallow or narrow mechanisms. After the U.S. Civil War, for example, some state constitutions required broad loyalty oaths for professionals, including doctors, ministers, and lawyers.[167] Moreover, they excluded from these professions anyone who had participated in the rebellion—a rather deep punishment of preventing their employment.

A targeted approach to purges would follow both segmented and individual targeting, applying purges only in some areas but not in others, depending on the circumstances, and applying them only to certain groups. For example, during a war, the government could declare that all insurgent leaders or foreign fighters or a definable class of irreconcilables would be purged from all government and military positions. It could also announce a weaker purge—such as a loyalty oath—for all reconcilables who defect. This graduated and targeted system of purges would help distinguish between segments of the enemy and create incentives for reconciliation among the lower-level fighters.

Finally, an evolutionary approach to purges suggests that it would be possible to purge collaborators or insurgents for a time, and then reinstate them at some future date. This process could be formally stated (a delay rule for reinstatement) or could rely on norms evolving over time. The latter process appears to have taken place in Germany after World War II. In the early years, association with the Nazis was a practical bar to engagement in politics. But "after the passage of time, such past political service became acceptable, even desirable."[168] Once the legitimacy and stability of the new regime was no longer in doubt, it became possible to include those with experience from the Nazi era.

## Truth Commissions

The most prominent alternative to vengeance through legal justice is exposing the truth. In transitional situations, truth commissions have been used to reveal the injustices and crimes of the past in lieu of, or in conjunction with, prosecutions. Discovering the truth is seen as desirable, or even perhaps necessary, because it helps determine and clarify abuses, reverses the self- or regime-imposed culture of silence and secrecy, begins the process of psychological closure, and enables forgiveness.[169] Some see truth commissions as a second-best solution, needed because trials would be destabilizing; others see truth commissions as independently helpful, perhaps more effective than vengeance at fostering closure.[170] At the same time, however, there may be important reasons not to seek out the truth, including negative consequences, such as social unrest and violence; lack of political interest; other more urgent priorities such as reconstruction; alternative mechanisms for reconciliation such as local traditions; and a culture that opposes addressing conflict head-on.[171] These factors may caution against a truth commission in the interest of peace.

According to Priscilla Hayner's comprehensive study of truth commissions since World War II, most truth commissions share four features: they focus on the past, they investigate patterns of abuses rather than a particular event, they are temporary, and they are sanctioned and empowered by the state.[172] Others have added that truth commissions usually involve an elite group of commissioners who have moral authority and that truth commissions usually incorporate popular participation as a way of getting to the truth—they are social and political processes.[173] The structure of truth commissions differs depending on the situation, but most often, the aims of truth commissions include discovering abuses, responding to the needs of victims, contributing to justice and accountability, providing recommendations for institutional reform, promoting reconciliation, and fulfilling obligations under human rights law.[174] Hayner finds that a best practice for designing a successful truth commission is to give it a deadline of one to two years.[175]

The conventional understanding of the aims and best practices for truth commissions fit poorly with the realities of turbulent transitions. For starters, focusing only on past issues and a past pattern of abuses may be difficult, if not impossible. Not only is conflict ongoing, but the sites of atrocities or crimes may be in the midst of a war zone, making evidence collection difficult. Relatedly, the suggestion that truth commissions be temporary is perhaps the most inapposite to turbulent transitions, in which the conflict may continue indefinitely or at least into the unforeseeable future. Temporary truth commissions may expire before the conflict is actually over. Moreover, that truth commissions must be sanctioned by the state is neither true nor desirable in ongoing conflicts. First, insurgents may be as likely to use a truth commission as the counterinsurgent state, particularly if they gain control over a territory or seek to enhance their legitimacy. For example, the African National Congress (ANC) during apartheid twice created a commission to investigate its own abuses, thus becoming the only armed resistance group to create a truth commission. The ANC's second truth commission even included independent commissioners in order to have greater credibility.[176] Second, state-sanctioned truth commissions might backfire in situations of conflict if they are seen as illegitimate. If they appear one-sided, they may undermine rather than add to the credibility of the commission. Finally, truth commissions that focus on popular participation or that take advantage of expansive mandates push up against some harsh realities of conflict situations. Victims and perpetrators in conflict situations will be less likely to participate in turbulent truth commissions. Victims (and perpetrators) will fear the consequences of speaking out, and perpetrators will have little reason to come forward if they believe they can still win the conflict. A broad mandate may aggravate these risks, particularly if the actual capacity for protecting witnesses is limited.

Truth commissions in times of conflict also face political challenges. After the invasion of Afghanistan in 2001, a standing human rights commission with truth commission powers, the Afghan Independent Human Rights Commission

(AIHRC), was created to address past crimes.[177] The commission produced a report, only to face political challenges from both international and local communities. The AIHRC report was meant to be released in conjunction with a report by the UN High Commission for Human Rights that would outline in greater detail war crimes and human rights violations because the AIHRC report could not go so far for security reasons.[178] Yet, fearing for the safety of the UN staff, the UN report was not released, leaving locals cynical about the international community's commitment and increasing the security risks for the AIHRC members.[179] Perhaps more importantly, when it released its report, which did not specify names or affiliations of perpetrators, it was denounced by some as "anti-mujahidin."[180] Many who had fought with the mujahidin saw their work as patriotic service to the country against the Soviets and rejected transitional justice processes altogether.[181] In situations of conflict, who to target even for truth commissions is difficult not only because there are many interpretations of history and of the truth but also because many of the players may be necessary partners in the future.

In light of these challenges, consider the possibilities of minimalist, targeted, and evolutionary truth commissions. A minimalist truth commission could be either shallow, providing only limited reports and processes for truth-seeking, or narrow, having limited scope or authority. Hayner identifies a number of features necessary for designing truth commissions that are helpful in shaping a minimalist truth commission. Truth commissions have different powers of reporting, such as the ability to name perpetrators or make mandatory recommendations for structural reform; the commissions vary in the breadth of abuses that are investigated; they vary in which parties are investigated; and they delineate a particular time frame to investigate.[182] Within each of these four categories, narrow and shallow opportunities present themselves. The Guatemala truth commission had some shallow elements in that it could not name responsible individuals in its work and its reports had no judicial effect.[183] The Chilean truth commission had narrowing elements, in that it was not empowered to investigate situations of torture in which the victims were not killed.[184]

Targeted truth commissions investigate only certain groups or break up their work by geography. Targeting only certain groups for investigation can either reduce or increase the credibility of the commission. When targeting only the opposition or only the most heinous crimes of the opposition, the truth commission risks being seen as propaganda, particularly if the government is potentially guilty of crimes itself. However, targeting one's own group, as the African National Congress did, can increase the credibility of the organization. Targeting truth commissions by geography is also not totally unprecedented. Sri Lanka created a truth commission in which commissioners had authority over particular geographic areas; each took a different approach to their work, leading to inconsistency and variation.[185] On the one hand, this variation can be seen as unfair and problematic, undermining a single narrative or approach in the nation. But the segmentation and fragmentation of territory, coupled with the complexity of conflict situations, suggests that the conflict in each region might be substantially different. As a result, truth commissions of different scope and processes may be better able to adapt to local realities. In other words, there is no reason why all truth commissions must follow a national-scale, one-size-fits-all approach.

An evolutionary approach to truth commissions recognizes that truth can be pursued at different stages in time. As a starting point, truth commissions during conflict can be granted jurisdiction to cover crimes in the ongoing conflict, thus acting more like standing inspectors general than historical truth commissions. As importantly, in some places it may be politically difficult to pursue truth immediately, but that does not foreclose pursuing truth in the future. For example, the famous killing fields in Cambodia took place in the late 1970s and with fits and starts the country remained in civil war through the 1980s. In the early 1990s, prosecutions seemed impossible because so many of the leaders in the Cambodian government had been affiliated with the Khymer Rouge of the 1970s.[186] Yet at that time, U.S. Senator Charles Robb set aside funding to investigate the genocide, despite heavy resistance from the State Department that the people and the elites did not support such investigations and simply wanted to move on.[187] Robb's funds eventually went to collecting documents from the genocide era that might have been destroyed and to storing and organizing those documents. By the late 1990s when the last active Khymer Rouge leaders had left government and the Khymer Rouge had lost its power as an armed force within Cambodia, interest grew for prosecutions.[188] According to one poll, 80 percent believed the surviving leaders should be prosecuted for their crimes.[189] Now ready for prosecutions, the documents that were protected earlier could be helpfully used, though they could not be at the time of collection. The lesson is that thinking about transitional justice as organic and evolutionary requires preparing for future transitional justice projects, even if they may not be plausible today.

Putting together the challenges truth commissions face during conflict and the three frameworks for turbulent truth commissions, it is possible to revisit the four components of truth commissions and redesign the truth commission for times of conflict. This redesigned truth commission—the *turbulent truth commission*—will better adapt to the realities of conflict and will contribute to success in the conflict. Publicizing insurgent abuses will galvanize the population against the insurgency and government abuses will (hopefully) encourage more humane and careful government counterinsurgency operations. The turbulent truth commission is not so speculative: in great measure, the Afghan Independent Human Rights Commission (AIHRC) has innovated substantially in order to operate in the midst of conflict.

First, turbulent truth commissions have to be seen as a long-term commitment whose purview includes ongoing actions, not as a temporary process covering a limited past. They must be more like inspectors general or permanent human rights commissions than temporary truth commissions. For example, the Afghan Independent Human Rights Commission was created in 2001 by the Bonn Agreement and then codified in the 2004 Afghan Constitution. Its particular operations are governed by statute, but its existence is constitutional, rendering it a far more permanent body than the one to two years that is suggested as best practice for a truth commission. Additionally, the AIHRC investigates ongoing violations of the insurgency. Two of their reports in particular, *Insurgent Abuses against Afghan Civilians* and *Violations of International Humanitarian Law in Afghanistan*, address ongoing practices of the insurgency—not historical events from the Taliban or Soviet eras.[190]

Second, participation by the public would have to be limited in order to protect the public from retaliation. Because territories can shift hands quickly and unexpectedly, collaborators with the truth commission may be punished if their area falls into insurgent hands. As a result, the truth commissions would primarily have to be run by experts and government who operate either from publicly available materials or by quiet intelligence and information gathering. To some extent, the AIHRC has incorporated this lesson as well. The AIHRC recognizes that it operates in a "climate of fear" in which many are afraid to cooperate openly for retaliation by insurgents.[191] As a result, the AIHRC withholds the names of many of its interviewees.[192]

At the same time, limited public involvement cuts against the credibility of the truth commission, making it appear more like a government propaganda arm. The third requirement, then, is that truth commissions need to undertake policies to gain credibility. External involvement or monitoring may be one way to accomplish this goal.[193] For instance, a government could sanction an independent third party, such as the Red Cross, to act as its truth commission during the conflict or to monitor a government-sponsored commission. These ideas are not so far-fetched, as international law already recognizes the role of third-party protecting powers to guarantee the interests of states that have broken off diplomatic ties and as the Geneva Conventions establish a role for the Red Cross as a monitoring body during conflict.[194] Another way to improve the credibility would be to ensure that the truth commission is evenhanded, investigating actions by both sides.[195] Not all truth commissions have pursued this course, but in situations of conflict, evenhandedness may become more important to signal legitimacy and credibility.[196] The AIHRC, for example, investigated the indiscriminate and excessive use of force against civilians by U.S. forces and the shooting of protesters by Afghan forces in 2007.[197] These reports prevent any credible attempt to call the AIHRC's work "government propaganda," particularly when it investigates insurgents.[198]

With these modifications, turbulent truth commissions may seem disconnected from the goals of truth commissions. But that conclusion is unwarranted. Return to Priscilla Haynes's statement of the aims of truth commissions. Like conventional truth commissions, turbulent truth commissions are helpful in discovering abuses. Though it is true turbulent truth commissions may not allow for a full inquiry into the evidence and into some past incidents, due to the ongoing conflict and political constraints, they have a countervailing benefit of providing an ongoing truth commission that can deter crimes more effectively than a distant and speculative threat of eventual investigation. The deterrent is more than just moral or norm-based, as publicity will negatively impact either side's cause. In this manner, turbulent truth commissions may be better at addressing abuses, even if they cannot promise a full investigation of all past abuses. Second, justice and accountability are still served by an ongoing commission with limited participation because wrongdoers' actions are publicized. Turbulent truth commissions, like traditional counterparts, could be tasked with suggesting institutional reforms. And in cases where international human rights law applies, turbulent truth commissions contribute to fulfilling those obligations.

Turbulent truth commissions are less apt than traditional truth commissions at responding to the needs of victims and promoting reconciliation. Traditional truth commissions can allow for victim participation and are more likely to enable a full investigation of all past crimes. If one subscribes to the theory that these practices help victims, then turbulent truth commissions are clearly inadequate.[199] In terms of promoting reconciliation, turbulent truth commissions may actually reduce reconciliation between insurgents and supporters of the government because they will publicize the atrocities and crimes of the insurgents. Reconciliation will thus be less likely as the population gets increasingly alienated by the horrors of war. But note that in turbulent transitions, traditional truth commissions may also be ineffective in these areas. Traditional truth commissions will not begin proceedings for years or even decades because the conflict will not have ended. As time goes on, the needs of victims will go unaddressed. In Afghanistan, thirty years of war makes truth about earlier atrocities more difficult to determine. Moreover, in turbulent transitions, reconciliation is not an end in itself and may even be undesirable. Creating cleavages between groups may help separate irreconcilable insurgents from the population. Finally, it is worth noting that turbulent and traditional truth commissions are not mutually exclusive: if the conflict subsides over time, the operation of a turbulent truth commission during the conflict does not preclude the operation of a broader, more participatory truth commission later when the conflict has been contained or effectively managed. In this manner the needs of victims and reconciliation can still be attained.

As traditionally understood, truth commissions do not appear to be well suited to situations of conflict. They face hurdles in terms of information gathering, limited time-span, and credibility. Nonetheless, in turbulent transitions, it is possible to structure a turbulent truth commission—a truth commission that, though it has a narrower purview, can still bring to light atrocities and crimes on both sides of the conflict. Such an action would be helpful for the side that creates the commission, as it would provide an added incentive to act humanely, which is strategically valuable for winning over the population, and it would bring to light horrors that could turn the population against the enemy. More than just a mechanism of reconciliation after conflict, the turbulent truth commission would be a mechanism for success in the conflict.

## Reparations

Reparations are the final mechanism of transitional justice. As Eric Posner and Adrian Vermeule argue, the boundaries between reparations, normal legal remedies, and redistributive transfer programs are fuzzy, but reparations programs, however diverse, generally share some characteristics.[200] Perhaps the core quality of reparations is that they do not involve the "transfer from an identified individual wrongdoer to an identified individual victim of the wrong" but rather "relax[] one condition or the other, or both."[201] As a result, reparations feature a group paying an individual, an individual paying a group, or a group paying a group. Reparations take many forms in transitional justice, including money or in-kind payments to individuals and groups; restitution, the return of the very property taken from the owner; and apologies, which are implicit and symbolic forms of reparation.[202] Underlying these policies is a principle of reciprocity, in which violators and victims are connected, and a backward-looking sense of justice that seeks to compensate victims for their losses and, in systems in which the violator pays, to punish the violator for her crime.[203] As Martha Minow states, "restorative justice seeks to repair the injustice, to make up for it, and to effect corrective changes in the record, in relationships, and in future behavior."[204]

In turbulent transitions, reparations are problematic. Although determining the form of reparations may be a relatively simple policy choice, identifying who should pay and who should benefit is exceedingly difficult as a practical matter. The initial source of this problem is that the wrongdoer often is not the state, as is true in classic cases of reparations such as the U.S. internment of the Japanese during World War II, but instead an individual or group without sanction from the state. Nor is it even as simple as individuals or groups. The fluidity and changing nature of the conflict over time and across different geographies means that today's insurgent may be tomorrow's ally, and today's perpetrator may be tomorrow's victim. Spiraling violence and interconnected relationships make determining blameworthy parties difficult.[205]

In addition to the problem of identifying payers and beneficiaries, reparations in times of conflict create a disincentive for insurgents to reconcile. Few will willingly repair their relationship with the victim when the victim is still the enemy. Most importantly, however, the possibility of reparations may be a threat to the victim; once the courts are out of the picture, little will stop insurgents from retaliating against those who brought claims against them. In times of ongoing violence, publicity as one who brought a case to court may transform a person from past victim into future target.

A minimalist reparations policy could be shallow or narrow. Narrowness could apply to either or both factors: the payers and the victims. On the payer side, narrow policy might focus only on government crimes or only on the crimes of particular groups or individuals. On the victim side, narrow policy would suggest reparations only for those who suffered the harshest crimes. Shallow policies include, for example, symbolic reparations, such as an apology or a public monument. These policies are important but not as substantial or costly to the perpetrator as monetary compensation.

Targeted reparations would focus either on geographies or on populations. As with trials, amnesties, purges, and truth commissions, geographically determined reparations enable the state to adapt its policy to the needs of a particular community and the strategic value of reparations in that community. More interestingly, reparations can be targeted at specific populations that have suffered injuries and need to be won over to prevent their cooperation with the insurgency. For example, when the government causes an injury, reparations can follow the standard model: The government is to blame and can repair the relationship by paying the victim. It is important to note the strategic value of this interaction: by repairing the relationship, the government may help rebuild trust with the injured population and regain their support. Indeed, in Iraq and Afghanistan, victim compensation (though technically not part of a reparations program) has become a significant phenomenon and one that has been recognized as effective both as a matter of justice and as a matter of strategy.

The larger challenge for turbulent reparations is identifying wrongdoers when the government did not cause the injury. Here, a government pursuing a targeted reparations policy would focus on the victims rather than the perpetrator, and having identified them, could *still* pay to support the victims even though the government is not culpable as a matter of fact or historical legacy.[206] Compensating victims for their losses can be an effective strategic mechanism to solidify support in the population for the government. To be sure, the government may not need to focus its attention on victims of the insurgency, who already have cause to dislike the insurgency. But a strong government response in providing for survivors and victims will indicate to the community at large that the government is committed to and capable of supporting them. Moreover, the benefits will spill over into the community, particularly if the reparations program is designed to focus on compensation with high spillover effects. For example, instead of paying the victim directly in a lump sum (a fact that once known might make them a target for killing and robbery), in-kind and collective payments, such as providing a family with jobs or loans, may increase the spillover effects and enhance the gains in goodwill from reparations.

An evolutionary perspective suggests that reparations policy can grow and change over time. In addition to pursuing reparations far into the future via delay rules or informal mechanisms, rather than immediately during or after the conflict, governments can institute a ratcheted reparations policy. In the short term, it could pursue a shallow or narrow form of reparations, such as apologies, and in the longer term could expand that policy to incorporate monetary transfers. Seeing the conflict as operating in phases and changing over time means that reparations policy is as flexible as the other areas—and therefore need not be achieved all at once.

CONTEMPORARY CONFLICTS DO not present a clean break between war and peace. Conflict persists as reconstruction, civil affairs, and transitional justice are pursued. Turbulent transitional justice takes seriously the coexistence of transitional justice mechanisms and conflict, and it transforms transitional justice programs into instruments of lawfare—tools that can help bring the insurgency to an end. Although it cannot resolve the eternal debate between politics and justice, turbulent transitional justice argues for a broader set of approaches to navigating the balance between those poles, in order to better meet the challenges of conflict. And it requires and enables innovations in designing the mechanisms of transitional justice. Turbulent transitional justice requires the soldier to embrace justice and the humanitarian to embrace strategy. This precarious union of justice and strategy, each interacting with the other, each incompletely realized at any moment, enables the counterinsurgent to expand its legitimacy and win over the population from the throes of insurgency.

# PART THREE

## *The Reconstruction of Order*

# 5

# *Warfighting as Village-Building*

WITH WAR COMES the breakdown of order. Whether between states or within a state, war brings violence and destruction. When the war ends, attention turns to rebuilding infrastructure, reestablishing governance and the rule of law, and jumpstarting the economy. The Civil War was thus followed by the Reconstruction of the South; World War II brought with it the rebuilding of Germany and Japan. In conventional wars, reconstruction takes place after victory. Postconflict reconstructors seek to hold national elections, establish a market economy, and develop a professional, effective central government bureaucracy. They hope to build a stable national society that adheres to the highest ideals of the Western tradition: democracy, the rule of law, and free-market capitalism. Like conventional war, counterinsurgency involves destruction and reconstruction. Unlike conventional war, however, counterinsurgency's theory of reconstruction is not a postwar affair. Because counterinsurgency's transitions from war to peace are turbulent transitions, the reconstruction of order operates not after conflict but in its midst. As importantly, counterinsurgency strategy holds that defeating an insurgency requires rebuilding obligation between the people and their government.

Counterinsurgency's theory of reconstruction and state-building rejects the aspirational visions of order defined by electoral democracy, unfettered markets, and centralized bureaucracies and instead focuses on the dynamic relationship between warfighting and state-building. Turbulent reconstruction holds that warfighting can reinforce state-building and that state-building can, in turn, enhance warfighting. This process is easiest and most effective at the local level, so counterinsurgency embraces a bottom-up approach that grows organically from the local conditions and context: the population's capacities and needs, their traditions and preferences. Organic reconstruction reframes warfighting as village-building. The result is that counterinsurgents need to be attentive not only to local reconstruction but also to the variety of strategies that they can take to decentralizing operations and governance.

## Visions of Order

In the modern era, order is synonymous with the state. Scholars generally agree on what defines a state: a set of centralized, autonomous, and differentiated institutions that operate in a geographically bounded territory and have a monopoly on rulemaking within that territory.[1] Historically, the state has provided internal order, military defense, and internal security; maintained communication infrastructures such as roads, weights and measures, and coinage; and supported economic production and redistribution.[2] Contemporary commentators argue that effective modern states have ten basic functions: the rule of law, a monopoly on legitimate violence, administrative control, sound public finance policy, investment in human capital, citizenship rights via social policy, infrastructure, formation of the market, management of public assets, and effective public borrowing.[3] In other words, the state provides all the basic necessities that guarantee a stable order in the modern world. In providing these necessities, states are not independent of the broader social context. "States are parts of societies," growing organically from the traditions and conditions of the place.[4] The state shapes society's rules and structures and is itself continually transformed and influenced by social forces. Order arises out of ideological, military, political, and economic relationships in a society, and the state is a crucial part of that order.[5]

As important as the state is to the modern conception of order, the state is not the only form of social and political order. History provides countless examples of institutional orders that diverge from the state's union of hierarchical sovereignty and territorial limitations. Medieval Europe alone saw at least three different forms of order: feudalism, the Catholic Church, and the Holy Roman Empire. In each case, power was not exclusive within a territory and territorial jurisdiction was fluid rather than fixed. Feudalism was a decentralized form of political organization based on personal bonds and mutual dependence. The Church claimed authority over all believers—providing a clear hierarchy and no geographical limitations. And the Holy Roman Empire had a similar hierarchical and universal status.[6] In the late Middle Ages, new forms of political organization developed, each taking a different approach to hierarchy and territory. In France, the sovereign, territorial state emerged— uniting a centralized, hierarchical authority with exclusive power within its territory.[7] In Northern Germany and Southern Scandinavia, the Hanseatic League joined commercial and maritime towns in a confederation to improve trade, regulate economic activities, and even wage war. As a city-league, it had neither central, hierarchical authority nor territorial borders.[8] Italy developed a hybrid: the city-state. The Italian city-states had clear territorial boundaries but did not have a settled internal hierarchy. Towns annexed by major city-states retained considerable autonomy from their parent city, and internally, the city-state was plagued by factionalism and feuds, never developing a single authoritative king.[9]

Despite the variety of institutional structures, the state has much to offer in sustaining social and political order. The centralized, hierarchical, and territorially defined sovereign state can efficiently provide services to its members. Internationally, states speak with one voice for their constituents, enabling them to make and enforce agreements with other states. As a result, a system of states is relatively stable when compared to a universalizing empire.[10] Domestically, territorial limitations ease the burdens and scope of governance by minimizing the diversity of interests, facilitating cultural and national identity, and excluding the high costs of governing far-flung territories.[11] The hierarchical, sovereign state can provide uniformity in public and coordination goods, such as weights and measures, currency, legal rules, and enforcement. And it can mobilize the resources of the population through taxes, redistribution, and the punishment of free-riders.[12]

In addition to being efficient, the state is a moral entity. Thomas Hobbes, perhaps the most important philosopher of the state, saw the state as providing the moral good of security. Without states, people were engaged in an anarchical "war of all against all" in which life, famously, is "nasty, brutish, and short." The state puts an end to this anarchy and guarantees safety and security, enabling peace, order, and daily life. But more than just providing security, as philosopher Michael Walzer has argued, a state is founded in a political community, which has moral integrity because it unites and expresses the collective culture and beliefs of people, developed over generations.[13] Members of the state have the ability to shape their destiny—to pursue their own unique path of political and cultural development, to defend against invaders, to overthrow their government. The state therefore has a moral component: it can serve as an expression of the population's beliefs, commitments, and aspirations.

In much of the world, the central problem is not that the state is too strong and therefore oppressive, but rather that the state is too weak. These states are characterized, alternatively, as failed, failing, fragile, weak, endemically weak, aborted, ungovernable, shadow, anarchic, phantom, anemic, collapsed, and under stress.[14] Between 1955 and 1998, there were 136 cases of state failure among countries with more than 500,000 people, ranging from cases of revolutionary war and ethnic war to adverse regime change and genocide. Often these challenges seem intractable. Structural problems cannot be solved by replacing a leader,[15] and the external neighborhood around such states is usually weak, compounding the problems.[16]

Violence and state failure often go hand in hand. State failure can lead to violence, as in the case of Somalia, in which the absence of a state has perpetuated violence in the form of domestic civil war and offshore piracy. But violence can also lead to state failure, as in Iraq, in which the disbanding of the army, growth of the insurgency, and expansion of crime transformed an effective, if unjust, state into a barely functioning one. Political scientists have shown that wars are most likely not in places with ethnic or religious divisions but in places where the conditions are ripe for insurgency: a financially and bureaucratically weak state, political instability, rough terrain, and a large population.[17] Indeed, in seeking to gain political power and develop a counterstate, the insurgents themselves are engaged in a "process of competitive state-building."[18]

In responding to state failure or simply seeking to fortify state institutions, postconflict reconstruction offers a laundry list of necessary programs: writing constitutions, building governance, reducing corruption, establishing the rule of law, training police and prosecutors, holding elections, and encouraging market-based economic transactions. The dominant approach to postconflict reconstruction embraces an idealized vision of order for society and seeks, with haste, to implement that vision. Policymakers and commentators approach their task with one of two end-states: the vision of self-regulating order and the vision of centralized order. These visions of order are idealized images for the future of the society under reconstruction.

Those who start with the vision of self-regulating order believe either that electoral democracy or the creation of a market economy is the crucial component to a stable order.[19] Comparing corruption, human rights violations, poor public policy, and violence in the conflicted state with the liberal democracies of the West, they conclude that liberal democracy equals stability, prosperity, order, and peace. The advocates of state-building-as-democratization fundamentally believe that the central problem in failed, failing, or insurgent states is a lack of free and fair elections, though since the 1990s they have shifted emphasis from elections alone to elections plus liberal democratic institutions. With electoral democracy, the preferences of the population can be aggregated into public policy through their representatives, thereby channeling the insurgents' grievances from violence to politics. With democratically established constraints on government, the government will be unable to exploit its population and pursue heavy-handed tactics. Freedom follows.

Hence the focus of reconstruction is creating the institutions of liberal constitutional democracy: a constitution with federalism, a bill of rights, separation of powers, and, perhaps most importantly, elections.

The state-building-as-democratization vision is a Jeffersonian ideal, born of the American experience and its revolutionary philosophy. Under this idealized narrative, civil government grew out of the state of nature. In the state of nature, life was characterized by poverty, hardship, and uncertainty. The alternative to a state of nature was a civil government—a system in which laws set rules for people and property, judges adjudicated disputes as they arose, and laws and judgments were enforced. In the state of nature, people come together and, exercising reflection and choice, establish a social contract—a constitution—that determines the shape of their government. Political obligation arises out of popular participation and rational agreement with the social contract. Political order is maintained by the terms of the contract that creates the government. Consent is thus at the center of good government, and the primary fear is that the consented-to government will become oppressive and tyrannical, undermining the liberty and rights of the people.

A related self-regulating vision is the vision of the market. On this theory, economic development leads to political stability, so the core work of reconstruction must be economic: establishing and protecting private property, enforcing contracts, and promoting free trade and labor. This approach, state-building-as-market-formation, draws on caricatures of economic theory. In a market economy, people will rationally sell their labor and output to buyers. Over time, the society's supply and demand for employment, goods, and services will reach an equilibrium, based on aggregated individual preferences exercised through pricing and purchasing. Order follows, as market equilibrium is maintained by the aggregation of individual choices. All that is needed is for the state to enforce market prerequisites such as rules of property and contract. Moreover, the economic relationships between individuals at home and abroad will create interdependence, thereby discouraging individuals and states from waging war. Ensuring economic equilibrium and interdependence prevents violence and maintains order.

In response to the self-regulating visions of order, others begin with a vision of centralized order, which is either absolutist or administrative. Under the absolutist approach, the state of nature is a state of war, and peace is only achievable through a sovereign authority with absolute power to prevent conflict. When people decide to leave the state of nature and enter into civil government, they cede their liberties to a sovereign who has the power to ensure security throughout the population. Obligation derives from the shared need for security; order from the sovereign's power to prevent anarchy. The sovereign's expansive power is the "despotic power" of the state—the ability to exercise power without consulting or negotiating with civil society groups.[20] In recent years, the absolutist approach has had occasional supporters, more often than not among those who believe political and economic development is best achieved through strong, decisive leadership.

Of course, few today embrace creating sovereign states with power approaching absolutism. Far more adherents to the centralized vision of order argue that reconstruction must be directed at creating a centralized administrative state—at developing institutions.[21] Modern states are defined by large administrative bureaucracies that implement rules and provide services throughout society. From income taxes to driver's licenses, government operates in every sector of modern society and extends far into daily life, with its legitimacy deriving from its following impartial, fair, and clear rules. The twentieth-century social theorist Max Weber identified this feature of modern life as "rational-legal domination," and he contrasted it to forms of "charismatic domination" and "traditional domination" that he ascribed to other societies. Order in a bureaucratic state is provided by government; obligation by the fairness and reasonableness of the procedures the government follows. Modern adherents to the administrative approach to centralized order see reconstruction as building state administrative capacity throughout the territory. They focus on training national police forces, building courts, training judges and prosecutors, reforming national laws, and generally expanding the power of central government bureaucracies in local social, political, and economic affairs. Institutions are the key to a reconstructed order.

As promising as the conventional postconflict visions of order may seem, they clash with the dynamics of counterinsurgency and turbulent transitions. As an approach to turbulent reconstruction, the self-regulating and centralized visions of order are potentially, though not universally, disconnected from counterinsurgency strategy. The sources of the insurgency may have nothing to do with political democracy or market participation. Rather, they may be based on ethnic prejudice, religious fervor, ambition and desire for power, backlash against an overbearing and oppressive government, or ineffective government. Moreover, the self-regulating visions of order assume substantial prerequisites. Electoral democracy and a well-functioning market take for granted a relatively unified culture, shared social norms, internal peace, and, most importantly, a government that can enforce the laws and maintain security. In turbulent transitions, these factors cannot be assumed. In some areas the state may be powerless to enforce its will, and insurgents are empowered. The nation maybe divided by class, ideology, race, tribe, eth-nicity, or religion. Because both markets and democracy rely on competition and conflict to function properly, in states where order is fragile, the conflict and competition spurred by democracy or markets may end up destabilizing the country.[22] As Samuel Huntington has argued, "The primary problem is not liberty but the creation of a legitimate public order. Men may, of course, have order without liberty, but they cannot have liberty without order."[23]

The centralized visions of top-down state order also suffer from significant problems. In some cases, the authority of the state may itself be the cause of the insurgency. As a result, the centralized vision may only exacerbate disorder. To be sure, it is not that the enforcement of every particular policy will fuel the insurgency. Individual laws may often be unpopular without sparking demon-strations or insurgency. The problem arises when the government's actions (or inaction) create such widespread social dissatisfaction and disruption that the government loses the obligation of some of the people.[24] In other cases, the baseline power of government may be so weak that the centralized vision is simply unrealistic. Indeed, in territories controlled by the insurgency or fiercely contested by the insurgency, the government would not have the authority to implement its will, even if it tried. Administrative officials may be assassinated for trying to do their jobs, bribed into inaction, or coerced into skewing pol-icies toward particular groups. The state's fraying control over the territory makes the centralized visions an impractical mindset for shaping policy.

## *Postconflict Reconstruction as External Administration*

In establishing a self-regulating or centralized vision of order, the dominant approach is external administration—a foreign government, coalition, or in-ternational organization taking effective control over the territory in question with the goals of reconstruction, state-building, and modernization. External administration allows the external actor to confront problems in the state di-rectly or at least to have substantial influence over state policies. It is therefore thought to be more efficient than diffusing control and more effective than leaving authority with a potentially corrupt local government. External ad-ministration usually takes four forms: occupation, empire, international tran-sitional administration, and neotrusteeship. Most commentators see these as different strategies, though their similarities are perhaps greater than their dif-ferences: transitional administration and neotrusteeship differ in duration, though both grant authority to the international community; occupation and empire likewise differ in duration, though both empower a foreign nation.[25]

Few who study state-building have recognized the similarities between postwar occupation and other external forms of territorial administration, but occupation law has become ever more committed to transforming the occupied territory over its history.[26] Occupation law governs a territory being held during or after a war by an external power and is defined by its central tension between conservation and reform.[27] The conservationist strand sees occupation law as a way to maintain prewar governance, until a peace treaty is signed and the temporarily ousted sovereign can retake control.[28] The reformist strand sees that occupiers might need to change the laws in force in the country and has developed in three phases: security, humanity, and self-determination. The Hague Conventions allowed occupiers to change the laws in the country if needed to maintain their security; the Geneva Conventions allowed reform to protect humanitarian interests; and in the wake of the Iraq War, UN Security Council Resolution 1483 required the occupying forces "to promote the welfare of the Iraqi people through the effective administration of the territory, including . . . the creation of conditions in which the Iraqi people can freely determine their own political future," including political reforms and economic reforms.[29] This "new model of multilateral occupation"[30] required occupiers to become state-builders. Occupation law involves a foreign state with control over a territory and is seen as a strictly time-limited status.

All-out empire involves the direct management of territory as part of the imperial state. Sebastian Mallaby argues that throughout history, when weak states or ungoverned territories caused problems for great powers, the powers became empires to provide governance, and he argues that the United States should fill that role.[31] The most prominent supporter of this position, Niall Ferguson, argues that the United States needs to be more of an empire and develop imperial experts to understand the far corners of the globe that require government from afar.[32] Even liberals like Michael Ignatieff have seen the American project as an imperial one.[33] Empire usually involves a foreign state controlling a territory but, unlike in occupation law, it is defined by a long duration.

International transitional administration is perhaps the most prominent external state-building strategy.[34] Often authorized by the UN Security Council, transitional administration "has always been seen as a temporary, transitional measure designed to create the conditions under which conventional sovereignty can be restored."[35] In these situations, the United Nations will take on the "possession of full executive, as opposed to supervisory, authority" and seek to rebuild institutions of governance,[36] usually during or after peacekeeping or peace enforcement operations in the wake of conflict. One leading scholar says it comprises operations including "electoral assistance, human rights and rule of law technical assistance, security sector reform and certain forms of development assistance."[37] Another scholar makes the link to state-building even clearer, remarking that the purpose of international administration is to "facilitate the emergence of a new state."[38] Significantly, transitional administration assumes that the powers of the state are held only on a temporary basis.[39] In an important sense, occupation and transitional administration are parallel—they both involve external authority designed for a short-term, postconflict situation.

Just as occupation is parallel to transitional administration, so is empire parallel to trusteeship. Empires often involved a civilizing mission to enable self-government of the colony; trusteeship seeks to place in international control a territory that requires guidance prior to self-government. Trusteeship emerged after World War II as the successor to the League of Nations Mandate system. The Mandate system placed under external authority territories "inhabited by peoples not yet able to stand by themselves under the strenuous conditions of the modern world."[40] Under the UN Charter, trusteeship sought to "give the Trust Territories full statehood"[41] and excluded all member states.[42] By the early 1960s most trust territories had achieved independence or merged with independent states; the last trust territory, Palau, achieved independence in 1994.[43]

After the Cold War, and more prominently in the years after September 11, many commentators have argued for a new form of trusteeship.[44] The earliest advocates, appearing a decade before the proposal became popular, argued that governance assistance was ineffective and that delegation of governmental authority to the United Nations or direct UN trusteeship could be effective at addressing the problem of failed and weak states.[45] In Cambodia, for example, the UN Transitional Authority controlled five ministries directly, issued binding directives, and had the power to remove officials.[46] Though trusteeship was precluded by the United Nations' limitation of the category to former League Mandates, World War II territories, and some other areas, a new form of trusteeship would be even more effective at "saving failed states" because it would enable direct control of all government operations by a vigorous and active trustee.[47]

After the invasions of Afghanistan and Iraq, many commentators and scholars argued for applying a new form of trusteeship.[48] The most prominent advocates, Professors James Fearon and David Laitin, called it "neotrusteeship" or "postmodern imperialism" and defined it as the "complicated mixes of international and domestic governance structures that are evolving in Bosnia, Kosovo, East Timor, Sierra Leone, Afghanistan and, possibly in the long run, Iraq."[49] Neotrusteeship has four characteristics: a "remarkable degree of control" by the external actors; governance by a "complex hodgepodge of foreign powers, international and nongovernmental actors (NGOs), and domestic institutions, rather than a single imperial or trust power"; an international mandate; and a desire to "exit as quickly as possible."[50] Noting the problem of failed states and the possibility of neotrusteeship, Fearon and Laitin suggested encouraging interventions to bolster collapsed states and advocated creating international institutions to enable these operations.[51] Other scholars concurred, seeing intervention as requiring long-term trusteeship or else "leaving resentful occupants of the troubled area to figure out ways to strike back at the rich societies from which the interventions came."[52]

Importantly, the methods for implementing these visions of order—the external administration strategies—face many challenges. Indeed, one of the most important problems in state-building is the inability of international actors and local actors to work together as partners to develop political and economic institutions.[53] Perhaps the central challenge for international actors is the tension between efficiency in state-building activities and the necessity of local participation to guarantee sustainability. International actors can almost always design and implement programs faster, cheaper, and more easily than local actors, but simply providing those services is often ineffective and potentially counterproductive. One scholar has argued that the state-building process must be locally driven because it requires organizational design, political system design, a basis for legitimacy, and cultural and structural relevance. The latter two cannot be transferred across times and places; and the former two are almost impossible to implement because they are dependent on institutional culture and behavior, not scientific or even rational principles.[54] The conclusion is that "[e]very bit of technical assistance that displaces a comparable capability on the part of the local society should be regarded as a two-edged sword and treated with great caution."[55] Nonetheless, many NGOs and other international actors still provide services directly, undermining local administration, and perhaps even leading to popular backlash.[56] International and local actors conflict over cultural problems because external actors face a knowledge gap in understanding local customs and traditions, and in the process they might offend or undertake actions that are misguided. And the presence of international actors may also result in creating a "security welfare state"—a class of locals who are dependent on international aid for position and status and thereby work against genuine local development.[57]

In addition to local-international dynamics, international actors themselves cause a number of problems. The necessary resources for state-building are substantial but rarely forthcoming.[58] External actors often seek to exit immediately, despite the fact that state-building is a long-term process.[59] External actors rarely have a unified decision-making or strategic process because they are no longer a singular entity as empires or occupying forces once were. Modern state-building involves both internal and external stakeholders, ranging from local governments and organizations to international organizations, foreign states, nongovernmental organizations such as the Red Cross and Doctors without Borders, and global corporations and investors.[60] These actors are uncoordinated and often have conflicting goals and overlapping agendas.[61] The result is a variety of policies, diffuse accountability, and competition for scarce resources.[62]

External actors also suffer from a serious accountability gap. They seek to establish the rule of law, which is premised on following legal rules even when inconvenient, and at the same time, they often seek to evade legal liability and political responsibility.[63] The United Nations, for example, seeks to shield its members from the jurisdiction of the International Criminal Court,[64] just as the United States in Iraq sought to evade Iraqi courts for their soldiers and contractors who committed crimes.[65] International actors thus signal not only that they are above the law but also that the local legal system is insufficiently civilized for their citizens. This problem extends beyond legal liability for crimes. In Bosnia, for example, the UN High Representative and other international actors supported the president of Srpska when she dissolved the national assembly in 1997—and they then overruled the constitutional court when it declared the dissolution unconstitutional.[66] Political convenience trumped legal process, a fact made more obvious when the president was indicted by the International Criminal Tribunal for the former Yugoslavia.[67]

As great as these problems are, they are only compounded by the dynamics of armed conflict, in particular, that the presence of an international actor may actually inflame the conflict rather than quell it. Under the accidental guerrilla theory of insurgency warfare, when international or governmental actors respond to violence with heavy-handed or overwhelming force, they may fall into the radical insurgents' trap—uniting ordinary locals and radical insurgents together in an insurgency against the intervention. The locals fight not for the radical ideology but merely to repulse the intervention. External action in internal conflicts will also inevitably amount to taking sides in the conflict because it will create winners and losers; even humanitarian aid and developing governance create winners and losers. The alienated losers will be able with relative ease to join the ranks of the opponents of the external actor. Action thus often results in backlash.

Ultimately, the trouble with the conventional postconflict reconstruction approach is that it was not designed to address turbulent transitions, and it therefore neglects the spirit of counterinsurgency. The conventional visions of order imagine an idealized end-state, rather than starting with the messy realities of life on the ground. In doing so, they undervalue the importance of time in turbulent transitions—the recognition that the reconstruction of order proceeds over a long period of time, often in uncomfortable, imperfect, and unpredictable ways. The conventional visions of order advocate for a top-down approach that focuses on elite-level representative politics, large metropolitan systems of justice and order, and central government authority. In doing so, they ignore the diversity of turbulent transitions—the fact of segmented and fragmented territory, the many causes that motivate insurgents and their sympathizers at the local level, and the variation in local environmental, social, and political conditions. These top-down approaches also assume a willing countryside and a receptive population, when, in fact, they are as likely to find a skeptical, cautious, and fearful population in an isolated countryside. The conventional visions of order focus on institutions—elections, markets, executive power, and bureaucracy—rather than on functions, such as dispute resolution, regulation of behavior, popular legitimacy, and effective provision of basic goods and services. In doing so, they ignore the nature of popular support and backlash in turbulent transitions. The people must accept the mechanisms of order, and prepackaged institutional structures may be difficult, if not impossible, to implement. Finally, the conventional visions of order assume a peaceful environment in which democracy or market freedom, centralized authority or bureaucratic rules can spread freely across the land. In doing so, they are blind to the violent, contentious nature of turbulent transitions. The turbulent nature of transitions suggests that grandiose visions of order are misguided. Reconstruction takes place in the midst of war, and its success depends, in no small part, on the winds of war.

## *Turbulent Reconstruction: Warfighting as State-Building*

"Preparation for war has been the great state building activity."[68] Throughout history, rulers needed soldiers, arms, money, and other resources in order to wage war effectively. To acquire these means of warfare efficiently, they created administrative institutions that could extract these resources from the population. As Charles Tilly has said, "[w]ar made the state, and the state made war."[69] Fortuitously, and perhaps unwittingly, counterinsurgency embraces the symbiotic relationship between state-building and warfighting, and explicitly elevates it into military doctrine.

To be sure, there are many theories of state-building. In *The Origins of Political Order*, Francis Fukuyama summarizes some of the most important: the social contract theory that states were established to create security or promote public goods like property rights; the hydraulic theory that state-formation arose from the need for large-scale irrigation projects; population density and growth theories; geographic theories that stress circumscribed valleys versus mountainous or expansive areas; charismatic theories focusing on religion and individual leaders; and warfighting and violence theories.[70] How, why, when, and where any particular state formed likely requires a mix of these theories, with the elements influencing each other in complex and interconnected ways. Counterinsurgency's theory of reconstruction draws on many of these theories: the importance of geography, population density, and religion and leadership. But the central lesson of turbulent transitions is that warfighting and state-building operate simultaneously and, therefore, they will have interactive effects. Counterinsurgency's theory of reconstruction seeks to harness these effects to reconstruct social and political order. Although warfighting cannot be said to be the sole factor in creating states (many parts of the world have seen wars without the creation of states), it has been central to state-building around the world.[71]

The relationship between warfighting and state-building is defined by what S. E. Finer called the "extraction-coercion" cycle.[72] Tilly explains it best:

> In an idealized sequence, a great lord made war so effectively as to become dominant in a substantial territory, but that war making led to increased extraction of the means of war—men, arms, food, lodging, transportation, supplies, and/or the money to buy them—from the population within that territory. The building up of war-making capacity likewise increased the capacity to extract. The very activity of extraction, if successful, entailed the elimination, neutralization, or cooptation of the great lord's local rivals; thus, it led to state making. As a by-product, it created organization in the form of tax-collection agencies, police forces, courts, exchequers, account keepers; thus it again led to state making. To a lesser extent, war making likewise led to state making through the expansion of military organization itself, as a standing army, war industries, supporting bureaucracies, and (rather later) schools grew up within the state

apparatus. All of these structures checked potential rivals and opponents. In the course of making war, extracting resources, and building
up the state apparatus, the managers of states formed alliances with
specific social classes. The members of those classes loaned resources,
provided technical services, or helped ensure the compliance of the
rest of the population, all in return for a measure of protection
against their own rivals and enemies.[73]

Through this process of extracting resources and coercing internal and
external actors, rulers consolidated control and built the state. The state-
building process required public authorities to engage not only in warmaking
and extraction but also in adjudication to settle internal disputes and redistribution to promote production of goods necessary for the military.[74] In France,
for example, maintaining the army became the "chief task of the state's financial administration" and required taxing and stimulating industrial production. "Economic life could not be left to itself, because it was supposed to
serve the ends dictated by *raison d'etat*."[75] The creation of state institutions
could, in turn, also be used by private actors, providing order and predictability to private transactions and relationships.[76] As importantly, the international system fortified the state-building process, as rulers of consolidated
states could speak for their constituents, enforce external agreements, and
exist simultaneously with other territorially delimited states.[77]

To be sure, the process of state-building was not without resistance. The
long and arduous road to the modern state involved "death, suffering, loss of
rights and unwilling surrender of land, goods, or labor" and "resistance was
often concerted, determined, violent, and threatening to the holders of
power."[78] At the same time, the warfighting and state-building process often
looked more like an organized crime racket—creating external threats in
order to extract internal power and control over people—than a social contract or political society defined by shared norms.[79]

In addition to tax collection, military conscription, police forces, judicial
institutions, and the war bureaucracy, rulers have used a number of other
tactics for facilitating state formation. In order to better identify, monitor,
and communicate with the population, states have promoted the use of sur-
names and given names instead of just single names, pushed linguistic centralization on local peoples, and conducted periodic censuses.[80] War has
been used to build national identity, creating a shared culture, historical narrative, and unified community.[81] States also bargained with the population
for authority, in the process creating rights, obligations, and claims against

the state.[82] Indeed, the benefits of state-building—from public goods to improvement in health and security—can be seen as expanding warfighting capacity while simultaneously building allegiance to the state. As one commentator has said of nineteenth-century Germany, "[c]onscription and Bismarck's welfare program were two sides of the same flag: one showed the young man how powerful was the State and how limitless its claim on him, the other showed him how much the State could do for him."[83]

Precisely how did this process of extraction and coercion take place? In the context of European state formation from 1000 A.D. onward, Tilly argues that rulers in different areas followed one of three strategies: coercion-intensive, capital-intensive, and capitalized coercion. Under the coercion-intensive approach, in areas with few cities and little concentrated capital, such as Russia and Brandenburg, rulers "squeezed the means of war from their own populations and others they conquered," creating top-down state institutions.[84] In areas with developed commercial towns, such as the Italian city-states and Northern European states, rulers made bargains with capitalists. As a result, the structures of town and maritime commerce became state institutions.[85] Finally, in England and France, areas with limited commerce, rulers combined the coercive- and capital-intensive modes of state formation, "incorporating capitalists and sources of capital directly into the structures of their states."[86] This process, of course, took hundreds of years. In just the military sector, Tilly argues that prior to 1300, armed forces were recruited through personal service contracts based on specific needs, seasons, and circumstances. Between 1300 and 1700, these arrangements shifted to contractor-supplied mercenary systems of vassals and militias. At the same time, tax farmers and fiscal contractors grew in influence. After 1700, militias and mercenaries were merged into state military structures and the fiscal actors became integrated as part of the state financial administration.[87] Of the three approaches, Tilly argues, war proved the capitalized-coercion strategy most effective, as the Italian city-states and Northern European city-leagues gave way to the national state.[88]

Scholars have qualified Tilly's account by stressing the relationship between local actors and political rulers. Two crucial factors determined which path different European areas took: the power of the towns (which were the burgeoning middle-class economic actors) and the decisions of rulers to align with the towns or to align with the nobles against the towns. Where towns bargained with political rulers, as in France, states emerged because state authority and capital resources could be integrated and mutually supporting, nobles bought off with money or titles. Where political actors worked with local nobles and lords against the towns, as in northern Germany and southern Scandinavia, economic resources developed independently of political power through city-leagues, confederations defined more by economic interest than political hierarchy. In the city-leagues, economic, political, military, and administrative power were never integrated into a national state. By integrating political and economic power, emerging national states like France were better able to gain uniformity in weights and measures, establish a currency, provide a legal system for disputes, and protect property than were the decentralized city-leagues. As a result, the state proved better at reducing transaction costs, preventing freeriding, providing collective goods, and extracting resources. Warfighting and state-building were linked because the state created an internal hierarchy that was most effective at mobilizing society's resources. And that mobilization was ultimately dependent on an alliance between rulers and middle-class economic actors, not the nobles.[89]

The accounts of state formation in Europe suggest that counterinsurgents must integrate economic, political, and military power in order to build institutions and hierarchy that can both coerce internal and external deviants and extract resources effectively and legitimately from the population. This aim will undoubtedly prove difficult. But counterinsurgents must consider resources and logistics as part of their overall strategy, as intertwined with turbulent reconstruction. Turbulent reconstruction requires contracting with local firms and using local labor.[90] Insourcing rather than importing is crucial to the success of turbulent reconstruction. To be sure, insurgents will deliberately seek to disrupt the counterinsurgent's ability to extract manpower, resources, and production from the population, through terror, intimidation, and violence. If the conflict is overlain with identity-based cleavages, working with one side over another may only deepen the conflict rather than mitigate it. And counterinsurgents may operate in areas with little commercial strength and therefore may need to create economic opportunities even as they incorporate economic actors into the regime. But given the relationship between warfighting and state-building, limited warfighting may lead only to limited state-building.[91] The key issue, then, is how counterinsurgents can mobilize the population at the nexus of warfighting and state-building.

## The Local Origins of Counterinsurgency Strategy

Mobilization is crucial to counterinsurgency's dynamics. Insurgencies seek to destroy the bonds of obligation between a people and their government. Counterinsurgents respond by separating the insurgents from the population and reforging the bonds of obligation with the people. They seek to develop a sustainable order in which the insurgency cannot gain a toehold. As a result, in any given area, both the government and the insurgents are competing for control. The heart of the counterinsurgent's enterprise is therefore mobilizing the people's energies in favor of the counterinsurgent and, by implication, against the insurgency. In the process, they will establish a "normative system for resilient, full-spectrum control over violence, economic activity and human security."[92]

Understanding how political order is constructed in counterinsurgency requires first distinguishing between power and violence. As the philosopher Hannah Arendt explains, power is traditionally understood as domination, command, and obedience—the ability of a person to control the actions of others. Under this approach, violence is just a particular aspect of power. Mao thus noted that power comes from the barrel of a gun, and Weber focused on the monopoly of violence as defining state power. Arendt, however, offered a different explanation of power. Rooting power in a tradition linking ancient Athens and eighteenth-century Enlightenment thought, Arendt argued that power "corresponds to the human ability not just to act but to act in concert. Power is never the property of an individual; it belongs to a group and remains in existence only so long as the group keeps together." To be "in power," she argued, is to be empowered by a group.[93] As a result, political institutions are powerful only because they have the support of the people; once the "living power of the people ceases to uphold them," they will "petrify and decay."[94] Violence, in contrast, is rooted in individual strength, and the use of weapons and other implements simply augments the natural strength of the individual.[95] Violence can garner obedience through fear, but it does not create power. In fact, violence is a substitute for power—it is used *because* the person is powerless, because she has not been empowered by the group. Counterinsurgency's theory of competitive control is grounded in the Arendtian version of power: Power resides with the population, and the counterinsurgent, to gain control, must be empowered by the people. Violence is reserved for those irreconcilable insurgents who would never empower the government. As Edmund Burke wrote in 1775, "the use of force alone is but *temporary*. It may subdue for a moment; but it does not remove the necessity of subduing again: and a nation is not governed, which is perpetually to be conquered."[96]

This approach to power also implies a theory of the *sources* of power among the people. Societies, as sociologist Michael Mann has argued, are "constituted of multiple overlapping and intersecting . . . networks of power," rooted in ideological, economic, military, and political relationships.[97] These relationships are interactive, overlapping, and often organized into institutions for accomplishing goals. The requirement for full-spectrum control in counterinsurgency acknowledges these sources of social power and directs operations at each of these relationships in order to shape the society's order and direction.[98] Full-spectrum reconstruction, unlike conventional approaches that focus primarily on electoral democracy, market economics, or executive or bureaucratic control, takes a much wider view of the sources of power in society and recognizes that power is rooted in the complex relationships and interactions that create popular acceptance.

Gaining full-spectrum power, however, is not enough. For the counterinsurgency to be truly successful, it must create a resilient order. In the midst of turbulent transitions, the possibility of backsliding means that an irresolute counterinsurgent will be unlikely to gain the support of the population. If the counterinsurgent's order is likely to collapse in the near future, the people will be less likely to support it, knowing that when the insurgents come to power, retribution for cooperation with the counterinsurgent is likely. Resilient order, however, cannot be built overnight. As Samuel Huntington once wrote, a resilient community depends on "the scope of support for [political] organizations and procedures and their level of institutionalization."[99] Increasing the scope and institutionalization of support takes time because, as Huntington argued, strong organizations are adaptable, complex, autonomous from social groups, and coherent.[100] Adaptable organizations evolve with the turbulence in transitions, unlike rigid organizations that assume a static environment. Complex organizations have overlapping power structures and relationships, preventing an individual or group from consolidating power. Autonomous organizations treat people impersonally, rejecting patronage and withstanding changes in social structure. Coherent organizations have a united community and are thus more stable than fragmented communities. The characteristics of resilient order imply that top-down and sector-based approaches are poorly suited to reconstruction. Order has a complex, dynamic, and organic quality—it is greater than the sum of its aggregated parts.

Creating a resilient, full-spectrum order may appear virtually impossible across a vast territory. But unlike the conventional visions of reconstruction, which assume a national polity and therefore focus on national policies, counterinsurgency embraces the fragmentation and segmentation of territory in addition to the diversity of motives and dynamics in an area. Initially, counterinsurgents must diagnose the particular area in which the insurgency takes place. Different nations—such as Iraq and Afghanistan—will have different histories, state structures, and social traditions and, as a result, require different strategies. Even within a country, areas may differ: city may be different from country, north from south, impersonal social environments from clan-dominated environments. Because "what works in this province may not work in the next," the counterinsurgent will find that order in the nation will only come from order in the provinces, order in the provinces only from order in the districts, and order in the districts only from order in the villages. To craft a resilient, full-spectrum order, the counterinsurgent looks first to the village.

This local focus has significant consequences. Perhaps most importantly, it means that counterinsurgents must act like anthropologists or sociologists in understanding the population. Because anthropology seeks to understand "other societies from within their own framework," it has long played a role in counterinsurgency operations.[101] The discipline was born from the imperial powers' need to understand and govern colonial peoples, and anthropologists played significant roles in World War I, World War II, and Vietnam.[102] The *Counterinsurgency Field Manual* itself embraces the anthropologist's perspective, directing counterinsurgents to study the society, social structure, culture, language, powers and authorities, and interests in a community.[103] It even requires "immersion in the people and their lives to achieve victory."[104] This sociological approach suggests that counterinsurgents should embed themselves with the people. One commentator has called this a "whole of place" approach: counterinsurgents on bases in the field should get to know their neighbors, live off the local economy, and be social rather than fearful of the population.[105] Others have argued that counterinsurgents should actually live in the villages, rather than commuting to the villages from military bases.[106] The benefits of such intimate local connections are significant. Developing close, trusting relationships with local leaders enables counterinsurgents to identify not only the whereabouts and plans of the insurgents but also the needs, habits, and traditions of the community, which are essential for reconstructing order. Given how quickly local dynamics can change in turbulent transitions, this kind of granular information can only emerge from the local community.[107] Counterinsurgency, in essence, benefits from a "holistic, total understanding of local culture."[108]

The political theory of counterinsurgency therefore finds inspiration less in thinkers like John Locke, Thomas Hobbes, Adam Smith, and Max Weber and more in Montesquieu and John Stuart Mill. The idea that legitimate government had to be centered on the local community was central to the thought of the celebrated French philosopher. In his treatise on government, *The Spirit of the Laws*, Montesquieu wrote that republican government—government in which the people ruled as a democracy or aristocracy—required a small size to maintain a virtuous population and government.[109] In small republics, he wrote, "the public good is better felt, better known, lies nearer to each citizen; abuses are less extensive there."[110] In other words, at the local level, people have a better understanding of their collective needs, and because people know each other and the needs of society, corruption is less likely. Small republics thus empower local communities to determine their needs and to address them. If the locals can shape their own policies (as counterinsurgents would say, if the host nation can do it tolerably), the likelihood of government action or inaction alienating the population and pushing them to insurgency will be severely diminished.

The focus on local politics has a second virtue—it enables counterinsurgents to accommodate diversity and differences throughout the territory. Montesquieu spent a considerable part of his treatise discussing the importance of connecting law and government to the local conditions. He argued that many features influenced the "general spirit" of a population: the climate, religion, laws, maxims of government, their past history, manners and customs, wealth, and commercial enterprises.[111] At times Montesquieu took this approach to its most extreme—ascribing governmental types to particular races, territorial features, or climates. But despite these often unwarranted and offensive stereotypes, his basic prescription that different contexts must be treated differently remains inescapable. "Laws should be so appropriate to the people for whom they are made," he wrote, "that it is very unlikely that the laws of one nation can suit another."[112] Montesquieu's commitment to diverse institutional arrangements aligns well with the counterinsurgent's maxim that "what works in this province may not work in the next." For counterinsurgents, applying one-size-fits-all policies will likely fail to address the diverse causes and divergent conditions in insurgent territories. Likewise, for foreign counterinsurgents, simply assuming that their home country's system of law or government can be translated into a foreign context may prove perilous. Rejecting the "general spirit" of the population may unwind rather than strengthen the ties that bind a people.

In *Considerations on Representative Government*, John Stuart Mill, the nineteenth-century British philosopher and statesman, rejected Montesquieu's "naturalist" position and instead argued that natural factors were only important inasmuch as they influenced three basic conditions that any government must have to exist: (1) "The people for whom the government is intended must be willing to accept it; or at least not so unwilling, as to oppose an insurmountable obstacle to its establishment." (2) "They must be willing and able to do what is necessary to keep it standing." (3) "[T]hey must be willing and able to do what it requires of them to enable it to fulfil [*sic*] its purposes."[113] Each of these principles are far easier to fulfill in a local community than at the national level. At the local level, people are most closely connected to their government, most likely to defend themselves, and most able to participate in reconstructing their society.

Mill's three conditions also form the foundation necessary for government to provide order. For Mill, all governments face a tension between order and progress. Order is the principle of obedience; it involves "the preservation of peace, by the cessation of private violence."[114] Progress, on the other hand, is the principle of improvement.[115] Mill thought that progress was the aim of good government—improvement of the capacities, moral and intellectual, of the population—but that order was a necessary precondition for the existence of government. Without order, progress would be impossible. A people cannot expand their moral, intellectual, or even economic capacities if they live in a state of anarchy and chaos, violence and war. As a result, Mill's view of political development was evolutionary and incremental. He believed that order had to come before states could progress to greater levels of self-determination. As a population progressed in its capacities, it could rise to the extraordinary levels of popular understanding and commitment that true self-government requires of its citizenry. Governments, on Mill's model, should seek to remove the impediments to progress, but they must also do no harm in eroding the order and progress a people has already made.[116] In this manner, Mill pursued an incremental approach to designing government—one focused on the conditions in the country itself, on making progress, and on preventing backsliding.

The political theory of counterinsurgency thus begins with the conditions on the ground—with the realities of the population's situation and the characteristics of the population. Only by understanding the local context can the connection between the aggrieved population and the government possibly be repaired. Counterinsurgents must therefore first understand the population—its grievances, its needs, and its hopes—and they must then direct all their energies toward mobilizing the population.

## *Organic Reconstruction: Warfighting as Village-Building*

Uniting the extraction-coercion cycle and bottom-up localism, counterinsurgency sees warfighting as village-building. Establishing security, public goods and institutions, and order at the local level is the first step toward creating widespread order throughout the entire country. Counterinsurgents identify a particular locale and then attempt to gain full-spectrum control within that community, working with and through the population to ensure security and provide essential services. They begin the process of building administrative institutions that can extract resources from the population, coerce remaining insurgent sympathizers, and provide public goods and services. Once that community is secure and the village-building process is underway, counterinsurgents can then expand their area of operations to additional areas.

Known as the "oil spot" or "ink spot" theory of counterinsurgency, this approach was first articulated by the French General Joseph-Simon Gallieni (1849–1916). Having served in the Sudan, Gallieni took over French colonial operations in Tonkin, Indochina, in 1892 with the goal of pacifying the Black Flag pirates and insurgents in the northern part of the country. The basic idea of his *tache d'huile* or "oil spot" strategy was one of "progressive occupation." The French would secure a specific area and then provide basic services, build roads and infrastructure, and enable trade and economic activity. With such benefits, the local population would cooperate with the French.[117] Considered successful in Indochina, Gallieni then implemented the oil spot strategy in Madagascar from 1896 to 1905. He ended the practice of raids and burning villages and pushed his subordinates to learn about the local people and their customs, build schools, and provide medical services and food. Only when security was established would the frontiers of French operations be expanded. By 1897, effective opposition had ended and by 1905, when Gallieni left Madagascar, the island was considered to have been fully pacified.[118]

The oil spot theory enables counterinsurgents to apply the extraction-coercion cycle in a local community, an area that is limited enough in geographic scope that the counterinsurgents are able to provide security to the population day and night. Oil spot theory also facilitates gaining local understanding, receiving intelligence and information from the population, and building trust among the population and institutions. In doing so, it can better adapt to differences in local conditions. Because popular support follows control, if the counterinsurgent concentrates only on a few oil spot areas, the insurgency will build up its control in areas outside the counterinsurgent's attention. As a result, counterinsurgents will eventually have to retake consolidated insurgent territories using traditional warfighting operations or conduct disruptive operations in insurgent territories to prevent or delay the insurgent from consolidating its counterstate.

Two examples of state-building as village-building are particularly instructive. From June 1948 to July 1960, the Malayan Communist Party sought to

mobilize ethnic Chinese in Malaya to overthrow the British colonial government and (after 1957) the Malaysian government.[119] During the Emergency,
insurgents drew on "shortages of food, the high cost of living, the continuing
corruption, and the increasing repression of labor" to gain adherents.[120] From
1948 to 1950, the British pursued a "search and destroy" strategy that alienated the population.[121] By the end of 1951, the insurgency was nearly 8,000
strong, with an additional 10,000–15,000 regular workers.[122] In May 1950, Lt.
Gen. Sir Harold Briggs took command, intending to shift strategies. He reset-
tled rural ethnic Chinese living on the borders of the insurgent-filled jungles
into camps where they could be separate and secure from the insurgency. In
addition, he sought to strengthen civil administration, better coordinate government activities, build roads, and hold the border areas that had been
cleared.[123] In February 1952, Sir Gerald Templer took command with a mandate for further reform. Finding squalor in the resettlement camps, Templer
coined the term "hearts and minds." He determined to treat the population
well, hear and address their grievances, and apply political, economic, cultural, spiritual, and military power.[124]

Central to Templer's strategy was recasting the resettlement camps into
"New Villages." In addition to increased security in the 500 New Villages,
Templer wanted to provide improved conditions across the full-spectrum of
services: clean water, schools, community centers, basic medical care, labor
and agricultural employment opportunities, land titles, youth programs like
scouts and cubs, places of worship, trees around the main streets, an illumi-
nated perimeter, and Home Guards comprised of New Villagers providing
local security.[125] In addition, he created village councils with power to impose
limited local taxes, repair and build roads, and conduct other capital projects
using grants from the federal government. By July 1954 some 200 village councils were in operation, giving locals the opportunity to share in their own governance and shape their community's development.[126] Finally, starting in
September 1953, Templer declared certain regions "white areas"—portions of
the country that were deemed free of insurgency and where restrictions such as
curfews and food control measures would not apply.[127] The result was a clearly
progressive approach to village building: villages would be secured initially;
make progress in social services, economic development, and governance; and
finally be declared "white areas" with greater freedom. To be fair, not all villages proceeded according to plan. Some village programs suffered from bad
planning, social services took longer to establish in remote areas, and not all
village councils were successful at spreading effective self-government.[128] Still,
the New Villages Program is generally considered to have been effective. By

1954 the insurgency had been reduced to 6,000, by 1955 to 3,000, and by 1958 to only 400 members. The Malaysian government declared the Emergency over in 1960.[129]

Without commitment and sound design, however, mere focus on the village level may not be successful. In the second half of 1961, the Vietnamese government of Ngo Dinh Diem began a "strategic hamlets" program, in part influenced by the example of New Villages in Malaya.[130] Diem believed the program would separate the communist insurgency from the population, secure villages, and build support for the government, while mobilizing the population to become self-reliant and economically secure.[131] As a "strategic" hamlet, the program embraced full-spectrum control, aspiring to establish security through a hamlet-based militia, democracy through local elections, and economic development through small programs that would be debated, chosen, and implemented by villagers with only limited funding and oversight from outside.[132] Through active participation of the population, the strategic hamlet would lead to community solidarity.[133] For Diem, the strategic hamlet would simultaneously address the problems of communism, underdevelopment, and disunity. Democratic decentralization provided a new model for postcolonial development, one that navigated between the heavy-handedness of authoritarianism and Western-style national democracy, which would lead to fragmentation of the state.[134]

Unfortunately, the program failed to meet these aspirations. As an initial matter, the program was designed with little involvement from the Americans and was thus not aligned with American strategy.[135] Moreover, Diem's desired pace of implementation—16,000 hamlets within 12 months—was completely unrealistic.[136] After one month, the government claimed that over 1,300 fortified hamlets had been created, resulting in the "creation" of strategic hamlets in which security was in fact absent.[137] Indeed, by November 1963, over one-third had either fallen into communist hands or were at risk of such a fate.[138] Diem also had a nostalgic vision of village life, so he wrongly assumed that peasants would support the program and establish security almost immediately.[139] Finally, it did not help that the head of the program was secretly supporting the Viet Cong.[140] The failure of the program suggests less about the promise of local initiatives than the importance of consolidating security at the local level.

Around the same time, however, the U.S. Special Forces were having considerable success at implementing an oil spot strategy in Darlac province, South Vietnam, through the Civilian Irregular Defense Group (CIDG) program. From November 1961 until the end of 1962, the Special Forces "worked hand in hand with the people to fortify their village; they constructed shelters and an early-warning system and closely regulated the movement of people in and out of the area. They also armed and trained local volunteers to help protect the village from attacks by guerrillas."[141] By April 1962, 40 villages had been voluntarily secured through the program; by August, 200 villages were in the program. And at the end of 1962, when the government declared Darlac province clear, 38,000 armed civilians provided security to 300,000 civilians and a few hundred square miles of territory.[142] Yet, despite the success of the program, which had been run through the CIA, the U.S. Army soon took control over CIDG because it wanted the Special Forces to engage in conventional offensive military operations rather than counterinsurgency.[143] As the Special Forces left a partially trained Vietnamese contingent in the villages and the government began to confiscate weapons from the villagers, security deteriorated.[144]

The Marines Combined Action Platoon (CAP) program in Vietnam followed a similar course. In the late 1960s, the Marines established CAPs consisting of 15 Marines and 34 locally recruited paramilitary "popular forces." The CAP would live among the people in a village in order to provide security. Despite the technical challenge of language barriers and the strategic problem of not operating in a contiguous area to ensure that insurgents cannot operate in the interstitial spaces between villages, the CAP program produced results. Casualty rates in CAP areas were lower than in search and destroy missions, the villages scored almost 1.5 points higher than non-CAP villages on the 5-point pacification scale, and only one CAP village was ever overrun in the history of the program. Yet, the army disapproved of the CAP strategy, with one general commenting that the Marines "don't know how to fight on land, particularly against guerrillas."[145]

Malaya and Vietnam show the promise and pitfalls of a village-building strategy. At its best, village-building can divide the population from insurgents, provide security, empower political self-governance, and provide employment in a matter that creates a virtuous cycle of improvement and solidarity. When implemented hastily or irresolutely, however, village-building may prove unhelpful to the reconstruction of order.

## Nongovernmental and Communitarian Counterinsurgency

Counterinsurgency's local approach requires radically decentralizing operations. At the local level, counterinsurgency frequently takes two forms: nongovernmental counterinsurgency and communitarian counterinsurgency.

Nongovernmental counterinsurgency starts at the local level, and it relies on powerful actors, networks, and groups to build order in that particular community. In any local area, certain actors or groups—clans, tribes, families, organizations—will command authority and power. Nongovernmental counterinsurgency seeks to win over those actors and groups and provide full-spectrum control through their organizations instead of establishing new organizations. Because nongovernmental counterinsurgency relies upon existing power structures, it neither encroaches on the authority and jurisdiction of local actors who may fear the creation of a new social order nor involves counterinsurgents in reinventing organizations. Moreover, because the local actors have considerable local knowledge, nongovernmental counterinsurgency reduces the inevitable knowledge gap that counterinsurgents often face when entering a local community. At the same time, however, nongovernmental counterinsurgency poses considerable risks. Counterinsurgents cannot control local actors, who may exploit their relationship with the counterinsurgent to hoard resources, switch sides in the midst of the conflict, exploit the population for gain, abuse the population through violence and fear, or pursue their own feuds and power struggles. If local actors engage in human rights abuses, create a climate of fear, or discriminate among portions of the population, the people may turn against both the local actors and the counterinsurgent, instead embracing insurgents who promise better conditions. These risks are compounded by the counterinsurgent's knowledge gap, which makes it difficult to monitor and assess local agents.

In other words, local empowerment through nongovernmental counterinsurgency risks sanctioning, even supporting, warlordism. Warlords are primarily interested in their own benefit, not the reconstruction of the state.[146] Working with warlords might condone the use of violence against the population and undermine the moral authority of the counterinsurgent.[147] At the same time, the term "warlord" encompasses many meanings and practices, and some warlords may even provide social services, making their form of warlordism an effective form of governance.[148] Moreover, warlords may also be the primary or only route to stability and security, and rejecting cooperation outright may rob the counterinsurgents of effective leaders who wish to "transition from 'warlord to ward leader.'"[149] Whether to coerce or co-opt warlords is therefore best determined on a case-by-case basis. Military and law enforcement power, prosecution and amnesty, and reduced, transparent, and dispersed funding may help diminish the influence of warlords.[150] But ultimately, as the Chinese thinker Hu Shi argued during the 1920s, because warlordism is the product of disorder, developing impartial administration is the only sustainable solution.[151] At its worst, therefore, nongovernmental counterinsurgency can backfire, aggravating tensions in a community, reducing support for the government, and supporting and sanctioning human rights violations, fear, and violence. At its best, nongovernmental counterinsurgency is merely a first step. Future steps will involve developing institutions of administration that do not rely on patronage or other personality- or clan-based networks of power.

In recent years, nongovernmental counterinsurgency has been hotly debated, particularly in the context of working with tribes in Iraq and Afghanistan. The experience working with tribes in Al Anbar province, Iraq, for example, is generally considered a successful case of using local powerholders as a strategy to improve security and reestablish order. Throughout the 1980s and 1990s, Saddam Hussein directly and indirectly shifted power to Anbar's tribes. Needing Ba'athists at the front in the war with Iran, Saddam was forced to rely on the tribes for support. Moreover, his erosion of civil society groups, such as trade unions, forced people to revert to tribes for their social welfare needs. The power of the tribes grew so great that, by 1996, Saddam created the High Council of Tribal Chiefs and provided tribes with judicial, security, and taxation powers.[152] After the U.S. invasion in 2003, the tribal sheikhs' power was threatened both by U.S. plans to establish a new, democratic, central government and by Al Qaeda in Mesopotamia.[153] Though they initially sided with Al Qaeda, in 2005 tribal leaders began to worry that Al Qaeda's international goals clashed with their local interests and that Al Qaeda was capturing their revenue sources. To deter the tribes from defecting, Al Qaeda killed key tribal leaders. But by late 2006 two leaders, Sheikh Sattar al Rishawi and Fasal al-Gaoud, formally began to act against Al Qaeda.[154] The Awakening, as it was known, had begun. During this same period in 2005 and 2006, some in the U.S. military believed that Anbar was "beyond repair."[155] However, the military then shifted its policy, focusing primarily on working with the tribes against Al Qaeda instead of seeking to establish a separate government-run structure for security and economic development. They allowed local sheikhs' militias to guard their own neighborhoods instead of relying on Iraqi police, and they paid the sheikhs directly, rather than disbursing funds through open-bid contracts, which undermined the sheikhs' power.[156] To be sure, facilitating the Awakening posed significant dangers. As a third party supporting both the tribes and government, the United States risked alienating the government of Iraq and even undermining its longer-term goal of creating an effective, democratic central government. It also risked taking sides in intertribal and inter-sect feuds and tensions.[157] Was supporting the Awakening the right policy? In the short term, it not only reduced violence but also provided an "Iraqi-led, bottom-up" solution based on civil society, rather than a top-down plan for political reconciliation that U.S. strategists had initially imagined.[158] At the same time, as one commentator put it at the time, it could have "play[ed] out in ways that may be good or bad, but [were] fundamentally unpredictable."[159]

In the fall of 2009 and spring of 2010, commentators and policymakers debated whether a form of nongovernmental counterinsurgency—a tribal engagement strategy—could succeed in Afghanistan.[160] Commentators argued that working with Afghan tribes could provide security and governance, and interdict external support for insurgents, in a manner that was culturally sensitive to local conditions.[161] Others countered that the tribes were no longer the primary form of social identification in much of Afghanistan because decades of war had increased the powers of mullahs and militia commanders and weakened tribal identity.[162] And some held that it would be difficult to identify the right local leaders to work with, and even then, supporting local militias might only lead to strengthening the power of warlords and further fragmentation of power in Afghanistan.[163]

Consider one brief snapshot that illustrates the complexities in pursuing a nongovernmental strategy. In January 2010 the United States embraced an opportunity to work with the Shinwari tribe in Eastern Afghanistan, after the tribe pledged to support the government against Taliban insurgents.[164] Weeks later, the partnership met its first challenge, as two Shinwari subtribes began fighting against each other over a long-standing land dispute.[165] Similarly, in Arghandab district in Kandahar, the Special Forces began training villagers to conduct local security. This Local Defense Initiative (LDI) was not sanctioned by the Karzai government, which worried that when the United States leaves, the militias would not support the government and would end up spawning future conflict. To reduce the possibility of creating warlords, LDI was not supposed to provide the militias with weapons or salaries, and each militia would have to operate under the authority of a group of tribal elders rather than a single individual. This program too immediately met challenges, as the local volunteers eventually convinced the military to pay them $10 per day, in return for both providing security and participating in local reconstruction projects.[166]

Ultimately, it is difficult to say whether nongovernmental counterinsurgency is advisable. Each situation presents a complex history, changing ground-level dynamics, and varying power structures in society. The risks are great, but in some cases, nongovernmental counterinsurgency may be the best path to stability. To reduce the risks of warlordism, some have advocated for modifying tribal engagement to focus instead on local communities, not just tribes, and have suggested linking the central government and the local community to prevent the fragmentation of power.[167] In doing so, they have articulated a different species of decentralized reconstruction: communitarian counterinsurgency.

Like nongovernmental counterinsurgency, communitarian counterinsurgency begins at the local level. Unlike nongovernmental counterinsurgency, communitarian counterinsurgency does not rely on local powerholders but rather seeks to build community solidarity, strength, and the full spectrum of social power from the bottom up. Importantly, communitarian counterinsurgents eschew forcing uniform national solutions or central government authority in local communities. Instead, they decentralize strategy, programs, and authority to the most granular, local level possible. "Small is beautiful," the *Counterinsurgency Field Manual* says, because small programs are tailored to local conditions and can often remain below the enemy's radar.[168] Communitarian counterinsurgents also seek to link programs to national or central government authority, but in limited ways. In other words, bottom-up localism is the inspiring principle of communitarian counterinsurgency. It centers attention on a particular local community, and it designs programs from the ground up to address the conditions and needs of that community.

Perhaps the best example of the communitarian approach to counterinsurgency is the National Solidarity Program (NSP), designed and implemented in Afghanistan starting in 2003. The NSP empowers communities to identify their own reconstruction needs and to plan, manage, and monitor projects to address those needs. Under the NSP, villages elect Community Development Councils (CDCs) by secret ballot, and the CDCs then hold public and participatory meetings to determine community needs and design a recovery plan. The NSP then provides block grants between $20,000 and $60,000 per community for specific projects within the community's plan.[169] Communities must provide at least 10 percent of the costs of the project, in terms of labor, materials, or other costs, and all financial records must be available publicly.[170] According to the World Bank, which is the largest financier of the NSP, around 90 percent of projects have focused on "bringing drinking water and irrigation to the villages, paving rural roads and bridges, constructing school buildings and community centers, and electrifying village communities."[171] For these projects, over 80 percent of labor has come from the local communities, reducing costs and increasing employment and income.[172]

By all accounts, the NSP has thus far been successful. As of August 2008, the NSP affected over 17 million Afghans in all 34 provinces in the country.[173] By March 2009, the NSP had established over 21,800 CDCs.[174] In addition to providing almost a 20 percent economic rate of return,[175] the programs are 30 percent cheaper than those implemented by foreign NGOs, and insurgents are wary of attacking the projects for fear of alienating the local communities.[176] The NSP strengthens social bonds through participation in community development, includes young people and women in decision making, and incorporates the central government while pursuing a bottom-up strategy of local empowerment and self-government.[177] Ashraf Ghani and Clare Lockhart note that "[m]any representatives maintain that as a result of this program they—for the first time in their lives—feel like citizens of a state, they have rights, and they are not just people who are subject to the whims of a distant authority."[178] Finally, the NSP evades the problems of nongovernmental counterinsurgency: identification of local power-brokers and entrenchment of warlords. Its programs are transparent, solidaristic, empowering to the local population—and linked to the government.

The National Solidarity Program lends credence to the pragmatist and progressive philosopher John Dewey's view that "[t]he local is the ultimate universal."[179] For Dewey, democracy meant more than simply elections or political representation. Rather, "democracy is . . . the idea of community life itself."[180] Democratic communities involved individuals working together to take an active role in shaping their destiny as a group and seeking to expand those activities precisely because they were good for the community as a whole.[181] Local community thus enables people to find meaning: they build a shared identity and harmony, and they are empowered to shape their future.[182] At the local level, Dewey argued, it was possible to unite the political, economic, spiritual, familial, and cultural in a manner that is truly democratic because it relies on the people's values, deliberations, and collective choices. This Deweyan philosophy—one that unites democracy, community solidarity, and economic empowerment—is at the heart of communitarian counterinsurgency strategy. At the local level, political obligation and legitimacy can be at their strongest.

As effective as they are at adapting to the local context, nongovernmental and communitarian strategies themselves have contextual limitations. They will be best suited to areas in which there is a strong social structure and in which the population is relatively small and isolated. Each are essential because the communitarian and nongovernmental approaches assume that locals can effectively govern themselves, which is difficult to do in large, dispersed population areas where people have divergent feelings about social and political authority. Significantly, the social structure and small-society requirements are often related, but they need not be. In many areas of Afghanistan, for example, the Taliban have assassinated *maliks* and *ulemas* (local political and religious leaders), filling their places with Taliban commanders and religious leaders. Those areas might fail the strong-social-structure prong even if they pass the small-and-isolated-areas prong of the test. The only way to determine where such an approach can succeed is to conduct individual assessments: district by district, valley by valley, village by village. A bottom-up approach would root this analysis with the soldiers, Marines, and civilians on the ground who would know best the local conditions. The corollary to this caveat is that in the major cities, surrounding areas, and relatively open or densely populated rural areas, central government authority and programs will likely be more prominent.

## Decentralized Governance Strategies

In nongovernmental and communitarian counterinsurgencies, the relationship between the central authorities and the local actors or community can be precarious. Designing this relationship, however, is critical to successful counterinsurgency. The structure of governance not only shapes whether order can be established on the ground but also determines how legitimate and how sustainable that order is. Though the relationship between the center and the peripheries will inevitably be dynamic, evolving over time, counterinsurgents can pursue six strategies when designing governance structures.

*Formal decentralization* grants authority to the local communities and limits the role of the central government. At its most extreme, pure decentralization may even mean secession or autonomy for a particular province or district. The Northwest Frontier Province (NWFP) and Federally Administered Tribal Areas (FATA) in Pakistan are examples of areas in which local control is so expansive that the national government rarely operates in those regions.

Most prominent as a strategy of British imperial governance, *indirect rule* was defined by Donald Cameron, governor of the Tanganyika territory, as "the principle of adapting for the purposes of local government, the institutions which the native peoples have evolved for themselves, so that they may develop in a constitutional manner from their own past, guided and restrained by the traditions and sanctions which they have inherited."[183] The goal is to "maintain and support native rule" rather than "to impose a form of British rule with the support of native chiefs."[184] Under indirect rule, the role of the regional and central governments becomes managing the local actors: playing them off of each other, occasionally conducting shows of force, and otherwise maintaining the balance of power among factions, regions, and groups. The implicit bargain struck between the center and the communities is that the local actors recognize the authority of the central government, and the central government grants the local actors considerable autonomy. Indirect rule, of course, suffers from a number of problems. It requires strong social norms or traditions for the local and central authorities to continue this state of affairs. These traditions are challenged by globalization and modern values of human rights and democracy, which reject a government of local strongmen controlling the community through mafia-like authority. Indirect rule is also inherently unstable. When local actors change or the leader of the central government changes, the entire system risks collapsing, as the balance of power inevitably shifts. As a result, it is by no means a sustainable solution to the structure of order. Indirect rule also requires local actors who actually have the capacity to govern the community, which may be unlikely in counterinsurgency.

Often working in conjunction with indirect rule is the *auxiliary approach*. Simply put, the auxiliary approach requires the central government to purchase allegiance from the local actors through money, titles, or other benefits. The auxiliary approach is not without its challenges. Losing support of local actors or communities is possible if the other side provides greater compensation or more appealing benefits. As importantly, the auxiliary approach requires that the central authorities have funds to spend. In feudal and post-feudal Europe, funding came from spoils of external wars of conquest, which fortuitously enabled transition from an auxiliary approach to institutional state-building over time. In the colonial era, funding came from the colonial power. In this manner, the British bankrolled the internal wars and alliances of the Afghan state in the 1880s and 1890s.[185] In the modern era, funding would most likely have to come from the international community or from illicit trade. The former is unlikely to flow in a consistent manner; the latter brings with it social pathologies and dependencies that are inherently and instrumentally undesirable to a well-functioning social order.

*State incorporation* goes further than the auxiliary approach, involving local actors directly in the central government. In a nongovernmental counterinsurgency, this may mean that the state fills its rolls of officials with members of a local power network. For example, in postcolonial Kenya, Jomo Kenyatta filled the army with his Kikuyu tribesmen in order to shift power away from the Kamba and Kalenjin tribes, which had been favored during the

British era.[186] In a communitarian counterinsurgency, this may mean that local leaders become part of a provincial or central parliament.

Another option is to establish *parallel structures*, in which the community-level structures exist and operate alongside state institutions at the local level. This approach may be effective in the area of dispute resolution, where state-run courts and traditional adjudication could coexist, but it may be less effective to have overlapping institutions when it comes to governance and security.

The final strategy, the strategy used in the National Solidarity Program and the one perhaps most aligned with counterinsurgency theory, is *democratic experimentalism*.[187] Under democratic experimentalism, the central government sets and enforces goals, priorities, and basic procedural rules; collects information and data from local governments; and shares information and best practices to enable mutual learning in different locales. Local governments are given considerable discretion to design and implement solutions. Democratic experimentalism empowers local populations through participation in self-government; fosters creative, bottom-up solutions that are tailored to the local conditions; and enables testing many different approaches to a problem within a single country. An analogy from technology might be helpful. Democratic experimentalism could be called a "platform approach" to government. Just like with technology platforms that provide basic infrastructure and functionality and then allow users to customize their experience and develop their own programs and applications, the platform strategy has the central government providing the basic framework of rules, oversight, and funding but allows the local communities to customize the reconstruction and development process in a way that is participatory and locally responsive. Instead of the central government providing services, it sets basic goals and guidelines and the communities provide themselves with the services they need.

In addition to the National Solidarity Program, democratic experimentalism has been used in a wide variety of settings. In Minneapolis, the Neighborhood Revitalization Program has given residents a "seat at the table" and made them partners in local development—not just recipients of the city's services and public works. Residents of each city neighborhood help set priorities and determine their needs in conjunction with city officials. In Chicago, city officials adopted a radical new policing strategy by creating partnerships with neighborhoods, nonprofits, and public agencies. At "beat meetings," residents and police discuss safety problems in the neighborhood and work together to establish priorities and solve them.[188] Scholars have even shown the power of democratic experimentalism in areas as diverse as the reg-ulation of nuclear power plants, procurement of sophisticated military hard-ware, environmental regulation, and child-protective services.[189]

Democratic experimentalism incorporates government and empowers local communities. In doing so, it evades the greatest risk of poorly designed nongovernmental and communitarian counterinsurgency strategies: that they become an antigovernment counterinsurgency, that is, a counterinsur-gency strategy that is defined not only by the absence of government support and involvement but also by actual hostility toward the government. To understand the allure of antigovernment counterinsurgency, consider the po-sition of Afghanistan under the Karzai government in 2009 and early 2010. During the debate over U.S. strategy in Afghanistan in the fall of 2009, skep-tics of a troop increase argued that counterinsurgency requires a legitimate government partner and that the Karzai government's corruption and foot-dragging made success difficult if not impossible. The logic of the argu-ment makes sense given the conventional paradigm for counterinsurgency in which there is a government seeking to regain control of territory it has lost to an insurgency. The problem is that the conventional approach assumes that government authority and anti-insurgency sentiment go together. In Afghani-stan, the conventional wisdom among the military during that time was that operations must support the Government of the Islamic Republic of Afghani-stan. The belief is that supporting the government is necessarily anti-insurgency. As a logical matter, this conclusion may be unwarranted: a local community could be both anti-insurgency and antigovernment. It could prefer *local self-government* to both central government authority and the insurgency. The result is that it might be possible to have an antigovernment counterinsur-gency strategy—a strategy that seeks to build local resilience and self-govern-ment that is both autonomous from central government control and decidedly anti-insurgency.

Antigovernment counterinsurgency would focus on building local resil-ience, solidarity, and strength and on community-based mechanisms of jus-tice, security, governance, and economic development. However, the antigovernment approach would not explicitly link these institutions to the central government for fear of sparking local backlash or corrupting the local organizations and processes. Although an antigovernment counterin-surgency strategy may be successful in the short term in reducing violence and building stability and order, because it relies upon local animus toward the government to craft that stability, it risks the fragmentation of the state. In situations where secession or autonomy is inevitable, this may well be an appropriate strategy. In cases where hope remains for a unified state, it is unclear whether the antigovernment approach is desirable: it may fragment the state and impede state consolidation or, at some point in the future, empower the local community to a position in which it is willing to bargain with the state to establish closer ties. Over a long period of time, state consolidation may still be possible, but the risks of failure are substantial.

IN THE END, counterinsurgency's approach to the reconstruction of order is not visionary. It does not presume that the aspirational future can be achieved immediately, but it rather seeks to take deliberate, progressive steps toward greater order and stability. Organic reconstruction—the process of warfighting as village-building—requires a patient, long-term commitment to creating security, improving full-spectrum services and control in the village, and transitioning over time from heavily fortified areas to normalcy. Perhaps in no area are these tasks more difficult than building the rule of law and designing a new constitutional order.

# 6

## The Organic Rule of Law

THE RULE OF law is one of those few but fortunate concepts that has universal support. It has been called a "panacea for the ills of countries in transition" and an "elixir" that "promises to remove all the chief obstacles on the path to democracy and market economies."[1] The orthodox view is that the rule of law is "good for everyone."[2] And who could disagree? To stand against the rule of law is to stand with absolutism—against democracy, prosperity, peace, order, human rights, and liberty.

In a competition with the insurgents for full-spectrum control of society, the rule of law is therefore a powerful tool: it helps regulate behavior, resolve disputes, and enable the creation or revision of social rules. Indeed, by the end of 2009, the United States had spent $1.27 billion on rule-of-law programs in Iraq.[3] From 2002 to 2010, civilian expenditures on rule-of-law programs in Afghanistan amounted to $904 million.[4] In addition to the United States, the World Bank, United Nations, foreign governments such as the United Kingdom, and nongovernmental organizations (NGOs) spend considerable sums on rule-of-law programs. So important is the rule of law to strategic success that the *Counterinsurgency Field Manual* declares that "[e]stablishing the rule of law is a key goal and end state in COIN."[5] Insurgents are likewise well aware of law's power. In Afghanistan, for example, the Taliban provides legal adjudication in order to win over the population and address their local needs, particularly with respect to land, water, and other civil disputes.[6] Taliban courts not only help resolve disputes through adjudication but also demonstrate to the population that the insurgency can provide a stable, efficient, and effective social order.

The universal appeal of the rule of law, however, masks a deep problem—that the rule of law is almost impossible to define. The rule of law has a "know it when I see it" quality that evades precise definition.[7] Indeed, as one scholar has noted, the rule of law has been used to support political programs "from Hayekian libertarianism, to Rawlsian social welfare liberalism, to Lee Kuan Yew's soft authoritarianism, to Jiang Zemin's statist socialism, to a Sharia-based Islamic state."[8] As a result of its extraordinary breadth, some have become fed up with the rule of law. Joseph Raz called the rule of law a "slogan used by supporters of ideas which bear little or no relation to the one it originally designated."[9] And the formidable political theorist Judith Shklar said the rule of law was "meaningless thanks to ideological abuse and general over-use"; it is nothing more than a "self-congratulatory rhetorical device."[10]

Without theoretical clarity, those who are tasked with building the rule of law are lost both conceptually and operationally. They are unsure of the "essence" of the rule of law and the "basic rationale" for promoting the rule of law.[11] And the central problem rule-of-law practitioners face is that they know an endpoint of the rule of law—the model of Western-style systems—but they do not know how those systems develop. As a result, they operate under a simple assumption: "if the institutions can be changed to fit the models, the rule of law will emerge."[12]

Thinking about the rule of law from the perspective not of existing stable systems but of the messy, conflict-ridden reality of turbulent transitions shows that many of the definitions used to capture the rule of law are insufficient, problematic, and potentially counterproductive. Counterinsurgency's rule of law is not idealistic or universal. Rather, it is *organic*, rooted in local conditions and commanding popular support. The organic rule of law embraces traditional dispute resolution mechanisms, rather than relying solely on state-run courts, and it advocates for community-oriented policing rather than a top-down professional policing approach. Perhaps most strikingly, when thinking about law and justice, counterinsurgency requires moving beyond criminal law and security and instead considering the full range of civil disputes and behaviors that law governs.

## What Is the Rule of Law?

Defining the rule of law is difficult, if not impossible, as definitions often turn on resolving deeply contested normative issues.[13] In international development, definitions of the rule of law sometimes incorporate stability, security, democracy, market economics, and even human flourishing. Given the complexity and scope of most definitions, looking to the particular components of the rule of law provides a better guide to understanding its meaning. The elements of the rule of law can be broken down into five broad categories: minimalist, substantive, institutional, security, and cultural.

*The Minimalist Approach*. Minimalist approaches to the rule of law center on the qualities necessary for a legal system to exist.[14] At the most basic level, a legal system requires rules that govern people's conduct, ways to change those rules, ways to address uncertainty or disputes about the rules, and ways to enforce the rules.[15] Without these components as a bare minimum, legal philosophers argue, it is impossible to have a legal system in a complex society. Minimalist philosophers do not specify particular institutional arrangements for a legal system. For example, one does not need an American-style adversarial court system or even a European-style inquisitorial court system to address uncertainty or disputes; a council of elders might work just as well. Moreover, one need not have a professional police force to enforce the laws; some combination of social pressure, internalization of norms, and legal enforcement might be as effective. What is important is just that there is some way to address these basic functions.

Having a legal system is not enough for the *rule* of law. Paramount is the need for supremacy of law, the idea that government officials and ordinary citizens are *all* subject to law.[16] The supremacy of law implies a form of anti-politics that supports the familiar desire for a "government of laws not men."[17] Many minimalists derive from the idea of law ruling that the laws must be public, clear, stable, and predictable.[18] Without these requirements, the law cannot guide individual conduct, and therefore it would be unable to shape ordinary citizens' behavior or the behavior of officials.[19] The assumption is that if the law is capable of guiding conduct, people will act in accordance with law instead of relying on extrajudicial methods of resolving disputes, such as violence.[20] Of course, it may be possible to have rules that can guide conduct without their being public, clear, stable, or predictable. Broad standards might be as predictable as precise rules if people share the same social norms, and frequent changes in the laws might not be destabilizing if people learn of the changes quickly and are willing and able to adapt. Ability to guide conduct is a function of knowledge—publicity, clarity, stability, and predictability are simply proxies.

Minimalist definitions of the rule of law also stress nonarbitrariness.[21] At a most basic level, nonarbitrariness means that the laws are evenly applied *according to their own terms*.[22] Some commentators, however, have gone further, requiring equality for all citizens, regardless of gender or ethnicity, class or caste.[23] This expansive vision of nonarbitrariness amounts to a substantive requirement for equality of treatment beyond mere equivalence according to the terms of the law itself. A true minimalist takes a much narrower approach: As Joseph Raz has argued, "[the rule of law] is not to be confused with democracy, justice, equality (before the law or otherwise), human rights of any kind or respect for persons or for the dignity of man."[24]

*The Substantive Approach.* Although most definitions of the term "rule of law" include minimalist components, few in the international realm limit the rule of law to its minimalist conception. Most definitions include some substantive component, whether human rights, democracy, or economic principles of contract and property. Some who adhere to the substantive approach do so for principled reasons, others because they have interwoven their commitments to liberalism and the rule of law, and some use the term instrumentally for its rhetorical power, perceived neutrality, and widespread acceptance.[25] For each substantive value—human rights, democracy, and economic principles—there are two approaches to understanding the relationship between the substantive value and the rule of law. One group sees the rule of law as an instrument for furthering the substantive value; another group sees the substantive value as an inherent and constitutive part of the rule of law. For example, some have argued that the rule of law is the foundation for democracy, a necessary element for democracy to exist and flourish.[26] Others have instead insisted that "democracy is an inherent element in the rule of law."[27]

The difference between the instrumental and inherent views of substantive values within the rule of law is perhaps best seen with human rights. The rule-of-law practitioner field largely grew out of efforts to promote human rights in Latin America in the 1980s.[28] With a greater desire for treating human rights as "justiciable claims rather than mere aspirations," practitioners sought to develop legal institutions that could enforce these claims.[29] For example, the American Bar Association's Rule of Law Initiative includes as one of its goals increasing awareness of international human rights law and teaching lawyers how to address human rights violations in court.[30] As a result of this interest in promoting human rights through law, a set of definitions has emerged that treats the goal or purpose of the rule of law as promoting human rights.[31]

In addition to this instrumental vision, another set of definitions argues that the rule of law includes human rights inherently. For example, the UN Peacekeeping Operations Handbook defines the rule of law as "[a] principle of governance in which all persons, institutions and entities, public and private, including the State itself, are accountable to laws that are publicly promulgated, equally enforced and independently adjudicated, and which are consistent with international human rights norms and standards."[32] Other aid groups and scholars have similarly defined the rule of law as incorporating human rights.[33] When it comes to defining the particular human rights included, most definitions fail to specify which human rights norms are necessary. The UN Development Program, for example, does not specify what counts as human rights to be pursued in Afghanistan. Instead it uses as one (somewhat baffling) metric, the percentage of "laws passed in the last two years incorporating the principles of human rights."[34] The few who do specify human rights have diverse ways of determining *which* human rights are necessary to the rule of law. One set of scholars include rights specified in the Universal Declaration of Human Rights, the International Covenant on Civil and Political Rights (ICCPR), the Convention on the Elimination of All Forms of Discrimination against Women, the International Convention on the Elimination of All Forms of Racial Discrimination, and the Convention against Torture.[35] The *Counterinsurgency Field Manual* includes rights specified in the Universal Declaration and the ICCPR but not in the other treaties. And one commentator argues that the rule of law must uphold "the rights of marginalized groups, such as women and racial and religious minorities," even if this principle would conflict with *sharia* law and caste systems.[36]

The last major substantive category is economic rules of contract and property, and again there are some who see the rule of law as establishing foundations for a market economy and others who see the rule of law as requiring market principles to even exist. The economist Hernando de Soto thus argues that "formal law is the foundation of the market system, essential to the development of corporations, limited liability contracts and an adequate business environment."[37] In contrast, a famous World Bank study, *Governance Matters*, which has been influential in shaping the World Bank's governance projects, includes enforceability of contracts in its definition of the rule of law.[38] A later iteration of the same report justifies this inclusion: "[T]hese indicators measure the success of a society in developing an environment in which fair and predictable rules form the basis for economic and social interactions, and importantly, the extent to which property rights are protected."[39] The rule of law, on this vision, requires contracts and property rights of a certain kind. Indeed, some studies use the security of property rights as a metric for the rule of law itself.[40] Perhaps the most important, though somewhat subtle, advocate for incorporating market principles into the rule of law was Friedrich Hayek. Hayek defined the rule of law based on clear and predictable rules that would facilitate his vision of the free market.[41]

*The Institutional Approach.* Many in international discourse think of the rule of law in terms of legal institutions and focus on codes, courts, and the legal profession. Some aid workers focus on reforming the laws themselves—on

modernizing legal codes to revise ancient and outdated provisions or on replacing the codes completely.[42] The most frequently cited institutional goal of the
rule of law is the existence of an independent judiciary.[43] The extraordinary
focus on judicial institutions stems in part from viewing the rule of law as a
quality inherent in stable societies that have such institutions. In essence, this
"rule of law orthodoxy" is premised on a "build it and they will come" approach
that assumes that if the institutions existed, they would not be abused and
would serve their intended purposes.[44] Some commentators and practitioners
go even further, arguing that the rule of law requires the separation of powers
and a judiciary that takes one case at a time.[45]

By centering the rule of law on the judiciary, rule of law practitioners focus
on organizations that support the courts—lawyers, bar associations, prosecutors, and legal education systems. As a result, much of the rule-of-law aid effort
is focused on strengthening or building top-down, state-controlled legal institutions: "Training and salaries for judges and court staff are increased ... [and]
reform efforts target the police, prosecutors, public defenders, and prisons."[46]
Some reformers focus on a civil society that can hold officials accountable;
others on legal education, civic education, and legal profession reform; and at
least one group of advocates stress most aspects of a modern liberal democratic
society:[47] "On the institutional level, the rule of law involves courts, legislatures, statutes, executive agencies, elections, a strong educational system, a free
press, and independent nongovernmental organizations (NGOs) such as bar
associations, civic associations, political parties, and the like."[48] In recent years,
some academic commentators have gone further, arguing that the respect for
the rule of law is an element of culture, and therefore that programs need to
focus on instilling respect for law into the people's culture.[49]

*The Security Approach.* Another set of rule-of-law elements fits under the
category of security, and it is often called the "law and order" approach. Some
have argued that security was "never part of the philosophical basis of the rule
of law," though others have noted that at its core the "rule of law should protect against anarchy and the Hobbesian war of all against all."[50] Law and order
programs usually focus on "cops, courts, and corrections" or "police, prosecutors, and prisons." They are sometimes considered part of security sector
reform, which includes programs to reform the military, intelligence agencies,
judicial bodies, prisons, human rights commissions, traditional justice systems,
and the civilian agencies and civil society groups that manage or oversee those
institutions.[51] On this theory, the rule of law focuses on the institutions in
society that provide security to the population, in particular, safety from violence and crime.

*The Cultural Approach*. Many commentators and scholars (though fewer practitioners) stress that the rule of law has, for lack of a better term, a cultural component—based on social practices or history.[52] Here, the rule of law is seen as socially constructed and dependent on the particular conditions of the time and place. The cultural approach requires realizing that promoting the rule of law is not a technocratic, neutral process but rather is "inherently political" because it involves addressing basic questions of justice, rights, and the distribution of resources.[53] The rule of law must therefore be separated from liberalism, and instead it is linked to the political values of the particular society.[54] The reason is that the rules are meaningless if they are ignored in practice; they become mere words on parchment, rather than felt obligations that are followed by most of the population most of the time.[55] Under this cultural and sociological approach, in transitional settings, the people's experience with their prior regimes will have a significant impact on how they understand justice and injustice and also will influence the nature of the legal system they are willing to accept for the future.[56] For adherents to the cultural approach, efforts to build the rule of law that ignore local values and traditions may appear to the local population to look more like an imposition of values, even imperialism.[57] However good the intentions, those efforts will be fruitless.

## The Rule of Law during Conflict

In the midst of conflict, attempts to build the rule of law are shaped by the dynamics of turbulent transitions. The core dynamics of conflict—the possibility of backsliding into conflict, the need for popular support, the evolution of the conflict, the segmentation of territorial control, and the partiality of any action—have important implications for defining the rule of law. They suggest that the rule of law during conflict is best defined by its minimalist and cultural components.

Minimalist goals are at the core of the rule of law because they best capture the absolute minimum necessary for the phrase "rule of law" to make any sense: a legal system and its supremacy. In turbulent transitions, minimalist definitions and components are clear and simple, making it easier for international actors and the host-nation to agree on the goals. They also provide minimal disruption to local power structures and cultural values because they take no position on particular structures or substantive values.[58] As a result, they are less likely to be deemed imperialistic in their aims, and they provide great flexibility in adapting to local conditions. This minimalist approach also has the virtue of limiting an external actor's substantive interactions with the population. By not specifying particular cultural or institutional arrangements as goals, the formalist approach reduces the likelihood of backlash from overreaching policies and creates an opportunity for culturally relevant and effective institutions. The challenge to minimalism stems not from its efficacy within the host-nation but from the perspective of outsiders: international actors may be unlikely to support rule-of-law programs if they promote substantive ends that international groups oppose, such as incorporating sharia into the legal system.[59] But this is precisely the point in turbulent transitions: the population's support is paramount and the rule of law must be driven by their needs and values, not those of outsiders.

At the same time, however, the minimalist component of the rule of law threatens to obscure the possibility of the rule of law as a factor in shaping the conflict itself. Choices between types of institutions and substantive values can have profound effects in times of conflict. Using tribal councils instead of state-run courts, for example, may empower certain factions over others; supporting certain substantive rights over others may win over certain groups and alienate others. In turbulent transitions, where popular support is necessary to success, the particular design will make a strategic difference. It can either build support or alienate the people or, more precisely, particular groups of people. The virtue of minimalist definitions is that they articulate the core of the rule of law and enable diversity beyond the core. The vice of minimalist definitions is that they threaten to ignore the particular choices made to accomplish minimalist goals.

Like the minimalist element, the cultural component is central to building the rule of law. Indeed, military lawyers thinking about counterinsurgency operations have recognized that systems that do not reflect local values might fail or result in heavy-handed tactics. As the *Rule of Law Handbook* states,

> [f]rom a moral perspective, it is problematic for a state to impose a legal system that does not reflect its society's values. From a practical perspective, the failure of a legal system to become internalized can devastate the official legal infrastructure either because of constant resistance (through political or more violent means) or by requiring the state to rely on its coercive power to resolve more legal disputes than it has the capacity to handle.[60]

This commitment to local culture and values is nothing more than a restatement of the fundamental principle of counterinsurgency: legitimacy. The idea of creating a culturally relevant rule of law assumes that people embrace their culture and therefore accept and support it. Given that the counterinsurgent must "foster development of effective governance by a legitimate government," looking to local values may be the easiest path.[61]

Even though the cultural element is important in turbulent transitions, culture itself might be malleable. During wartime, identities may be transformed as disparate local, tribal, and affinity groups are brought together under a single party in the war, or they may be hardened as the war enables locals to pursue blood feuds and rivalries under the cover of the war's broader aims. Moreover, new identities might be created through the war, as happened with the Panjshiri Afghans during the 1980s and 1990s.[62] The fluidity of cultural commitments and identity destabilizes the idea of a culture-specific rule of law. In wartime, it may be impossible to even identify a fixed culture: practices and identities may be in constant flux. As a result, returning to prewar institutions may or may not be effective and reclaiming traditional mechanisms may require their modification to meet new realities.

Despite these caveats, the minimalist and cultural components of the rule of law align well with counterinsurgency and the dynamics of turbulent transitions. Because they do not require fixed and uniform institutional forms or involve specific substantive values, the minimalist and cultural components allow for variation across different geographies, according to the segmentation of territorial control, and they enable dynamic changes that evolve over time. Moreover, their adaptability permits the design of systems that can maximize popular support and mitigate the likelihood of backlash.

In contrast, the security, institutional, and substantive approaches to the rule of law are problematic in counterinsurgency. That security or "law and order" issues are important to the rule of law during times of conflict is evident. Turbulent transitions suggest that widespread violence is always possible. Securing the population is therefore a necessary part of any operation, and the popular "clear-hold-build" formulation of counterinsurgency doctrine indicates that it is helpful to secure an area from ongoing violence before full-scale civil and development programs take place. Security is essential because, in the midst of outright violence, it is difficult to even think about building a legal system. Still, the law and order approach focuses too narrowly on crime and punishment. It does not address civil disputes, such as land and water disputes, contract disagreements, or other disputes related to everyday life. Given the importance of popular support and a full-spectrum approach, the law and order approach is thus insufficient. It marginalizes so many of the rules and procedures that ordinary people use on a daily basis—and upon which they make a judgment about the efficacy of government.

The idea that the rule of law *requires* substantive goals is problematic in turbulent transitions. The substantive rule of law assumes that the alternative futures for a country are a legal system with substantive values or a legal system without substantive values. This is a mistake, as there is a third possibility: neither a legal system nor substantive values. For a legal system to exist, officials must value and accept the law as guiding their behavior.[63] If the war-peace distinction is robust, one might presume that a legal system will be established after the war ends. But in turbulent transitions, it is possible that war will simply continue indefinitely or that the regime that eventually emerges will have officials who do not respect or follow the law—and also do not respect substantive values. In other words, the insurgents could take over and establish a counterstate that rejects both law and substantive values. It is for this reason that counterinsurgency "favors peace over justice."[64] It assumes that a stable society is preferable to the anarchy of insurgent violence or civil war, even if that means accepting second-best solutions on substantive values. The goal is a workable legal system, not the best legal system.

This goal of a workable legal system demonstrates another problem with including substantive values as a constitutive part of the rule of law: the different perspectives of actors. International actors have one view as to what is legitimate or substantively desirable, a view that is often based on an end-state of Western liberal democracies. The host-nation's population may have a different view of how to configure their society. For example, some have argued that democracy may not be necessary or even the best route to effective political and economic order.[65] Others have argued that a one-size-fits-all approach to economic development and institutional configurations within developing countries is likely to be less effective than a country-by-country approach.[66] In the case of human rights, significant clashes may emerge on topics from the death penalty to the relationship between religious law and state law.

Promoting these substantive goals may be desirable but it is not the same as promoting the rule of law. Indeed, there may be significant tradeoffs between pursuing substantive goals and establishing a minimalist rule of law or defeating the insurgency. Separating substantive goals like democracy from the minimalist goal of a legal system helps reiterate that the choices made are not "technical," but rather political. The particular substantive choices made could empower certain actors, create or exploit divisions between rival groups, and alienate whole populations. All operations in conflict situations amount to taking sides in the conflict.

Similarly, institutional definitions of the rule of law present serious problems. Focusing on particular institutional arrangements confuses the goal of the rule-of-law enterprise, which is a legal system, with the goal of a legal system that has a particular configuration in institutions and their support structures. In reality, the particular institutions are merely means to the end of a legal society; they are not the goals themselves.[67] Legal systems require rules that govern behavior, ways to change those rules, ways to address uncertainty in the rules or disputes about the rules, and ways to enforce the rules.[68] These goals do not require any particular institutional configuration. Courts may be unnecessary if other dispute resolution mechanisms such as mediation and arbitration are pervasive or if tribal councils are available.[69]

Concentrating on particular institutional arrangements also narrows the possibilities for designing institutions that will have built-in popular support and legitimacy, necessary conditions for preventing backlash. For example, despite considerable time and resources focused on creating an Afghan judicial system, more than 80 percent of social conflicts are resolved by nongovernmental dispute mechanisms, such as local and tribal councils (the *shura* or *jirga*).[70] The *shura* and *jirga* are seen as accessible, fair and trusted, less corrupt than state courts, linked with local values, effective, and meeting human rights and international standards.[71] In addition, the goal of these councils is primarily peacemaking and reconciliation, not creating winners and losers. As one court official put it, "jirgas do the jobs that courts in Kandahar are unable to do" because they are self-enforced through social pressure and can end enmities between disputants rather than just ending the dispute.[72] Given these local perceptions and practices, it should be no surprise that some practitioners have suggested creating a hybrid form of justice in Afghanistan that incorporates the *shura* and *jirga* into the formal legal system, particularly with respect to civil disputes and minor crimes.[73] Not only would a hybrid system better fit with popular preferences, but incorporating traditional mechanisms into a system of justice would also reduce the burden on newly created court systems that are underresourced and may not be accessible everywhere in the country.[74]

Institutional definitions also focus inordinately on continuity throughout the nation and across time, instead of embracing the segmentation and fragmentation of territorial control and the evolutionary nature of conflict. The segmentation and fragmentation of territory imply that different areas within a country can and in some cases may need to have different systems of the rule of law. The evolutionary development of conflict suggests that the rule-of-law institutions need to be flexible and dynamic, changing in structure as the conflict escalates or subsides.

Finally, the institutional approaches that focus on building a culture of the rule of law miss the fact that institutions and culture are not autonomous.[75] They exist in an organic relationship, with each in part constituting the other. Legal institutions require support from the people, and at the same time support grows from effective institutions. And legal institutions and a culture of respect for law cannot be separated from the broader context of turbulent transitions from conflict into peace.

## Two Concepts of Law

The difficulty in defining the rule of law, particularly during times of conflict, reflects a deeper challenge—how to think about what law is and how it works. At its core, the debate over the nature of law is driven by two divergent starting points: the formal and the sociological.[76] The formal view defines law and social order by what is technically law, the laws on the books and the institutions of government. The sociological view looks at what is actually happening in society, how people behave, and what people believe. Understanding these two views and their interplay is central for grasping the role of law in society—and in counterinsurgency.

In most complex modern societies, the source of social order seems obvious: it is created and sustained by the legal institutions and legal rules that govern interactions between people.[77] Law is the command of the sovereign authority in society, and compliance is guaranteed by the threat of force.[78] The state's commands are announced through documents such as constitutions, laws, regulations, and judicial opinions. Order is enforced through institutions like courts, legislatures, executive and administrative officers, and police, which can impose punishments, financial or penal.[79] People comply with the law for instrumental reasons—they are worried about punishments and the coercive power of the sovereign if they do not obey her commands. The state's power is what enforces legal rules and prevents society from a descent into chaos.

Importantly, this formal vision sees the legal system as largely autonomous, as independent of social and political contexts.[80] People in society see laws as constraints on their behavior and comply for fear of sanction. Lawyers see social behaviors as inputs that they must consider according to the precise terms of the law and then deem legal or illegal. Each sphere—society and law—is autonomous and interprets the other through its own lens.[81] Social consequences, political context, and judge's preferences are not thought to be relevant to law. Law is a technical and logical enterprise. What is considered legitimate under the formal approach is what is legal: decisions and actions that go through the procedures of the legal system and are enforced according to its terms. It does not matter if one disagrees with an outcome or even if all of society disagrees with an outcome; the process and authority of the state grants legitimacy to the law.[82]

The opposing vision of law is sociological or behavioral, and it begins from a very different starting point. Instead of considering a complex, modern society, imagine the anthropologists who were the first to live with tribes in the islands of Polynesia. When they arrived, they were shocked to find that the state of nature was not a chaotic war of all against all. Even though the locals did not have state or bureaucratic institutions, they still had ways of resolving disputes, systems of governance, and shared norms that guided their conduct. So the anthropologists asked themselves: What else could we call this except a legal system? It may look different from Western structures, but it serves exactly the same functions.[83] From this starting point, anthropologists and sociologists argued that these systems of social order were best understood as a legal system, even though they were not created by or connected to a state.[84] Even as anthropologists in the early twentieth century challenged the formalist approach to legal institutions, a group of legal theorists known as the "legal realists" challenged the formalist approach to legal doctrine. They argued that social context and consequences were part of legal interpretation and that the law was not a perfectly logical, coherent system of rules, independent of society. As Oliver Wendell Holmes Jr. put it, "[t]he life of the law has not been logic; it has been experience."[85] The legal anthropologists and realists share a sociological approach that sees law and legal order as "social practice" and as responsive to social conditions.[86] What is most important for this model is people's actual behavior and beliefs.

Under the sociological approach, unlike the formal approach, legal institutions are "embedded in social life."[87] What sustains the social order is social norms, beliefs, and a sense of community obligation.[88] The formal laws that do exist are merely reflections of popular consciousness and beliefs, and judges will interpret laws in a manner that aligns with social experience and beliefs.[89] Compliance is driven by the people's sense of obligation, self-interest, and an idea of reciprocity.[90] Coercion is often unnecessary.[91] Under the sociological approach, legitimacy requires that "the relevant public regards [a behavior] as justified, appropriate, or otherwise deserving of support for reasons beyond fear of sanctions or mere hope for personal reward."[92] Where formal legitimacy is supported by process and authority, sociological legitimacy is supported by popular belief and behavior.

Neither the formalist nor the sociological ideal is precisely accurate for understanding society, and the two approaches are not mutually exclusive. Consider the failings of the formal approach. It is not true that all laws are coercive. Some laws enable action or facilitate social relations, such as laws of marriage and wills. Failure to comply with these laws does not trigger a violation of law with a corresponding sanction but rather a legal nullity—an incorrectly executed will, for example, is simply invalid.[93] Moreover, not all laws are followed; norms and behaviors are as important to understanding the implementation of legal rules as are the written rules themselves. The prohibition on underage drinking, for example, is substantially underenforced on college campuses. Likewise, not all order is premised on formal laws.[94] Social order is sustained through a complex interplay of practices.[95] In some traditional societies, there are few codified laws or formal structures; legal disputes are resolved by discussion, arbitration of local elders, and other practices, rather than state coercion, cops, and corrections. Even in a modern, legalistic society, some areas may rely more on social norms than law. In his study of cattle ranchers in Shasta County, California, Robert Ellickson showed that norms of neighborliness play a greater role than the laws on the books in managing disputes and shaping behavior in that community. When it came to cattle issues, Shasta County featured "order without law."[96] If these practices are consistent over time, what difference besides a formalistic definition separates them from constituting a legal order? Additionally, command and coercion cannot sustain a legal system over time. Formal legal systems need some level of sociological acceptance to continue. If the coercive sovereign has no sociological support, she is likely to find an insurgency in her country or, upon her death, a revolution.[97] Such uncertainty does not have the persistence associated with a legal order.

At the same time, the sociological approach to law is insufficient for understanding the nature and concept of law. Most importantly, it cannot tell us what is law and what is not.[98] Behavior and beliefs are shaped by more than just social rules, structures, and conventions. Education, religion, and the size and homogeneity of the population will all shape the behavior of the people.[99] But those factors do not fit naturally with any intuitions about what constitutes law. Moreover, formalist coercion is an important function of law. Many in society will not follow the law based solely on obligation or reciprocity and must be therefore coerced into behaving in accordance with social rules.

Both the formal and sociological visions of law and legal order have much to offer in situations of counterinsurgency, and embracing both visions suggests a spectrum between the formal and sociological approaches to law that implies that each vision can influence the other. The greatest risk, however, is of a gap or disconnect between the formal and sociological visions—for clarity, between law and norms. Law and norms need not be precisely overlapping and, in fact, they rarely are. But too great a disconnect between law and norms can be problematic. Laws that remain on the books far after the norms of society change will most likely be ignored. However, if they are enforced, they may prevent conduct that everyone in society approves—and that might be normatively desirable or even necessary for social welfare. The result in either case may be the denigration of the laws, resulting in backlash, protest, and perhaps even revolution. The lesson is that the law cannot remain static but must evolve because society evolves. Impatient laws may also create problems. If law changes too quickly, it may far outpace the population's beliefs and behaviors. If these impatient laws are unenforced, they may do injury to the legitimacy of law—revealing it as mere parchment guarantees with little real-world applicability. And if the impatient laws are enforced, they may spark backlash among a population that rejects them. At the root of this problem is the fact that law is relatively easy to change, while norms are relatively hard to change. Those who seek change through law without attending to underlying norms risk alienating the people. The disconnect between law and norms creates instability, space for dissent, protest, and backlash. In stable societies, this instability is usually channeled into the political process; in unstable societies, it may be fuel for violence and insurgency. Stability requires minimizing the gap between laws and norms.

The prospect of revolt due to a disconnect between laws and norms raises the issue of legitimacy. As one scholar comments, legitimacy

> is believed to be the key to the success of legal authorities. If authorities have legitimacy, they can function effectively; if they lack it it is difficult and perhaps impossible for them to regulate public behavior. As a result those interested in understanding how to maintain the social system have been concerned with identifying the conditions that promote legitimacy; those seeking social change have sought to understand how to undermine it.[100]

Whether legal or sociological, legitimacy is "the perceived obligation to comply with the directives of an authority, irrespective of the personal gains or losses associated with doing so."[101] In the case of legal legitimacy, it is maintained by the authority and procedures established by law; in the case of sociological legitimacy, by the beliefs of the population.

The interplay and disconnect between norms and law parallel the interplay and disconnect between sociological and legal legitimacy. At the most fundamental level, formal legitimacy is predicated on sociological legitimacy.[102] Although most laws are respected because they are passed through legal procedures—such as the constitutional requirement of Congress passing legislation and the president signing it—the legitimacy of the overall system does not rest on formal legal processes as much as it relies on the fact that people today accept it as governing society.[103] People may embrace the legal system for moral, traditional, or utilitarian reasons, but their ultimate justification for seeing the overall system as legitimate must be based on some deeper value, not on the procedures that instituted the system. If the legal system contradicts a deeply held value and cannot or will not incorporate it, the legal system will face serious challenges.[104] At the same time, however, once the legal system has been accepted as a matter of sociological legitimacy, legal legitimacy has independent power.[105] The process followed grants legitimacy to an outcome, even if people disagree with the outcome. However, disconnects in legitimacy are possible. A law, such as the prohibition of alcohol in the 1920s, can be legally legitimate and sociologically illegitimate. Legitimacy gaps, just like gaps in norms and law, can undermine social order. In stable societies, divergences might be channeled constructively into politics; in unstable societies, divergences might mean war.

## Counterinsurgency's Rule of Law

The parallels between legal and military theory are uncanny. Conventional warfare is a highly structured enterprise, defined by orderly, bureaucratic armies waging civilized war on pitched battlefields. Success in conventional war requires applying force and coercing the enemy into submission. Formalist conceptions of law are likewise highly structured, defined by orderly rules enforced by bureaucratic institutions. Compliance in a formalistic legal world, like in conventional warfare, is the result of enforcement by coercion. In addition, both conventional war and formalist law see their realm as autonomous, as largely independent of social context.

Counterinsurgency flips conventional warfare on its head. Insurgency warfare is not highly structured but embedded in the social context, defined by the fluidity of the insurgents and their interactions with the people. Success in counterinsurgency is a function not of force, but of gaining popular support. Sociological conceptions of law are likewise not highly structured but embedded in the social context, defined by the behaviors and beliefs of the people themselves. Compliance in a sociological legal world is the result of gaining popular support for practices or behaviors.

The parallel between counterinsurgency and sociological conceptions of law is not mere coincidence. They both focus on the population because they recognize that both war and law operate in a social and political context. The creation of law is necessarily a political act, the determination of a policy that is institutionalized so as to apply to everyone in society. War is also political because it involves applying force to implement a policy for all in a society. War and law are simply different mechanisms for maintaining social order, and sustainable social order is ultimately dependent on the population's beliefs and behaviors.[106]

This insight is nothing more than a revival of Clausewitz's concept of war, though revisited in an important way. Clausewitz's dictum that "war is politics by other means" reflects the political foundations of warfare, and it transforms warfare from a separate sphere of social life to a mere extension of conflict resolution in social life.[107] War is but one means of resolving conflict—politics is another, and law is a third.[108] Each are ways of organizing dissent, protest, challenges to power, and opposing visions of what is best for society. Hence, if war is politics by other means, politics and law are war by other means.[109] Once it is clear that war, politics, and law are each different pathways for achieving social order, it is necessary to understand the sources of power that can implement—or forestall—establishing order. Clausewitz again is helpful. Clausewitz argued that power in a complex society was rooted in the trinity of the military, the government, and the population.[110] For Clausewitz and his followers in conventional warfare, war required confronting these sources of power—and destroying them. Victory was a function of coercion over the enemy, so military, government, and population needed to be defeated physically, practically, or spiritually. Note the parallel to the formal conception of legal order: laws are enforced by external institutions, like the police, against unwilling citizens.

Yet coercion is not the only way to achieve order in society. The sociological conception of law argues that an orderly society can exist if people have shared beliefs and norms and behave in accordance with them. Institutions can be made legitimate not by their authority and process but by social acceptance. Counterinsurgency embraces the same theory. It seeks to create legal systems, government, and security grounded in local values and responsive to the people's needs and concerns. In other words, where conventional warfare seeks to destroy the sources of social power, counterinsurgency seeks to build the sources of social power: popular support, government authority, and national security. Although all three sources in the trinity are important to the success of counterinsurgency, popular support is first among equals. The reason is similar to the priority of sociological to legal legitimacy. Legal legitimacy provides a firm foundation for practices that maintain social order: they are accepted by the population because of the processes and authority of the government. But legal legitimacy is bounded by the constraints of sociological legitimacy. If the population utterly rejects a policy or legal structure, it will remove its support or begin a revolution. Sociological legitimacy is thus the foundation upon which legal legitimacy is built. The result is that the state can then focus on a few outliers. As Tom Tyler has written, "if many or most of the people within a society are voluntarily following the rules, authorities are freed to direct their coercive force against a smaller subset of community residents who do not hold supportive internal values."[111] So too in counterinsurgency. Gaining popular support is the foundation upon which government authority and national security are built. Counterinsurgency thus seeks to use war, politics, law, and other means to build social strength in the trinity of military, government, and the population. This power in the population leaves the military only a few irreconcilables who need to be confronted with military force. Like conventional war, counterinsurgency is total war. Unlike conventional war, counterinsurgency's vision of total war is primarily constructive, not destructive.

Counterinsurgency's law is ultimately sociological, grounded in the beliefs and behaviors of people, in the norms of the society. Formalist approaches to law can be deeply problematic in counterinsurgency. Enforcing legal rules created by government authorities may be counterproductive if the government has no popular support and the legal rules or institutions are anathema to the population's beliefs, behaviors, and norms. Saying "technically it is legal" when undertaking actions may be unimportant or even counterproductive if legal and sociological legitimacy diverge substantially and the population abhors the "technically legal" action that is taken. Ultimately, a stable and sustainable political and social order can only exist with popular support. Implementing an institutional rule-of-law vision from the top-down, without popular support and participation, is therefore akin to waging conventional warfare in the midst of a counterinsurgency campaign.

As a result, a minimalist and culturally linked approach to defining the rule of law is preferable to institutional and security-based approaches. The minimalist component focuses on finding some way of making rules, adjudicating disputes, and enforcing rules, but it does not specify particular institutions or mechanisms that can accomplish those tasks. Rather, it recognizes that there might be many ways to achieve those goals. The cultural component argues that the particular mechanisms should be dependent on the social conditions and context of the place and should be driven by practices the people believe are legitimate.

This notion of the rule of law can be called *organic.* The organic rule of law grows naturally out of the conditions of the place—its culture, popular preferences, and traditions—and at the same time it fulfills the central function of the rule of law, a legal system that has supremacy in society. It does not declare commitments to institutional or substantive values outside the context of a particular society, preferring instead to identify local traditions, preferences, and values and allow them to guide the shaping of institutions and substantive values. In many situations, the rule of law may look similar to those of justice systems in Western states—professional police, adversarial court systems, and impartial judges. But in some situations, and even in some areas within a particular country, the rule of law may take on a different manifestation. At the extreme, tribal councils may take the place of courts in resolving disputes. Land and water issues may be addressed through equitable mediation rather than adversarial court systems. And criminal justice remedies may involve addressing broader tensions between families and clans, rather than just punishing individual wrongdoers. In turbulent transitions, the organic rule of law holds that the most important factor in establishing a legal system is ensuring popular support for the system.[112] It therefore starts with a diagnosis of the capacities and practices of the people themselves. From that foundation, it pursues a rule of law that is tailored to the local conditions and context.

Perhaps most importantly, the organic rule of law is not limited to criminal law, "law and order," or security concerns. Its minimalist commitment to rules of behavior, ways to resolve disputes, and ways to change the rules extends well beyond security and criminal law issues. Indeed, if counterinsurgency is 20 percent military and 80 percent civil affairs, then the organic rule of law requires a similar proportion of effort spent on criminal versus civil disputes. In Afghanistan, for example, the central drivers of disputes are land and water issues.[113] Counterinsurgents must therefore focus their energies on more than just police, prosecutors, and prisons. Because the neutral and reconcilable population seeks effective and efficient ways to go about their daily lives, counterinsurgents must provide for the rule of law in everyday affairs. Focusing primarily on criminal law issues in counterinsurgency is like focusing primarily on kill-capture military operations. Real victory can only come from civilian affairs—from outgoverning the insurgency, not outfighting it.

Rooted in the community, the organic rule of law cannot be established through "technical assistance," as orthodox reformers characterize their work. Laws are created for policy reasons, and the same is true of the rule of law. In answering the policy question of how society should be governed and public goods provided, the rule of law gives one answer—an answer that has opponents in authoritarianism, pure populism, and warlordism. Just as the idea of a legal system governing society is a policy choice, so too are the particular arrangements of that legal system. Rule-of-law choices are therefore the very archetype of a political choice. One notable consequence is that the choice of rule-of-law structures must be embraced by the political elites in the community. If the powerholders in a community, just like the population at large, disapprove of the rule of law promulgated, they will rebel against it or operate around it. The organic rule of law thus recognizes that the powerful must want to restrain themselves under the system of law. They may embrace restraint for moral reasons or, more likely, for self-interested reasons.[114] But without their support, the rule of law is a lost cause.

Ultimately, the organic rule of law is an inherently transitional concept. It is not a fixed entity adhering to an idealized vision of what the rule of law could be, but rather a dynamic, ever-changing midpoint between the contentious and violent reality of war and the aspiration for long-run stability. The rule of law will likely vary across places based on the seriousness of the conflict and the segmentation of territory. It will likely be incomplete, providing partial justice and imperfect processes. And it will likely be impure, featuring hybrid forms of justice that incorporate varying sociologically accepted traditions instead of a single formalist institutional framework.

## *Structuring Hybrid Justice: The Case of Afghanistan*

Perhaps the greatest challenge in facilitating the organic rule of law during counterinsurgency is navigating between formal and traditional methods of resolving disputes. In many places, formal state-sanctioned and state-run courts are not the primary method for resolving disputes. In Malawi, 80 to 90 percent of disputes are resolved through traditional processes; in Bangladesh, 60 to 70 percent of local disputes are addressed through the *salish*; Sierra Leone places 85 percent of the population under the jurisdiction of customary law; 80 percent of Burundians use local institutions; and 90 percent of land transactions in Mozambique and Ghana are governed by customary tenure.[115] Indeed, in Afghanistan since 2001, the central challenge in building the rule of law has been the tension between formal and traditional forms of justice—between the state-run system of courts and the local and tribal systems of *shura* and *jirga*, councils of community leaders who mediate conflicts. The question in Afghanistan—and one that may arise in other counter-insurgencies—is how to handle the two systems of justice.

Some background may be helpful. The primary issue in Afghan law and governance for over a century has been the relationship between the central government and local communities. Since the 1880s, the central government in Kabul has repeatedly attempted to expand its authority and influence in rural communities by establishing formal judicial structures that would replace or co-opt traditional, nonstate mechanisms for resolving disputes and regulating behavior.[116] Whenever the central government has sought to change local structures quickly, it has faced massive resistance. For example, during the 1970s, the government of Daoud Khan made incremental changes, only to be challenged by radicals who wanted quicker transformation. When the modernists took power and pursued "massive land redistribution, abolition of marriage payments, elimination of rural debts, and secular government," they were "met with suspicion and then armed resistance in the countryside."[117] They learned that "the strength of the Afghan government was illusory. The state had encapsulated existing tribal and regional groups but had never broken their power at the local level."[118]

Despite the centralizing tendencies of its leaders, the Afghan government has never had the power to enforce its will in the countryside.[119] The government's authority has largely been limited to urban areas and irrigated agricultural plains. Villages and communities in the mountains, deserts, and other areas were often too remote or poor for the government to administer effectively and efficiently.[120] This divide in the rule of law persists even today, as two-thirds of urban Afghans bring claims to the state courts and 45 percent of rural Afghans prefer *shuras* or *jirgas*.[121] While the central government has not recognized traditional law as legitimate, officials have often used the policy of indirect rule in governing their districts. Officials would permit the use of traditional mechanisms to maintain social order and only intervene in significant disputes. Members of the community therefore bargained in the shadow of state intervention and could use the possibility of state intervention as a threat in order to improve the chances of a mediated settlement.[122]

Throughout the Afghan countryside, law was a mix of state law, customary or traditional law, and Islamic sharia law.[123] State structures were weak, but social norms and processes took their place.[124] Centered in Southern Afghanistan but adopted with revision throughout the country was a code of ethics and behavior known as Pashtunwali, which focuses on revenge, hospitality, and sanctuary and is defined by a commitment to honor and equality.[125] These guiding principles create a culture that requires people to respect property and refrain from injuring each other. The revenge principle allows injured parties to pursue retribution themselves. The hospitality principle—which requires hosts to protect and take care of guests or travelers even if the host has a feud with the guest—enables safe freedom of movement in the absence of a police force. And the sanctuary provision allows for a weaker person to seek protection from a stronger one and is particularly applicable in the case of persons fleeing to a new community.[126]

In addition to this developed and internalized code of social norms and behavior, Afghan society established dispute-resolution processes in order to maintain community harmony. Councils of community leaders, *shura* or *jirga*, resolve disputes equitably through mediation and arbitration rather than adjudication. Equality in Afghan society means political nondomination, so *shura* and *jirga* seek reconciliation to correct injuries to property or honor, rather than the outright victory of one side over another.[127] The reconciliation process requires both sides to accept an outcome because Pashtunwali's commitment to honor commands that a family take revenge for a violation, even if retribution involves a blood feud or could take generations to fulfill. State involvement, including throwing someone in jail, is seen as irrelevant and even inappropriate.[128] Because damage is inflicted against the individual rather than the public, state intervention misses the point: restoring honor requires individual action.

The recent history of Afghanistan has not significantly changed the importance of nonstate forms of justice. Due to decades of continuous war, starting with the Soviet Invasion, state institutions grew weaker, even nonexistent, in many places throughout the country. Traditional governance and justice filled the gap.[129] At the same time, however, local military commanders displaced the power of landowners and tribal elders and the Islamic clergy (*ulema*) likewise grew in influence. Village *shuras*, collective assemblies of local communities that began in Pashtun areas as *jirgas*, also spread.[130] Throughout the countryside, people seek swift, efficient justice, particularly to deal with pressing land and water issues.[131]

Since 2002 the government and international community have sought to reassert the government's authority through formal institutions, though these efforts have faced serious challenges independent of the cultural commitment to nonstate institutions. In many places courts simply do not exist.[132] Around 80 percent of prosecutors are unqualified, 40 percent of judges have not finished introductory training and exams, and public defense attorneys are virtually nonexistent, a problem for such an impoverished country.[133] Corruption is a pervasive problem, undermining the legitimacy of the system. And the level of violence renders prosecutors and judges insecure, resulting in either corruption for protection or flight from the area.

In this context, the central issue in establishing the rule of law in Afghanistan is identifying the appropriate relationship between the central government and local communities, between formal and traditional justice. In general, the Afghan government has been hostile to incorporating traditional institutions into the formal justice system.[134] The international community is similarly skeptical, as development practitioners have historically neglected the study of traditional justice systems and their contribution to overall social order. None of the World Bank's seventy-eight justice-sector projects from 1994 to 2006, for example, addressed links between informal and formal systems.[135] Despite the general disregard for traditional systems, they are incredibly important. Many societies resolve disputes primarily based on traditional principles; in places where the formal state structures are illegitimate or weak, traditional systems constitute the legal system; and perhaps most significantly, purely formal or top-down approaches to building the rule of law have generally failed to improve access to justice for the most vulnerable in society.[136]

In practice, traditional justice systems may provide a number of benefits: practical, social, and structural. Traditional systems are often seen as enabling faster resolution of cases, following local norms and values, being cheaper and more geographically accessible, and being more accessible to people who are illiterate or do not understand legal procedures.[137] They tend to be trusted because they are seen as fair and not corrupt, and as such people generally have greater satisfaction with outcomes from traditional justice than formal courts.[138] Much of the legitimacy of traditional mechanisms comes from their linkage to the social community. Traditional mechanisms focus on community and collective interests and seek to maintain and strengthen community unity. As a result they are often entrenched and embedded in the social structure itself.[139] Traditional mechanisms often gain support of the population not through formal process and legal legitimacy but through a focus on equity, mediation, and agreement of the parties. Processes are voluntary and flexible, instead of focusing on winning and losing or on legal technicalities. They tend to be run by locals instead of outsiders appointed from the central government, they involve a high degree of public participation, and enforcement comes from community agreement and social pressure rather than formal coercion.[140]

At the same time, traditional systems generally share a number of failings. They tend to exclude women and often engage in practices that violate human rights. They are poorly suited to addressing disputes between peoples who do not see themselves as part of the same community and to addressing complex legal issues involving government, corporations, and major crime. And they can also be subject to elite capture.[141]

Given these benefits and drawbacks, ignoring traditional systems in favor of formal systems is unlikely to succeed. In particular, their embedded character in society renders wholesale transition to formal, state systems difficult if not impossible. As Afghan history has shown, attempts to revise the local systems from the center have proven unsuccessful unless undertaken slowly and incrementally. At the same time, formal systems enable consistency of practices, legitimate processes, and better protection of human rights. Moreover, in complex communities like big cities or in complex litigation, such as crime syndicates or corporate issues, formal systems are far more effective than traditional structures. Given the tradeoffs between these systems, the focus must be on how both can coexist.

In recent years a few practitioners and scholars have turned to identifying possible options for how to design hybrid justice systems. Synthesizing this work yields four models for hybrid justice structures: abolition of traditional justice, incorporation as a lower court, separate systems with regulation, and a commission system. Across all these models, decisions will have to be made on whether the state should codify traditional laws, refer disputes to traditional courts, and enforce traditional justice decisions.

## Abolition of Traditional Justice

The most obvious strategy is to deny a hybrid approach altogether by only recognizing formal justice and working to abolish traditional justice processes. This approach has the advantages of mimicking models of justice well known to lawyers trained in the West, ensuring human rights and due process are followed in court, and fitting nicely with the formalistic approach to the rule of law. Perhaps most importantly, it would build state power and control throughout the country's territory.

On the other hand, rejecting traditional justice presents insurmountable problems. In the transitional phase to formal structures, the courts will be ineffective and inefficient. Overrun with cases and seeking to enforce state-driven justice in areas unfamiliar with those processes, the formal system may be seen as illegitimate and culturally offensive. In systems where corruption is pervasive, expanding the role of courts increases the corruption in society and reinforces the belief that the government and its institutions are corrupt, undermining the ability of the government to gain the trust and confidence of the population. This approach may also undermine or erode social order and community, which is intertwined with traditional justice practices. The result may be to increase the vulnerability of the population and reduce their ability to resolve disputes peaceably—factors that can lead people to support an insurgency. This approach is also likely to be impossible to implement. From the perspective of the reformers, this approach is incredibly costly in terms of money, resources, and time, and it requires engagement across the entire geography. From the perspective of the population, traditional justice may be used in part because they reject the idea of government control itself.[142] Expanding the state's role will only inflame public opinion in these areas or result in the widespread ignoring of state-run justice coupled with a de facto system of traditional justice.

## Incorporation as a Lower Court

A second option is to incorporate traditional justice into the formal system, as if the *shura* or *jirga* were a lower court. On this model, a state would have both formal and traditional dispute mechanisms, and parties could choose which forum to bring their cases. Just like decisions by a trial-level court in the formal system, however, decisions made by the traditional justice system could be appealed to formal courts that would review decisions for compliance with national and international legal norms. The appeal of this system is self-evident. Review by formal courts ensures that traditional justice does not violate human rights and due process norms, and it protects against local elites capturing the justice system. Moreover, this structure lowers the cost of spreading state power and authority because it incorporates preexisting local dispute mechanisms. It also respects local customs, traditions, and social structures.

However, this structure also faces considerable challenges. Allowing for appeals to the formal system will reduce the efficiency and efficacy of local justice, important features of a legitimate justice system. Traditional justice processes are efficient and effective precisely because they achieve finality quickly; an appeal would undermine those benefits. More significantly, this structure is likely to corrupt traditional justice. It introduces the possibility of bribery and corruption into the system. Community justice processes are not considered corrupt because the participants all know each other and are bound by social ties and bonds of honor and reputation. Once distant formal officials are introduced, the social norms that prevent corruption locally are no longer applicable. In societies in which corruption is a substantial problem, there is little to stop parties from bribing officials at the appeals stage. Incorporating traditional justice into formal structures may also eviscerate the ability of traditional justice to function. Through appeals, government becomes an adjudicator of disputes. In a place like Afghanistan, however, traditional mechanisms enforce decisions through agreement via mediation and arbitration, rather than coercive power. This absence of coercive power is what allows "the players to come to an acceptable compromise agreement instead of standing on principle."[143] In addition, this approach will be hard to implement.[144] Not only do people reject state intervention in community affairs in places like Afghanistan, but the resources required to create an appeals system are considerable. In most parts of Afghanistan, low literacy rates, poor recording of decisions, lack of knowledge of the new system, hardship in traveling to courts, and the creation of the courts and their supporting elements are all challenges that would have to be overcome.

## Separate Systems with Regulation

A third option is to legitimize both the formal and traditional systems of justice and to constrain some of what the traditional system can address; in other words, to clarify the jurisdiction of both types of justice systems. On this approach, the central government would establish basic constraints or regulations on the traditional system. For example, it could require compliance with some basic human rights, establish formal court jurisdiction over major crimes (such as murder) and complex criminal enterprises, allow traditional justice to address major crimes but ban particular punishments, or create safeguards for basic minority rights. It could also require the filing of traditional judgments in a state court, providing a clearer record of how disputes were resolved and acting as a first step to transition toward greater state involvement in local justice. Formal courts would still be open to anyone bringing a case, but individuals would have a choice of the traditional process as well. Forms of this kind of proposal have been suggested by the UN Development Program and commentators, with particular focus on having a human rights unit that could monitor decisions.[145]

The benefits of such an approach are considerable. The separate systems approach retains traditional justice and is therefore more legitimate, easier to implement, and connected to local practices, tradition, and values. The possibility of forum shopping and of the threat of a formal court case would enable mediation and arbitration, just as it has historically in Afghanistan. And the balance between the two systems could vary by location. In cities, a robust formal court system could function successfully given the challenges to maintaining social cohesion and norm-based justice. In rural areas and areas without much state control, traditional systems would function legitimately. Over time, the balance between formal and traditional systems could fluctuate as particular communities grow in size and as the state exercises greater effective control in particular regions.

Despite these benefits, there are some drawbacks to a separate systems approach. State power would be limited, particularly in far-flung portions of the country. Decisions would be unreviewable, meaning that violations of rights and the regulations would still be possible. It may be difficult to convince local communities to narrow the scope of traditional justice mechanisms. And the international community may reject a model that envisions law so differently than the formal court-centered system common in the West.

## Commission System

The fourth option is a referral system. Under this approach, a commission would hear of disputes and recommend to the governor which ones should be certified for mediation by a commission following semitraditional processes. The model for this approach is the Commission on Conflict Mediation (CCM), created in Khost province, Afghanistan, in 2006, and composed of six elders chosen by a *jirga*. The CCM works with the provincial government to identify conflicts, and the governor ultimately decides which conflicts the CCM will address. The CCM gathers evidence and investigates the dispute, arbitrates between the parties with a government representative present, and then debates the resolution privately. It tells each party the outcome privately before announcing the resolution publicly, and the parties can reject or accept the outcome with no penalty for rejecting it. The process has been relatively successful. During the first 18 months, 31 cases were referred to the CCM; 18 were resolved, 3 referred to court, 10 were pending. The longest case was open for 6 months, and most of the cases are land disputes (many involving the nomadic Kuchi people). The process works because the CCM members' personal credibility is at stake in the process.[146]

The complexity of the referral system renders its benefits and drawbacks more uncertain than the other models. Under the referral system, the state retains a substantial amount of power and retains a link between community leaders and political leaders. It also prevents human rights and due process issues through state involvement, and retains popular legitimacy and efficacy through the involvement of local leaders. At the same time, the referral system faces serious resource constraints. The number and variety of disputes throughout a province is likely to overwhelm a commission that is tasked with determining which disputes can be addressed through traditional solutions. At the district level, the process may be more effective, but it may still be difficult to implement in districts and villages with unmanageable terrain. Moreover, the introduction of political supervision raises the possibility that the governor's certification of a dispute for mediation could be subject to corruption or bribery.

Regardless of which model is picked, designers of a hybrid system must consider whether to codify traditional laws, to refer disputes from formal systems to the traditional system, and to enforce traditional justice decisions. Codifying traditional laws has the benefits of clarity and reducing capture of the traditional process by local elites, but it ultimately would undermine the entirety of traditional justice. Traditional justice is defined by its flexibility—it is more akin to mediation or equity court than to a principled court with winners and losers determined by particular laws.[147] Codifying traditional laws prevents the flexibility necessary to maintain social stability and community peace. Traditional justice does not assume a single transaction between strangers that results in a conflict; rather, it is designed for a small community in which everyone knows each other and conflicts between individuals require the family or tribe to be involved.[148] In these repeated transactions between groups, flexibility and consensus are necessary. Making referrals to the traditional justice system, on the other hand, is likely to be a beneficial practice. Referrals will reduce the caseload of formal courts and enable the state to remove itself from difficult cases better addressed by local actors who understand local conditions and challenges.[149] The state must also consider whether it will enforce traditional decisions. Enforcing traditional decisions has the virtue of extending state control and creating clarity about which judgments are official and legitimate. However, if state control is generally rejected, then state enforcement might be counterproductive if it sparks antigovernment backlash or undermines effective and socially acceptable traditional forms of justice.

Given the importance of the rule of law to counterinsurgency, great care and thought is necessary in designing a hybrid justice system for a state. Though particular designs will be contentious, the greatest challenge will be embracing a mindset that looks first to the conditions on the ground. The counterinsurgent must accept that justice will not be uniform and formalistic, but rather varied and contextual.

## Policing in Counterinsurgency

By all accounts an effective police force is essential to providing security and ensuring the rule of law. The conventional approach to police reform sees postconflict policing as one component in reforming the entire criminal justice system. The *Counterinsurgency Field Manual* captures the conventional postconflict reconstruction practice well: "[T]he police are only a part of the rule of law. Police require support from a law code, judicial courts, and a penal system. Such support provides a coherent and transparent system that imparts justice."[150] The place of police within the justice system may seem self-evident: Police need updated and modern laws to identify what behaviors constitute crimes. Trained lawyers then prosecute suspects, knowledgeable judges preside over trials, and courts house those proceedings. Prisons hold the guilty. If any piece of this process is missing, security under the rule of law will remain elusive. As a result, efforts to train police will be insufficient—perhaps even counterproductive—if they are not integrated into a comprehensive strategy to reform the entire justice system.[151]

Under the conventional approach, reformers face a daunting task. They will have to recruit, vet, and train the police, ensuring that the police are not corrupt, factionalized, or selected due to nepotism or ethnicity. Police need training in "basic police procedures, such as patrolling and crime-scene protection, physical security, corrections, civil disturbance operations, traffic control, use of force, special unit training, such as counterdrug or counterterrorist operations, human rights."[152] To be effective at tracking down criminals, the police must be skilled in investigation, debriefing local witnesses, forensics, apprehension, and crime scene protection.[153] In the longer term, police development must focus on responsiveness and accountability. A responsive police force, the conventional model suggests, has a 911 program, in which individuals can "summon police assistance regardless of social and political standing."[154] The "call-and-response" program demonstrates to the people that the police are working on their behalf. Accountability under the conventional model requires a series of overseers: courts, legislatures, an independent media, and compliant procedures. These checks guarantee that the police follow and enforce the laws, and they contribute to the police's legitimacy. Additionally, reformers must engage the rest of the justice system. They will need to identify which laws will apply after regime change and which laws will be purged or amended. They will have to train prosecutors and judges and rebuild infrastructure such as courts, police stations, and prisons. And they will need to reform the central government's policing institutions, such as the ministry of the interior, in order to develop top leadership who are honest, effective, and accountable.[155]

In Afghanistan and Iraq, police reform has not proceeded as the conventional postconflict reformers would have advised. After the fall of the Taliban in Afghanistan in 2001, Germany took the lead role in police training programs and embraced the conventional vision of a professional police force providing law and order through the enforcement of the laws. As the insurgency grew in strength over the next few years, the United States adopted a different vision for the Afghan National Police (ANP): assisting in military operations against insurgents.[156] Under the U.S. vision, the ANP would participate in U.S. and Afghan National Army patrolling, thereby acting as "little soldiers" who could clear and hold territory.[157] Rather than use the police for conventional civilian law enforcement, the U.S. military (placed in control of police reform in 2005) saw the police as an auxiliary to the army, increasing the number of boots on the ground, improving local knowledge, and providing an Afghan "face" to the operations. Those who held firm to the conventional vision of policing chafed at this role. As one ANP officer put it, "[f]iring rockets is not the job of police officers."[158]

The Iraqi experience likewise betrayed a divide between the conventional and militarized approaches to establishing and reforming the police forces. After the U.S. invasion of Iraq, the police force, like the military, disbanded, leaving the United States to reestablish a police presence throughout the country. The initial police reform strategy faced significant resource constraints and left police poorly equipped. In May 2004 President Bush transferred authority for police training from the State Department to the Department of Defense.[159] Over the next few years, civilian and military agencies would clash over the very purpose of the police forces: the military wanted to "put[] Iraqi guns on the street in order to reduce pressure on coalition forces."[160] In contrast, the Department of Justice wanted to "create an efficient, lightly armed, civilian police service that utilized community-policing techniques and operated in conformity with Western democratic standards of professional law enforcement."[161] As a result, the police became an "auxiliary force to fight the insurgency," with the Iraqi National Police (INP) functioning as "heavy police units" that were "virtually indistinguishable from a military force."[162] By 2006, a Shi'a political leader had purged the INP's ranks of Sunnis, and the INP was participating in sectarian violence and death squads.[163]

Both the conventional and militarized approaches to the role of police are derived from the professional model of policing adopted in America in the mid-twentieth century.[164] Developed by early-twentieth-century progressive and liberal reformers, the professional model was a conscious break from the political model of policing that dominated the late nineteenth century. Under the political model, local political leaders and machines provided authority and resources to police officers, resulting in a decentralized, locally based approach to policing. Police officers engaged in a variety of neighborhood social services: they ran soup kitchens, prevented public alcohol consumption, and participated extensively in community life through foot patrols.[165] As "adjuncts to local political machines," the police could be corrupt and discriminatory, even fixing elections when necessary.[166] Objecting to the corruption and geographical variation that accompanied the political model, the twentieth-century reformers sought to create a more professional police force. Reformers eliminated patronage hires, establishing a civil service model for police. They transformed police departments into centralized hierarchies, with a clear division of labor and standard, routinized practices. And they redefined the day-to-day activities of policing from "social work" to controlling crime through motorized patrols, call-and-response, and the investigation of crimes.[167] In this new world of professional policing, citizens were not participants in providing public order, but mere bystanders—eyewitnesses. Anything more would make them vigilantes. Citizens would provide "just the facts," as *Dragnet*'s Sergeant Friday would say. Indeed, the idea of keeping police distant from the community was so strong that some communities banned patrol officers from living in the areas they patrolled. Under the professional model, the police were legitimate because they followed established procedures with little discretion and because they were tasked only with the narrow goal of enforcing the laws.[168]

Embedded in the professional model were actually two different approaches to policing, the Crime Fighting and the Criminal Justice System approaches, which parallel the approaches implemented in Afghanistan and Iraq.[169] Under the Crime Fighting approach, police are seen as warriors. Society is defined by "friend and foe, good and bad, citizens and lawbreakers," and only the police can keep the forces of evil from harming innocent citizens.[170] The centralized, hierarchical organization of Crime Fighters parallels military hierarchy, with police officers subject to strict rules prescribing their behavior, hierarchical chains of command and supervision, and routinized and standardized duties.[171] Indeed, even the Crime Fighting image of the police as "the thin blue line" has military origins. The *London Times* journalist Walter Russell coined the phrase "the thin red line" to describe the British infantry at the 1854 Battle of Balaclava during the Crimean War. Rudyard Kipling then popularized the term in his poetic description of

British infantry, "Tommy." Red soon turned to blue, and the new phrase was adopted by Los Angeles Police Chief William Parker in the 1950s.[172] The Crime Fighting approach goes so far in the direction of militarization that it even ignores many of the traditional functions of police: "preventing crime, maintaining order, resolving disputes, providing social and emergency services, and, in some places, even traffic enforcement."[173] Bill Stuntz captures the idea well:

> [T]he culture of most police departments was both authoritarian and adversarial. Toughness was prized; the goal was to go after the bad guys and catch them, and to convince potential bad guys that their lives would be unpleasant if they made the wrong choices. In carrying out that task, police officers had no allies apart from their fellow officers; the law-abiding portions of the population were either ignored or seen as hostile.[174]

Under the Criminal Justice System approach, the police are understood not as warriors but as the front lines in a larger legal process that controls crime through incarceration, deterrence, and rehabilitation.[175] By punishing and threatening to punish violations of the law, police keep criminals behind bars and deter potential criminals from harming innocent people. Policing is redefined as "law enforcement," as arresting those who violate the law and then prosecuting them. The professional police officer is focused on "incident-driven policing"—patrols to prevent incidents, call-and-response after an incident, and investigations to determine what happened during the incident and provide the foundation for prosecution.[176] As a result, the Criminal Justice System approach integrates police into the rest of the legal system but still keeps the police separate from the community at large.[177]

Though it has been applied in Iraq, Afghanistan, and other reconstruction situations, the professional approach to policing is fundamentally disconnected from counterinsurgency's principles and strategies. Professional policing establishes a hierarchical organization with routinized and standardized practices for rank-and-file officers. Counterinsurgency requires a decentralized organization with expansive discretion to junior officers to experiment and adapt to local conditions. Professional policing seeks to be autonomous from the community, providing only limited opportunities for citizen involvement as witnesses. Counterinsurgency mandates embedding into the community and seeks to include community members as full participants in all activities. Professional policing is reactive, focused on particular incidents.

Counterinsurgency is proactive, focused on creating sustainably secure conditions. Professional policing uses force and coercion through arrests, prosecution, and incarceration. Counterinsurgency prefers to deploy a full spectrum of social, political, economic, military, and cultural power to win over the population. Professional policing's legitimacy derives from following established procedures and professional neutrality. Counterinsurgency's legitimacy stems from popular support. Counterinsurgency strategy thus rejects many of the major tenets of both the Crime Fighting and Criminal Justice approaches to policing.

The disconnect between the professional policing approach and counterinsurgency strategy is all the more surprising because the professional approach has long been rejected in American police strategy circles in favor of a community policing approach that aligns almost perfectly with the civil affairs elements of counterinsurgency strategy. In the 1970s, police chiefs and scholars began to question the heart of the professional policing model. Crime had been on the rise since the 1960s. Studies showed that patrolling, call-and-response, and investigations had little effect on reducing crime and fear or on improving popular satisfaction with the police. Many citizens, particularly minorities, grew hostile to overly aggressive policing tactics. Police officers tired of routinized work. And local communities increasingly turned to private security guards and community crime control programs to improve their security.[178]

Skeptical of the professional approach, police chiefs and scholars developed a new approach to policing: problem-oriented and community policing.[179] Community policing rests on three pillars: problem solving, community engagement, and organizational flexibility and adaptability.[180] Instead of taking an incident-based or law enforcement approach to policing, in which police are primarily reactive to particular crimes or attempted crimes, community policing requires police to proactively address a "wide range of behavioral and social problems that arise in a community"—the underlying factors that enable crime.[181] Incidents could be clustered and analyzed by the time of day, the characteristics of the persons involved, the triggers of the behavior at question, and the locations in which the crimes take place.[182] For example, under the conventional approach to rape, police would simply respond quickly, seek to determine whether a rape occurred, and then try to apprehend the perpetrator. Under the community policing approach, the police role expands to include educating men and women about safety and consent, teaching self-defense courses, improving safe movement through better lighting and late-night transit programs, and grappling with the physical and mental anguish that victims suffer.[183] Instead of just apprehending perpetrators, the police seek to reduce the likelihood that crimes will take place in a community and improve the overall security of the community. On this model, the laws on the books are not only used to arrest and prosecute individuals but also to provide police with a resource to persuade individuals to change their behavior. Loiterers, for example, can be warned of their behavior rather than immediately arrested.[184]

In order to solve social and behavioral problems, police must be engaged with the community rather than detached from it. Police communicate and cooperate with all citizens in the community to better understand the community's needs, develop effective programs, and incorporate citizen participation.[185] The police must "treat people with respect and sensitivity" and be careful not to use unnecessary force.[186] In engaging with communities, police can either broadly develop relationships with the community "in hopes that this will reduce tensions, create a reservoir of goodwill, and ultimately enable the police and the community to work together to solve community problems," or they can undertake a more directed form of engagement in which "the initial objective is to deal with a specific problem. . . . [If] the police conclude that it could be eliminated or significantly reduced by some form of community involvement, they then set out to bring about such involvement."[187] This latter form may be more successful because it directs the community's involvement at a concrete problem, thereby giving the community a stake in a particular problem and solution, rather than just a general sense that the police are interested in cooperation. Community police work with a variety of community groups, including local government, nongovernmental civic organizations, business, and religious institutions.[188] Through community engagement, the police "stimulate and buttress a community's ability to produce attractive neighborhoods and protect them against predators."[189]

Effective problem-solving and community engagement require police forces to be flexible and adaptable. Community police need the flexibility to design programs that are tailored to the local conditions, and because information is rooted in the community itself, decentralization enables the police to have greater local knowledge and to develop better solutions to local problems.[190] Moreover, under a decentralized system, officers in frequent contact with community members develop close relationships and trust.[191] Community policing thus requires a flatter structure and greater discretion to individual officers.[192] Headquarters "preach the values and state the principles and broad objectives," but the local districts have considerable discretion in developing programs tailored to their local conditions.[193]

Accountability likewise differs in community policing. Because officers each have more discretion, they need a strong, shared set of norms to prevent overreaching and corruption.[194] A strong code of values and other forms of guided discretion provide one check on police abuses.[195] Community support provides another. Because the community participates in an open decision-making process with the police—one that includes identifying problems, exploring solutions, and implementing them—the community not only will inform police of unacceptable or unworkable solutions but also will understand the constraints under which the police operate.[196] Additionally, administrative controls such as education, training, promotions and rewards, disciplinary actions, and supervision can be effective means of accountability.[197] Notably, institutionalizing civilian oversight boards, which tend to have an adversarial culture, has proved only to strain relationships between the police and the community.[198]

Just as counterinsurgency flips conventional warfare on its head, so too does community policing flip professional policing on its head. Community policing addresses problems instead of reacting to particular crimes; it embeds the police into the community instead of distancing them; and it mandates a flexible and dynamic organization instead of a centralized hierarchy. Legitimacy derives not only from professionalism and the laws being enforced through prosecution but also from community participation, understanding, and support.[199] One scholar puts it well: "When the goal is to reclaim violent neighborhoods and thereby return control of the streets to the law-abiding population, the police stay where that population lives. Policing becomes more about winning and holding territory than about catching and punishing criminals."[200]

The community policing approach works because it relies on social dynamics derived from human behavior. In situations where the collective action of many people is necessary, behavior is often self-reinforcing. If "some individuals conclude that those around them are inclined to contribute, they will respond by contributing in kind, prompting still others to contribute, and so forth and so on until a highly cooperative state of affairs takes root. But if some individuals conclude that others are free riding, then they will respond by free riding too, spurring others to do the same, and so forth and so on until a condition of mass noncooperation becomes the norm."[201] This dynamic, reciprocal behavior implies that punishment for committing a crime is less of a motivator of conduct than are social norms in a community.[202] As a result, what is most important is whether individuals will respect the security of others and their perception that others will reciprocate; whether the community will protect themselves by vigilance in their neighborhoods and by taking an interest in community activities and organizations; and whether the police and the community will develop a norm of cooperation and trust.[203] In areas with a strong social norm of reciprocity, cooperation and interest in neighbors, and trust in the police, crime will decline. Where citizens are atomized and withdrawn from community life, trust and reciprocity grow weaker and crime rises.[204]

Although the professional policing approach has dominated police reform during reconstruction, community policing is in far greater alignment with counterinsurgency strategy. Both require integration with the community. Both involve addressing the broad social issues that cause disorder. Both seek out popular support to identify problems, develop solutions, implement programs, and legitimize the government's actions. And perhaps most importantly, both understand that the use of force, while important, is insufficient for success. Arrest and prosecution in community policing are the equivalent of killing and capturing in counterinsurgency. They are necessary, but they are only a limited part of a full-spectrum strategy and cannot by themselves result in victory.

Indeed, despite its relatively recent origins in American policing circles, the use of community policing methods is not totally unheard of in past counterinsurgency operations. During the Malayan Emergency from 1948 to 1960, the British adopted a rudimentary community-policing approach as part of their police reform program. From 1948 to 1951, the British expanded the Malayan police force considerably, adding regular police forces and "special constables" who served as auxiliaries to the military forces. Undertrained, underequipped, and drawn primarily from Malayans, the police forces were corrupt and abused their power, creating hostility from ethnic Chinese and fueling the insurgency.[205] When Sir Gerald Templer took command in 1952, he tapped Sir Arthur Young, the commissioner of the London Metropolitan Police, to direct police reform efforts. In addition to improving training and recruiting a more diverse police force, Young sought to change the police's mentality from a "police state" to public service.[206] Under "Operation Service," police officers were expected to assist the population. Police officers helped civilians get care at government clinics, farmers apply for government land, children cross roads, and even, in one case, a woman deliver her baby in the absence of a midwife.[207] Young changed the Malay name for police station from "lock-up room" to "police house," and police were told that promotions depended not only on performing ordinary duties but also on engaging with the local community.[208] Although some commentators have seen Operation Service primarily as a public relations exercise, it was, in fact, a shift in the direction of community policing—an understanding that police must be "recognized as friends, and not enemies, of the average citizen."[209]

The intersection of policing and counterinsurgency strategy was also well known by imperial thinkers. In the classic *Imperial Policing*, British Major General Sir Charles W. Gwynn established four principles for effective policing: civil control over the police, minimum use of force, firm and timely action, and civil-military cooperation.[210] Of these, perhaps most important was the principle of the minimum use of force. Gwynn argued that "excessive severity may antagonize the population" and that "punitive measures . . . may awaken sympathy with the revolutionaries."[211] In contrast to standard military operations, a counterinsurgency is "a battle of wits."[212] It thus required providing general rather than definite orders to officers, and applying the minimum force rather than maximal power.[213]

Modern policing innovations suggest helpful techniques for policing in counterinsurgency. Police have developed strategies for "hot spots," areas where crime is most prevalent. In these areas, community policing strategy shifts to more offensive operations, just as counterinsurgency relies more on military force in "hot spots." Effective policing in "hot spots" requires both changing the physical environment that is facilitating the criminal activity in the hot spot and increasing patrols, crackdowns, and searches.[214] Under the "pulling levers" approach, police "deploy enforcement, services, the moral voice of communities, and deliberate communication in order to create a powerful deterrent to particular behavior by particular offenders."[215] By using a variety of levers—from threats of prosecution to warnings to community pressure—police can change behavior and address community problems. For example, police in Lowell, Massachusetts, recognized that local gangs had strong hierarchies and codes of behavior. After younger gang members were involved in homicides, the police confronted the older members, cracking down on their gambling parlors. The police told the older members that the crackdowns were due to the younger members' participation in the homicide. Even though the "police could not control the shooters, . . . the older members could and did."[216] Other police innovators have argued for third-party policing, a process by which police "persuade or coerce organizations or non-offending persons, such as public housing agencies, property owners, parents, health and building inspectors, and business owners to take some responsibility for preventing crime or reducing crime problems."[217] Working through private actors enables the police to indirectly address problems in the community. Community policing advocates have also focused on measuring performance through effects-based metrics. Instead of measuring the number of police or arrests, success is measured, among other things, by the reduction in crime and fear and the increase in everyday social and commercial activity in the neighborhood. Effects of operations, not the operations themselves, are the guide.

The alignment of community policing with counterinsurgency has important implications. It suggests that attempts to use the police to assist conventional military forces in clearing territories of insurgents, including taking part in conventional battles, are misplaced. In counterinsurgency, the police should primarily operate as a community policing force. As a corollary, conventional military forces should primarily undertake operations clearing areas of insurgents. To the extent that additional forces are necessary for clearing and other targeting operations, counterinsurgents should provide or recruit more military forces. To be sure, between conventional military operations to retake an insurgent-held territory and a more stable situation in which community policing can operate lies the turbulent security environment that pervades counterinsurgency operations: times when the military has largely cleared an area of insurgents, but when subversives remain, engaging in limited attacks, creating fear in the population, and disrupting the reconstruction of order. Conventional military force is too heavy-handed and community policing too passive.

In those turbulent times, counterinsurgents must focus most of their attention on developing paramilitary or gendarmerie forces: forces designed and trained in the small unit tactics that define the majority of counterinsurgency operations. Among other things, they are trained in patrolling day and night, conducting searches and ambushes, and operating and maintaining curfews. They are the crux of security operations in counterinsurgency because they are designed for precisely the diverse and complex realities of turbulent transitions and the consolidation of order. Indeed, both the military and the police are secondary and auxiliary to a robust gendarmerie force.

As a result, security in counterinsurgency is provided in three phases: Conventional military forces like the army initially clear an area of insurgents. Gendarmerie or paramilitary forces then stabilize the area, with military forces remaining to ensure that the insurgents do not retake the territory. During this phase, community policing forces begin to be trained. Once the area is relatively stable, military and paramilitary forces are gradually reduced and the community police force takes on greater responsibility. Importantly, police forces themselves are not primarily used for either clearing or stabilization operations. The division between police and military or paramilitary forces is crucial for building popular support for the rule of law. Blurring the line changes the nature of the police: they become accustomed to different use-of-force rules, rules of engagement, and legal accountability standards. It postpones developing a mindset of community engagement. As David Bayley and Robert Perito put it, "police contribute to counterinsurgency by winning the allegiance of the population; the military contribute to counterinsurgency by eliminating immediate threats of violence."[218]

Moreover, those who argue that police forces cannot be successful without reform of the judicial system, training of prosecutors and judges, and construction of prisons are likewise mistaken in how they envision the role of policing. Under a community policing model, the police can make incredible headway in improving and maintaining security and safety in a community even in the absence of a strong judicial system. To the extent that a judicial system is necessary for punishing individuals, monitoring their behavior, and preventing them from future misconduct, it is not clear that the formal justice system is the only workable set of institutions. In fact, community policing aligns as well with traditional systems of justice. In Afghanistan, for example, most disputes, civil and criminal, are not taken to police or courts but rather to traditional dispute resolution bodies such as the *shura* and *jirga*. These bodies deliberate on the appropriate way to resolve a conflict that takes account of not only the individual's culpability but also the community's well-being. This process of community involvement, equitable resolution of disputes, and social pressure to ensure enforcement aligns well with community policing's reliance on local participation, problem solving, and social norm creation. Indeed, just as the professional policing approach and formal justice system are integrated, with each relying on the other for the system to succeed in providing a top-down, state-run social order, community policing and traditional justice can be integrated to provide a system of order that is contextual and reliant on strong community norms and engagement.

As importantly, instead of envisioning the police as a national force, controlled by a central government ministry of the interior and providing security throughout the country, community policing would mobilize communities to secure their own villages and valleys. An attack on the police would be an attack on the community itself—on fathers, sons, and brothers. A united community under attack would not tolerate insurgents or their sympathizers. The Local Defense Initiative, a program started in Afghanistan in the fall of 2009 to support local militias that seek to secure their own villages, is one example of such a program. Another is the Home Guards program that mobilized Chinese living in the New Villages during the Malayan Emergency to provide security for the New Villages. In both cases, the idea was that local people can take part in providing their own security. They will not only have access to the best information about local needs and threats but also be best able to design programs that will improve security in the particular community. This local focus strikes at the heart of the tendency to see police reform as a technical, apolitical process; rather, counterinsurgency's police strategy is integrally interconnected with local political dynamics.[219]

THE ORGANIC RULE of law demands a bottom-up approach and anthropological mindset to managing disputes and ensuring public safety and security. It is tailored to local needs and preferences, is driven by popular support and engagement, and is constantly in flux, growing and developing with local conditions. Hybrid justice systems and community policing strategies are driven by the organic approach to the rule of law. They reject idealized visions of top-down, one-size-fits-all institutional orders, and instead embrace the diversity and complexity of turbulent transitions. They provide a first step— an incremental step—toward stability and order. And their commitment to ground-level realities and local support provides the popular legitimacy that is necessary for building the rule of law.

# 7

# *Counterinsurgency and Constitutional Design*

FEW THINK OF counterinsurgency as linked to constitutional design.[1] Counterinsurgency recognizes powerful individuals and groups vying for political power through force and fear. Constitutional design assumes equal individuals creating a social contract through reflection and choice. Counterinsurgency often takes place in failed states far from the European tradition. Constitutional design assumes a society that has a basic level of traditions, institutions, and manners in line with European Enlightenment philosophy. Counterinsurgency exists when a community is fractured to the point of violence. Constitutional design assumes a peaceful, relatively unified community. Counterinsurgency is bottom-up. Constitutional design is top-down. Counterinsurgency establishes answers to core political questions over a long period of time, with turbulent transitions constantly placing those answers in jeopardy. Constitutional design assumes a single founding moment, in which the core questions of politics are resolved once and for all.[2]

Despite these differences, constitutional design is crucial to counterinsurgency. In Iraq and Afghanistan, counterinsurgency and constitutional design took place simultaneously. Both enterprises required high-level political agreement and ground-level acceptance, and both involved politics, law, and security. Indeed, counterinsurgents have, on occasion, recognized the importance of constitutions to strategic success. Sir Robert Thompson once wrote that "the greatest importance should be attached to the Constitution, from which all authority is derived," and he argued that the abrogation of the constitution in Vietnam was an important source of instability.[3] In the midst of turbulent transitions, in which constitution-making and counterinsurgency may take place simultaneously, the central question is how these two activities influence each other. The answer requires rethinking the conventional paradigm of modern constitutional design: a founding, often postconflict, moment in which the structures of government can be crafted to provide order for generations to come. Counterinsurgency, however, suggests a turbulent approach. Counterinsurgents shape constitutional design by influencing the choice of constitution-makers, the constraints or parameters they face, and the underlying constitutional culture in the society. At the same time, the design of the constitution can shape the course of counterinsurgency operations by entrenching bottom-up, evolutionary, and fragmented structures that embrace the organic approach.

## Counterinsurgency as Constitutional Design

Most counterinsurgents do not think of themselves as participating in the process of constitutional design, but counterinsurgency can actually be a form of constitutional design. The leading political science theory conceives of constitutions as bargains among competing groups.[4] Constitutions should not be understood as contracts, which imply mutual exchange between parties, normative agreement and obligation, and enforcement through external sanctions—features often missing from constitutions.[5] Rather, constitutions arise out of a "coordination dilemma," the fact that society needs a set of institutional structures in order to coordinate basic functions, achieve stability, and unify civic culture.[6] Elite groups compete, compromise, and eventually develop a "focal equilibrium," a set of governance structures to which all groups will acquiesce.[7] The constitution codifies this predictable set of rules for elites, lowering their level of fear and establishing signals for those out of power to coordinate to prevent incumbents from violating the constitution. Through elite buy-in and vigilance, the constitution becomes "self-enforcing."[8] To be sure, popular opinions influence elite behavior, but elites, not the masses, determine the particular provisions chosen and are thus the central actors in the constitution-making process.[9]

Coordination theory presupposes the elite parties who participate in the constitution-making process; it does not explain how they come to participate. When counterinsurgency and constitution-making occur simultaneously, the counterinsurgent will have considerable influence, although not complete power, over who participates in the constitution-making process. If a third-party counterinsurgent is initiating the constitution-making process, it may think of itself as above the competition between groups jockeying for influence in the drafting process. But the counterinsurgent could handpick the participating groups and thus have considerable power over the final constitutional structure. With this power comes great risk. Self-enforcing constitutions require elites in society to agree to their terms, so a counterinsurgent who exercises undue, top-down influence may create a constitution that does not have elite support. Without self-enforcement, sustaining the constitutional order may require the third-party counterinsurgent's power, threatening to mire the counterinsurgent in local constitutional politics for decades, lest withdrawal brings constitutional collapse.[10] More often than not, however, a third-party counterinsurgent will not have a completely free hand in choosing constitutional designers or in designing the constitution. Rather, the counterinsurgent will be one actor among many, and it will have to work with other powerholders to determine who will participate in the drafting. This more open, participatory reality can help create a self-enforcing constitution by including the relevant stakeholders in the constitution-making process—and by increasing the legitimacy of the process itself.

Iraq's constitution-making process is an exemplary case: the Coalition Provisional Authority (CPA), although initially reluctant, eventually acquiesced to negotiations with the other groups in society to determine who would be included in the drafting process. At first, the CPA wanted a new Iraqi constitution to "be drawn up by expert Iraqis, and then presented to the public and endorsed by a referendum."[11] Ayatollah Ali Sistani, a powerful Shia cleric, found the plan unacceptable, and he announced that the only legitimate approach would involve elections to a constitutional assembly, followed by popular ratification.[12] The CPA thus found itself in a difficult position: "Either it accepted an elected body that might not prove amenable to its pressures, or it had to face the possibility of rejection of the constitution if it were produced by an appointed group, no matter how 'representative' they appeared to be."[13] In order to mollify Sistani, the CPA pronounced the November 15 agreement, which provided for direct election to the constitutional convention.[14] The November 15 agreement demonstrates that the CPA had a central role in determining the procedures for participation in the constitution-making process but still had to work with other powerful actors in society to negotiate an acceptable structure for that process. Which groups participated was neither predetermined nor dictated by the counterinsurgent. But in exerting influence over the process of who was included, the counterinsurgent had considerable power to shape the ultimate outcome of the constitution.

After the drafters of the constitution are chosen, counterinsurgents can still have a significant influence on the drafting of the constitution due to the constraints facing the drafters. Jon Elster famously distinguished between two types of constraints endemic to the constitution-writing process: "Upstream constraints are imposed on the assembly before it starts to deliberate. Downstream constraints are created by the need for ratification of the document the assembly produces."[15] Because constitutional conventions are usually established by an initiator, such as a legislature, executive, or occupying power, the initiating authority can place "upstream" constraints on the constitution writers regarding matters of procedure or substance.[16] In the United States, for example, the Continental Congress mandated that the Philadelphia Convention revise the Articles of Confederation, not create a new constitution.[17] Although the drafters may seek to exceed such constraints, as the American founders did, the cost of doing so is at least a strong disincentive and may even be prohibitive. At the same time, downstream constraints exist in the drafters' knowledge of the ultimate need for ratification. Drafters must consider the preferences of the ratifying body, whether it be a legislature, the executive, or the public via referendum.[18] For example, during the Philadelphia Convention, the drafters were constrained by the divisions between the small and large states and the Northern and Southern states.

This static model of upstream constraints and downstream ratification preferences does not tell the whole story. The initial upstream and downstream constraints may change dramatically if some intervening event modifies the ratifiers' preferences.[19] Concerned by these new preferences, the initiator may change the rules of the game, announcing new upstream constraints that the drafters must consider. Even if the initiator does not react, the drafters still face new downstream constraints based on the change in the ratifiers' preferences. As constraints shift, so will the constitutional provisions that the drafters can choose to include or exclude.

Under this dynamic model, three factors are important for determining the potential for changes in the drafting room: the power of the initiator, the type of ratifying body, and the character of the intervening event. Depending on the initiator's power over the constitutional assembly and within the society, the initiator's changing of the upstream constraints may have more or less influence over the drafters. Occupiers and waning regimes, for example, will have varying degrees of authority. The type of ratifying body will also influence the extent of change in ratifiers' preferences. If the body is an assembly with relatively long terms of office, for example, it may be insulated from changes in popular preferences. If the ratifying body is the populace, then popular preferences are themselves the constraints facing drafters, so changes in the public's view will have direct and immediate impact. Finally, the character of the intervening condition is significant. Power dynamics in society may change due to foreign interventions or wars, insurgencies, economic troubles, natural disasters, famines, or even the simple evolution of preferences over time. Each type of intervening condition will impact power dynamics in different ways.

Counterinsurgency provides a clear illustration of the dynamic nature of upstream and downstream constraints. Counterinsurgency's turbulent transitions are constantly reshaping ground-level power dynamics and influencing popular preferences. Because the constitutional drafting process occurs simultaneously, successful or failed counterinsurgency operations will undoubtedly change the population's preferences, thereby implicating the constitution. For example, the counterinsurgent's decisions to ally with or empower certain groups may have an effect on the status of those groups within society. Groups may be stigmatized by their affiliation, empowered through cooperation, or even exalted because excluded. Security operations can also influence ground-level power dynamics. Excessive shows of force or brutal tactics such as torture may delegitimize the counterinsurgent and create a backlash within society that results in greater support for particular factions. Backlash against the counterinsurgent may undermine the counterinsurgent's approach to political institutions more generally; a loss of legitimacy for the occupier may lead to a loss of legitimacy for the occupier's values. Not to be excluded, the insurgents' tactics may also affect ground-level dynamics. Insurgents may attack particular factions or assassinate leaders, diminishing or increasing sympathy for those factions. Any of these factors can reshape power dynamics in society, and if the power shifts are substantial enough, they will be felt in the drafting room.

In addition to influencing the parties who write the constitution and the constraints faced by drafters, counterinsurgents can actually act as constitutional designers themselves. To understand how counterinsurgency is a form of constitutional design, it is necessary to distinguish a country's formal and informal constitutions.[20] The formal constitution is the written constitution, which lays out the legal institutions that frame society. Scholars often refer to it as the "Big-C constitution." The informal constitution is more difficult to define. Lord Bolingbroke, writing in the 1730s, described it as the "assemblage of laws, institutions and customs . . . that compose the general system."[21] More recently, scholars have defined the informal, or "small-c constitution," as "consist[ing] of the body of rules, practices, and understandings, written or unwritten, that *actually* determines who holds what kind of power, under what conditions, and subject to what limits."[22]

The distinction between formal and informal constitutions tracks the distinction between the law on the books and the law in practice or between formalistic and sociological views of law. Whether defining law or constitutions, formalists look to commands of an authoritative person or document. Sociologists look instead to practices that have operated consistently over a long period of time with popular acceptance.[23] Historically, the association of constitutions with the formal, written constitution is an invention of the late eighteenth century. From the ancient Greeks until Lord Bolingbroke's day, the word "constitution" meant both what people agreed to explicitly and what customs the people followed.[24] Only after the French Revolution did the meaning of the term "constitution" decisively shift in the direction of formal, written constitutions.[25] Importantly, informal constitutionalism makes formal constitutionalism possible. If informal constitutional values diverge too greatly from the written constitution, the latter will be little more than a façade constitution.[26] A façade constitution can declare aspirational principles and adopt power structures for government, but such provisions and principles are ineffective and potentially delegitimized because they are not followed in practice.[27] Many African constitutions, for example, have not been well tailored to their social context and have been either ignored or manipulated, thereby undermining constitutionalism and the rule of law.[28] The formal and informal constitutions thus need to be relatively well aligned.

Counterinsurgents are constitutional designers because they are inevitably involved in shaping the shared norms and practices of society—the informal constitution. Through village-building, fortifying traditional and state-run forms of justice, establishing policing practices, and reconciling with former enemies, the counterinsurgent determines the actual practices for how power is exercised. In so doing, counterinsurgents are, in effect, designing the "constitution" in its most basic, ancient interpretation. Additionally, the nature of the informal constitution influences the success of the formal constitution. Because popular support and practice undergird any formalistic legal system, changes in the beliefs and practices of the people will inevitably alter the trajectory of the formal legal system. In sum, the decisions counterinsurgents make on seemingly narrow, local concerns have consequences of a constitutional magnitude: they directly influence the informal constitution and indirectly shape the formal constitution.

## Constitutional Design as Counterinsurgency

Just as counterinsurgency can be a form of constitutional design, the reverse is equally true—constitutional design can be a form of counterinsurgency. Counterinsurgency seeks to build a legitimate, stable set of political structures that channel power within a society; constitutions provide particular canals through which public power is legitimately channeled. It is possible, then, to use the constitution as a tool to assist the counterinsurgent in building these political structures and channeling power within society.

Counterinsurgency-inspired constitutional provisions have the potential to narrow the gap between the uncertainty on the ground and the stability constitutions require. Instead of seeing the constitution as presupposing a degree of legitimacy and public power, and primarily acting as a constraint on government power, constitutional designers should see the constitution as a tool to help *build* legitimacy and public power. Indeed, constitutions have often been understood as empowering and enabling self-government rather than just restraining government power.[29] This idea, known as the "constitution as instrument," holds that constitutions are needed to empower the government to address "things needing to be done in the future."[30] When a government is not empowered to act, it cannot ensure "peace or stability for [its] populations or control [its] territories" or provide "any reasonable distribution of social goods."[31] The idea of "constitution as instrument" is central to constitutional design during counterinsurgency because counterinsurgents need to build state power and self-government in order to win over the population and end the insurgency. To be sure, constitutions with or without counterinsurgency-inspired provisions will help empower government to some degree. But constitutions inspired by counterinsurgency may accelerate the development of effective self-governance.

Counterinsurgency-inspired constitutions act as an effective focal point for action.[32] The specific provisions in the constitution's text will provide guidance to local leaders and counterinsurgents on setting up governance structures, facilitating development, and empowering leaders. In failed states, and particularly in failed states without a tradition of democracy or self-government, even the basic issues of setting up civil society organizations, creating local governments, or conducting elections can be incredibly difficult.[33] Constitutionalizing these basic structural components will both enable local populations to create and participate in these structures and reduce future debate and conflict over how to establish those structures. Although there are considerable upfront costs in constitutionalizing a provision, the provision will likely be more durable because parties have expended so much effort in coming to an agreement.[34] In other words, constitutionalizing these structures accelerates their establishment through ease of coordination.[35] Statutes could also establish these structures, but in failed and failing states, a constitution may be preferable not only because it might be promulgated with greater fanfare and distributed more widely across the country but also because it would likely be read aloud and discussed at local gatherings. Constitutionalizing these provisions thus announces loudly and clearly what powers the people have to govern themselves. Statutes are meek in comparison.

Additionally, the constitution provides a clear signal that empowers and thereby legitimizes local leadership and holds them accountable. Constitutionalizing these structures signals—to both the domestic population and international organizations—the identity of the political officials responsible for establishing and delivering basic social services. The signaling effect also applies to the leaders themselves, who will self-identify as serving in constitutionally created posts. They will likely feel a greater sense of responsibility and will certainly feel a greater sense of authority, both of which should strengthen the legitimacy of their positions. Crucially, with empowerment comes accountability. Constitutionalizing the lessons of counterinsurgency informs domestic and international communities of who is accountable for progress or failure. Accountability will help prevent local leaders from passing the blame either upward to the central government or across to the counterinsurgent.

Constitutions also provide an opportunity to empower the government through building a shared, unified national identity. It is for this reason that many constitutions provide detailed discussions of national symbols. The 1977 Afghan constitution, for example, specifies that the nation's flag "consists of black, red and green colors arranged horizontally in fixed proportions from top downwards with the national emblem of the state affixed in its upper left hand corner."[36] The constitution of Bangladesh specifies the design of the national emblem as "the national flower Shapla (nymphaeanouchali) resting on water, having on each side an ear of paddy and being surmounted by three connected leaves of jute with two stars on each side of the leaves."[37] Provisions for national symbols, anthems, and even languages and religions can help create or unify a nation under the constitutional order.

Despite these benefits, constitutional theory suggests three counterarguments to constitutionalizing the lessons of counterinsurgency: endurance, flexibility, and moral rights. The endurance counterargument claims that because constitutions are meant to be lasting documents, presentist concerns are inappropriate.[38] This response, however, is based on a faulty assumption: that constitutions are meant to, and do, exist for long periods of time. In fact, on average, constitutions only last nineteen years.[39] Given this short life span, and the turbulent evolution of insurgency situations, constitutions may be better conceived not as eternal documents but rather as structures to achieve immediate governance goals. Even the American Constitution, despite the semidivine reverence for the wisdom of the founders, was born, in part, from messy compromises and short-sighted interests. The U.S. Constitution, for example, dodged one of the most pressing long-term issues for the nation—slavery—by compromising on the Three-Fifths Clause and a time-limited provision for ending the slave trade.[40] These short-term fixes enabled the Constitution to come into being. They were not designed for all time because both sides assumed that conditions would change over time allowing the nation to address the issue of slavery. Even if a constitutional designer had endurance as a goal, the endurance counterargument assumes a level of pre-constitutional stability that is absent in insurgencies. If the shared norms and practices of society are undecided, establishing a constitution for all time necessarily places that constitution on shaky ground.

The flexibility counterargument claims that entrenching provisions designed for short-term projects undermines future generations' ability to adapt to changed conditions. The flexibility counterargument, however, elides specificity and flexibility. A constitution can be both specific in counterinsurgency-inspired provisions and flexible in allowing change over time. Indeed, such a constitution is precisely what is needed during an insurgency. Specificity takes important issues off the table for debate, enabling focal-point solutions that direct actors toward their duties. Specificity also creates the demand for flexibility, because actors will want to keep the constitutional provisions up-to-date according to the changing circumstances.[41] Flexibility enables a country to reduce the gap between the views on the ground—the informal constitution or sociological law—and the formal, written constitution. In the midst of turbulent transitions and state-building during war, counterinsurgents seek a constitution that is at once specific and flexible. Specificity enables action, empowering government actors. Flexibility allows for change as the conflict evolves in time. To ensure flexibility, the constitution could include time-limited provisions, renewable provisions, provisions that give locales a choice of pathways to follow, and diverse amendment procedures that entrench different provisions to different degrees. Additionally, interim constitutions may be an effective way to incorporate counterinsurgency-inspired provisions while not entrenching them.[42] Indeed, scholars have shown that constitutions that are flexible, but not so flexible as to undermine the need for serious bargaining over the constitutional provisions, have the greatest endurance.[43]

The moral rights counterargument claims that accommodating insurgency conditions in the constitution, even partially, may condone unacceptable or immoral practices, thus contravening human rights. Conversely, specifying rights that are presently unattainable may help bring those rights into effect.[44] Extreme divergences between human rights and local practices must be guarded against, but some compromise—between the realities on the ground and constitutional aspirations—will be necessary to ensure the success of the constitutional project. In Iraq, for example, advocating for the strict separation of church and state would have been counterproductive, as the decision to make Islam the state religion was "entirely uncontroversial."[45] However, if the counterinsurgent forces upon a new nation an idealistic constitution that runs counter to the nation's traditions and culture, the constitution may be ignored, jettisoned, or used as a mere political tool. The success of some kind of constitutionalism may be preferable to the failure of any kind of order.[46]

So what would a counterinsurgency-inspired constitution look like? One of the crucial lessons of turbulent transitions is that counterinsurgency proceeds in phases over a long period of time—evolving from the provision of security to building sustainable social, political, and economic institutions. This lesson suggests two design strategies. First, time-limited and renewable constitutional provisions may be helpful. For example, provisions that grant the military or occupying security forces greater powers for a short period of time may be helpful for ensuring that the "clear" phase of clear-hold-build is effective and legitimate. Second, establishing an interim constitution that exists for a relatively long period of time, until stability can be confidently predicted, may be useful. An interim constitution could delineate the scope of an occupying force's mission and operations. It could assist the counterinsurgent's initial offensive operations by identifying certain groups, practices, or actions as unconstitutional. And it could outline a clear path to sovereignty, one that passes authority from the counterinsurgent to the domestic population as certain goals are met.

The local focus of counterinsurgency suggests that effective counterinsurgency requires anchoring the constitution in the particular conditions, cultures, and characteristics of a place. As the *Counterinsurgency Field Manual* notes, "if it works in this province, it might not work in the next."[47] No design structure, therefore, should be seen as universally applicable—context matters. Focusing on the uniqueness of the place means that constitutional designers should try to address local grievances, incorporate cultural norms, include neotraditional governance structures, and, above all, know the population.

Constitutional designers should attempt to address and neutralize local grievances, thereby depriving insurgency networks of discontented potential recruits. The most evident forms of local grievance relate to human rights and divided societies. During the 1950s, for example, Sir Gerald Templer took measures toward social and political equality for all groups in Malaya.[48] Addressing the grievance—a history of the Chinese not having political and social rights—reduced the number of disaffected Chinese and thus the number of possible recruits to the insurgency. The problem of divided societies is evident in Iraq. The Shia, Sunni, and Kurds all had local grievances. The Shia had experienced a history of repression and lack of political control despite being a majority of the population.[49] The Sunni, having held power for so long, were now anxious about the future.[50] And the Kurds, who had experienced persecution, were unwilling to cede relative autonomy to a majoritarian Arab state.[51] Neutralizing these grievances by finding a way for the three groups to coexist was, and remains, a central challenge. Constitutional mechanisms such as federalism, concurrent majorities, minority vetoes, partition, and secession are but a few of the possible solutions.[52]

In addition to these national-level local grievances, there may be community-level local grievances. Particular tribal, minority, cultural, or linguistic groups may have concerns that, if addressed, would increase their likelihood of supporting the counterinsurgent's government-in-creation. Designing structures to address these grievances will obviously depend on the particular grievance and situation. The important lesson is that addressing national and community grievances will assist in counterinsurgency because it will eliminate the fuel for disaffection and insurgency.

Keeping a constitution relevant and winning the support of the population require drafting a constitution that fits within the basic preconstitutional values and philosophy of the population—even when these cultural norms may contravene widely held beliefs or preferred approaches of the counterinsurgent or constitution drafters. For example, despite America's constitutional commitment to having no established state religion, Iraq and Afghanistan are both Islamic states: Iraq's constitution allows Islam to be "a source" of law, and Afghanistan's constitution provides that no law can be contrary to Islam.[53] A pure separation of Islam and the state was never even considered.[54] Even the Japanese constitution, imposed from outside by General MacArthur after World War II, retained the emperor in a titular position, despite the obvious incongruence with American ideas of democracy, because eliminating the emperor from the political system would have caused considerable upheaval within Japan.[55]

Local areas may also have unique cultural traditions and may have traditional governance structures that can be incorporated into the constitution.[56] Because local populations will be familiar with the structure and functions of traditional governance, they may be more inclined to accept and embrace them compared to externally devised and culturally unfamiliar structures. Additionally, incorporating traditional governance structures will help keep the constitution socially relevant and linked to power realities on the ground. Of course, traditional institutions will likely need to be updated and reformed in order to comport with modern ideas of human rights and democracy. Hence, the governance structures should be "neotraditional"—including the core of the traditional institutions, but revising practices of composition and eligibility to meet international norms.

Ultimately, insurgency and counterinsurgency depend on the support, or at least the acquiescence, of the population. As a result, counterinsurgents must know who is in the population. The most effective ways to gain detailed knowledge of the population cannot be accomplished at the constitutional level, but a constitution can provide helpful authority by requiring a census of the population.[57] More controversially, a constitution could require issuance of identification cards.[58] Both mechanisms could potentially assist in identifying members and groups within the population and within specific areas of the country. Each may also have significant risks, such as putting a list of a minority ethnicity in the hands of a corrupt majority-dominated government. But these risks must be evaluated on a case-by-case level.

The local nature of counterinsurgency also suggests constitutional provisions for multiple tiers of government and for full-spectrum constitutional provisions at the local level. Tiered constitutions—constitutions with subnational governance structures specified down to the precinct level—align well with counterinsurgency. Constitutionalizing local government has the potential to accelerate the counterinsurgent's project because the constitution would act as a focal point providing clear governance structures for local peoples to follow, while simultaneously pushing counterinsurgents toward transferring control to local people. Because core elements of counterinsurgency—providing social services and security—occur at the municipal level (or the equivalent), strengthening local public authorities is vital to undermining the insurgency and winning over the population. Moreover, including the populace more directly in political action, via participation in local governance, may aid in building legitimacy in public institutions. The result may be increased acceptance of both democracy and freedom.[59] Establishing local government structures will also immediately create many local officeholders. With constitutional sanction, these officeholders will be formally empowered and accountable, thus facilitating legitimacy in their operations. And as these officials learn how to work the machinery of government, they will gain valuable skills in politics and governance, eventually forming a skilled class of future provincial and national leaders. As a result, constitutionalizing local government might actually be a way to protect constitutional rights. Because "local governments are often uniquely well positioned to give content to the substantive constitutional principles that should inform the consideration of [certain] public questions," they may facilitate and protect a burgeoning rights-based regime.[60]

Afghanistan provides perhaps the best example of a constitution that fails to decentralize authority and empower local actors. Advocates of a presidential system, instead of a parliamentary system, contended that a strong, centralized state authority would make it more likely for Afghanistan to develop an effective government.[61] As a result of this "principle of centralization," the Afghan government's structure is deeply disconnected from the local nature of counterinsurgency and turbulent reconstruction. District and provincial governors are not elected by their constituents but instead appointed by the president. Police forces are not local, but lodged within the Ministry of the Interior. And the massive centralized bureaucracy creates the risk of corrupt patronage hires and distance from local conditions and needs.[62] The result is a centralized system that does not align with counterinsurgency's requirement of local mobilization.

At the local level, counterinsurgency is a full-spectrum operation, requiring the counterinsurgents to go beyond military operations and a "kill-capture" philosophy. They must enable security, build governance and political structures, facilitate capacity-building and delivery of social services, and aid economic development and reconstruction. Constitutional design can facilitate each of these areas.

Ensuring security for the population is perhaps the most important factor for a successful counterinsurgency. Although the military and foreign counterinsurgency forces can provide some level of security, indigenous security forces will ultimately be responsible. Constitutionalizing the security services can at once empower and hold them—and the political leaders to whom they report—accountable for security conditions. Creating provincial- and district-level gendarmerie and police chief positions that report to the respective political bodies, and delineating their mode of selection, would help quickly establish persons responsible for training, patrols, and operations. Moreover, the constitution could mandate reporting and transparency, enable complaints and accountability, and establish controls and limits on the gendarmerie and police. Indeed, the South African constitution's provisions might act as a model, as they create a police force, establish political responsibility for the police force, and place limits and controls on the police.[63]

Counterinsurgency often requires building legitimate political structures from scratch. Because so many of the tasks government must accomplish are local, such as sewage maintenance, trash collection, and rebuilding infrastructure, local political structures are perhaps the best way to achieve these goals. Local participation is also likely the best way to build legitimacy—local government can enable "*self*-government and self-*government*."[64] As a result, constitutional designers should consider specifying political structures at the provincial, district/municipal, and precinct/village levels. In some cases, it might be possible to use traditional governance structures at the precinct or district level, but in many cases new institutions would be required. The constitution would need to mandate either how bodies at the precinct or district level should be selected or the procedures for choosing a selection mechanism. Identifying the body or bodies with primary responsibility for ensuring and providing social services and security would go a long way to empowering and holding accountable specific actors at the local or regional level. For example, in Afghanistan, National Solidarity Program created Community Development Councils (CDCs) and empowered them to set priorities and implement development projects. The CDCs may serve as a model for empowering local actors in politics and security as well. Finally, constitutional designers should consider reporting mechanisms that link the levels of governance.[65] Precincts could provide information to districts, and districts may need to provide progress reports to provinces.

Although the U.S. Constitution does not constitutionalize local government structures and functions, several other countries' constitutions do, and their provisions could be used as models. South Africa specifies the objects, composition, election, and even internal procedures of local governments and municipalities.[66] The Dutch constitution establishes election processes and structures for provinces and municipalities.[67] And the Indonesian constitution identifies ways to create provinces, regencies, and municipalities.[68]

In counterinsurgency, provision of basic social services is essential not only for sustaining a basic quality of life but also for preventing insurgency. Absence of basic services often correlates directly with insurgency, as populations see public power as less effective and legitimate and are willing to embrace insurgency.[69] Constitutional designers might facilitate the delivery of social services in two simple ways. They could include a provision that allows a district or municipality to create public services authorities—such as water, sewage, and trash collection boards, or even fire companies—that would organize and supervise the provision of public services. For example, the Dutch constitution specifies a process for the creation or dissolution of water control boards and for other public bodies.[70] In addition, constitutional designers could provide for community empowerment projects, such as the Afghan CDCs.[71] Constitutionalizing these organizations would encourage local entities to act, involve the population in resolving challenges in their communities, and provide an officially sanctioned path for development organizations and NGOs to provide aid.

Reconstructing a society and building a functioning economy take money. Community-driven reconstruction and development would benefit from fiscal decentralization to prevent waste, corruption, transaction costs, and delays in money transfers from the federal to the local governments, and to direct money toward the populations that can best identify and act upon the challenges they face.[72] The constitution could require that part of the national budget be devolved to the provinces, districts, and precincts.[73] The specific proportion could be established by law, but the constitution would mandate fiscal decentralization to encourage local development. The constitution could also grant local governments the power to levy taxes in order to ensure a consistent stream of revenue for community-driven reconstruction and development.[74] Fiscal decentralization places trust and responsibility in the hands of the local populations and their leaders. It encourages action through empowerment and fosters accountability.

Undergirding these counterinsurgency-inspired constitutional provisions is the philosophy of democratic experimentalism. The structure of each counterinsurgency-inspired provision involves two elements: the constitution (akin to the central government) establishing a set of priorities and goals, and then the local governments who are empowered to implement those goals as best suits local conditions. The ability to create local utilities boards and the decentralization of budgetary authority, for example, both involve central power over the ultimate priorities and acceptable structures of the state-building enterprise but also enable local flexibility and participation in crafting solutions. For counterinsurgents, constitutional design must enable locally designed and crafted policies—even as it ultimately connects public policy to the central government's authority.

## Solon's Gambit

After writing the Athenian constitution, the lawgiver Solon was asked whether he had devised the best constitution for Athens. He is said to have responded, "The best they could receive."[75] When they occur simultaneously, counterinsurgency and constitutional design are intimately interconnected.

Counterinsurgency may influence the creation of constitutional order and available constitutional provisions. Constitutional design can craft structures that assist counterinsurgents in their endeavor to establish a legitimate, stable government with political participation and functioning public power. The lessons of counterinsurgency for constitutional design follow from the law-giver Solon's remark: the lawgiver must devise the best constitution a people can receive. Solon's gambit is the gambit of any constitutional designer inter-ested in bridging the realities of the present with the ideals of political and constitutional philosophy. In the case of insurgency, the constitutional de-signer must gamble that compromise today to build sturdy foundations of order, stability, and shared values will lead eventually to the development of higher ideals and greater political and social justice. Even as they focus inexo-rably on the details of the moment, modern Solons must ultimately maintain a deep and abiding faith in the future—that with firm foundations, the con-stitution and the nation will adapt and develop over time.

# Conclusion

"VICTORY IS WON and pacification ends," David Galula wrote in *Pacification in Algeria*, "when most of the counterinsurgent forces can safely be withdrawn, leaving the population to take care of itself with the help of a normal contingent of police and Army forces."[1] The goal of counterinsurgency is not simply warfighting or defeating the insurgents but rather facilitating a stable, secure society. Counterinsurgency is embedded in a broader social context, and actions that are not narrowly "military" can contribute to—and may even be vital to—success. As with warfighting, legal operations are likewise embedded in a social context. They must be considered as intertwined with local politics and preferences, rather than as operating in an autonomous realm. The result is that both counterinsurgency and legal operations during counterinsurgency must take a bottom-up, locally driven, contextual approach.

If we embrace the idea that law and war are both embedded in society, a set of core principles emerges for understanding how law operates during war—and how law and war are related. Perhaps most importantly, counterinsurgents want the population to follow a certain set of behaviors. Force may be one option to achieve behavioral compliance, but law is another. Law gains compliance by building support for procedures. If the population embraces the legal process, the government can enforce the outcomes of the process, and the people will accept that enforcement and adapt their behavior. The power of law, in other words, is to legitimate the use of power—to achieve behavioral compliance through consent, rather than force. But as important as legal process is, law without legitimacy is no savior. Following the technical dictates of the law is rarely comforting if the rules or the outcomes are so wildly out of sync with popular opinion. Perfect legalism in an illegitimate regime is still likely to be illegitimate, and practices that have no connection to the local social context—practices that do not have a minimal level of social acceptance—are unlikely to legitimate the exercise of power. Thus, nonstate justice systems might be essential to providing civil justice. Community policing may be more effective at reducing violence in some contexts. And justice and reconciliation programs will have to reflect local values and preferences. The rule of law, in other words, must be organic, linking law and society, embedded in the community.

Just as law operates in society, so too does strategy, and as a result law and military strategy are interconnected. Law is not irrelevant to strategic success. Nor are law and strategy autonomous fields, with law merely operating as a humanitarian constraint on warfighting. Rather, law is in constant dynamic tension and collaboration with strategy. Counterinsurgency strategy shapes legal norms and requirements, even as the law channels and constrains military operations. The principle of exemplarism—of strategic self-interest— holds that counterinsurgents should follow the law independent of any benefits based on the enemy's reciprocity. In determining whether enemies can be targeted with military force, the principles of distinction and proportionality can be adapted to counterinsurgencies in order to incorporate the win-the-population strategy. And counterinsurgency embraces the rule of law as a mechanism for rebuilding order and obligation in a fragmented society. Indeed, counterinsurgency holds that following the law is essential to success and that building the rule of law is in part constitutive of success.

Law is therefore inevitably an instrument of counterinsurgency—as are military, political, economic, social, and other operations. Each arena is embedded in the social context, and counterinsurgency can draw upon actions in any of these areas in order to win the population's support. Constitutions can be designed in ways that further counterinsurgent success. Transitional justice and reconciliation can bring an end to conflict. Rule-of-law operations can provide public goods to communities seeking certainty and predictability in the midst of chaos. Importantly, because law is embedded in society, because it can be an instrument for legitimating power, it is not fixed for all time. Social norms change, policy preferences change, and, with them, the law can adapt and change. Particularly in the context of turbulent transitions, where war moves to fits and starts toward peace, laws and even constitutions need not be seen as eternal. They can evolve as the conditions evolve.

## Lessons for Counterinsurgents

These broad features of law lead to some concrete lessons for how counterinsurgents, lawyers, and policymakers should think about the role of law during counterinsurgencies. This is not an exclusive list of lessons, and these lessons are not to be applied uncritically. But they provide a starting point for thinking about how to integrate law into counterinsurgency operations more smoothly and more systematically.

## 1. Interpret the Laws of War to Align with Counterinsurgency Strategy

In a number of areas, the laws of war can be interpreted in a manner that both advances their humanitarian goals while better aligning with counterinsurgency strategy. The reformist strand in occupation law can require more democratic participation on the part of the local population. The rules of distinction and proportionality can be interpreted to account for the strategic costs of civilian casualties, not just the humanitarian costs. And the approach to detainee affairs can be decentralized to create adaptable procedures that better balance security and liberty.

## 2. Laws Are Resources, Not Just Constraints

Counterinsurgents can use legality to enhance their legitimacy by following the law and building the rule of law. In following the laws of war when conducting airstrikes, following local and international law in detainee affairs, and in building civil and criminal justice systems, counterinsurgents can gain legitimacy in the eyes of the population. Effective communication is essential— journalists, government officials, and the population itself will need to be educated on what the law requires and how the counterinsurgent is meeting (and perhaps even exceeding) those requirements. Indeed, legal education can also make clear when insurgents fail to follow the laws and may help build public support against them.

## 3. Justice Can Help End the War

Transitional justice programs like prosecutions, truth and reconciliation programs, amnesties, and purging or lustration are not simply postconflict processes. In the midst of counterinsurgency, they can be approaches to reconciliation and reintegration—and they can help end the conflict. Counterinsurgents must consider these programs as integral to their strategy, not as an afterthought.

## 4. Building the Rule of Law Is Central to Counterinsurgency

The need to win-the-population and the relationship between warfighting and state-building suggest that building the rule of law is an important part of counterinsurgency and one that should be integrated into operational planning.

Civil and criminal justice and effective policing are critical public goods that governments provide to their people. Counterinsurgents who support these institutions engage in state-building while denying the insurgents the support of the people.

## 5. Design Institutions for the Conditions

Because law is embedded in society, law must be seen through the eyes of the community. The context—war or peace, development, geography, history, religion, social norms—shapes how the community understands law and the legal process. In interpreting the laws of war, building the rule of law, or designing transitional justice programs, the local context is critical. Any institution or program—from a constitution to a local court—should be designed taking the local context into account with as much granularity as possible.

## 6. Lawyers as Warriors, Warriors as Lawyers

Lawyers must take on a broader role in counterinsurgency, working more closely with strategists and warriors to develop legal operations and assess the strategic ramifications of legal issues. Lawyers cannot be seen as just saying what the law is—they are integral to connecting law and strategy. Similarly, warriors cannot ignore law except when approaching its outer bounds. They too must work to integrate legal operations into their strategy.

## *The Counterinsurgent's Constitution*

The word *constitution* today most frequently indicates a written charter of government, a piece of parchment framing the institutions of public authority within a territory. But its meaning does not end there. For the ancients, the constitution was not a written document, but the entire assemblage of laws, rules, norms, and structures that governed society. Even into the eighteenth century, *constitution* signified a system beyond the rules codified in print, or even in law. Both the modern idea of the constitution as a charter of government and the ancient idea of the constitution as the assemblage of customs for governance hint at perhaps the most profound meaning of the word. They indicate that a constitution is inextricable from the very fabric of life itself. It is the basic core of how a society operates. It captures the character of society and its people. Indeed, the term "constitution" was frequently used in earlier times to mean the disposition, character, mindset, and inherent capacities of an individual.

The counterinsurgent's constitution is more than a set of laws, codified into the laws of war, and it is more than the legal, political, and social structures that govern the rule of law during turbulent transitions. It is the very disposition of the counterinsurgent: the character and mindset that counterinsurgents bring to bear on any problem arising in the midst of small wars. The successful counterinsurgent must elevate the organic approach to the level of disposition. The counterinsurgent must make second nature the win-the-population strategy, full spectrum operations, dynamic and evolutionary programs, and the bottom-up approach that focuses on mobilizing the population and building local power.

Embracing the dynamic nature of small wars does not leave us adrift, unmoored from principle or guidance. Small wars are wars among the people. Popular support and legitimacy drive their dynamics, political and social order are their ultimate aim. Success in counterinsurgency operations therefore requires embracing an organic approach that is rooted in the population itself—in its traditions and history, its needs and preferences, its capacities and aspirations. The organic approach means more than accepting the bland platitudes of "hearts and minds" or "putting a local face" on operations. It mandates immersion in the local community, and it involves participating in local affairs with the goal of empowering the people.

The organic approach cautions against hubris by making stark the counterinsurgent's limitations. Local knowledge—that most scarce resource—is highly prized. Without it, counterinsurgents cannot understand what the people consider legitimate, how they are fragmented, and what traditions they hold in law, governance, and culture. Without it, they will not be able to rebuild the people's sense of obligation to the government. As importantly, the organic approach suggests that counterinsurgents are not the most significant actor—nor the one with the most control—in shaping the destiny of the conflict. That role falls to the local population. Even a well-executed organic counterinsurgency could therefore fail based on the independent decisions of the people. Counterinsurgents can attempt to better understand what drives the people and to shape their decisions, but they cannot fully control the people's destiny.

Progressive counterinsurgency and its organic species are, of course, not the only strategies available in waging war against insurgents. The repressive counterinsurgency strategy seeks to crush the insurgents and the people. The minimalist counterinsurgency strategy aspires to little more than short-term stability, however precarious it may be. Counterterrorism strategies seek to kill, capture, and disrupt the most extreme insurgent operations, leaving untouched supporters whose actions fall short of violent plots. And containment strategies may keep an insurgent counterstate at bay.

The promise of progressive counterinsurgency is that it can create a sustainable order in a territory. It can create a better future for the people, protecting them from violence and fear and enabling them to shape their common destiny. The problem with progressive counterinsurgency is that it requires so much of counterinsurgents: time, resources, local knowledge, and mobilization of full-spectrum efforts. Counterinsurgents cannot imagine quick victory through military operations, though they must imagine a drawn-out conflict in which military operations will be insufficient. They cannot expect the creation of national democracy overnight, though they must expect politically abhorrent compromises that facilitate stable order. They cannot anticipate peaceful economic development through a market economy, though they must anticipate economic activities to fuel warfighting on both sides of the conflict. They cannot hope for a legal system with the characteristics of Western rule of law, though they must hope for a legal system in which law rules. They cannot foresee the universal achievement of human rights, though they must foresee messy moral compromises that might make incremental progress. With so many requirements, so many risks, and so much uncertainty, progressive counterinsurgency is not to be undertaken lightly. But in the age of small wars, its dynamics must not be ignored.

*Notes*

1.    Modern warfare takes many forms: commentators write about civil wars, insurgencies, hybrid wars, and transnational warfare, among other things. Despite minor differences, I use the terms "insurgency," "guerrilla warfare," and "small wars" interchangeably. Guerrilla warfare is "a strategy of armed resistance that uses small, mobile groups to inflict punishment through hit-and-run strikes while avoiding direct battle when possible and seeks to win the allegiance of at least some portion of the noncombatant population." Jason Lyall, *Do Democracies Make Inferior Counterinsurgents? Reassessing Democracy's Impact on War Outcomes and Duration*, 61 INT'L ORG. 167, 175 (Winter 2010) (ordinal numbering omitted). "Guerrilla" is Spanish for "small war." The term arose during Napoleon's invasion of Spain in 1807 when his forces faced persistent attacks by local resistance fighters. After 1945, guerrilla warfare transformed into insurgency warfare through the increased material support for guerrillas as part of the Cold War's proxy wars, the spread of radical ideologies, and a flourishing in guerrilla warfare doctrine. These three factors transformed the resistance of guerrillas into the revolutionary war of insurgents, who crucially seek to overthrow and replace the local political order. See Stathis Kalyvas & Laia Balcells, *International System and Technologies of Rebellion: How the Cold War Shaped Internal Conflict*, 104 AM. POL. SCI. REV. 415, 419-421 (2010). Despite the difference in guerrilla tactics and insurgency warfare, insurgencies are distinguished from conventional war precisely by the use of guerrilla tactics.

It is also important to note that insurgencies are not the same as civil wars. Insurgencies are asymmetric, with rebels challenging a state through guerrilla tactics. Many civil wars, however, are symmetrical, with each side using the same style of warfare. Conventional civil wars are fought between mobilized armies and feature, for example, trench warfare, artillery, and troops marching against each other into battle to defend and gain territory. The U.S. Civil War is paradigmatic, though more recent conventional civil wars include the Biafran conflict in Nigeria in the late 1960s, and the conflicts between Abkhazia and Georgia and between Nagorno

Karabakh and Azerbaijan in the early 1990s. Civil wars can also be symmetrical and unconventional. These wars—such as the ongoing conflict in Somalia, the civil war in the Central African Republic in the 1990s, and the civil war in Congo-Brazzaville in the mid-1990s—are characterized by militias with low levels of military capacity or organization. All sides use small arms, but they "exercised limited state-building and made little effort to indoctrinate the population or mobilize it." Id. at 418-419. Insurgencies are asymmetric political struggles. The dynamics of state versus insurgent and the strategies of insurgency and counterinsurgency inevitably differ from the dynamics and strategies of symmetric and less political forms of warfare.

2.  T. E. LAWRENCE, SEVEN PILLARS OF WISDOM 193 (1991). Lawrence's phrase was recently popularized by JOHN A. NAGL, LEARNING TO EAT SOUP WITH A KNIFE: COUNTERINSURGENCY LESSONS FROM MALAYA AND VIETNAM (2005).

3.  CICERO, PRO MILONE, chap. 4; SIR ROBERT THOMPSON, DEFEATING COMMUNIST INSURGENCY 66 (1966); David J. Kilcullen, *Countering Global Insurgency*, 28 J. STRATEGIC STUD. 597, 612 (2005); ROGER TRINQUIER, MODERN WARFARE 40 (1964, 2006); THE U.S. ARMY/MARINE CORPS COUNTERINSURGENCY FIELD MANUAL ¶¶ D-38, 1–132 (2007).

4.  FIELD MANUAL ¶ 1–2.

5.  See, e.g., Gian P. Gentile, *A Strategy of Tactics: Population-centric COIN and the Army*, PARAMETERS (Autumn 2009), at 5.

6.  See DAVID GALULA, COUNTERINSURGENCY WARFARE 4 (1964) (an insurgency is a "protracted struggle conducted methodically, step by step, in order to attain specific intermediate objectives, leading finally to the overthrow of the existing order") (emphasis omitted); see also FIELD MANUAL, at ¶ 1–2 ("an insurgency is an organized, protracted politico-military struggle designed to weaken the control and legitimacy of an established government, occupying power, or other political authority while increasing insurgent control").

7.  FIELD MANUAL at ¶ 1–9.

8.  TOM R. TYLER, WHY PEOPLE OBEY THE LAW 27 (2006).

9.  See Richard H. Fallon, *Legitimacy and the Constitution*, 118 HARV. L. REV. 1787, 1794–95 (2005) for a discussion of legal legitimacy that distinguishes between substantive and authoritative legitimacy. Fallon also argues for an independent category of moral legitimacy.

10. Id. at 1795.

11. Erin Simpson, The Perils of Third-Party Counterinsurgency, unpublished PhD dissertation, Harvard Univ. 2010 (arguing that third-party COIN faces challenges in selection effects, information gathering, and domestic political constraints).

CHAPTER 1

1.  The terms "laws of war," "laws of armed conflict," and "international humanitarian law" (IHL) are now often used synonymously, though they have different emphases. Historically, "war" implied conflict between states. "Armed conflict" expands

the scope to lesser hostilities, while IHL emphasizes a particular purpose of law. See David Wippman, *Introduction: Do New Wars Call for New Laws*, in NEW WARS, NEW LAWS?: APPLYING THE LAWS OF WAR IN 21ST CENTURY CONFLICTS 1, 1 n.1 (David Wippman & Matthew Evangelista eds., 2005).

2. See THE U.S. ARMY/MARINE CORPS COUNTERINSURGENCY FIELD MANUAL (2007).

3. FIELD MANUAL at ¶ 1–128.

4. Strategy can exist at many levels, from technical details and operations to political goals. See EDWARD N. LUTTWAK, STRATEGY 87–91 (2001). I use strategy to indicate an overall approach, encompassing particular operations.

5. Indeed, even when the enemy gives up, it does so from fear of destruction. See CARL VON CLAUSEWITZ, ON WAR 227 (Michael Howard & Peter Paret eds., Princeton Univ. Press, 1976) (1832).

6. FREDERICK THE GREAT, MILITARY INSTRUCTION FROM THE LATE KING OF PRUSSIA, TO HIS GENERALS 119 (Major Foster trans., London, J. Cruttwell, 4th ed. 1797). On Jomini, see AZAR GAT, THE ORIGINS OF MILITARY THOUGHT FROM THE ENLIGHTENMENT TO CLAUSEWITZ 115 (1989).

7. CLAUSEWITZ, ON WAR, at 258 and 227; see also id. at 577 ("[T]he grand objective of all military action is to overthrow the enemy—which means destroying his armed forces").

8. Id. at 595–596.

9. The military's definition of the term "center of gravity" is "[t]he source of power that provides moral or physical strength, freedom of action, or will to act." Dept. of Def., Joint Publication 1–02: Dictionary of Military and Associated Terms 81 (2001) (as amended through October 17, 2008).

10. CLAUSEWITZ, ON WAR, at 596, 259, 260.

11. Id. at 89.

12. WILLIAM C. MARTEL, VICTORY IN WAR: FOUNDATIONS OF MODERN MILITARY POLICY 52 (2007).

13. The German strategist Erich Ludendorff described total war as involving the entire territory, requiring the population to mobilize the economic power of the state, supporting their morale, preparing before the war, and having a single leader. Id. at 53. For a modern take on a variation of total war, see QIAO LIANG & WANG XIANGSUI, UNRESTRICTED WARFARE (1999).

14. MARTEL, VICTORY IN WAR, at 71.

15. Some international law scholars have noted the kill-capture nature of warfare. Professor Frédéric Mégret argues that the laws of war are necessarily based on "war," which is a social construction "beyond which humanitarian lawyers feel they cannot go." Frédéric Mégret, Non-Lethal Weapons and the Possibility of Radical New Horizons for the Laws of War: Why Kill, Wound and Hurt (Combatants) at All? 9, 18–19 (July 1, 2008) (unpublished manuscript), available at http://ssrn.com/abstract=1295348; see also Mark Weisburd, *Al-Qaeda and the Law of War*, 11 LEWIS & CLARK L. REV. 1063, 1071 (2007) ("[B]elligerent states attempt to

prevent their adversaries from causing future harm by destroying their military forces; obviously, killing or capturing the members of an adversary's forces will destroy those forces. If one could not kill members of the opposing military on sight, or capture members of enemy armed forces without going through time-consuming procedural steps, the delay imposed on military operations could be significant and the risks of defeat greatly increased.").

16. Eyal Benvenisti, *The Legal Battle to Define the Law on Transnational Asymmetric Warfare*, 20 DUKE J. COMP. & INT'L L. 339, 340 (2010).

17. This is the conventional approach: international humanitarian law is a "compromise between humanity and military necessity." Marco Sassòli, *Targeting: The Scope and Utility of the Concept of "Military Objectives" for the Protection of Civilians in Contemporary Armed Conflict*, in WIPPMAN, NEW WARS, NEW LAWS? at 181, 183–184. The foundational importance of kill-capture applies even if other approaches are followed. Eric Posner has argued that the laws of war seek to limit costly military technologies, thus freeing resources for production and consumption. Eric A. Posner, *A Theory of the Laws of War*, 70 U. CHI. L. REV. 297, 297 (2003). Given the primacy of military technology to Posner's theory, his approach also grounds the laws of war in the kill-capture strategy.

18. See Nathaniel Berman, *Privileging Combat? Contemporary Conflict and the Legal Construction of War*, 43 COLUM. J. TRANSNAT'L L. 1, 4–5 (2004).

19. General Orders No. 100, in RICHARD SHELLY HARTIGAN, LIEBER'S CODE AND THE LAW OF WAR 45 (1983).

20. Burruss M. Carnahan, *Lincoln, Lieber, and the Laws of War: The Origins and Limits of the Principle of Military Necessity*, 92 AM. J. INT'L L. 213, 214 (1998).

21. See HARTIGAN, LIEBER'S CODE, at 22; Grant R. Doty, *The United States and the Development of the Laws of Land Warfare*, 156 MIL. L. REV. 224, 230 (1998); Theodor Meron, *Francis Lieber's Code and Principles of Humanity*, 36 COLUM. J. TRANSNAT'L L. 269, 279 (1998).

22. Carnahan, *Lincoln, Lieber, and the Laws of War*, at 213.

23. General Orders No. 100 at art. 14.

24. Id. at art. 15, art. 16.

25. Id. at art. 17.

26. Meron, *Francis Lieber's Code*, at 271.

27. 1868. St. Petersburg Declaration Renouncing the Use, in Time of War, of Explosive Projectiles under 400 Grammes Weight, December 11, 1868, 18 Martens Nouveau Recueil (ser. 1) 474, reprinted in DOCUMENTS ON THE LAWS OF WAR 53, 54 (Adam Roberts & Richard Guelff eds., 3d ed. 2000).

28. Id. at 55.

29. Adam Roberts & Richard Guelff, *Introduction* to DOCUMENTS ON THE LAWS OF WAR, at 5.

30. Id. at 10; see also L. C. GREEN, THE CONTEMPORARY LAW OF ARMED CONFLICT 47, 113, 192 (2d ed. 2000). Under Article 1, the "laws, rights, and duties of war" apply

to armies, militia, and volunteer corps that are commanded by a person responsible to subordinates, that show a distinctive emblem, that carry arms openly, and that follow the laws and customs of war. Hague Convention (IV) Respecting the Laws and Customs of War on Land, Annex art. 1, October 18, 1907, 36 Stat. 2277, 1 Bevans 631 [hereafter Hague IV Annex].

31. Sassòli, *Targeting*, at 202.

32. Hague IV Annex at art. 20.

33. Id. at arts. 22, 23, 25.

34. For example, 1899 Hague Declaration 2 Concerning Asphyxiating Gases, July 29, 1899, 26 Martens Nouveau Recueil 998, reprinted in DOCUMENTS ON THE LAWS OF WAR, at 59, 60–61, banning the use of projectiles to spread asphyxiating gases, states that the Declaration is "only binding to the contracting Powers." Such rules were derived from the contractual approach to the laws of war that emerged in the seventeenth century. See STEPHEN C. NEFF, WAR AND THE LAW OF NATIONS 147–151 (2005); see also Eric A. Posner, *Terrorism and the Laws of War*, 5 CHI. J. INT'L L. 423, 427–430 (2005).

35. See Posner, *Terrorism and the Laws of War*, at 428.

36. 1899 Hague Declaration 2 Concerning Asphyxiating Gases, July 29, 1899, 26 Martens Nouveau Recueil 998, reprinted in *Documents on the Laws of War*, at 59, 60–61.

37. See Posner, *Terrorism and the Laws of War*, at 429.

38. See JOHN KEEGAN, THE FIRST WORLD WAR 213–215 (1998); David Turns, *Weapons in the ICRC Study on Customary International Humanitarian Law*, 11 J. CONFLICT & SECURITY L. 201, 219 & n. 117 (2006).

39. NEFF, WAR AND THE LAW OF NATIONS, at 340; see also DOCUMENTS ON THE LAWS OF WAR at 195 ("The central concern of all four 1949 Geneva Conventions is thus the protection of victims of war").

40. Geneva Convention for the Amelioration of the Condition of the Wounded and Sick in Armed Forces in the Field, August 12, 1949, 6 U.S.T. 3114, 75 U.N.T.S. 31 [hereafter GC I]; Geneva Convention for the Amelioration of the Condition of the Wounded, Sick, and Shipwrecked Members of Armed Forces at Sea, August 12, 1949, 6 U.S.T. 3217, 75 U.N.T.S. 85 [hereafter GC II]; Geneva Convention Relative to the Treatment of Prisoners of War, August 12, 1949, 6 U.S.T 3316, 75 U.N.T.S. 135 [hereafter GC III]; Geneva Convention Relative to the Protection of Civilian Persons in Time of War, August 12, 1949, 6 U.S.T. 3516, 75 U.N.T.S. 287 [hereafter GC IV].

41. JEAN S. PICTET, ICRC, COMMENTARY, I GENEVA CONVENTION FOR THE AMELIORATION OF THE CONDITION OF THE WOUNDED AND SICK IN ARMED FORCES IN THE FIELD 136 (Jean S. Pictet ed., 1952).

42. See, e.g., Rosa Ehrenreich Brooks, *War Everywhere: Rights, National Security Law, and the Law of Armed Conflict in the Age of Terror*, 153 U. PA. L. REV. 675, 711–743 (2004); see also Adam Roberts, *The Laws of War in the War on Terror*, in INTERNATIONAL LAW AND THE WAR ON TERROR 175, 182–184 (Fred L. Borch & Paul S. Wilson eds., 2003).

43. Brooks, *War Everywhere*, at 714. But see Hamdan v. Rumsfeld, 548 U.S. 557, 630–631 (2006); Derek Jinks, *September 11 and the Laws of War*, 28 YALE J. INT'L L. 1, 39–41 (2003) (arguing that noninternational armed conflicts extend not just to internal conflicts but to transnational conflicts on a fortiori grounds of creating a comprehensive system).

44. Brooks, *War Everywhere*, at 715–720.

45. Id. at 720–725.

46. Id. at 726 (emphasis omitted).

47. Id. at 729–736.

48. Id. at 736–743.

49. One challenge Brooks does not discuss—the absence of reciprocity from terrorist groups—does not have this feature. For a discussion of reciprocity in the war on terror, see Derek Jinks, *The Applicability of the Geneva Conventions to the "Global War on Terrorism,"* 46 VA. J. INT'L L. 165, 190 (2005).

50. Memorandum from President George W. Bush on Humane Treatment of Taliban and al Qaeda Detainees (February 7, 2002), available at http://www.gwu.edu/~nsarchiv/NSAEBB/NSAEBB127/02.02.07.pdf.

51. See John C. Yoo & James C. Ho, *The Status of Terrorists*, 44 VA. J. INT'L L. 207, 209–215 (2003).

52. Memorandum from Jay S. Bybee, Assistant Attorney Gen., to Alberto R. Gonzales, Counsel to the President, and William J. Haynes II, Gen. Counsel of the Dep't of Def. 4–10 (January 22, 2002), available at http://news.findlaw.com/hdocs/docs/doj/bybee12202mem.pdf.

53. Memorandum from Alberto R. Gonzales, White House Counsel, to President George W. Bush (January 25, 2002), available at http://www.gwu.edu/~nsarchiv/NSAEBB/NSAEBB127/02.01.25.pdf.

54. William Taft, Op-Ed., *Guantanamo Detention Is Legal and Essential*, FIN. TIMES (London), January 12, 2004, at 19.

55. President's Address before a Joint Session of the Congress on the United States Response to the Terrorist Attacks of September 11, 2 PUB. PAPERS 1140, 1141 (September 20, 2001) [hereafter President's Address].

56. David Luban, *The War on Terrorism and the End of Human Rights*, PHIL. & PUB. POL'Y Q., Summer 2002, at 9, 10.

57. Gabor Rona, *Interesting Times for International Humanitarian Law: Challenges from the "War on Terror,"* 27 FLETCHER F. WORLD AFF., Summer/Fall 2003, at 55, 69.

58. See Luban, *War on Terrorism*, at 12.

59. See CHRISTOPHER GREENWOOD, ESSAYS ON WAR IN INTERNATIONAL LAW 431–432 (2006) ("In the language of international law there is no basis for speaking of a war on Al-Qaeda or any other terrorist group, for such a group cannot be a belligerent, it is merely a band of criminals"); Mark A. Drumbl, *Judging the 11 September Terrorist Attack*, 24 HUM. RTS. Q. 323, 323 (2002)

(arguing that terrorism is a criminal act and should be addressed via international criminal law); Jordan J. Paust, *Post-9/11 Overreaction and Fallacies Regarding War and Defense, Guantanamo, the Status of Persons, Treatment, Judicial Review of Detention, and Due Process in Military Commissions,* 79 NOTRE DAME L. REV. 1335, 1340–1343 (2004); Jordan J. Paust, *War and Enemy Status after 9/11: Attacks on the Laws of War,* 28 YALE J. INT'L L. 325, 326 (2003) (arguing Al Qaeda is not a state, so war is impossible); Jordan J. Paust, There Is No Need to Revise the Laws of War in Light of September 11th, at 3–4 (ASIL Task Force Paper, November 2002), available at http://www.asil.org/taskforce/paust.pdf.

60. For discussion of the applicability of Common Article 3, see Jinks, *September 11 and the Laws of War,* at 45–49; see also Anthony Dworkin, *Military Necessity and Due Process: The Place of Human Rights in the War on Terror,* in WIPPMAN, NEW WARS, NEW LAWS? at 53, 55. For a discussion of the applicability of Common Article 2, see Jinks, *Applicability of the Geneva Conventions,* at 177–178.

61. Kenneth Roth, *The Law of War in the War on Terror,* FOREIGN AFF., January–February 2004, at 2, 7.

62. Rona, *Interesting Times,* at 58; see Wippman, *Introduction,* at 8; Brooks, *War Everywhere,* at 681; Roth, *Law of War in the War on Terror,* at 2.

63. Luban, *War on Terrorism,* at 12.

64. Id. at 13.

65. Id.

66. Brooks, *War Everywhere,* at 706.

67. Id. at 745; see also Pierre-Richard Prosper, War Crimes at Large Ambassador, Address at the Royal Institute of International Affairs in London (February 20, 2002), quoted in Roberts, *The Laws of War in the War on Terror,* at 225 ("[T]he war on terror is a new type of war not envisioned when the Geneva Conventions were negotiated and signed"); Sean D. Murphy, *Evolving Geneva Convention Paradigms in the "War on Terrorism": Applying the Core Rules to the Release of Persons Deemed "Unprivileged Combatants,"* 75 GEO. WASH. L. REV. 1105, 1106 (2007) (noting that the international/noninternational armed conflict distinction does not fit the transnational nature of global terrorism).

68. Wippman, *Introduction,* at 6; see also Weisburd, *Al Qaeda and the Laws of War,* at 1080, 1085.

69. See, e.g., Wippman, *Introduction,* at 4; Noah Feldman, *Choices of Law, Choices of War,* 25 HARV. J. L. & PUB. POL'Y 457, 457–458, 470 (2002) (concluding that "terrorist attacks on the United States, planned from without, cannot definitively be categorized as either war or crime. They are crime from the perspective of provenance, war from the perspective of intentionality, probably crime from the perspective of identity, and very possibly war from the perspective of scale"); Ronald J. Sievert, *War on Terrorism or Global Law Enforcement?,* 78 NOTRE DAME L. REV. 307, 308–310 (2003).

70. RICHARD A. POSNER, NOT A SUICIDE PACT 5 (2006).

71. Id. at 31–32.

72. Id. at 72, 147–148.
73. BRUCE ACKERMAN, BEFORE THE NEXT ATTACK 13–14 (2006).
74. Id. at 38; see id. at 89, 171.
75. Id. at 42.
76. Id. at 172.
77. Id. at 1–9.
78. Id. at 4.
79. On human rights, see Brooks, *War Everywhere*, at 746–747; extrastate hostilities, see Roy S. Schöndorf, *Extra-State Armed Conflicts: Is There a Need for a New Legal Regime?*, 37 N.Y.U. J. INT'L L. & POL. 1, 3–4 (2004). Administrative measures are discussed in Monica Hakimi, *International Standards for Detaining Terrorism Suspects: Moving Beyond the Armed Conflict-Criminal Divide*, 33 YALE J. INT'L L. 369, 373 (2008); and tribunals in Allison Danner, *Beyond the Geneva Conventions: Lessons from the Tokyo Tribunal in Prosecuting War and Terrorism*, 46 VA. J. INT'L L. 83, 87–88 (2005). The central text advocating for statutory systems, which would provide enhanced legitimacy to legal operations, is BENJAMIN WITTES, LAW AND THE LONG WAR 1–17 (2008). Noah Feldman discusses the ad hoc approach in Feldman, *Choices of Law, Choices of War*, at 477.
80. Brooks, *War Everywhere*, at 751.
81. See, e.g., Douglas Jehl and Thom Shanker, *For the First Time since Vietnam, the Army Prints a Guide to Fighting Insurgents*, N.Y. TIMES, Nov. 13, 2004, at A12.
82. See, e.g., Spencer Ackerman, *The Rise of the Counterinsurgents*, WASH. INDEP., July 27, 2008, http://washingtonindependent.com/426/series-the-rise-of-the-counterinsurgents. Prominent counterinsurgency strategist John Nagl even appeared on Comedy Central's *The Daily Show with Jon Stewart*. The Daily Show with Jon Stewart: Interview with Lt. Col. John Nagl (Comedy Central television broadcast August 23, 2007), available at http://www.thedailyshow.com/watch/thu-august-23-2007/lt-col-john-nagl.
83. Professor Robert Sloane has argued that terrorism is different in kind from traditional insurgency but for different reasons; namely, terrorists reject noncombatant immunity and are structured in networks instead of hierarchies. Robert D. Sloane, *Prologue to a Voluntarist War Convention*, 106 MICH. L. REV. 443, 450 (2007). Military strategists more precisely see terrorism as largely fitting *within* the concept of insurgency—as a tactic used by insurgents.
84. David Kilcullen, Countering Global Insurgency 17–18 (November 30, 2004), available at http://smallwarsjournal.com/documents/kilcullen.pdf [hereafter Kilcullen, Countering Global Insurgency]; see also DAVID KILCULLEN, THE ACCIDENTAL GUERRILLA: FIGHTING SMALL WARS IN THE MIDST OF A BIG ONE, at xv (2009).
85. Professor Philip Bobbitt makes this point, but curiously prefers to refer to "terrorists" and "states of terror." What defines terrorists, he says, is that they attack civilians and that they are opposed to the constitutional order of the era. See PHILIP BOBBITT, TERROR AND CONSENT 27 (2008). Precision suggests distinguishing

between these elements and referring to insurgents as those who oppose the constitutional order by violent means, whether as terrorists, guerrillas, or counterstates.
This distinction also suggests terrorism can exist apart from insurgency. Where
insurgency and terror overlap, political claims of insurgents can often be channeled into political mechanisms. The residual cases of pure terrorism will be few
and can be addressed through conventional means.

86. President's Address at 1140–1142.

87. Kilcullen, Countering Global Insurgency, at 1; see also ROBERT M. CASSIDY,
COUNTERINSURGENCY AND THE GLOBAL WAR ON TERROR, at vii (2006).

88. Kilcullen, Countering Global Insurgency, at 15.

89. Stephen J. Hadley and Frances Fragos Townsend, Op-Ed., *What We Saw in London*,
N.Y. TIMES, July 23, 2005, at A13.

90. Richard W. Stevenson, *President Makes It Clear: Phrase Is "War on Terror,"* N.Y.
TIMES, Aug. 4, 2005, at A12.

91. See generally, e.g., JAMES S. CORUM, FIGHTING THE WAR ON TERROR: A
COUNTERINSURGENCY STRATEGY (2007) (recommending a counterinsurgency
strategy to address security challenges in Iraq and Afghanistan).

92. Philip Johnston, *Ministers Ditch "War on Terror" to Avoid Glorifying Terrorists*,
DAILY TELEGRAPH (London), Jan. 17, 2008, at 2.

93. John J. Kruzel, *U.S. Should Use Counterinsurgency Methods in War on Terror, General
Says*, AM. FORCES PRESS SERVICE, February 28, 2007, available at http://www.
defenselink.mil/news/newsarticle.aspx?id=3218.

94. Condoleezza Rice, Sec'y, U.S. Dep't of State, Remarks on Transformational
Diplomacy at Georgetown University (February 12, 2008) (transcript available
at http://2001-2009.state.gov/secretary/rm/2008/02/100703.htm); Robert M.
Gates, Sec'y, U.S. Dep't of Def., Speech at National Defense University (September 29, 2008) (transcript available at http://www.defenselink.mil/speeches/
speech.aspx?speechid=1279).

95. U.S. Dep't of Def., National Defense Strategy 7–8 (June 2008), http://www.
defenselink.mil/pubs/2008NationalDefenseStrategy.pdf.

96. Id. at 17.

97. U.S. Dep't of Def. Directive 3000.07, at 4(a) (2008), available at http://www.dtic.
mil/whs/directives/corres/pdf/300007p.pdf.

98. I take the phrase "the likely war" from VINCENT DESPORTES, LA GUERRE
PROBABLE (2007).

99. Robert M. Gates, Sec'y, U.S. Dep't of Def., Remarks at the Association of the U.S.
Army (October 10, 2007) (transcript available at http://www.defenselink.mil/
speeches/speech.aspx?speechid=1181).

100. Rice, Remarks on Transformational Diplomacy.

101. Eliot A. Cohen, Preface to U.S. Gov't Interagency Counterinsurgency Initiative,
U.S. Government Counterinsurgency Guide (January 2009), available at http://
www.state.gov/documents/organization/119629.pdf.

102. Gates, Speech at National Defense University.

103. See, e.g., Department of Defense, Quadrennial Defense Review Report 85, February 2010, available at http://www.defense.gov/qdr/; THE CNA CORP., NATIONAL SECURITY AND THE THREAT OF CLIMATE CHANGE (2007), available at http://securityandclimate.cna.org/report/.

104. DAVID GALULA, PACIFICATION IN ALGERIA 1956–1958 168 (1963, RAND ed. 2006).

105. DAVID GALULA, COUNTERINSURGENCY WARFARE 4 (1964) (emphasis omitted); see also FIELD MANUAL ¶ 1–2 ("[A]n insurgency is an organized, protracted politico-military struggle designed to weaken the control and legitimacy of an established government, occupying power, or other political authority while increasing insurgent control").

106. David Kilcullen, *Counter-insurgency* Redux, SURVIVAL, Winter 2006–2007, at 111, 112.

107. FIELD MANUAL ¶ 1–3.

108. Kilcullen, Countering Global Insurgency, at 22–23, 26–27.

109. GALULA, COUNTERINSURGENCY WARFARE, at 7–8.

110. Id. at 11; KILCULLEN, THE ACCIDENTAL GUERRILLA, at 9.

111. FIELD MANUAL ¶ 1–75, ¶ 1–28; Kilcullen, *Counter-insurgency* Redux, at 119; Kilcullen, Countering Global Insurgency at 37. The word "grievance" is not used exclusively in this article to connote, as it sometimes does in political science, a grievance created by ethnic or religious difference or lack of political rights. See James D. Fearon and David D. Laitin, *Ethnicity, Insurgency, and Civil War*, 97 AM. POL. SCI. REV. 75, 75–76, 79 (2003). Neither counterinsurgents nor these political scientists focus solely on these grievances, though they recognize that such grievances can be produced by wars and can challenge peaceful resolution. Id. at 88.

112. FIELD MANUAL ¶ 1–9.

113. See generally, AHMAD NIZAR HAMZEH, IN THE PATH OF HIZBULLAH (2004). Insurgent groups frequently develop civil government and administrative capacity. See, e.g., Sandesh Sivakumaran, *Courts of Armed Opposition Groups: Fair Trials or Summary Justice?*, 7 J. INT'L CRIM. JUSTICE 489 (2009) (describing courts run by the Frente Farabundo Marti para la Liberacion Nacional (FMLN) in El Salvador and the Liberation Tigers of Tamil Eelam (LTTE) in Sri Lanka); ZACHARIAH MAMPILLY, REBEL RULERS: INSURGENT GOVERNANCE AND CIVILIAN LIFE DURING WAR (2011) (discussing governance structures and administrative programs of the LTTE and Sudan People's Liberation Movement/Army (SPLM/A)); GALULA, PACIFICATION IN ALGERIA, at 20, 45 (describing rebel organization in Algeria as having military, justice, and tax divisions, and as conducting dispute resolution in person in the villages); ELI BERMAN, RADICAL, RELIGIOUS, AND VIOLENT 16–18, 121–156 (2009) (describing groups that provide mutual aid, social services, and focusing on Hamas in particular); THOMAS RID AND MARC HECKER, WAR 2.0 144 (2009) (describing Hezbollah's service programs).

114. FIELD MANUAL ¶ 1–2.

115. Id. ¶ 1–4.

116. FIELD MANUAL at ¶ 1–14.

117. Id. at ¶ 1–128.

118. Id. at ¶¶ 3–84 to 3–88.

119. Id. at ¶ 1–128.

120. David W. Barno, *Fighting "The Other War": Counterinsurgency Strategy in Afghanistan, 2003–2005*, MIL. REV., September–October 2007, at 32, 34.

121. See Peter R. Mansoor and Mark S. Ulrich, *A New COIN Center-of-Gravity Analysis*, MIL. REV., September–October 2007, at 46–48.

122. Id. at 46.

123. David Kilcullen, *"Twenty-Eight Articles": Fundamentals of Company-Level Counterinsurgency*, MIL. REV., May–June 2006, at 103, 107.

124. See FIELD MANUAL at fig. 5–1.

125. See id. fig. 5–2; ¶¶ 5–36 to 5–41.

126. Id. ¶ 5–38.

127. Id. ¶¶ 5–38 to 5–39.

128. See id. fig. 5–4.

129. Peter W. Chiarelli and Patrick W. Michaelis, *Winning the Peace: The Requirement for Full-Spectrum Operations*, MIL. REV., July–August 2005, at 4, 9 fig. 3; see BING WEST, THE STRONGEST TRIBE: WAR, POLITICS, AND THE ENDGAME IN IRAQ 79 (2008).

130. Chiarelli and Michaelis, *Winning the Peace*, at 10–12.

131. FIELD MANUAL ¶ 5–45.

132. See id. ¶¶ 5–54 to 5–55, D-38.

133. Id. ¶ D-39.

134. Id. ¶ 5–48. Economic aid has been found to decrease violence in counterinsurgency in limited contexts. See Eli Berman, Jacob N. Shapiro and Joseph H. Felter, Can Hearts and Minds Be Bought? The Economics of Counterinsurgency in Iraq 37 (Nat'l Bureau Econ. Res., Working Paper No. 14606, 2008), available at http://www.nber.org/papers/w14606.

135. Field Manual ¶¶ 5–19, 5–28.

136. Id. tbl. 5–1.

137. Id.

138. Id. ¶ 5–19.

139. See Media Roundtable with Gen. David H. Petraeus, Commanding Gen., Multi-Nat'l Force Iraq, in Iraq (September 4, 2008), available at http://www.mnf-iraq.com/index.php?option=com_content&task=view&id=22229&Itemid=131.

140. Kilcullen, Countering Global Insurgency, at 15.

141. Id. at 20.

142. Id.

143. Id. at 27. An analogy to the human body may be helpful. The body has many internal systems—the cardiovascular system and the nervous system, for instance—and the person participates in a social system and an environmental ecosystem. Id. at 22.

144. Id. at 2.
145. Id. at 37.
146. Id. at 22, 37–40, 43–44.
147. FIELD MANUAL at ¶¶ 1-149–1-154.

CHAPTER 2

1. Stanley McChrystal, Commander, International Security Assistance Force, Tactical Directive, July 6, 2009, available at: http://www.nato.int/isaf/docu/official_texts/Tactical_Directive_090706.pdf.

2. JEAN-MARIE HENCKAERTS AND LOUISE DOSWALD-BECK, 1 CUSTOMARY INTERNATIONAL HUMANITARIAN LAW 3–8 (2005); see also Legality of the Threat or Use of Nuclear Weapons, Advisory Opinion, 1996 I.C.J. 226, 257 (July 8) [hereafter Nuclear Weapons Opinion] ("The first [principle constituting the fabric of humanitarian law] is aimed at the protection of the civilian population and civilian objects and establishes the distinction between combatants and non-combatants; States must never make civilians the object of attack and must consequently never use weapons that are incapable of distinguishing between civilian and military targets.").

3. Nuclear Weapons Opinion at 257; HELEN DUFFY, THE "WAR ON TERROR" AND THE FRAMEWORK OF INTERNATIONAL LAW 228–229 (2005); Gabriel Swiney, *Saving Lives: The Principle of Distinction and the Realities of Modern War*, 39 INT'L L. 733, 733 (2005).

4. L. C. GREEN, THE CONTEMPORARY LAW OF ARMED CONFLICT 103 (2d ed. 2000) (quoting EMMERICH DE VATTEL, 3 LE DROIT DES GENS §§ 9–10 [Charles G. Fenwick trans., 1916]).

5. Cf. Nathaniel Berman, *Privileging Combat? Contemporary Conflict and the Legal Construction of War*, 43 COLUM. J. TRANSNAT'L L. 1, 43 (2004) (describing how the possible justifications for granting POW status include protection of civilians and soldiers).

6. Protocol Additional to the Geneva Conventions of 12 August 1949, and Relating to the Protection of Victims of International Armed Conflicts (Protocol I) art. 48, June 8, 1977, 1125 U.N.T.S. 3 [hereafter Protocol I].

7. Hague Convention (IV) Respecting the Laws and Customs of War on Land, Annex art. 1, October 18, 1907, 36 Stat. 2277, 1 Bevans 631 [hereafter Hague IV Annex].

8. Geneva uses "fixed distinctive sign" instead of emblem. See Geneva Convention for the Amelioration of the Condition of the Wounded and Sick in Armed Forces in the Field, art. 13, August 12, 1949, 6 U.S.T. 3114, 75 U.N.T.S. 31 [hereafter GC I]; Geneva Convention for the Amelioration of the Condition of the Wounded, Sick, and Shipwrecked Members of Armed Forces at Sea, art. 13, August 12, 1949, 6 U.S.T. 3217, 75 U.N.T.S. 85 [hereafter GC II]; Geneva Convention Relative to the Treatment of Prisoners of War, art. 4, August 12, 1949, 6 U.S.T 3316, 75

U.N.T.S. 135 [hereafter GC III]; Geneva Convention Relative to the Protection of Civilian Persons in Time of War, art. 4, August 12, 1949, 6 U.S.T. 3516, 75 U.N.T.S. 287 [hereafter GC IV].

9. Protocol I at art. 44(3). This weaker approach does not change the general state practice of using uniforms to establish distinction. See id. at art. 44(7).

10. See Protocol I at art. 50. The provision defines civilians as any person not belonging to any of four categories: armed forces, persons meeting four criteria similar to those in the Hague Convention, unrecognized government armed forces, and participants in a *levée en masse*. See GC III at art. 4(A)(1), (2), (3), (6).

11. See, e.g., Rosa Ehrenreich Brooks, *War Everywhere: Rights, National Security Law, and the Law of Armed Conflict in the Age of Terror*, 153 U. Pa. L. Rev. 675, 729–736 (2004) (arguing that the war on terror blurs the line between civilian and combatant).

12. See Michael N. Schmitt, *Humanitarian Law and Direct Participation in Hostilities by Private Contractors or Civilian Employees*, 5 Chi. J. Int'l L. 511, 535–536 (2005) (describing the revolving door problem).

13. See ICTY, Final Report to the Prosecutor by the Committee Established to Review the NATO Bombing Campaign against the Federal Republic of Yugoslavia, 39 I.L.M. 1257, 1277 (2000).

14. Protocol I at art. 51(3) (emphasis added); Protocol Additional to the Geneva Conventions of 12 August 1949, and Relating to the Protection of Victims of Non-International Armed Conflicts (Protocol II) art. 13(3), June 8, 1977, 1125 U.N.T.S. 609 [hereafter Protocol II]. The "unless and for such time" language reveals the tension between status- and conduct-based forms of distinction. Under this provision, conduct matters; thus the revolving door combatant, fighting by day and a civilian by night, is protected at night because her conduct is civilian. See ICRC, Commentary on the Additional Protocols ¶ 1944 (Yves Sandoz, Christophe Swinarksi, and Bruno Zimmermann eds., 1987) [hereafter AP Commentary] ("Once he ceases to participate, the civilian regains his right to the protection"); id. ¶ 4789 ("as he no longer presents any danger for the adversary, he may not be attacked"). The discomfort with this approach comes from the idea that ongoing involvement, like conscription, gives a status of combatant that should not disappear when a person drops his weapon. See Schmitt, *Humanitarian Law*, at 535–536.

15. Protocol I at art. 52(2) (emphasis added).

16. Id. at art. 51(5) (defining as indiscriminate attacks whose humanitarian consequences are disproportionate to the military advantage gained) (emphasis added).

17. See AP Commentary at ¶ 1943 (finding hostilities includes "not only the time that the civilian actually makes use of a weapon, but also, for example, the time that he is carrying it, as well as situations in which he undertakes hostile acts without using a weapon"); see also Daphne Richemond, *Transnational Terrorist Organizations and the Use of Force*, 56 Cath. U. L. Rev. 1001, 1022 (2007).

18. See MICHAEL WALZER, JUST AND UNJUST WARS 146 (1977); James A. Burger, *International Humanitarian Law and the Kosovo Crisis: Lessons Learned or to Be Learned*, 82 INT'L REV. RED CROSS 129, 132 (2000), available at http://www.icrc. org/web/eng/siteengo.nsf/html/57JQCS; J. W. Crawford III, *The Law of Non-combatant Immunity and the Targeting of National Electrical Power Systems*, 21 FLETCHER F. WORLD AFF. 101, 101–102 (1997).

19. ICRC, Summary Report, Third Expert Meeting on the Notion of Direct Participation in Hostilities, Geneva, Switz., 22 (October 23–25, 2005), available at http://www.icrc.org/Web/eng/siteengo.nsf/htmlall/participation-hostilities-ihl-311205/$File/Direct_participation_in_hostilities_2005_eng.pdf.

20. See Jean-François Quéguiner, Direct Participation in Hostilities under International Humanitarian Law 2 (November 2003) (unpublished manuscript), available at http://www.ihlresearch.org/ihl/pdfs/briefing3297.pdf; ICRC, Summary Report, Third Expert Meeting on the Notion of Direct Participation in Hostilities, at 23. Of course, "military activity" does little to clarify the meaning of hostilities.

21. Marco Sassòli, *Targeting: The Scope and Utility of the Concept of "Military Objectives" for the Protection of Civilians in Contemporary Armed Conflict*, in NEW WARS, NEW LAWS?: APPLYING THE LAWS OF WAR IN 21ST CENTURY CONFLICTS 186 (David Wippman and Matthew Evangelista eds., 2005).

22. AP Commentary at ¶ 1679; see also id. at ¶ 4787 (direct participation in hostilities "implies that there is a sufficient causal relationship between the act of participation and its immediate consequences").

23. Id. at ¶ 1942.

24. Id. at ¶ 1945.

25. Nils Melzer, Interpretive Guidance on the Notion of Direct Participation in Hostilities under International Humanitarian Law 51, 53 (2009).

26. Id. at 54.

27. Michael N. Schmitt, *The Principle of Discrimination in 21st Century Warfare*, 2 YALE HUM. RTS. & DEV. L.J. 143, 149 (1999).

28. See W. Hays Parks, *Air War and the Law of War*, 32 A.F. L. REV. 1, 113–145 (1990).

29. See WALZER, JUST AND UNJUST WARS, at 146.

30. Richemond, *Transnational Terrorist Organizations and the Use of Force*, at 1022–1023.

31. ICTY, Final Report to the Prosecutor by the Committee Established to Review the NATO Bombing Campaign against the Federal Republic of Yugoslavia, at 1277.

32. Id.; Bankovic v. Belgium, No. 52207/99, ¶ 71 (Eur. Ct. H.R. December 12, 2001), available at http://cmiskp.echr.coe.int/tkp197/view.asp?item=1&portal=hbkm&action=html&source=tkp&highlight=bankovic&sessionid=28563015&skin=hudoc-en.

33. ICTY, Final Report to the Prosecutor by the Committee Established to Review the NATO Bombing Campaign against the Federal Republic of Yugoslavia, at 1278.

34. This is not to argue that militaries will want to, or should, attack such facilities. The strategic and legal analysis is more involved. The point here is that seemingly

"nonmilitary" objects play a crucial role in insurgencies, perhaps even greater than conventional military objects.

35. See ANDREW F. KREPINEVICH JR., THE ARMY AND VIETNAM 172 (1986).

36. Many understand "active" and "direct" to refer to the "same quality and degree of individual participation in hostilities," particularly since the French texts of the Geneva Conventions and the Additional Protocols use the same phrase, "participent directement." See Melzer, Interpretive Guidance, at 43. But there is disagreement. See Mark David "Max" Maxwell and Richard V. Meyer, *The Principle of Distinction: Probing the Limits of Customariness*, ARMY LAW., March 2007, at 1, 5; ICRC, Summary Report, Third Expert Meeting on the Notion of Direct Participation in Hostilities, at 29; see also Ryan Goodman, *The Detention of Civilians in Armed Conflict*, 103 AM. J. INT'L L. 48, 52 n. 18 (2009). As an interpretive matter, as discussed here, the distinction between "active" and "passive" may prove more practically effective than that between "direct" and "indirect."

37. See THE U.S. ARMY/MARINE CORPS COUNTERINSURGENCY FIELD MANUAL ¶¶ 3–84 to 3–88 (2007).

38. Id. at ¶ 3–87.

39. Id. at ¶ 3–88.

40. Id.

41. See Goodman, *The Detention of Civilians in Armed Conflict*, at 55–57.

42. Dale Stephens, *Counterinsurgency and Stability Operations: A New Approach to Legal Interpretation* in NAVAL WAR COLLEGE, 86 INT'L LAW STUD. 289, 301 (2010).

43. Schmitt, *The Principle of Discrimination in 21st Century Warfare*, at 150.

44. Protocol I at art. 51(5).

45. To be sure, the principle of distinction, because of the difficulty of applying it in practice, also requires discretion. See Maxwell and Meyer, *The Principle of Distinction*, at 5; see also 2 HENCKAERTS AND DOSWALD-BECK, CUSTOMARY INTERNATIONAL HUMANITARIAN LAW, at 121–122; W. Hays Parks, *Memorandum of Law: Executive Order 12333 and Assassination*, ARMY LAW., December 1989, at 4.

46. See Protocol I at art. 51(5); see also Schmitt, *The Principle of Discrimination in 21st Century Warfare*, at 151.

47. See Stanley McChrystal, ISAF Commander's Counterinsurgency Guidance 2 (August 26, 2009), available at http://www.nato.int/isaf/docu/official_texts/counterinsurgency_guidance.pdf.

48. Protocol I at art. 51(5).

49. See, e.g., Sarah Sewall, *Introduction* to FIELD MANUAL at xxv–xxvi; FIELD MANUAL at ¶ 1–141.

50. GC III at art. 99; see Protocol I at art. 45; see also Report on Terrorism and Human Rights, Inter-Am. C.H.R., OEA/Ser.L/V/II.116, doc 5 rev. 1 corr. ¶ 68 (2002) (noting that "the combatant's privilege . . . is in essence a license to kill or wound enemy combatants and destroy other military objectives").

51. GREEN, THE CONTEMPORARY LAW OF ARMED CONFLICT, at 185; Schmitt, *The Principle of Discrimination in 21st Century Warfare*, at 150–152.

52. 10 U.S.C. § 2734 (a) (2006).

53. Id. § 2374 (b).

54. U.S. Dep't of Army, Reg. 27–20, Claims, at 108 (February 8, 2008).

55. For example, solatia are paid through personal and operational appropriations rather than claims. See id. ¶ 10–11; id. at 108.

56. Id. ¶ 10–11; see also U.S. Dep't of Air Force, Instr. 51–501, Tort Claims ¶ 4.22 (December 15, 2005).

57. A condolence payment could be defined as "any monetary compensation made by the U.S. military directly to victims, or their survivors, who suffer physical injury, death, or property damage as a result of U.S. military or coalition operations." See Jonathan Tracy, Campaign for Innocent Victims in Conflict (CIVIC), Condolence Payments 1 (July 2006), available at http://www.civicworldwide.org/storage/civic/documents/condolence%20payments%20current.pdf.

58. See id. at 4, 10.

59. Int'l & Operational L. Dep't, Judge Advoc. Gen. Legal Ctr. & Sch., Operational Law Handbook 152 (2007) [hereafter Handbook].

60. Id.; see also John Fabian Witt, *Form and Substance in the Law of Counterinsurgency Damages*, 41 LOY. L.A. L. REV. 1455, 1469–1470 (2008).

61. Handbook at 152–153.

62. Gov't Accountability Off., The Defense Department's Use of Solatia and Condolence Payments in Iraq and Afghanistan, GAO-07-699, at 1 (May 2007) [hereafter GAO Report].

63. Ctr. for L. & Mil. Operations, Judge Advoc. Gen. Legal Ctr. & Sch., 1 Legal Lessons Learned from Afghanistan and Iraq 179 (2004) [hereafter CLAMO].

64. GAO Report at 2 n.3.

65. Id.

66. See Tracy, Condolence Payments at 6; see also id. at 7 (noting that CERP's goal is focusing "on labor intensive and urgent humanitarian relief and reconstruction projects" and directing that "[p]rojects should be implemented rapidly to reinforce a positive perception upon the Iraqi economy and by providing employment opportunities to the Iraqi people").

67. GAO Report at 20.

68. Id.

69. Tracy, Condolence Payments, at 6 n. 8.

70. See Witt, *Form and Substance in the Law of Counterinsurgency Damages*, at 1456; CLAMO at 175; CIVIC, Civilian Claims Act Frequently Asked Questions 2, http://www.campaign4compensation.org/FAQs.html (last visited August 20, 2009) [hereafter CIVIC, CCA].

71. See Witt, *Form and Substance in the Law of Counterinsurgency Damages*, at 1473–1475, 1477; CIVIC, CCA, at 2; CIVIC, Adding Insult to Injury: US Military Claims

System for Civilians 1–2, available at http://www.civicworldwide.org/storage/
civic/documents/civic%20military%20claims%20white%20paper.pdf [hereafter
CIVIC, Claims].

72. Tracy, Condolence Payments, at 6.

73. Id. at 5.

74. Id.

75. See G.A. Res. 60/147, ¶ 20, U.N. Doc. A/RES/60/147 (December 16, 2005); Protocol I at art. 91.

76. Jonathan Tracy, *Responsibility to Pay: Compensating Civilian Casualties of War*, HUM. RTS. BRIEF, Fall 2007, at 16, 16–17.

77. For a nuanced account of the relationship between technology and warfare, see MARTIN VAN CREVALD, TECHNOLOGY AND WAR (1989).

78. U.S. Dep't of Def. Directive 3000.3, at 3.1 (1996), available at http://www.dtic.mil/whs/directives/corres/pdf/300003p.pdf; see also Ingrid Lombardo, Chemical Non-Lethal Weapons—Why the Pentagon Wants Them and Why Others Don't, Center for Nonproliferation Studies, June 8, 2007, http://cns.miis.edu/stories/070608.htm (defining NLW as "a weapon or piece of equipment whose purpose is to affect the behavior of an individual without injuring or killing the person. NLW are also intended not to cause serious damage to property, infrastructure, or the environment"); Frédéric Mégret, Non-Lethal Weapons and the Possibility of Radical New Horizons for the Laws of War: Why Kill, Wound and Hurt (Combatants) at All? 8 (July 1, 2008) (unpublished manuscript), available at http://ssrn.com/abstract=1295348 (defining NLWs as weapons that "lay claim, in descending order of priority, to (i) not causing death, (ii) not causing injury, and (iii) not causing substantial pain").

79. See Joan M. Lakoski, W. Bosseau Murray, and John M. Kenny, The Advantages and Limitations of Calmatives for Use as a Non-Lethal Technique, Penn State Applied Research Laboratory 2 (October 3, 2000), available at http://www.sunshine-project.org/incapacitants/jnlwdpdf/psucalm.pdf; Lombardo, Chemical Non-Lethal Weapons.

80. See Douglas Pasternak, *Wonder Weapons*, U.S. NEWS & WORLD REP., July 7, 1997, at 38, 40–41. Other lists of nonlethal weapons are available in Nick Lewer, *Introduction* to THE FUTURE OF NON-LETHAL WEAPONS 2–4 (Nick Lewer ed., 2002); Brian Rappert, *Towards an Understanding of Non-Lethality*, in THE FUTURE OF NON-LETHAL WEAPONS, at 54.

81. David P. Fidler, *The International Legal Implications of "Non-Lethal" Weapons*, 21 MICH. J. INT'L L. 51, 55–57 (1999).

82. James C. Duncan, *A Primer on the Employment of Non-Lethal Weapons*, 45 NAVAL L. REV. 1, 14–21 (1998); Fidler, *International Legal Implications*, at 56.

83. On terminological problems, see Duncan, *Primer on the Employment*, at 5–6; see also Fed'n Am. Scientists Working Group on Biological Weapons, Non-Lethal Chemical and Biological Weapons 2 (November 2002) [hereafter FAS, Working

Group] ("[A] categorical distinction between lethal and non-lethal agents is not scientifically feasible."), available at http://www.fas.org/bwc/papers/nonlethal-CBW.pdf. On their design, see Fidler, *International Legal Implications*, at 55.

84. Convention on Prohibitions or Restrictions on the Use of Certain Conventional Weapons Which May Be Deemed to Be Excessively Injurious or to Have Indiscriminate Effects, Amended Protocol II, 35 I.L.M. 1206, art. 2 (1996).

85. Protocol for the Prohibition of the Use in War of Asphyxiating, Poisonous or Other Gases, and of Bacteriological Methods of Warfare, June 17, 1925, 26 U.S.T. 571, 94 L.N.T.S. 65.

86. Convention on the Prohibition of the Development, Production, Stockpiling and Use of Chemical Weapons and on Their Destruction art. 2, January 13, 1993, S. Treaty Doc. No. 103–121, 1974 U.N.T.S. 45 [hereafter CWC]. There is disagreement as to whether the CWC applies to antimateriel chemical weapons that might have the effect of death or incapacitation. Compare Fidler, *International Legal Implications*, at 72 (supporting this reading), with David A. Koplow, *Tangled Up in Khaki and Blue: Lethal and Non-Lethal Weapons in Recent Confrontations*, 36 GEO. J. INT'L L. 703, 738 (2005) (rejecting this reading).

87. By prohibiting riot control agents (RCA) in military operations, the CWC has enabled the United States to interpret the treaty as allowing the use of RCA in international operations other than war, such as peacekeeping operations, humanitarian and disaster relief, hostage rescue, and counterterrorist operations. See Fidler, *International Legal Implications*, at 74; Koplow, *Tangled up in Khaki and Blue*, at 739–740.

88. SIrUS stands for Superfluous Injury or Unnecessary Suffering. On the definition of the term, see Fidler, *International Legal Implications*, at 87; see also ICRC, The SIrUS Project: Towards A Determination of Which Weapons Cause "Superfluous Injury or Unnecessary Suffering" (Robin M. Coupland ed., 1997), http://www.loc.gov/rr/frd/Military_Law/pdf/SIrUS-project.pdf.

89. See Donna Marie Verchio, *Just Say No! The SIrUS Project: Well-Intentioned, but Unnecessary and Superfluous*, 51 A.F. L. REV. 183, 201–202, 204 (2001). For a critique of the SIrUS project's suggested criteria, see id. at 199–212.

90. FIELD MANUAL ¶ 1–150.

91. Lombardo, Chemical Non-Lethal Weapons.

92. See John B. Alexander, Nat'l Def. Indus. Ass'n, Putting Non-Lethal Weapons in Perspective 4 (March 2000), http://www.dtic.mil/ndia/nld4/alexander.pdf. Some even argue that NLWs should be mandatory in some circumstances. See Mégret, Non-Lethal Weapons and the Possible of Radical New Horizons for the Laws of War, at 5.

93. Jared Silberman, *Non-Lethal Weaponry and Non-Proliferation*, 19 NOTRE DAME J.L. ETHICS & PUB. POL'Y 347, 348 (2005).

94. See generally Ryan H. Whittemore, Air-Delivered Non-Lethal Weapons in Counterinsurgency Operations 4 (April 2008) (unpublished research report, available at https://

www.afresearch.org/skins/rims/q_mod_beoe99f3-fc56-4ccb-8dfe-670c0822a153/q_
act_downloadpaper/q_obj_722ffbd4-ac73-4b1c-808d-5980405fa19c/display.
aspx?rs=enginespage) (arguing that air power is seen as counterproductive in counterinsurgency because of its collateral damage and arguing that nonlethal weapons might
give air forces a greater role than merely advisory or monitoring).

95. Duncan, *Primer on the Employment*, at 56.

96. In addition to the perspectives presented here, some have indicated that opposition may be rooted in a "static technological perspective fixated on lethal force";
see David P. Fidler, *"Non-Lethal" Weapons and International Law*, in THE
FUTURE OF NON-LETHAL WEAPONS, at 26, 35, or as another commentator put
it, a "tendency to see conventional weapons as *defining* of war." See Mégret, Non-
Lethal Weapons and the Possibility of Radical New Horizons, at 11.

97. It is worth noting that many of the deaths were due to insufficient medical attention after the hostages were rescued. See Koplow, *Tangled Up in Khaki and Blue*,
at 769–781.

98. See Nat'l Inst. Just., U.S. Dep't Just., The Effectiveness and Safety of Pepper Spray
Research for Practice, No. 195739, at 1, 10–13 (April 2003).

99. FIELD MANUAL ¶ 1–152.

100. Robin Coupland, "Calmatives" and "Incapacitants"—Questions for International
Humanitarian Law Brought by New Means and Methods of Warfare with New
Effects, reprinted in The Open Forum on the Chemical Weapons Convention:
Challenges to the Chemical Weapons Ban 24 (May 1, 2003), http://www.sussex.
ac.uk/spru/hsp/publications; see also FAS, Working Group, at 3 (arguing that the
potential for abuse suggests prevention of weapons in the first place).

101. See Duncan, *Primer on the Employment*, at 11.

102. Brad Knickerbocker, Op-Ed., *The Fuzzy Ethics of Nonlethal Weapons*, CHRISTIAN
SCI. MONITOR, Feb. 14, 2003, at 2; Lombardo, Non-Lethal Chemical Weapons.

103. For example, cigarettes can be used as torture devices. Alexander, Putting Non-
Lethal Weapons in Perspective, at 3–4.

104. See id.; Duncan, *Primer on the Employment*, at 10; Fidler, *International Legal
Implications*, at 65.

105. See, e.g., Alexander, Putting Non-Lethal Weapons in Perspective, at 2 (criticizing
the fact that incineration is allowed but blinding is not).

106. See James D. Fry, *Contextualized Legal Reviews for the Methods and Means of
Warfare: Cave Combat and International Humanitarian Law*, 44 COLUM.
J. TRANSNAT'L L. 453, 490–518 (2006).

107. For an argument that nonlethal gas should be used in counterinsurgency operations depending on public opinion, see FRANK KITSON, LOW-INTENSITY OP-
ERATIONS 140 (1974).

108. See BENJAMIN WITTES, LAW AND THE LONG WAR 151–182 (2008); Jack L.
Goldsmith & Neal Katyal, Op-Ed., *The Terrorists' Court*, N.Y. TIMES, July 11,
2007, at A19.

109. RICHARD A. POSNER, NOT A SUICIDE PACT 64–65 (2006); Michael B. Mukasey, Op-Ed., *Jose Padilla Makes Bad Law*, WALL. ST. J., August 22, 2007, at A15.

110. See POSNER, NOT A SUICIDE PACT, at 92.

111. Gabor Rona, *Legal Frameworks to Combat Terrorism: An Abundant Inventory of Existing Tools*, 5 CHI. J. INT'L L. 499, 502 (2005); Kenneth Roth, *After Guantánamo: The Case against Preventive Detention*, 87 FOREIGN AFF., May/June 2008, at 9, 12.

112. Jack M. Beard, *The Geneva Boomerang: The Military Commissions Act of 2006 and U.S. Counterterror Operations*, 101 AM. J. INT'L L. 56, 56–57 (2007); Jennifer Daskal, *How to Close Guantanamo*, WORLD POL'Y J., Fall 2007, at 29, 30–32; Deborah H. Pearlstein, *We're All Experts Now: A Security Case against Security Detention*, 40 CASE W. RES. J. INT'L L. 577, 577–580 (2008) (arguing that even if valid under U.S. and international law, preventive detention schemes are counterproductive).

113. John B. Bellinger, III, Legal Advisor, U.S. Dep't of State, Legal Issues in the War on Terrorism, Speech (October 31, 2006), available at http://www.state.gov/s/l/2006/98861.htm.

114. Matthew C. Waxman, Administrative Detention: The Integration of Strategy and Legal Process 27, 10–12 (Brookings Inst., Counterterrorism and American Statutory Law Series No. 2, 2008), http://www.brookings.edu/~/media/Files/rc/papers/2008/0724_detention_waxman/0724_detention_waxman.pdf.

115. Robert Chesney & Jack Goldsmith, *Terrorism and the Convergence of Criminal and Military Detention Models*, 60 STAN. L. REV. 1079, 1080–1081 (2008).

116. Id. at 1126.

117. Id. at 1127–1131.

118. See Daniel Kahneman, Jack L. Knetsch, & Richard H. Thaler, *The Endowment Effect, Loss Aversion, and Status Quo Bias*, J. ECON. PERSP., Winter 1991, at 193, 194 (1991); William Samuelson & Richard Zeckhauser, *Status Quo Bias in Decision Making*, 1 J. RISK & UNCERTAINTY 7 (1988).

119. See Waxman, Administrative Detention, at 5–6.

120. For a discussion of the detention regime in Iraq, see Robert M. Chesney, *Iraq and the Military Detention Debate: Firsthand perspectives from the Other War*, 2003–2010, 51 VA. J. INT'L L. 549 (2011).

121. See Al Maqaleh v. Gates, 620 F. Supp. 2d 51, 53 (D.D.C. 2009).

122. David Kilcullen, Countering Global Insurgency 43 (November 30, 2004), http://smallwarsjournal.com/documents/kilcullen.pdf [hereafter Kilcullen, Countering Global Insurgency].

123. Id. at 37.

124. Along these lines, it could follow the existing approach in the laws of war that allows for the detention of those who are a threat to security but are not direct participants in hostilities. See Goodman, *Detention of Civilians in Armed Conflict*, at 53.

125. Convention against Torture and Other Cruel, Inhuman or Degrading Treatment or Punishment art. 3, December 10, 1984, S. Treaty Doc. No. 100–120 (1988), 1465 U.N.T.S. 85.

126. Abram Chayes & Antonia Handler Chayes, The New Sovereignty: Compliance with International Regulatory Agreements 3 (1995).

127. See generally Anne-Marie Slaughter, A New World Order (2004) (describing transnational networks of officials).

128. Waxman, Administrative Detention, at 11.

129. Id. at 16.

130. Id. at 17–18.

131. Id. at 18.

132. Id. at 17.

133. Id. at 18–19, 21.

134. See Matthew C. Waxman, *Detention as Targeting: Standards of Certainty and Detention of Suspected Terrorists*, 108 Colum. L. Rev. 1365, 1387–1388, 1391–1393 (2008).

135. See Andrew K. Woods, *The Business End*, Fin. Times Mag. (London), June 27, 2008, available at http://www.ft.com/cms/s/2/71c42ec0-40ca-11dd-bd48-0000779fd2ac.html.

136. See Chesney & Goldsmith, *Terrorism and the Convergence of Criminal and Military Detention Models*, at 1088–1089.

137. Cf. Anne-Marie Slaughter & William Burke-White, *The Future of International Law Is Domestic (or, The European Way of Law)*, 47 Harv. Int'l L.J. 327, 339 (2006).

138. Id. at 340.

139. See, e.g., Eyal Benvenisti, International Law of Occupation 182 (1993) (noting that governments have sought to avoid the distinction of occupant, except for Israel with respect to territories occupied during the 1967 war). For a helpful typology of occupations, see Adam Roberts, *What Is a Military Occupation?*, 1984 Brit. Y.B. Int'l L. 249 (1985).

140. Hague IV Annex at art. 42.

141. Int'l Humanitarian L. Res. Initiative [IHLRI], Application of IHL and the Maintenance of Law and Order, 2 Military Occupation of Iraq 2 (April 14, 2003), available at http://www.ihlresearch.org/iraq/pdfs/briefing3423.pdf [hereafter IHLRI, Application of IHL]. Once status as an occupant is triggered, the occupant must follow the law of occupation, which includes articles 42–56 of the 1907 Hague Regulations and articles 47–78 of the Fourth Geneva Convention.

142. See, e.g., Adam Roberts, *Transformative Military Occupation: Applying the Laws of War and Human Rights*, 100 Am. J. Int'l L. 580, 580 (2006).

143. Benvenisti, International Law of Occupation, at 27.

144. See id.; see also Eyal Benvenisti, *The Security Council and the Law on Occupation: Resolution 1483 on Iraq in Historical Perspective*, 1 IDF L. Rev. 19, 20 (2003).

145. See Gregory H. Fox, *The Occupation of Iraq*, 36 Geo. J. Int'l L. 195, 199 (2005) ("Occupiers are assumed to remain only for the limited period between the cessation of hostilities and the conclusion of a final peace treaty. That treaty determines the fate of the occupied territory, most likely returning it to the ousted de jure sovereign").

146. CARSTEN STAHN, THE LAW AND PRACTICE OF INTERNATIONAL TERRITORIAL ADMINISTRATION 115–116 (2008).

147. See id. at 119–120.

148. Paul Bowers, Int'l Aff. & Def. Sec., Iraq: Law of Occupation, 2003, H.C. 03/51, at 18.

149. See STAHN, THE LAW AND PRACTICE OF INTERNATIONAL TERRITORIAL ADMINISTRATION, at 120; Fox, *The Occupation of Iraq*, at 199; Thomas D. Grant, Iraq: How to Reconcile Conflicting Obligations of Occupation and Reform, ASIL Insights, June 2003, at 3, available at http://www.asil.org/insigh107a1.cfm; Yoram Dinstein, Legislation under Article 43 of the Hague Regulations: Belligerent Occupation and Peacebuilding 10 (Program on Humanitarian Pol'y & Conflict Res., Occasional Paper Series, Fall 2004).

150. See OSCAR M. UHLER ET AL., ICRC, COMMENTARY, IV GENEVA CONVENTION RELATIVE TO THE PROTECTION OF CIVILIAN PERSONS IN TIME OF WAR 273 (Jean S. Pictet, ed.) (1958) [hereafter Geneva IV Commentary]; IHLRI, International Assistance in Occupied Territory, 2 Military Occupation of Iraq 2 (April 22, 2003), http://www.ihlresearch.org/iraq/pdfs/briefing3424.pdf [hereafter IHLRI, International Assistance].

151. Geneva IV Commentary at 273; IHLRI, International Assistance, at 2.

152. Hague IV Annex at art. 43 (emphasis added).

153. BENVENISTI, INTERNATIONAL LAW OF OCCUPATION, at 13–14.

154. Hague IV Annex at art. 48.

155. Id. at art. 49.

156. GC IV at arts. 27, 49, 51.

157. BENVENISTI, INTERNATIONAL LAW OF OCCUPATION, at 28–31; see also STAHN, THE LAW AND PRACTICE OF INTERNATIONAL TERRITORIAL ADMINISTRATION, at 117–118.

158. GC IV at art. 47.

159. Geneva IV Commentary at 273.

160. Id. at 274; GC IV at art. 64 ("The Occupying Power may, however, subject the population of the occupied territory to provisions which are essential to enable the Occupying Power to fulfill its obligations under the present Convention. . . . ").

161. Hague IV Annex at art. 44, 45, 47; GC IV at art. 51, 33.

162. Hague IV Annex at art. 46; GC IV at art. 27.

163. GC IV at art. 55, 56, 58.

164. See, e.g., Charter of Economic Rights and Duties of States, G.A. Res. 3281 (XXIX), art. 16(1), U.N. GAOR, 29th Sess., Supp. No. 31, U.N. Doc. A/Res/3281 (December 12, 1974); G.A. Res. 3171 (XXVIII), at 52, U.N. GAOR, 28th Sess., U.N. Doc. A/9400 (December 17, 1973); Declaration on Principles of International Law concerning Friendly Relations and Co-Operation among States in Accordance with the Charter of the United Nations, G.A. Res. 2625 (XXV), at 123–124, U.N. GAOR,

25th Sess., Supp. No. 16, UN Doc. A/8028 (October 24, 1970); see also BENVENISTI, INTERNATIONAL LAW OF OCCUPATION, at 184–187.

165. STAHN, THE LAW AND PRACTICE OF INTERNATIONAL TERRITORIAL ADMINISTRATION, at 143.

166. See S.C. Res. 1483, U.N. SCOR, 58th Sess., 4761st mtg. at 2, U.N. Doc. S/RES/1483 (May 22, 2003); see STAHN, THE LAW AND PRACTICE OF INTERNATIONAL TERRITORIAL ADMINISTRATION, at 144.

167. S.C. Res. 1483 at 2 (emphasis added).

168. Id. (emphasis added).

169. Id.

170. See Dinstein, Legislation under Article 43 of the Hague Regulations, at 1.

171. See Melissa Patterson, *Who's Got the Title? or, The Remnants of Debellatio in Post-Invasion Iraq*, 47 HARV. INT'L L.J. 467, 467–468 (2006).

172. See Grant, Iraq: How to Reconcile Conflicting Obligations of Occupation and Reform, at 4; Marten Zwanenberg, *Existentialism in Iraq: Security Council Resolution 1483 and the Law of Occupation*, 86 INT'L REV. RED CROSS 745, 763 (2004), available at http://www.icrc.org/Web/eng/siteengo.nsf/htmlall/692EHY/$File/irrc_856_Zwanenburg.pdf.

173. BENVENISTI, INTERNATIONAL LAW OF OCCUPATION, at 29–30.

174. Professor Eric Posner's hypothesis—that occupation law is often violated because of enforcement difficulties grounded in the absence of reciprocity between the parties—makes sense in the context of a defeated power in conventional warfare. See Eric A. Posner, *Terrorism and the Laws of War*, 5 CHI. J. INT'L L. 423, 430 (2005).

175. IHLRI, Application of IHL, at 2–3.

176. Id. at 3.

177. DAVID KILCULLEN, THE ACCIDENTAL GUERRILLA: FIGHTING SMALL WARS IN THE MIDST OF A BIG ONE 108 (2009).

178. For discussion of the various potential sources of legitimacy for the CPA's reforms, see Fox, *The Occupation of Iraq*, at 246–247. For a skeptical account of CPA's actions, see David Scheffer, *Beyond Occupation Law*, 97 AM. J. INT'L L. 842 (2003). For a critique of CPA's actions, see Ctr. for Econ. & Soc. Rts., Beyond Torture: U.S. Violations of Occupation Law in Iraq (2004), available at http://www.cesr.org/downloads/Beyond%20Torture%20US%20Violations%20of%20Occupation%20Law%20in%20Iraq.pdf.

179. FIELD MANUAL at ¶ 1–154.

180. Ruth Wedgwood, Op-Ed, *The Rules of War Can't Protect Al Qaeda*, N.Y. TIMES, Dec. 31, 2001, at A11.

181. John Yoo, Editorial, *Terrorists Have No Geneva Rights*, WALL ST. J., May 26, 2004, at A16.

182. Posner, *Terrorism and the Laws of War*, at 427–430; see also Dan Belz, *Is International Humanitarian Law Lapsing into Irrelevance in the War on International*

*Terror?*, 7 THEORETICAL INQUIRIES L. 97, 117 (2006) (noting that "[u]tilitarian laws will only be found where the reciprocity element is still present, inducing both sides to decrease their aggregate costs").

183. Eric Posner, Editorial, *Apply the Golden Rule to al Qaeda?*, WALL ST. J., July 15–16, 2006, at A9.

184. On combatant's privilege, see Allen S. Weiner, Hamdan, *Terror, War*, 11 LEWIS & CLARK L. REV. 997, 1007 (2007). On the degradation of the laws, see Mark Weisburd, *Al-Qaeda and the Law of War*, 11 LEWIS & CLARK L. REV. 1063, 1086 (2007). On the unsustainability of law, see Kenneth Anderson, *Who Owns the Rules of War?*, N.Y. TIMES MAG., April 13, 2003, at 38, 43.

185. Eyal Benvenisti, *The Legal Battle to Define the Law on Transnational Asymmetric Warfare*, 20 DUKE J. COMP. & INT'L L. 339, 340 (2010).

186. Bruno Simma, *Reciprocity*, in 4 ENCYCLOPEDIA OF PUBLIC INTERNATIONAL LAW 29, 30 (Rudolf Bernhardt ed., 1992).

187. Dan Belz, *Is International Humanitarian Law Lapsing into Irrelevance*, at 98; Robert O. Keohane, *Reciprocity in International Relations*, 40 INT'L ORG. 1, 1 (1986).

188. Keohane, *Reciprocity in International Relations*, at 1; Francesco Parisi & Nita Ghei, *The Role of Reciprocity in International Law*, 36 CORNELL INT'L L.J. 93, 93–94 (2003); Simma, *Reciprocity*, at 29–30. In a centralized system, the central authority can impose and enforce norms; in a decentralized system, reciprocity plays a much larger role. See RENÉ PROVOST, INTERNATIONAL HUMAN RIGHTS AND HUMANITARIAN LAW 123 (2005).

189. In game theory, this is known as a prisoner's dilemma problem. ROBERT AXELROD, THE EVOLUTION OF COOPERATION (1984); Keohane, *Reciprocity in International Relations*, at 8–9.

190. Richemond, *Transnational Terrorist Organizations and the Use of Force*, at 1026.

191. See Keohane, *Reciprocity in International Relations*, at 4; Michael D. Gottesman, *Reciprocity and War: A New Understanding of Reciprocity's Role in Geneva Convention Obligations*, 14 U.C. DAVIS J. INT'L L. & POL'Y 147, 152, 170 n. 97 (2008).

192. Most commentators on asymmetry and the laws of war suggest that asymmetry will lead to greater violations on both sides and to undermining IHL itself. See, e.g., Stefan Oeter, Comment, *Is the Principle of Distinction Outdated?*, in INTERNATIONAL HUMANITARIAN LAW FACING NEW CHALLENGES 53, 56–59 (Wolff Heintschel von Heinegg & Volker Epping eds., 2007); Michael N. Schmitt, *Asymmetrical Warfare and International Humanitarian Law*, in INTERNATIONAL HUMANITARIAN LAW FACING NEW CHALLENGES 11, 47.

193. See, e.g., PROVOST, INTERNATIONAL HUMAN RIGHTS AND HUMANITARIAN LAW, at 136 (discussing the tension between humanity and military efficacy).

194. I take this term from Michael Signer, *City on a Hill*, DEMOCRACY, Summer 2006, at 33, 34. Signer applies the term to foreign policy, not law. Robert Sloane has recently argued for a unilateral or voluntarist war convention to bind states. Terrorists,

he notes, do not share human rights norms, and reciprocity fails because they are structured in networks not hierarchies. Sloane, *Prologue to a Voluntarist War Convention*, at 477–478. However similar his conclusions, his paradigm remains fixed on the war on terror, and he roots the failure of reciprocity in different sources from this insurgency-based analysis. Sloane focuses on the networked structure of terrorists; I confront directly the strategic foundations of reciprocity: equivalence, cost-reduction, and the benefits of defection.

195. See MARK OSIEL, THE END OF RECIPROCITY: TERROR, TORTURE, AND THE LAW OF WAR 329–390 (2009).

196. This is distinct from what Eric Posner and Jack Goldsmith call coincidence of interest, "a behavioral regularity among states [that] occurs simply because each state obtains private advantage from a particular action (which happens to be the same action taken by the other state) irrespective of the action of the other." JACK L. GOLDSMITH & ERIC A. POSNER, THE LIMITS OF INTERNATIONAL LAW 27–28 (2005). Goldsmith and Posner argue that if coincidence of interest drives state compliance regardless of the other state's action, there would be no need for codification of international law. Id. Agreements driven by coincidence of interest thus must have a "thin" cooperative element. Id. at 88–89. Counter-insurgency's exemplarist groundwork offers no opportunity for even thin cooperation because insurgents will not cooperate. But that does not mean there is no reason to codify agreements in situations driven by purely unilateral self-interest.

197. See NEFF, WAR AND THE LAW OF NATIONS, at 74.

198. PROVOST, INTERNATIONAL HUMAN RIGHTS AND HUMANITARIAN LAW, at 131.

199. Id.; see also W. Michael Reisman & William K. Leitzau, *Moving International Law from Theory to Practice: The Role of Military Manuals in Effectuating the Law of Armed Conflict*, in THE LAW OF NAVAL OPERATIONS 1 (U.S. Naval War C., International Law Studies Series No. 64, Horace B. Robertson, Jr. ed., 1991).

200. Protocol I at art. 54.

201. See René Provost, *Starvation as a Weapon: Legal Implications of the United Nations Food Blockade against Iraq and Kuwait*, 30 COLUM. J. TRANSNAT'L L. 577, 605 (1992).

202. See Gottesman, *Reciprocity and War*, at 181–182.

203. See Charles J. Dunlap Jr., Law and Military Interventions: Preserving Humanitarian Values in 21st Century Conflicts 4, Carr Ctr. For Hum. Rts. Pol'y (2001) (unpublished manuscript), available at http://www.hks.harvard.edu/cchrp/Web%20Working%20Papers/Use%20of%20Force/Dunlap2001.pdf (describing "lawfare").

204. PROVOST, INTERNATIONAL HUMAN RIGHTS AND HUMANITARIAN LAW, at 161.

205. Protocol II at art. 1.1.

206. See PROVOST, INTERNATIONAL HUMAN RIGHTS AND HUMANITARIAN LAW, at 161.

207. See, e.g., Douglas J. Feith, *Law in the Service of Terror—The Strange Case of the Additional Protocol*, NAT'L INT., Fall 1985, at 36, 42–45.

208. See PHILLIP BOBBITT, TERROR AND CONSENT 130 (2008).

209. See id.

210. JON ELSTER, ULYSSES AND THE SIRENS (1985); JON ELSTER, ULYSSES UNBOUND (2000).

211. JANE MAYER, THE DARK SIDE: THE INSIDE STORY OF HOW THE WAR ON TERROR TURNED INTO A WAR ON AMERICAN IDEALS 327 (2009).

212. See Chesney, Iraq and the Military Detention Debate.

213. See DAVID ARMITAGE, THE DECLARATION OF INDEPENDENCE: A GLOBAL HISTORY (2007).

214. See, e.g., Ryan Goodman & Derek Jinks, *International Law and State Socialization: Conceptual, Empirical, and Normative Challenges*, 54 DUKE L.J. 983 (2005); Ryan Goodman & Derek Jinks, *How to Influence States: Socialization and International Human Rights Law*, 54 DUKE L.J. 621 (2004).

215. See, e.g., Hersh Lauterpacht, *Recognition of Insurgents as a De Facto Government*, 3 MOD. L. REV. 1, 1–2 (1939); Lester Nurick & Roger W. Barrett, *Legality of Guerrilla Forces under the Laws of War*, 40 AM. J. INT'L L. 563, 563 (1946); George Grafton Wilson, *Insurgency and International Maritime Law*, 1 AM. J. INT'L L. 46 (1907); see also NEFF, WAR AND THE LAW OF NATIONS, at 268–273.

216. Cf. Gabriella Blum, On a Differential Law of War 52 HARV. INT'L L.J. 163 (2011).

217. Roy S. Schöndorf, *Extra-State Armed Conflicts: Is There a Need for a New Legal Regime?*, 37 N.Y.U. J. INT'L L. & POL. 1, 3–6 (2004); Sloane, *Prologue to a Voluntarist War Convention*; Geoffrey S. Corn & Eric T. Jensen, Transnational Armed Conflict: A "Principled" Approach to the Regulation of Counter-Terror Combat Operations (forthcoming *Israel L. Rev.*), available at http://papers.ssrn.com/sol3/papers.cfm?abstract_id=1256380.

218. On Hezbollah, see AHMAD NIZAR HAMZEH, IN THE PATH OF HIZBULLAH (2004). On the Tamil Tigers, see ZACHARIAH MAMPILLY, REBEL RULERS: INSURGENT GOVERNANCE AND CIVILIAN LIFE DURING WAR (2011); see also Sandesh Sivakumaran, *Courts of Armed Opposition Groups: Fair Trials or Summary Justice?*, 7 J. INT'L CRIM. JUSTICE 489, 494 (2009). On the Taliban, see Issam Ahmed, *New Taliban Code: Don't Kill Civilians, Don't Take Ransom*, C.S. MONITOR, July 31, 2009, available at http://www.csmonitor.com/World/Asia-South-Central/2009/0731/p06s19-wosc.html (describing the 60-page Taliban Code of Conduct, titled "The Islamic Emirate of Afghanistan's Rules for Mujahideen"); but see Thomas Jocelyn & Bill Roggio, *Mullah Omar Orders Taliban to Attack Civilians, Afghan Women*, Long War Journal, July 28, 2010, available at http://www.longwarjournal.org/archives/2010/07/mullah_omar_orders_t.php. Of course, the Taliban also issued these directives as propaganda.

219. For a magisterial tract that takes this nexus seriously, see PHILLIP BOBBITT, THE SHIELD OF ACHILLES: WAR, PEACE, AND THE COURSE OF HISTORY (2002). For

a practical illustration, see Kelly D. Wheaton, *Strategic Lawyering: Realizing the Potential of Military Lawyers at the Strategic Level*, ARMY LAW., September 2006, at 1.

220. BOBBITT, SHIELD OF ACHILLES, at 5.

221. ARTHUR EYFFINGER, THE 1899 HAGUE PEACE CONFERENCE 204, 230, 232 (1999).

222. BOBBITT, SHIELD OF ACHILLES, at 6.

223. See WALZER, JUST AND UNJUST WARS, at 24–25 ("What is war and what is not-war is in fact something that people decide. . . . As both anthropological and historical accounts suggest, they can decide, and in a considerable variety of cultural settings they have decided, that war is limited war—that is, they have built certain notions about who can fight, what tactics are acceptable, when battle has to be broken off, and what prerogatives go with victory into the idea of war itself").

224. BOBBITT, TERROR AND CONSENT, at 437–438.

225. See, e.g., YORAM DINSTEIN, THE CONDUCT OF HOSTILITIES UNDER THE LAW OF INTERNATIONAL ARMED CONFLICT 1–2 (2006) ("Should nothing be theoretically permissible to a belligerent engaged in war, ultimately everything will be permitted in practice—because the rules will be ignored."); AP Commentary at ¶ 1390 ("[W]ithout these concessions, *which take reality into account*, it would never have been possible to arrive at such detailed texts and at provisions which were so favourable to the victims of war.") (emphasis added).

226. As Phillip Bobbitt notes, "[w]ithout legal reform . . . we are in the paradoxical position of putting ourselves at a potentially fatal disadvantage: if we adhere to law as it stands, we disable effective action against terror; if we act lawlessly, we throw away the gains of effective action." BOBBITT, TERROR AND CONSENT, at 395–396.

CHAPTER 3

1. See STEPHEN C. NEFF, WAR AND THE LAW OF NATIONS 102 (2005).

2. The Latin text appears as *inter bellum et pacem nihil est medium*. See GROTIUS, IUS BELLUM ET PACIS, Bk III, Ch XXI, I; CICERO, PHILIPPICA VII.

3. NEFF, WAR AND THE LAW OF NATIONS, at 178.

4. Janson v. Dreifontein Consolidated Mines Ltd. L.R. [1902] A.C. 484; see also Phillip C. Jessup, *Should International Law Recognize an Intermediate Status between Peace and War?*, 48 AM. J. INT'L L. 98 (1954). At least one commentator suggests this statement should be read as something like a clear-statement rule grounded in separation of powers concerns, to ensure the judiciary has clarity as to when municipal law does not apply. See Georg Schwarzenberger, *Ius Pacis ac Belli*, 37 AM. J. INT'L L. 460, 468 (1943).

5. NEFF, WAR AND THE LAW OF NATIONS, at 179.

6. Id. at 194.

7. WILLIAM EDWARD HALL, A TREATISE ON INTERNATIONAL LAW 941, A. Pearce Higgins, ed., (8th ed. 1924); see Schwarzenberger, *Ius Pacis ac Belli*, at 472.

8. U.N. Charter, Art. 2(4).

9. See Military and Paramilitary Activities (Nicaragua v. U.S.), 1986 I.C.J. 14, paras. 92–116 (June 27); cf. Legality of the Threat or Use of Nuclear Weapons, Advisory Opinion, 1996 I.C.J. 226, para. 46 (July 8) (noting that armed reprisals in times of peace are unlawful). See also NEFF, WAR AND THE LAW OF NATIONS, at 318, 362.

10. See Geneva Convention for the Amelioration of the Condition of the Wounded and Sick in Armed Forces in the Field, arts. 2, 3, August 12, 1949, 6 U.S.T. 3114, 75 U.N.T.S. 31 [hereafter GC I]; Geneva Convention for the Amelioration of the Condition of the Wounded, Sick, and Shipwrecked Members of Armed Forces at Sea, arts. 2, 3, August 12, 1949, 6 U.S.T. 3217, 75 U.N.T.S. 85 [hereafter GC II]; Geneva Convention Relative to the Treatment of Prisoners of War, arts. 2, 3, August 12, 1949, 6 U.S.T 3316, 75 U.N.T.S. 135 [hereafter GC III]; Geneva Convention Relative to the Protection of Civilian Persons in Time of War, arts. 2, 3, August 12, 1949, 6 U.S.T. 3516, 75 U.N.T.S. 287 [hereafter GC IV].

11. ICRC, COMMENTARY, III GENEVA CONVENTION RELATIVE TO THE TREATMENT OF PRISONERS OF WAR art. 3, at 36, available at http://www.icrc.org/ihl. nsf/COM/375-590006?OpenDocument.

12. Protocol Additional to the Geneva Conventions of August 12, 1949, and Relating to the Protection of Victims of Non-International Armed Conflicts (Protocol II) art. 1.1, June 8, 1977, 1125 U.N.T.S. 609 [hereafter Protocol II].

13. Id. at art. 1.2.

14. Jessup, *Should International Law Recognize an Intermediate Status*, at 100.

15. See, e.g., FRITZ GROB, THE RELATIVITY OF WAR AND PEACE (1949).

16. Schwarzenberger, *Ius Pacis ac Belli*, at 479.

17. Myres S. McDougal, *Peace and War: Factual Continuum with Multiple Legal Consequences*, 49 AM. J. INT'L. L. 63 (1955).

18. W. Michael Reisman, *International Law after the Cold War*, 84 AM. J. INT'L L. 859, 861 (1990).

19. Joint Chiefs of Staff, Joint Pub. 3–07.3, Joint Tactics, Techniques, and Procedures for Peacekeeping Operations, A-1 (1994).

20. Susan L. Turley, *Note: Keeping the Peace, Do the Laws of War Apply?*, 73 TEX. L. REV. 139, 140 (1994).

21. Id. at 140, 154.

22. See Peter J. Spiro, *War Powers and the Sirens of Formalism*, 68 N.Y.U. L. REV. 1338, 1354 (1993) (noting the difficulty of humanitarian and peacekeeping operations for war powers determinations); Jane E. Stromseth, *Understanding Constitutional War Powers Today: Why Methodology Matters*, 106 YALE L.J. 845, 887 (1996) (noting that it is difficult to translate the Founders' views on war powers to peace enforcement and peacekeeping operations).

23. On covert actions, see Jules Lobel, *Covert War and Congressional Authority: Hidden War and Forgotten Power*, 134 U. PA. L. REV. 1035 (1986). On the distinctness of peace enforcement and peacekeeping operations, see Jane E. Stromseth,

*Rethinking War Powers: Congress, the President, and the United Nations*, 81 GEO. L.J. 597, 670 (1993); see also Jane E. Stromseth, *Collective Force and Constitutional Responsibility: War Powers in the Post–Cold War Era*, 50 U. MIAMI L. REV. 145, 162–166 (1995).

24. Christopher Coleman, in Kate Greene, *International Responses to Secessionist Conflicts*, 90 PROC. AM. SOC'Y INT'L L. 296, 308–309 (1996).

25. See, e.g., Ronald J. Sievert, *War on Terrorism or Global Law Enforcement?*, 78 NOTRE DAME L. REV. 307 (2003); RICHARD A. POSNER, NOT A SUICIDE PACT 5 (2006); Rosa Ehrenreich Brooks, *War Everywhere: Rights, National Security Law, and the Law of Armed Conflict in the Age of Terror*, 153 U. PA. L. REV. 675 (2004); Monica Hakimi, *International Standards for Detaining Terrorism Suspects: Moving beyond the Armed Conflict–Criminal Divide*, 33 YALE J. INT'L L. 369 (2008).

26. Noah Feldman, *Choices of Law, Choices of War*, 25 HARV. J. L. & PUB. POL'Y 457 (2002).

27. See Roy S. Schöndorf, *Extra-State Armed Conflicts: Is There a Need for a New Legal Regime?*, 37 N.Y.U. J. INT'L L. & POL. 1 (2004); Geoffrey S. Corn, *Hamdan, Lebanon, and the Regulation of Hostilities: The Need to Recognize a Hybrid Category of Armed Conflict*, 40 VAND. J. TRANSNAT'L L. 295, 296 (2007); Kathryn L. Einspanier, *Note: Burlamaqui, The Constitution, and the Imperfect War on Terror*, 96 GEO. L.J. 985 (2008).

28. Carsten Stahn, *Jus Post Bellum: Mapping the Discipline(s)*, 23 AM. U. INT'L L. REV. 311, 316, 327 (2008). See also CARSTEN STAHN & JANN K. KLEFFNER, EDS., JUS POST BELLUM: TOWARDS A LAW OF TRANSITION FROM CONFLICT TO PEACE (2008).

29. Brian Orend, *War*, STANFORD ENCYCLOPEDIA OF PHILOSOPHY, July 28, 2005, available at http://plato.stanford.edu/entries/war/#2.3; see also Stahn, *Jus Post Bellum: Mapping the Discipline*, at 322.

30. Stahn, *Jus Post Bellum: Mapping the Discipline*, at 334.

31. See Roger Cohen, *In Balkans: Power Shift*, N.Y. TIMES, Aug. 18, 1995 (noting talk of a "mini-Marshall plan"); James Bennet, *On Eve of African Relief Talks, Aid Donors Argue over Numbers*, N.Y. TIMES, Nov. 22, 1996 (mentioning desire for a multilateral Marshall-type of plan); David Firestone, *Bremer Cites Marshall Plan in Bid for Iraqi Aid*, N.Y. TIMES, Sept. 23, 2003; Editorial, *Afghanistan's Marshall Plan*, N.Y. TIMES, Apr. 19, 2002; NORBERT EHRENFREUND, THE NUREMBERG LEGACY (2007).

32. Despite the relatively decisive victory in World War II, when the Allied Forces moved into Germany in the later stages of the war, they worried about Nazi guerrilla operations. For a discussion of the Nazi's plans for guerrilla warfare and the Allied response, see PERRY BIDDISCOMBE, WERWOLF! THE HISTORY OF THE NATIONAL SOCIALIST GUERRILLA MOVEMENT 1944–1946 (1998).

33. See, e.g., Richard Sannerholm, *Legal, Judicial and Administrative Reforms in Post-Conflict Societies: Beyond the Rule of Law Template*, 12 J. CONFLICT & SECURITY L. 65 (2007).

34. See Sannerholm, *Legal, Judicial and Administrative Reforms in Post-Conflict Societies*, at 65 (emphasis added).

35. Jane E. Stromseth, *Post-Conflict Rule of Law Building: The Need for a Multi-Layered, Synergistic Approach*, 49 WM. & MARY L. REV. 1443, 1447, 1448 (2008).

36. Stromseth, *Post-Conflict Rule of Law Building*; David Tolbert & Andrew Solomon, *United Nations Reform and Supporting the Rule of Law in Post-Conflict Societies*, 19 HARV. HUM. RTS. J. 29 (2006).

37. JON ELSTER, CLOSING THE BOOKS: TRANSITIONAL JUSTICE IN HISTORICAL PERSPECTIVE 1 (2004) (emphasis added).

38. RUTI G. TEITEL, TRANSITIONAL JUSTICE 3, 12 (2000).

39. TEITEL, TRANSITIONAL JUSTICE, at 69 (emphasis added).

40. Louise Arbour, *Economic and Social Justice for Societies in Transition*, 40 N.Y.U. J. INT'L L. & POL. 1, 3 (2007).

41. See TEITEL, TRANSITIONAL JUSTICE, at 12. The most prominent debate on transitional justice, stemming from the Nuremberg Tribunals was actually between two legal philosophers. See H. L. A. Hart, *Positivism and the Separation of Law and Morals*, 71 HARV. L. REV. 593 (1958); Lon L. Fuller, *Positivism and Fidelity to Law—A Reply to Professor Hart*, 71 HARV. L. REV. 630 (1958).

42. *Symposium, When the Fighting Stops: Roles and Responsibilities in Post-Conflict Reconstruction*, 38 SETON HALL L. REV. 1365 (2008), November 2, 2007, Seton Hall University School of Law; Ruth Wedgwood, Harold K. Jacobson, *Forward, Symposium: State Reconstruction after Civil Conflict*, 95 AM. J. INT'L L. 1 (2001).

43. David Tolbert & Andrew Solomon, *United Nations Reform and Supporting the Rule of Law in Post-Conflict Societies*, 19 HARV. HUM. RTS. J. 29, 30–31 (2006).

44. See also Simon Chesterman, *From State-Failure to State-Building: Problems and Prospects for a United Nations Peacebuilding Commission*, 2 J. INT'L L. & INT'L REL. 155, 156–157 (2005) (describing peacebuilding operations).

45. Center for Strategic and International Studies & Association of the United States Army, Post-Conflict Reconstruction: Task Framework 2 (2002), available at http://www.csis.org/media/csis/pubs/framework.pdf.

46. John J. Hamre & Gordon R. Sullivan, *Toward Postconflict Reconstruction*, WASH. Q., Autumn 2002, at 85, 89.

47. Chesterman, *From State-Failure to State-Building*, at 155.

48. CSIS & Association of the U.S. Army, Post-Conflict Reconstruction, at 2.

49. See, e.g., Chesterman, *From State Failure to State-Building*, at 163; David Wippman, *Sharing Power in Iraq*, 39 NEW ENG. L. REV. 29 (2004) ("In the absence of security, you can achieve little else."); CSIS & Association of the U.S. Army, Post-Conflict Reconstruction, at 3–5.

50. Hamre & Sullivan, *Toward Postconflict Reconstruction*, at 90.

51. See Subir Bhaumik, *Maoist Rebels Set Preconditions for Talks*, BBC NEWS, February 10, 2010, available at: http://news.bbc.co.uk/2/hi/south_asia/8507525.stm; *A Spectre Haunting India: Maoist Rebels Are Fighting a Brutal Low-Level War with*

*the Indian State*, THE ECONOMIST, August 13, 2006, available at: http://www. economist.com/world/asia/displaystory.cfm?story_id7799247.

52.  See Jayshree Bajoria & Carin Zissis, *The Muslim Insurgency in Southern Thailand*, Council on Foreign Relations Backgrounder, September 10, 2008, available at http://www.cfr.org/publication/12531/muslim_insurgency_in_southern_thailand. html#5; see also International Crisis Group, Thailand: Political Turmoil and the Southern Insurgency, Policy Briefing No. 80, August 28, 2008, available at http:// www.crisisgroup.org/library/documents/asia/south_east_asia/b80_thailand_ political_turmoil_and_the_southern_insurgency.pdf.

53.  See International Crisis Group, Southern Philippines Backgrounder: Terrorism and the Peace Process, July 13, 2004, available at http://www.crisisgroup.org/library/ documents/asia/south_east_asia/080_southern_philippines_backgrounder_ terrorism_n_peace_process.pdf.

54.  THE U.S. ARMY/MARINE CORPS COUNTERINSURGENCY FIELD MANUAL ¶ 1–2 (2007).

55.  Id. at ¶ 1–3; U.S. Army, Field Manual 3.24.2: Tactics in Counterinsurgency, at ¶ 2–22 (2009) [hereafter Field Manual: Tactics], available at: http://www.fas.org/ irp/doddir/army/fmi3-24-2.pdf.

56.  See Field Manual: Tactics, at ¶¶ 1–88, 1–92 to 1–96.

57.  ZACHARIAH MAMPILLY, REBEL RULERS: INSURGENT GOVERNANCE AND CIVILIAN LIFE DURING WAR (2011); see also Sandesh Sivakumaran, *Courts of Armed Opposition Groups: Fair Trials or Summary Justice?*, 7 J. INT'L CRIM. JUSTICE 489, 494 (2009).

58.  DAVID GALULA, PACIFICATION IN ALGERIA 1956–1958 20, 45 (1963, RAND ed. 2006).

59.  See generally AHMAD NIZAR HAMZEH, IN THE PATH OF HIZBULLAH (2004); ELI BERMAN, RADICAL, RELIGIOUS, AND VIOLENT 16–18, 121–156 (2009) (describing groups that provide mutual aid, social services, and focusing on Hamas in particular); THOMAS RID & MARC HECKER, WAR 2.0 144 (2009) (describing Hezbollah's service programs).

60.  See DAVID KILCULLEN, THE ACCIDENTAL GUERRILLA 34–38 (2009). Kilcullen demonstrates the Accidental Guerrilla Syndrome in West Java, Afghanistan, Pakistan's Federally Administered Tribal Areas, and Iraq. The same effect can be seen in the context of the Malayan communist insurgency, see SIR ROBERT THOMPSON, DEFEATING COMMUNIST INSURGENCY 20, 26 (1970), and perhaps also in the Maoist insurgency in Nepal, see Sara Shneiderman & Mark Turin, *The Path to Jan Sarkar in Dolakha District: Towards an Ethnography of the Maoist Movement*, in HIMALAYAN "PEOPLE'S WAR": NEPAL'S MAOIST REBELLION (Michael Hutt, ed., 2004). For a rigorous academic treatment of the formation of rebel groups, see ROGER D. PETERSON, RESISTANCE AND REBELLION 14 (2001) (describing the triggering stages as including formation of resentment, security concerns, status issues, and community norms of reciprocity).

61. Sarah Sewall, *Introduction*, in FIELD MANUAL, at xxvii.
62. FIELD MANUAL at ¶ 1–132.
63. KILCULLEN, THE ACCIDENTAL GUERRILLA, at 60.
64. See FIELD MANUAL at figure 5–1.
65. David Kilcullen, *"Twenty-Eight Articles": Fundamentals of Company-Level Counterinsurgency*, MIL. REV., May–June 2006, at 103.
66. RORY STEWART, THE PRINCE OF THE MARSHES 400 (2006).
67. Kilcullen, *"Twenty-Eight Articles,"* at 107.
68. FIELD MANUAL at ¶ 1–113.
69. Field Manual: Tactics, at lx; FIELD MANUAL at ¶ 1–37; see also FIELD MANUAL ¶ 1–114 (describing legitimate systems throughout history, ranging from theocracy to monarchy to liberal democracy).
70. FIELD MANUAL at ¶ 1–118.
71. FIELD MANUAL at ¶¶ 5–51 to 5–80.
72. See JOHN HILLEN, BLUE HELMETS 79 (1998).
73. See PAUL F. DIEHL, INTERNATIONAL PEACEKEEPING 5 (1993).
74. TREVOR FINDLAY, THE USE OF FORCE IN UN PEACE OPERATIONS 85 (2002).
75. Id. at 357, 100, 358.
76. Id. at 56, 63–63, 66–70, 71–81.
77. Id. at 51.
78. Peacebuilding is the United Nations' preferred term for state- or nation-building and postconflict reconstruction. See SIMON CHESTERMAN, YOU, THE PEOPLE: THE UNITED NATIONS, TRANSITIONAL ADMINISTRATION, AND STATE-BUILDING 4 (2004).
79. An Agenda for Peace, Report of the Secretary General, June 17, 1992, para. 21, available at: http://www.un.org/Docs/SG/agpeace.html.
80. Id. at introduction.
81. See Alan James, *Is There a Second Generation of Peacekeeping?*, 1 INT'L PEACEKEEPING 110, September/November 1994; FINDLAY, THE USE OF FORCE IN UN PEACE OPERATIONS at 5–6.
82. HILLEN, BLUE HELMETS, at 26.
83. See FINDLAY, THE USE OF FORCE IN UN PEACE OPERATIONS, at 17.
84. S/25264 Report of SG pursuant to SC Res. 743, February 10, 1993 (emphasis added).
85. HILLEN, BLUE HELMETS, at 173–174.
86. FINDLAY, THE USE OF FORCE IN UN PEACE OPERATIONS, at 148; HILLEN, BLUE HELMETS, at 176.
87. HILLEN, BLUE HELMETS, at 177.
88. JOHN MACKINLAY, THE INSURGENT ARCHIPELAGO 2, 67–69 (2009). Though it is infrequently noted, the comparison between counterinsurgency and peacekeeping is not new. See FRANK KITSON, LOW-INTENSITY OPERATIONS 144–164 (1974).

89. For an excellent overview of the debate through the 1990s, see FINDLAY, THE USE OF FORCE IN UN PEACE OPERATIONS, at 154–159.

90. Report of the Panel on United Nations Peace Operations, A/55/305-S/2000/809, para. 12 [hereafter Brahimi Report], available at: http://www.un.org/peace/reports/peace_operations/.

91. Id. at para 20 (emphasis added).

92. Id. at para 13.

93. Id. at para 48.

94. Id. at executive summary.

95. Id. at para 51.

96. Stephen John Stedman, *Spoiler Problems in Peace Processes*, 22 INT'L SEC. 5, Autumn 1997.

97. Id. at 36–40.

98. Id. at 12–14.

99. On the segmentation and fragmentation of territory, see STATHIS KALYVAS, THE LOGIC OF VIOLENCE IN CIVIL WAR 12 (2006).

100. See BRUCE ACKERMAN, I WE THE PEOPLE (1993) (presenting the classic account of constitutional moments).

101. See, e.g., SANJIB BARUAH, DURABLE DISORDER (2005) (discussing insurgencies in Northeastern India).

102. Cf. L. T. HOBHOUSE, SOCIAL DEVELOPMENT 55–73 (1924).

103. See KALYVAS, THE LOGIC OF VIOLENCE IN CIVIL WAR, at 77.

104. Id. at 78.

105. Id. at 79.

106. Id. at 80.

107. Id. at 10–11.

108. GALULA, PACIFICATION IN ALGERIA, at 119.

109. Cf. ROGER TRINQUIER, MODERN WARFARE: A FRENCH VIEW OF COUNTER-INSURGENCY 42 (1964, 2006 ed.).

110. Kilcullen, *"Twenty Eight Articles,"* at 107.

CHAPTER 4

1. See Reuters, *Afghanistan Says It Enacted Law to Pardon War Crimes*, N.Y. TIMES, March 16, 2010, available at http://www.nytimes.com/2010/03/17/world/asia/17kabul.html; Jon Boone, *Afghanistan Quietly Brings into Force Taliban Amnesty Law*, THE GUARDIAN (U.K.), Feb. 11, 2010; Human Rights Watch, Afghanistan: Repeal Amnesty Law, March 10, 2010, available at http://www.hrw.org/en/news/2010/03/10/afghanistan-repeal-amnesty-law.

2. Transitional Justice is "that set of practices, mechanisms and concerns that arise following a period of conflict, civil strife or repression, and that are aimed directly at confronting and dealing with past violations of human rights and humanitarian

law." Naomi Roht-Arriaza, *The New Landscape of Transitional Justice* 2, in TRANSITIONAL JUSTICE IN THE TWENTY-FIRST CENTURY (Naomi Roht-Arriaza & Javier Mariezcurrena, eds., 2006). For other similar definitions, see JON ELSTER, CLOSING THE BOOKS: TRANSITIONAL JUSTICE IN HISTORICAL PERSPECTIVE 1 (2004) ("the processes of trials, purges, and reparations that take place after the transition from one political regime to another"); Ruti Teitel, *Transitional Justice Genealogy*, 16 HARV. HUM. RTS. J. 69 (2003) ("conception of justice associated with periods of political change, characterized by legal responses to confront the wrongdoings of repressive predecessor regimes").

3. Richard Pregent, *Building Rule of Law Capacity in Iraq*, 40 ISRAEL YEARBOOK ON HUMAN RIGHTS (2010).

4. Charles J. Dunlap, Jr., *Lawfare: A Decisive Element of 21st Century Conflicts*, 54 JOINT FORCES Q. 35 (3d Quarter 2009).

5. See Council on Foreign Relations (CFR), Lawfare: The Latest in Asymmetries, March 18, 2003, available at: http://www.cfr.org/publication/5772/lawfare_the_latest_in_asymmetries.html; David B. Rivkin Jr. & Lee A. Casey, Op-Ed., *Lawfare*, WALL ST. J., February 23, 2007.

6. CFR, Lawfare; Council on Foreign Relations (CFR), Lawfare: The Latest in Asymmetries—Part II, May 22, 2003, available at: http://www.cfr.org/publication/6191/lawfare_the_latest_in_asymmetries_part_two.html.

7. Id.

8. Philip Carter, *Legal Combat*, SLATE.COM, April 4, 2005, available at: http://www.slate.com/id/2116169. For a similar approach, see QIAO LIANG & WANG XIANGSUI, UNRESTRICTED WARFARE (1999).

9. See OTTO KIRCHHEIMER, POLITICAL JUSTICE 6 (1980).

10. ALEXANDRA BARAHONA DE BRITO, CARMEN GONZALÉZ-ENRIQUEZ, & PALOMA AGUILAR, EDS., THE POLITICS OF MEMORY: TRANSITIONAL JUSTICE IN DEMOCRATIZING SOCIETIES (2001); NEIL J. KRITZ, ED., TRANSITIONAL JUSTICE (1995); CARLA HESSE & ROBERT POST, EDS., HUMAN RIGHTS IN POLITICAL TRANSITIONS (1999); BRUCE ACKERMAN, THE FUTURE OF LIBERAL REVOLUTION (1992); PHILIPPE C. SCHMITTER ET AL., TRANSITIONS FROM AUTHORITARIAN RULE: LATIN AMERICA (1986). For the classic treatment of democratization during this period, see SAMUEL P. HUNTINGTON, THE THIRD WAVE: DEMOCRATIZATION IN THE LATE TWENTIETH CENTURY (1991). Some scholars have noted the emphasis on democratic transitions. See Eric A. Posner & Adrian Vermeule, *Transitional Justice as Ordinary Justice*, 117 HARV. L. REV. 761, 768 (2004).

11. Fionnuala Ni Aoláin & Colm Campbell, *The Paradox of Transition in Conflicted Democracies*, 27 HUM. RTS. Q. 172, 184 (2005).

12. See ELSTER, CLOSING THE BOOKS, at 3–24; Adriaan Lanni, Law and Order in Classical Athens (forthcoming Cambridge University Press).

13. See, e.g., NORBERT EHRENFREUND, THE NUREMBERG LEGACY (2007).

14. For modern references to the Marshall Plan, see Roger Cohen, *In Balkans: Power Shift*, N.Y. TIMES, Aug. 18, 1995 (noting talk of a "mini-Marshall plan"); James Bennet, *On Eve of African Relief Talks, Aid Donors Argue over Numbers*, N.Y. TIMES, Nov, 22, 1996 (mentioning desire for a multilateral Marshall-type of plan); David Firestone, *Bremer Cites Marshall Plan in Bid for Iraqi Aid*, N.Y. TIMES, Sept. 23, 2003; Editorial, *Afghanistan's Marshall Plan*, N.Y. TIMES, April 19, 2002. For a discussion of de-Ba'athification, see the discussion on purges and lustration *infra*.

15. In recent years, some scholars have noticed that something is different about contemporary transitional justice. Ruti Teitel notes that transitional justice is no longer an occasional occurrence, but has become increasingly common due to globalization and instability. See Teitel, *Geneology*, at 89–90, 92. Teitel's work goes furthest in considering transitional justice during conflict, as she notes that contemporary transitional justice must grapple with "political fragmentation, weak states, small wars, and steady conflict." Id. at 90. However, she only gestures at the implications, suggesting that international humanitarian law, human rights law, and criminal law are increasingly conflated. Id. at 91–92. In later work, she moves away from conflict and characterizes contemporary transitional justice as defined by regime change, the linkage between local and international law, and postconflict reconciliation. See Ruti Teitel, *The Law and Politics of Contemporary Transitional Justice*, 38 CORNELL INT'L L.J. 837 (2005). One set of scholars comment that Colombia began its transitional justice process "pre–post-conflict." See Lisa J. Laplante & Kimberly Theidon, *Transitional Justice in Times of Conflict: Colombia's Ley de Justicia y Paz*, 28 MICH. J. INT'L L. 49, 51 (2006). Laplante and Theidon provide the lone article on transitional justice during conflict. However, their work is a detailed case study of Colombia's Justice and Peace Law, not a broad, theoretical, or systematic treatment of the phenomenon of transitional justice during conflict. And two scholars, Fionnuala Ni Aoláin and Colm Campbell, have argued that the focus on transitions from nondemocracy to democracy has obscured the fact that transitions can occur from war to peace without a change in the political regime. See Aoláin & Campbell, *Paradox of Transition*, at 173, 195. They argue that in "conflicted democracies," such as Northern Ireland, a shift from violent conflict to political contestation was possible through institutional reform. Id. at 194–195. Despite these occasional suspicions about changes in the field, none of these scholars has fundamentally challenged the war-peace distinction. Transitional justice has remained a postconflict process. Note also that the past world of clean-cut transitions may itself be a myth. Great wars with formal ends, such as the U.S. Civil War and even World War II, featured postconflict violence and fear of insurgency.

16. Even the literature on Iraq and Afghanistan does not consider the relationship between transitional justice and ongoing conflict. On Iraq, see, e.g., M. Cherif Bassiouni, *Post-Conflict Justice in Iraq: An Appraisal of the Iraq Special Tribunal*, 38 CORNELL INT'L L.J. 327 (2005); Note, Danielle Tarin, *Prosecuting Saddam and*

*Bungling Transitional Justice in Iraq*, 45 VA. J. INT'L L. *467* (2005); Dana Michael Hollywood, *The Search for Post-Conflict Justice in Iraq: A Comparative Study of Transitional Justice Mechanisms and Their Applicability to Post-Saddam Iraq*, 33 BROOK. J. INT'L L. 59 (2007); Note, Daniel J. Hendy, *Is a Truth Commission the Solution to Restoring Peace in Post-Conflict Iraq?*, 20 OHIO ST. J. ON DISP. RESOL. 527 (2005). On Afghanistan, see, e.g., Laura A. Dickinson, *Transitional Justice in Afghanistan: The Promise of Mixed Tribunals*, 31 DENV. J. INT'L L. & POL'Y 23 (2002); Ahmed Nader Nadery, *Peace or Justice? Transitional Justice in Afghanistan*, 1 INT'L J. TRANSITIONAL JUSTICE 174 (2007); Barnett R. Rubin, *Transitional Justice and Human Rights in Afghanistan*, 79 INT'L AFF. 567 (May 2003); Rama Mani, Ending Impunity and Building Justice in Afghanistan, Afghanistan Research and Evaluation Unit, December 2003, available at http://unpan1.un.org/intradoc/groups/public/documents/APCITY/UNPAN016655.pdf.

17. See Miriam J. Aukerman, *Extraordinary Evil, Ordinary Crime: A Framework for Understanding Transitional Justice*, 15 HARV. HUM. RTS. J. 39, 44 (2002) (providing a list of goals for transitional justice).

18. See MARTHA MINOW, BETWEEN VENGEANCE AND FORGIVENESS 10 (1998); Aukerman, *Extraordinary Evil*, at 57–61; CARLOS SANTIAGO NINO, RADICAL EVIL ON TRIAL 164–185 (1996); ELSTER, CLOSING THE BOOKS, at 129–135.

19. Aukerman, *Extraordinary Evil*, at 80.

20. See, e.g., M. Cherif Bassiouni, *Accountability for Violations of International Humanitarian Law and Other Serious Violations of Human Rights* 9, in M. CHERIF BASSIOUNI, ED., POST-CONFLICT JUSTICE (2002); Aukerman, *Extraordinary Evil*, at 67–68.

21. Roht-Arriaza, *New Landscape*, at 3–4.

22. Aukerman, *Extraordinary Evil*, at 76.

23. MINOW, BETWEEN VENGEANCE AND FORGIVENESS, at 57.

24. See, e.g., id. at 24 ("To respond to mass atrocity with legal prosecutions is to embrace the rule of law"); Teitel, *Law and Politics*, at 838 (noting transitional justice has aspirations for the rule of law and nation-building); Juan E. Mendez, *In Defense of Transitional Justice* 1, 4, in TRANSITIONAL JUSTICE AND THE RULE OF LAW IN NEW DEMOCRACIES (James McAdams, ed., 1997) (focusing on democracy).

25. See, e.g., James McAdams, *Preface*, in McADAMS, TRANSITIONAL JUSTICE AND THE RULE OF LAW IN NEW DEMOCRACIES, at x; Mendez, *In Defense of Transitional Justice*, at 1.

26. NINO, RADICAL EVIL ON TRIAL, at vii, x.

27. RAMA MANI, BEYOND RETRIBUTION 91 (2002).

28. See, e.g., ACKERMAN, LIBERAL REVOLUTION, at 70–73; CLAUS OFFE, VARIETIES OF TRANSITION 82 (1997).

29. See Carla Hesse & Robert Post, *Introduction*, in HESSE & POST, HUMAN RIGHTS IN POLITICAL TRANSITIONS, at 18, 24; HUNTINGTON, THE THIRD WAVE, at 214.

30. Ronald C. Slye, *Amnesty, Truth, and Reconciliation: Reflections on the South African Amnesty Process* 179–182, in ROBERT I. ROTBERG & DENNIS THOMPSON, EDS., TRUTH V. JUSTICE (2000).

31. Michael Feher, *Terms of Reconciliation*, in HESSE & POST, HUMAN RIGHTS IN POLITICAL TRANSITIONS, at 326–327.

32. Nino is explicit on this point, see NINO, RADICAL EVIL ON TRIAL, at vii, x, but most of the major works on postauthoritarian transitions include some thinking about transitional justice and its relationship to establishing a stable democracy.

33. THE U.S. ARMY/MARINE CORPS COUNTERINSURGENCY FIELD MANUAL ¶ 5–8 (2007).

34. DAVID J. KILCULLEN, THE ACCIDENTAL GUERRILLA 87–109 (2009). For a critique of road-building as a tool in counterinsurgency, see Joshua Foust, The Strange Benefits of Paving Afghanistan, Registan.net, April 25, 2008, available at http://www.registan.net/index.php/2008/04/25/the-strange-benefits-of-paving-afghanistan/; Joshua Foust, *The Birth (and Death) of a Meme*, COLUM. JOURNALISM REV. September 10, 2008, available at http://www.cjr.org/behind_the_news/the_birth_and_death_of_a_meme.php?page=all%E2%80%9D; Joshua Foust, On the Roads Again in Afghanistan, Need to Know on PBS, August 31, 2010, available at http://www.pbs.org/wnet/need-to-know/voices/on-the-roads-again-in-afghanistan/3223/.

35. ACKERMAN, LIBERAL REVOLUTION, at 71.

36. HUNTINGTON, THE THIRD WAVE, at 231.

37. Ruti Teitel, *Bringing the Messiah through the Law* 177, in HESSE & POST, HUMAN RIGHTS IN POLITICAL TRANSITIONS; Bassiouni, *Accountability for Violations of International Humanitarian Law*, at 8 (political stability); NINO, RADICAL EVIL ON TRIAL, at vii, x; Mendez, *In Defense of Transitional Justice*, at 1, 4 (democracy); see Richard Goldstone, *Exposing Human Rights Abuses—A Help or Hindrance to Reconciliation?*, 22 HASTINGS CONST. L.Q. 607, 615 (1995); Slye, *Amnesty, Truth, and Reconciliation*, at 179–182 (reconciliation).

38. See RUTI TEITEL, TRANSITIONAL JUSTICE 51 (2000); ELSTER, CLOSING THE BOOKS, at 116–117 (peace v. justice); MINOW, BETWEEN VENGEANCE AND FORGIVENESS; ROTBERG & THOMPSON, TRUTH V. JUSTICE; Hesse & Post, *Introduction*, at 16–17 (reconciliation and punishment); Posner & Vermeule, *Transitional Justice as Ordinary Justice*, at 769 (political precautions and liberal commitments); Leslie Vinjamuri & Jack Snyder, *Advocacy and Scholarship in the Study of International War Crime Tribunals and Transitional Justice*, 7 ANN. REV. POL. SCI. 345 (2004) (pragmatism v. legalism).

39. For the classic account, see Diane F. Orentlicher, *Settling Accounts: The Duty to Prosecute Human Rights Violations of a Prior Regime*, 100 YALE L.J. 2537, 2548, 2549 (1991).

40. See Hesse & Post, *Introduction*, at 14 (describing this position using the Latin, *fiat justitia, ruat coelum*).

41. See Orentlicher, *Settling Accounts*, at 2458, 2458; see also Lisa Laplante, *Outlawing Amnesty: The Return of Criminal Justice in Transitional Justice Schemes*, 49 VA. J. INT'L L. 915, 917 (2009) (noting that "use of amnesty in the name of peace" often was unquestioned).

42. Orentlicher, *Settling Accounts*, at 2546 n. 32.

43. TEITEL, TRANSITIONAL JUSTICE, at 51.

44. See Hesse & Post, *Introduction*, at 16.

45. See id. at 16.

46. ELSTER, CLOSING THE BOOKS, at 190; see also Hesse & Post, *Introduction*, at 18 (noting that amnesties "can facilitate the reconciliation necessary for the establishment of a legitimate legal system").

47. Aukerman, *Extraordinary Evil*, at 39; see also Paul van Zyl, *Dilemmas of Transitional Justice: The Case of South Africa's Truth and Reconciliation Commission*, 52 J. INT'L AFF. 647, 651 (1999).

48. Van Zyl, *Dilemmas of Transitional Justice*, at 651.

49. TEITEL, TRANSITIONAL JUSTICE, at 51.

50. Teitel, *Geneology*, at 78–81.

51. MINOW, BETWEEN VENGEANCE AND FORGIVENESS, at 13. Most recently, some commentators have acknowledged that transitional justice "lies precisely in the space in which local actors seek to balance legality with politics, the demands of peace with the clamor for justice." Laplante & Theidon, *Transitional Justice in Times of Conflict*, at 52; see also MINOW, BETWEEN VENGEANCE AND FORGIVENESS, at 22 (describing the space between vengeance and forgiveness); TEITEL, TRANSITIONAL JUSTICE, at 54 (noting the tradeoff between criminal justice and other political goals); Posner & Vermeule, *Transitional Justice as Ordinary Justice*, at 769 (describing the balance of liberal norms and the need for consolidated institutions). There are tradeoffs between justice and political realism, but because both are necessary there is a fallacy in the strict dichotomy between justice and politics. McAdams, *Preface*, at xiv (recognizing tradeoffs); Ellen Lutz, *Transitional Justice: Lessons Learned and the Road Ahead*, in ROHT-ARRIAZA & MARIEZCURRENA, TRANSITIONAL JUSTICE IN THE TWENTY-FIRST CENTURY, at 327 (noting the fallacy in a strict dichotomy).

52. For the distinction between reconcilables and irreconcilables, see Media Roundtable: General David H. Petraeus, September 4, 2008, Multi-National Force Iraq, available at http://www.mnf-iraq.com/index.php?option= com_content&task= view&id=22229&Itemid=131. For the active and passive distinction, see FIELD MANUAL at ¶¶ 3-84–3-88.

53. See Laplante & Theidon, *Transitional Justice in Times of Conflict*, at 71.

54. See ANGELA J. DAVIS, ARBITRARY JUSTICE: THE POWER OF THE AMERICAN PROSECUTOR 6, 14, 169 (2007).

55. ELSTER, CLOSING THE BOOKS, at 118.

56. Id. at 119; see also TEITEL, TRANSITIONAL JUSTICE 45 (discussing liability in the Berlin Wall cases, which considered whether to hold responsible low level shooters or the policy makers).

57. One possible model not explored here is *maximalist transitional justice*, an approach in which there is a default rule of transitional justice in all cases with robust programs and only minimal exceptions for political needs. This approach, the opposite of minimalism, is relatively conventional in the literature, and so is not discussed here.

58. Sewall, *Introduction* xxv, in FIELD MANUAL.

59. CASS R. SUNSTEIN, ONE CASE AT A TIME 3 (1999).

60. Note, however, that Sunstein makes *both* a requirement for minimalism. Id. at 10–11. I suggest that *either* is enough for Minimalist Transitional Justice.

61. Id. at 11.

62. Id. at 10.

63. Cf. Mark Tushnet, *The Possibilities of Comparative Constitutional Law*, 108 YALE L.J. 1225 (1999) (describing in the context of using foreign law in constitutional interpretation, the differences between bricolage, using whatever materials are available, and selectivity, choosing particular materials intentionally from a larger set).

64. For reconcilable leaders, the appropriate prescription would be highly dependent on the context: Leaders of armed groups may reconcile only to become warlords, potentially causing backlash from a population that hoped for better. If those who are reconciled do not give up their private power, reconciliation might simply contribute to insecurity in the longer term. See Patricia Gossman, In the Tent or Out? Warlords and Legitimacy in Afghanistan, U.S. Institute of Peace Report (unpublished draft).

65. See *infra* the discussion on trials and amnesties.

66. See ACKERMAN, LIBERAL REVOLUTION, at 3, 70.

67. See Jacob E. Gerson & Eric A. Posner, *Timing Rules and Legal Institutions*, 121 HARV. L. REV. 543 (2007).

68. Cf. ACKERMAN, LIBERAL REVOLUTION, at 3, 70 (discussing the possibilities of a founding moment in transitional situations).

69. See RICHARD A. WILSON, THE POLITICS OF TRUTH AND RECONCILIATION IN SOUTH AFRICA: LEGITIMIZING THE POST-APARTHEID STATE 171 (2001); see also Laplante, *Outlawing Amnesty*, at 931.

70. Both transformations are linked to the growing power and influence of human rights institutions, see Kathryn Sikkink & Carrie Booth Walling, *Argentina's Contribution to Global Trends in Transitional Justice* 304–308, 313–321, in ROHT-ARRIAZA & MARIEZCURRENA, TRANSITIONAL JUSTICE IN THE TWENTY-FIRST CENTURY.

71. TEITEL, TRANSITIONAL JUSTICE, at 33–34.

72. Rome Statute of the International Criminal Court, preamble.

73. Catherine Jenkins, *"They Have Built a Legal System without Punishment": Reflections on the Use of Amnesty in the South African Transition*, 64 TRANSFORMATION: CRITICAL PERSP. ON S. AFR. 27, 29 (2007).

74. Garth Meintjes and Juan E. Méndez, *Reconciling Amnesties with Universal Jurisdiction*, 2 INT'L L.F. 76, 76–77 (2000).

75. See, e.g., Jo M. Pasqualucci, *The Whole Truth and Nothing but the Truth: Truth Commissions, Impunity and the Inter-American Human Rights System*, 12 B.U. INT'L

L.J. 321, 361–364 (1994); Brian D. Tittemore, *Ending Impunity in the Americas: The Role of the Inter-American Human Rights System in Advancing Accountability for Serious Crimes under International Law*, 12 Sw. J. L. & TRADE AM. 429 (2006).

76. 1988 Inter-Am. Ct. H.R. (ser. C) No. 4 (July 29, 1988) at para 166.

77. Laplante, *Outlawing Amnesty*, at 938–939.

78. Barrios Altos, 2002 Inter-Am. Ct. H.R. (ser. C) No. 75 (March 14, 2001) at para 41; see Laplante, *Outlawing Amnesty*, at 962.

79. Laplante, *Outlawing Amnesty*, at 964–965.

80. Case of the Mapiripán Massacre v. Colombia, 2005 Inter-Am. Ct. H.R. (ser. C) No. 134, P304 (September 15, 2005); see Laplante & Theidon, *Transitional Justice in Times of Conflict*, at 98–99.

81. Bámaca Velásquez Case, 2000 Inter-Am. Ct. H.R. (ser. C) No. 70, P201 (November 25, 2000) (holding that victims or kin have a right to have human rights violations identified); see Laplante & Theidon, *Transitional Justice in Times of Conflict*, at 87; Laplante, *Outlawing Amnesty*, at 963; U.N. Human Rights Comm., Communication No. 107/1981, P16, U.N. Doc. CCPR/C/19/D/107/1981 (July 21, 1983) (creating a right to have human rights violations considered by courts). On the right to a remedy, see Pasqualucci, *The Whole Truth and Nothing but the Truth*, at 349–359; Sherrie L. Russell-Brown, *Out of the Crooked Timber of Humanity: The Conflict between South Africa's Truth and Reconciliation Commission and International Human Rights Norms Regarding "Effective Remedies,"* 26 HASTINGS INT'L & COMP. L. REV. 227, 231–254 (2003). For a discussion of arguments courts use to strike or uphold amnesty laws under international treaties and constitutional provisions, see Naomi Roht-Arriaza & Lauren Gibson, *The Developing Jurisprudence on Amnesty*, 20 HUM. RTS. Q. 843, 860–869 (1998).

82. Laplante, *Outlawing Amnesty*, at 939.

83. See Prosecutor v. Furundzija, December 10, 1998, para. 155.

84. See Mendez, *In Defense of Transitional Justice*, at 14.

85. See PRISCILLA HAYNER, UNSPEAKABLE TRUTHS 186–195 (2001). For more background, see, e.g., Andrea Bartoli, Aldo Civico, & Leone Gianturco, *Mozambique—Renamo* 140–155, in CONFLICT TRANSFORMATION AND PEACEBUILDING: MOVING FROM VIOLENCE TO SUSTAINABLE PEACE (Bruce W. Dayton & Louis Kreisberg, eds., 2009).

86. See AHMED RASHID, DESCENT INTO CHAOS 93–94 (2009).

87. Nadery, *Peace or Justice?*, at 175.

88. Afghan Independent Human Rights Commission, A Call For Justice 9, 13 (2005), available at: http://www.aihrc.org.af/Rep_29_Eng/rep29_1_05call4justice.pdf.

89. MICHAEL SEMPLE, RECONCILIATION IN AFGHANISTAN 74 (2009).

90. Id. at 30.

91. Id. at 30–32.

92. Id. at 32.

93. Id. at 39, 42.

94. See Maria Jose Guembe & Helena Olea, *No Justice, No Peace: Discussion of a Legal Framework Regarding the Demobilization of Non-State Armed Groups in Colombia* 122–224, in ROHT-ARRIAZA & MARIEZCURRENA, TRANSITIONAL JUSTICE IN THE TWENTY-FIRST CENTURY.

95. Id. at 124.

96. Id. at 126.

97. Id. at 126.

98. Id. at 120.

99. Id. at 125–126.

100. Id. at 129.

101. Laplante & Theidon, *Transitional Justice in Times of Conflict*, at 79.

102. Id. at 82–86.

103. Id. at 87–95.

104. Id. at 95–97.

105. Id. at 99–100.

106. Id. at 101.

107. Timothy Longman, *Justice at the Grassroots? Gacaca Trials in Rwanda* 209, in ROHT-ARRIAZA & MARIEZCURRENA, TRANSITIONAL JUSTICE IN THE TWENTY-FIRST CENTURY. For an overview of local justice arguments and a criticism of the gacaca system, see Lars Waldorf, *Mass Justice for Mass Atrocity: Rethinking Local Justice as Transitional Justice*, 79 TEMP. L. REV. 1 (2006). For arguments that local justice is better than international justice at promoting accountability, facilitating the rule of law, improving reconciliation, and facilitating democracy, see Jose Alvarez, *Crimes of States/Crimes of Hate: Lessons from Rwanda*, 24 YALE J. INT'L L. 365, 477, 482 (1999); Mark A. Drumbl, *Punishment Post Genocide: From Guilt to Shame to Civis in Rwanda*, 75 N.Y.U. L. REV. 1221, 1323–1325 (2000); Note, Aneta Wierzynska, *Consolidating Democracy through Transitional Justice: Rwanda's Gacaca Courts*, 79 N.Y.U. L. REV. 1934 (2004).

108. Longman, *Justice at the Grassroots*, at 210–211.

109. Id. at 211.

110. Id. at 220.

111. See id. at 220–222 (describing logistical, participatory, retaliation, and manipulation concerns). For a general discussion of the gacaca, see PHIL CLARK, THE GACACA COURTS, POST-GENOCIDE JUSTICE AND RECONCILIATION IN RWANDA (2010). For a more general discussion of local justice, including the problem of enemies becoming neighbors, see ERIC STOVER & HARVEY M. WEINSTEIN, EDS., MY NEIGHBOR, MY ENEMY: JUSTICE AND COMMUNITY IN THE AFTERMATH OF MASS ATROCITY (2004).

112. SEMPLE, RECONCILIATION IN AFGHANISTAN, at 67.

113. Id. at 67–68.

114. Id. at 68.

115. See generally ELI BERMAN, RADICAL, RELIGIOUS, AND VIOLENT (2009).

116. Semple, Reconciliation in Afghanistan, at 68–69.
117. See J. M. Carrier & C. A. H Thomson, Viet Cong Motivation and Morale: The Special Case of Chieu Hoi at ix, RAND Memoranda 4830-2-ISA/ARPA, 1966, available at www.rand.org/pubs/research_memoranda/RM4830-2; J. A. Koch, The Chieu Hoi Program in South Vietnam, 1963–1971 at viii, Report 11–73 ARPA, 1973, available at http://www.rand.org/pubs/reports/2006/R1172.pdf.
118. Carrier & Thomson, Viet Cong Motivation and Morale, at x–xi.
119. Id. at 35.
120. Id. at xiv.
121. Koch, The Chieu Hoi Program, at viii; Carrier & Thomson, Viet Cong Motivation and Morale, at xv.
122. Lucian W. Pye, Observations on the Chieu Hoi Program xi, Rand Memoranda 4864-1-ISA/ARPA, 1966, available at http://www.rand.org/pubs/research_memoranda/2008/RM4864-1.pdf.
123. Id. at 12.
124. Id. at 16–18.
125. Id. at 18.
126. Id. at 19–25.
127. Id. at 25.
128. Austin Long, On "Other War": Lessons from Five Decades of RAND Counterinsurgency Research 45–49 (2006) (describing the challenge of protecting ralliers, following up to ensure no recidivism, and administrative issues).
129. Koch, The Chieu Hoi Program, at v–vii.
130. See Andrew K. Woods, *The Business End*, Fin. Times, June 27, 2008; see also Yochi J. Deazen, *Iraq's Counterinsurgency College: U.S. Military Aims to Temper Detainees' Religious Beliefs before Their Release*, Wall St. J., Sept. 18, 2008. For another example, see David Galula, Pacification in Algeria 1956–1958 185 (1963, RAND ed. 2006) (describing prison camps in Algeria that sought to separate the extreme insurgents from the moderates and pursued reeducation programs).
131. Kilcullen, The Accidental Guerrilla, at 164.
132. Teitel does discuss loyalty oaths. See Teitel, Transitional Justice, at 154.
133. Robert Ciadini, Influence 79, 86 (1985); see also Richard Katzev et al., *Can Commitment Change Behavior? A Case Study of Environmental Actions*, 9 J. Soc. Behav. & Personality 1, 13–26 (1994); see also T. Wang & R. Katzev, *Group Commitment and Resource Conservation: Two Field Experiments on Promoting Recycling*, 20 J. Applied Soc. Psych. 265—275 (2006) (finding that group commitments can be lasting but only with monitoring, while individual commitments lasted beyond the trial period).
134. For one scholar's thoughts on the relationship between community and loyalty oaths, see Sanford Levinson, *Constituting Communities through Words That Bind: Reflections on Loyalty Oaths*, 84 Mich. L. Rev. 1440 (1986).
135. Lutz, *Transitional Justice*, at 332; see also Sikkink & Walling, *Argentina's Contribution*, at 316–317, 321.

136. Sikkink & Walling, *Argentina's Contribution*, at 321; Lutz, *Transitional Justice*, at 331–332.

137. Sikkink & Walling, *Argentina's Contribution*, at 321.

138. James Cavallaro & Stephanie Brewer, *Reevaluating Regional Human Rights Litigation in the Twenty-First Century: The Case of the Inter-American Court*, 102 AM. J. INT'L L. 768, 819–820 (2008).

139. Id. at 820.

140. Id. at 820.

141. Id. at 820–821.

142. Id. at 821. One commentator has suggested that this form of "delayed justice" applies in South Korea as well as Argentina. See Sang Wook Daniel Han, *Transitional Justice: When Justice Strikes Back—Case Studies of Delayed Justice in Argentina and South Korea*, 30 HOUS. J. INT'L L. 653 (2008).

143. Cf. Grutter v. Bollinger, 539 U.S. 306, 343 (2003) ("We expect that 25 years from now, the use of racial preferences will no longer be necessary to further the interest we approved today"); cf. also BRUCE ACKERMAN, BEFORE THE NEXT ATTACK 131 (2007) (describing sunset provisions in an emergency constitution, requiring congressional reauthorization for continued executive power).

144. "Lustration" is the ancient practice of purification, and is perhaps a more accurate term because it can include purifying actions short of a total purge. See Roman Boed, *An Evaluation of the Legality and Efficacy of Lustration as a Tool of Transitional Justice*, 37 COLUM. J. TRANSNAT'L L. 357 (1999).

145. Posner & Vermeule, *Transitional Justice as Ordinary Justice*, at 778.

146. TEITEL, TRANSITIONAL JUSTICE, at 158.

147. Posner & Vermeule, *Transitional Justice as Ordinary Justice*, at 778; ELSTER, CLOSING THE BOOKS, at 208.

148. See TEITEL, TRANSITIONAL JUSTICE, at 158–159.

149. See id. at 159 (noting how few were excluded from office).

150. See id. at 165.

151. See id. at 169.

152. AIHRC, A Call For Justice, at 10–11.

153. JAMES DOBBINS ET AL., OCCUPYING IRAQ 52–53 (2009).

154. ALI A. ALLAWI, THE OCCUPATION OF IRAQ 155 (2007). The first order promulgated the de-Ba'athification policy. Id. at 150.

155. DOBBINS ET AL., OCCUPYING IRAQ, at 59. The number is contested. Allawi suggests it was over 400,000. ALLAWI, THE OCCUPATION OF IRAQ, at 157.

156. DOBBINS ET AL., OCCUPYING IRAQ, at 60.

157. Id. at 104.

158. Id. at 105.

159. Id. at 113. The number of people was estimated at 20,000, though some within the government thought it would be higher, around 50,000. See id. at 112 n. 25. Allawi puts the figure at around 30,000. ALLAWI, THE OCCUPATION OF IRAQ, at 150.

160. DOBBINS ET AL., OCCUPYING IRAQ, at 115–116.

161. Id. at 117.

162. Id. at 118.

163. Id. at 119. Allawi notes, however, that many in the U.S. administration were skeptical of Chalabi and had long sought to undermine his credibility. Chalabi's fall from favor also meant that the lion's share of the blame for de-Ba'athification could be ascribed to him. See ALLAWI, THE OCCUPATION OF IRAQ, at 281–282.

164. DOBBINS ET AL., OCCUPYING IRAQ, at 133–134.

165. Id. at 136. The framework and motivations for de-Ba'athification may have compounded this problem. Many considered de-Ba'athification to be "de-Sunnification." See ALLAWI, THE OCCUPATION OF IRAQ, at 152.

166. DOBBINS ET AL., OCCUPYING IRAQ, at 136.

167. See Cummings v. Missouri, 71 U.S. (4 Wall.) 277 (1866) (addressing ministers); see also *Ex Parte* Garland, 71 U.S. (4 Wall.) 333 (1866) (striking a federal statute directed at lawyers).

168. TEITEL, TRANSITIONAL JUSTICE, at 160–161.

169. Roht-Arriaza, *The New Landscape*, at 3–4.

170. See id. at 3 (seeing trials as destabilizing); MINOW, BETWEEN VENGEANCE AND FORGIVENESS, at 57 (noting the possibility of closure).

171. HAYNER, UNSPEAKABLE TRUTHS, at 185–186.

172. Id. at 14.

173. TEITEL, TRANSITIONAL JUSTICE, at 81.

174. HAYNER, UNSPEAKABLE TRUTHS, at 24–31.

175. Id. at 321–322.

176. See id. at 60–64.

177. Patricia Gossman, *Truth, Justice, and Stability in Afghanistan*, in ROHT-ARRIAZA & MARIEZCURRENA, TRANSITIONAL JUSTICE IN THE TWENTY-FIRST CENTURY, at 268–269.

178. Id. at 271.

179. Id.

180. Id.

181. Nadery, *Peace or Justice?*, at 177.

182. HAYNER, UNSPEAKABLE TRUTHS, at 322.

183. Id. at 46.

184. Id. at 36.

185. Id. at 74.

186. Id. at 196.

187. Id. at 197–198.

188. Id. at 199.

189. Id. at 199.

190. AIHRC, Insurgent Abuses against Afghan Civilians, December 2008, available at http://www.aihrc.org.af/2008_Dec/PDF_Anti_G/Eng_anti_G.pdf; AIHRC, Violations of International Humanitarian Law in Afghanistan, available at http://www.aihrc.org.af/IHL_practices_and_examples_final_Coalition_Vioalatioin.pdf [*sic*].

191. AIHRC, Insurgent Abuses, at 13.

192. See, e.g., id. at 17.

193. Cf. Eric A. Posner & Adrian Vermeule, *The Credible Executive*, 74 U. CHI. L. REV. 865 (2007).

194. See, e.g., Geneva Convention Relative to the Treatment of Prisoners of War, arts. 10, 11, August 12, 1949, 6 U.S.T 3316, 75 U.N.T.S. 135.

195. See ELSTER, CLOSING THE BOOKS, at 121.

196. HAYNER, UNSPEAKABLE TRUTHS, at 74–75.

197. AIHRC, Investigation: Use of Indiscriminate and Excessive Force against Civilians by US Forces Following a VBIED Attack in Nangahar Province on March 4, 2007, available at http://www.aihrc.org/2010_eng/Eng_pages/Reports/Thematic/Investigatoin.pdf [*sic*]; AIHRC, Investigation into the shooting of demonstrators in Sheberghan on May 28, 2007 available http://www.aihrc.org.af/rep_sheberghan_incedent_18_july_2007.htm.

198. See AIHRC, Insurgent Abuses; AIHRC, Violations.

199. It is, of course, not clear what is most effective. In some societies, community-based mechanisms may be better than national truth commissions. See Longman, *Justice at the Grassroots*. In other cases, traditional cleansing rituals may succeed at reconciliation and healing. See HAYNER, UNSPEAKABLE TRUTHS, at 186–195 (describing Mozambique's use of traditional rituals instead of transitional justice).

200. Eric A. Posner & Adrian Vermeule, *Reparations for Slavery and Other Historical Injustices*, 103 COLUM. L. REV. 689, 691 (2003); cf. MANI, BEYOND RETRIBUTION, at 5–6, 126–160 (discussing distributive justice concerns and retribution).

201. Posner & Vermeule, *Reparations for Slavery*, at 691.

202. See MINOW, BETWEEN VENGEANCE AND FORGIVENESS, at 94–107 (discussing payments), 107–112 (discussing restitution), 112–117 (discussing apologies and implicit and symbolic forms of reparation); Posner & Vermeule, *Transitional Justice as Ordinary Justice*, at 725–728 (discussing payments), 729–733 (discussing apologies and implicit and symbolic forms of reparation).

203. TEITEL, TRANSITIONAL JUSTICE, at 119, 134.

204. MINOW, BETWEEN VENGEANCE AND FORGIVENESS, at 91.

205. See STATHIS KALYVAS, THE LOGIC OF VIOLENCE IN CIVIL WAR 21, 82–83 (2004).

206. See HAYNER, UNSPEAKABLE TRUTHS, at 171 (noting the irony that in transitions from authoritarian states, democratic governments are saddled with the legacy costs, even as they are trying to reconstruct the state).

CHAPTER 5

1. See JOHN A. HALL & G. JOHN IKENBERRY, THE STATE 1–2 (1989); GIANFRANCO POGGI, THE STATE: ITS NATURE, DEVELOPMENT AND PROSPECTS 19 (1990); Charles Tilly, *Reflections on the History of European State-Making* 70, in THE FORMATION OF NATIONAL STATES IN WESTERN EUROPE (Charles Tilly and

Gabriel Ardant, eds., 1975); Samuel E. Finer, *State- and Nation-Building in Europe: The Role of the Military* 85–86, in TILLY AND ARDANT, THE FORMATION OF NATIONAL STATES IN WESTERN EUROPE (including community, nationality, and external recognition as factors). See also Montevideo Convention on the Rights and Duties of States, December 26, 1933, art. 1, 49 Stat. 3097, 165 U.N.T.S. 19.

2. Michael Mann, *The Autonomous Power of the State: Its Origins, Mechanisms, and Results* 120–121, in STATES IN HISTORY (John A. Hall, ed., 1986).

3. ASHRAF GHANI & CLARE LOCKHART, FIXING FAILED STATES 124 (2008).

4. JOEL S. MIGDAL, ATUL KOHLI, & VIVIENNE SHUE, EDS., STATE POWER AND SOCIAL FORCES 2 (1994). For an excellent treatment of the relationship between states and societies, see JOEL S. MIGDAL, STRONG SOCIETIES AND WEAK STATES (1988).

5. MICHAEL MANN, I THE SOURCES OF SOCIAL POWER: A HISTORY OF POWER FROM THE BEGINNING TO A.D. 1760 at 2 (1986).

6. HENDRIK SPRUYT, THE SOVEREIGN STATE AND ITS COMPETITORS 35, 34–58 (1994).

7. Id. at 77–108.

8. Id. at 109–129.

9. Id. at 130–150.

10. Id. at 158, 167–169.

11. Cf. ALBERTO ALESINA & ENRICO SPOLAORE, THE SIZE OF NATIONS (2005).

12. See, e.g., SPRUYT, THE SOVEREIGN STATE AND ITS COMPETITORS, at 155, 158–169.

13. Michael Walzer, *The Moral Standing of States: A Response to Four Critics*, 9 PHIL. & PUB. AFF. 209, 211 (Spring 1980).

14. See SETH KAPLAN, FIXING FRAGILE STATES 5–6 (2008) (defining fragile, failed, and LICUS countries); Robert I. Rotberg, *Failed States, Collapsed States, Weak States: Causes and Indicators* 4, 5, 9, in STATE FAILURE AND STATE WEAKNESS IN A TIME OF TERROR (Robert I. Rotberg, ed., 2003) (defining weak, failed, and collapsed states); Sebastian von Einsiedel, *Policy Responses to State Failure* 16, in MAKING STATES WORK (Simon Chesterman, Michael Ignatieff, & Ramesh Thakur, eds., 2005) (mentioning various names including endemically weak, aborted, ungovernable, shadow, anarchic, phantom, anemic).

15. See KAPLAN, FIXING FRAGILE STATES, at 6.

16. Michael Ignatieff, *State Failure and Nation-Building* 314, in HUMANITARIAN INTERVENTION: ETHICAL, LEGAL, AND POLITICAL DILEMMAS 299 (J. L. Holzgrefe and Robert O. Keohane, eds., 2003).

17. James D. Fearon & David D. Laitin, *Ethnicity, Insurgency, and Civil War*, 97 AM. POL. SCI. REV. 75 (2003).

18. STATHIS KALYVAS, THE LOGIC OF VIOLENCE IN CIVIL WAR 218 (2006).

19. For a discussion of how liberal democracy and market economics have shaped the peacebuilding paradigm, see Roland Paris, *Peacebuilding and the Limits of Liberal Internationalism*, 22 INT'L SEC. 54, 56–57 (1997). See also ROLAND PARIS, AT WAR'S END (2004).

20. Mann, *The Autonomous Power of the State*, at 113.

21. For a recent, and prominent, argument for "institutionalization before liberalization" (that is, for focus on building institutions prior to facilitating democracy and markets) see PARIS, AT WAR'S END.

22. Paris, *Peacebuilding and the Limits of Liberal Internationalism*, at 56, 74. See also PARIS, AT WAR'S END.

23. SAMUEL P. HUNTINGTON, POLITICAL ORDER IN CHANGING SOCIETIES 7 (1968).

24. T. H. GREEN, LECTURES ON THE PRINCIPLES OF POLITICAL OBLIGATION §94 (Paul Harris & John Morrow, eds., 1986).

25. Cf. Stephen Krasner, *Sharing Sovereignty: New Institutions for Collapsed and Failing States*, INT'L SECURITY, Fall 2004, at 90 (2004).

26. The exception is Steve Ratner, who notes a convergence between occupation and territorial administration. See Steven R. Ratner, *Foreign Occupation and International Territorial Administration: The Challenge of Convergence*, 16 EUR. J. INT'L L. 695 (2005).

27. See, e.g., Adam Roberts, *Transformative Military Occupation: Applying the Laws of War and Human Rights*, 100 AM. J. INT'L L. 580 (2006).

28. See Gregory H. Fox, *The Occupation of Iraq*, 36 GEO. J. INT'L L. 195, 199 (2005) ("Occupiers are assumed to remain only for the limited period between the cessation of hostilities and the conclusion of a final peace treaty. That treaty determines the fate of the occupied territory, most likely returning it to the ousted de jure sovereign").

29. S.C. Res. 1483, U.N. SCOR, 58th Sess., 4761st mtg. at para. 4, 8, U.N. Doc. S/RES/1483 (May 22, 2003).

30. See CARSTON STAHN, THE LAW AND PRACTICE OF INTERNATIONAL TERRITORIAL ADMINISTRATION 143 (2008).

31. Sebastian Mallaby, *The Reluctant Imperialist: Terrorism, Failed States, and the Case for American Empire*, FOR. AFF., (March/April 2002), at 2-7.

32. See NIALL FERGUSON, COLLOSUS: THE PRICE OF AMERICA'S EMPIRE (2004).

33. Michael Ignatieff, *The American Empire: The Burden*, N.Y. TIMES MAG.e, Jan. 5, 2003.

34. For an excellent general overview, see STAHN, THE LAW AND PRACTICE OF INTERNATIONAL TERRITORIAL ADMINISTRATION. Stahn puts into the category of international territorial administration four structures: mandates, trusteeship, occupation, and peacekeeping. See id. at 43.

35. Krasner, *Sharing Sovereignty*, at 98.

36. RICHARD CAPLAN, A NEW TRUSTEESHIP? THE INTERNATIONAL ADMINISTRATION OF WAR-TORN TERRITORIES 10 (2002).

37. SIMON CHESTERMAN, YOU, THE PEOPLE: THE UNITED NATIONS, TERRITORIAL ADMINISTRATION, AND STATE-BUILDING 5 (2004).

38. CAPLAN, A NEW TRUSTEESHIP?, at 13–16.

39. CHESTERMAN, YOU, THE PEOPLE, at 5.

40. League of Nations Covenant, art 22, para 1, available at http://www.yale.edu/lawweb/avalon/leagcov.htm (accessed Apr. 15, 2012).

41. TOM PARKER, THE ULTIMATE INTERVENTION: REVITALISING THE UN TRUSTEESHIP COUNCIL FOR THE 21ST CENTURY 12 (2003) (quoting UN Secretary General Trygve Lie).

42. UN Charter, art. 78.

43. Christian Eric Ford & Ben A. Oppenheim, *Neotrusteeship or Mistrusteeship? The "Authority Creep" Dilemma in United Nations Transitional Administration*, 41 VAND. J. TRANSNAT'L L. 55, 65–66 (2008).

44. Gerald B. Helman & Steven R. Ratner, *Saving Failed States*, 89 FOR. POL'Y 3 (1993); PARKER, THE ULTIMATE INTERVENTION; CAPLAN, A NEW TRUSTEESHIP?; James D. Fearon & David D. Laitin, *Neotrusteeship and the Problem of Weak States*, 28 INT'L SECURITY 5 (2004); Brian Deiwert, Note, *A New Trusteeship for World Peace and Security: Can an Old League of Nations Idea be Applied to a Twenty-First Century Iraq?*, 14 IND. INT'L & COMP. L. REV. 771 (2004); Krasner, *Sharing Sovereignty*.

45. Helman & Ratner, *Saving Failed States*, at 13–16.

46. Id. at 14.

47. Id. at 16.

48. See Martin Indyk, Op-Ed., *A U.S.-Led Trusteeship for Palestine*, WASH. POST, June 29, 2002, at A23; Suzanne Nossel, Op-Ed., *A Trustee for Crippled States*, WASH. POST, August 25, 2003, at A17; Paul Kennedy, Op-Ed., *UN Trusteeship Council Could Finally Find a Role in Postwar Iraq*, DAILY YOMIURI (Japan), May 9, 2003, available at http://www.globalpolicy.org/security/issues/iraq/after/2003/0511trusteeshipcouncil.htm; CAPLAN, A NEW TRUSTEESHIP?, at 7; Ignatieff, *State Failure and Nation-Building*, at 308; Martin Indyk, *A Trusteeship for Palestine?*, FOR. AFF., May/June 2003, at 51; Deiwart, Note, *A New Trusteeship for Peace and Security*; Fearon & Laitin, *Neotrusteeship and the Problem of Failed States*; PARKER, THE ULTIMATE INTERVENTION; Krasner, *Sharing Sovereignty*.

49. Fearon & Laitin, *Neotrusteeship and the Problem of Failed States*, at 7.

50. Id. at 7. Short duration, of course, is more characteristic of transitional administration than trusteeship, but this is more an indicator that these concepts should be seen as having convergent boundaries rather than being strictly delineated.

51. Id. at 28.

52. Robert O. Keohane, *Political Authority after Intervention*, in HUMANITARIAN INTERVENTION, at 296.

53. GHANI & LOCKHART, FIXING FAILED STATES, at 193.

54. FRANCIS FUKUYAMA, STATE-BUILDING (2004).

55. Id. at 88.

56. S. Frederick Starr, *Sovereignty and Legitimacy in Afghan Nation-Building* 116, in NATION-BUILDING (Francis Fukuyama, ed., 2006).

57. Fearon & Laitin, *Neotrusteeship and the Problem of Failed States* at 37; see also CAPLAN, A NEW TRUSTEESHIP?, at 11; Krasner, *Sharing Sovereignty*, at 99.

58. See Krasner, *Sharing Sovereignty*, at 99; cf. FERGUSON, COLOSSUS.

59. See Krasner, *Sharing Sovereignty*, at 99; Fearon & Laitin, *Neotrusteeship and the Problem of Failed States*, at 7.

60. GHANI & LOCKHART, FIXING FAILED STATES, at 176; see also Fearon & Laitin, *Neotrusteeship and the Problem of Failed States*, at 7 (noting the "complex hodgepodge of actors"); CAPLAN, A NEW TRUSTEESHIP?, at 21–23 (describing the sources of a "multiplicity of actors) as more international organizations, greater expectations for delivery, and the absence of local administrative capacity).

61. GHANI & LOCKHART, FIXING FAILED STATES, at 176.

62. Id.

63. CHESTERMAN, YOU, THE PEOPLE, at 146 (noting that transitional administrators are often above the law).

64. Fearon & Laitin, *Neotrusteeship and the Problem of Failed States*, at 35.

65. Coalition Provisional Order, No. 17, Status of Coalition Provisional Authority, MNF-Iraq, Certain Missions and Personnel in Iraq, June 27, 2004, available at http://www.iraqcoalition.org/regulations/20040627_CPAORD_17_Status_of_Coalition__Rev__with_Annex_A.pdf.

66. CAPLAN, A NEW TRUSTEESHIP? at 55.

67. Id.

68. Tilly, *Reflections on the History of European State-Making*, at 74; see also Otto Hintze, *Military Organization and the Organization of the State* 181, in I THE STATE: CRITICAL CONCEPTS (John A. Hall, 1994).

69. Tilly, *Reflections on the History of European State-Making*, at 42.

70. FRANCIS FUKUYAMA, THE ORIGINS OF POLITICAL AUTHORITY: FROM PREHUMAN TIMES TO THE FRENCH REVOLUTION 81–90 (2011).

71. Id. at 105 (noting the effect of war on state-building in China and Europe) and 111 (noting that not all wars lead to states).

72. Finer, *State-and Nation-Building in Europe*, at 96.

73. Charles Tilly, *War Making and State Making as Organized Crime* 521, in HALL, I THE STATE.

74. See CHARLES TILLY, COERCION, CAPITAL, AND EUROPEAN STATES, AD 990–1990 at 97 (1990).

75. Hintze, *Military Organization and the Organization of the State*, at 193–194.

76. See TILLY, COERCION, CAPITAL, AND EUROPEAN STATES, at 117–118.

77. See SPRUYT, THE SOVEREIGN STATE AND ITS COMPETITORS, at 155, 158; see also TILLY, COERCION, CAPITAL, AND EUROPEAN STATES, at 14.

78. Tilly, *Reflections on the History of European State-Making*, at 71.

79. Tilly, *War Making and State Making as Organized Crime*, at 508.

80. JAMES C. SCOTT, SEEING LIKE A STATE: HOW CERTAIN SCHEMES TO IMPROVE THE HUMAN CONDITION HAVE FAILED 64–73 (1998). On the census as a tool

of population control, see DAVID GALULA, COUNTER-INSURGENCY WARFARE 115–118 (1964); DAVID GALULA, PACIFICATION IN ALGERIA 1956–1958 at 99 (1963, RAND ed. 2006); ROGER TRINQUIER, MODERN WARFARE: A FRENCH VIEW OF COUNTERINSURGENCY 28–29 (1964, 2006 ed.).

81. See POGGI, THE STATE, at 27; Miguel Angel Centeno, *Limited War and Limited States* 90, in IRREGULAR ARMED FORCES AND THEIR ROLE IN POLITICS AND STATE FORMATION (Diane E. Davis and Anthony W. Pereira, eds., 2003).

82. TILLY, COERCION, CAPITAL, AND EUROPEAN STATES, at 101–102.

83. Centeno, *Limited War and Limited States*, at 88–89 (citing V. G. Kiernan, *Conscription and Society in Europe before the War of 1914–1918*, in M. R. D. FOOT, ED., WAR AND SOCIETY (1973) at 141).

84. TILLY, COERCION, CAPITAL, AND EUROPEAN STATES, at 30.

85. Id. at 150–151.

86. Id. at 30.

87. Charles Tilly, *Armed Force, Regimes, and Contention in Europe since 1650*, in DAVIS & PEREIRA, IRREGULAR ARMED FORCES AND THEIR ROLE IN POLITICS AND STATE FORMATION, at 52.

88. See SPRUYT, THE SOVEREIGN STATE AND ITS COMPETITORS, at 30.

89. SPRUYT, THE SOVEREIGN STATE AND ITS COMPETITORS, at 30–31, 91–92, 109–129, 159–169, 185. The alliances between different domestic constituencies also had significant effects on the development of accountable government. For an account of these coalitions and their consequences, see FUKUYAMA, THE ORIGINS OF POLITICAL ORDER, at 422–434.

90. Counterinsurgents have recently recognized this phenomenon. See David H. Petraeus, COMISAF's Counterinsurgency (COIN) Contracting Guidance, September 8, 2010, available at http://smallwarsjournal.com/blog/2010/09/comisafs-counterinsurgency-coi/.

91. Centano, *Limited War and Limited States*.

92. DAVID J. KILCULLEN, COUNTERINSURGENCY 152 (2010).

93. HANNAH ARENDT, ON VIOLENCE 44 (1969).

94. Id. at 41.

95. Id. at 44, 46.

96. Edmund Burke, Speech on Conciliation with the Colonies, in THE PORTABLE EDMUND BURKE (ed. Isaac Kramnick, 1999), at 260.

97. MANN, I THE SOURCES OF SOCIAL POWER, at 1–2.

98. See Peter W. Chiarelli & Patrick W. Michaelis, *Winning the Peace: The Requirement for Full-Spectrum Operations*, MIL. REV., July–August 2005, at 7; THE U.S. ARMY/ MARINE CORPS COUNTERINSURGENCY FIELD MANUAL ¶¶ 5-7 to 5-49 (2007).

99. HUNTINGTON, POLITICAL ORDER IN CHANGING SOCIETIES, at 12 (emphasis omitted).

100. Id. at 13, 17, 20, 22.

101. Montgomery McFate, *Anthropology and Counterinsurgency: The Strange Story of Their Curious Relationship*, MIL. REV., March–April 2005, at 26, 28.
102. Id. at 26, 28–36.
103. FIELD MANUAL, at ¶¶ 3-19 to 3-78.
104. Id. at ¶ 1–125.
105. Joshua Foust, From Whole-of-Government to Whole-of-Place, Registan.net, March 31, 2010, available at http://www.registan.net/index.php/2010/03/31/from-whole-of-government-to-whole-of-place.
106. Jim Gant, One Tribe at a Time 33 (2nd ed., 2009), available at http://www.steven-pressfield.com/wp-content/uploads/2009/10/one_tribe_at_a_time_ed2.pdf.
107. Cf. Michael T. Flynn, Matt Pottinger, & Paul D. Batchelor, Fixing Intel: A Blueprint for Making Intelligence Relevant in Afghanistan, Center for a New American Security Working Paper, January 4, 2010, available at http://cnas.org/node/3924.
108. McFate, *Anthropology and Counterinsurgency*, at 37.
109. MONTESQUIEU, THE SPIRIT OF THE LAWS, 2.2, 9.1 (trans. & ed. Anne M. Cohler, Basia Carolyn Miller, & Harold Samuel Stone, Cambridge Univ. Press, 1989). Citations to Montesquieu are to book and chapter numbers.
110. Id. at 8.16.
111. Id. at 1.3, 19.4.
112. Id. at 1.3.
113. JOHN STUART MILL, CONSIDERATIONS ON REPRESENTATIVE GOVERNMENT 207–208, in ON LIBERTY AND OTHER ESSAYS (ed. John Gray, Oxford Univ. Press 1989). For Mill's critique of the naturalist position, see 211.
114. Id. at 218–219.
115. Id. at 218.
116. Id. at 234.
117. FREDERICK QUINN, THE FRENCH OVERSEAS EMPIRE 143–144 (2000); PETER PARET, MAKERS OF MODERN STRATEGY 388 (1986); Thomas Rid, *The 19th Century Origins of Counterinsurgency Strategy*, 33 J. STRATEGIC STUD. 729 (2010).
118. QUINN, THE FRENCH OVERSEAS EMPIRE, at 153; see also Rid, *The 19th Century Origins of Counterinsurgency Strategy*.
119. Richard Stubbs, *From Search and Destroy to Hearts and Minds: The Evolution of British Strategy in Malaya 1948–60*, at 113, in COUNTERINSURGENCY IN MODERN WARFARE (Daniel Marston and Carter Malkasian, eds., 2008). See generally ANTHONY SHORT, THE COMMUNIST INSURRECTION IN MALAYA, 1948–1960 at 391–415 (1975); RICHARD STUBBS, HEARTS AND MINDS IN GUERRILLA WARFARE: THE MALAYAN EMERGENCY, 1948–1960 at 168–180 (2004).
120. Stubbs, *From Search and Destroy to Hearts and Minds*, at 114.
121. Id. at 115–118.
122. Id. at 114.
123. Id. at 118–119.
124. Id. at 113, 119, 121.

125. SHORT, THE COMMUNIST INSURRECTION IN MALAYA, at 404; Stubbs, *From Search and Destroy to Hearts and Minds*, at 122.

126. SHORT, THE COMMUNIST INSURRECTION IN MALAYA, at 402.

127. Stubbs, *From Search and Destroy to Hearts and Minds*, at 123.

128. STUBBS, HEARTS AND MINDS IN GUERRILLA WARFARE, at 190, 213–215.

129. Stubbs, *From Search and Destroy to Hearts and Minds*, at 114.

130. See Phillip E. Catton, *Counter-Insurgency and Nation-Building: The Strategic Hamlet Programme in South Vietnam 1961–1963*, 21 INT'L HIST. REV. 918, 923 (1999). There is some debate about when exactly the program started and whether Robert Thompson, who had worked in Malaya, provided the idea for the program. Catton finds that plans were underway prior to Thompson's suggestion of the program in the fall of 1961, see id. at 924, and that it was based on the 1957 land development and 1959 agroville programs, id. at 920–921. Krepinevich suggests that Thompson was the primary inspiration for the plan. See ANDREW F. KREPINEVICH JR., THE ARMY AND VIETNAM 66–67 (1988).

131. Catton, *Counter-Insurgency and Nation-Building*, at 919, 927.

132. Id. at 925, 929, 932, 935–936.

133. Id. at 922, 929–930.

134. Id. at 925, 938.

135. Id. at 923–924. The Americans knew of the program, but Diem saw the program as a way to regain control from an overbearing and meddlesome patron. See id. at 924.

136. Id. at 938–939. See also J. P. D. DUNBABIN, THE POST-IMPERIAL AGE: THE GREAT POWERS AND THE WIDER WORLD 118 (1994); JOHN A. NAGL, LEARNING TO EAT SOUP WITH A KNIFE: COUNTERINSURGENCY LESSONS FROM MALAYA AND VIETNAM 130 (2005).

137. KREPINEVICH, THE ARMY AND VIETNAM, at 68.

138. Bernard B. Fall, *South Viet-Nam at the Crossroads*, Int'l J. 19:2 (Spring 1964), 139, 145.

139. Catton, *Counter-Insurgency and Nation-Building*, at 939.

140. DUNBABIN, THE POST-IMPERIAL AGE, at 118.

141. KREPINEVICH, THE ARMY AND VIETNAM, at 70.

142. Id. at 71.

143. Id. at 72.

144. Id. at 72–73.

145. Id. at 172–176.

146. See Antonio Giustozzi, The Debate on Warlordism: The Importance of Military Legitimacy 5, 14, London Sch. Econ. Crisis States Res. Ctr., Discussion Paper No. 13, 2005, available at http://www.crisisstates.com/download/dp/dp13.pdf.

147. See U.S. Inst. of Peace, Unfinished Business in Afghanistan: Warlordism, Reconstruction, and Ethnic Harmony, 4–5 (2003), available at http://www.usip.org/pubs/specialreports/sr105.pdf; see also Jeremy I. Levitt, *Illegal Peace?: An Inquiry into the Legality of Power-Sharing with Warlords and Rebels in Africa*, 27 MICH. J. INT'L L. 495, 502, 506–508, 575, 577 (2006).

148. See Daniel Biró, The (Un)bearable Lightness of . . . Violence: Warlordism as an Alternative Form of Governance in the "Westphalian Periphery"?, in Inst. for Dev. & Peace, *State Failure Revisited II: Actors of Violence and Alternative Forms of Governance* 7, 33–43 (Tobias Debiel & Daniel Lambach eds., 2007), available at http://inef.uni-due.de/page/documents/Report89.pdf; Conrad Schetter, Rainer Glassner, & Masood Karokhail, *Beyond Warlordism: The Local Security Architecture in Afghanistan*, INT'L POL. & SOC'Y, June 2007, at 136, 137–148, 150.

149. See U.S. Inst. of Peace, Unfinished Business in Afghanistan, at 4–5.

150. James C. O'Brien, *Lawyers, Guns, and Money: Warlords and Reconstruction after Iraq*, 11 U.C. DAVIS J. INT'L L. & POL'Y 99, 100, 106–120 (2004).

151. Arthur Waldron, Research Note, *Warlordism versus Federalism: The Revival of a Debate?*, 121 CHINA Q. 116, 121–124 (1990).

152. Austin Long, *The Anbar Awakening* 74–75, SURVIVAL 50:2, 67–94 (2008).

153. John A. McCary, *The Anbar Awakening: An Alliance of Incentives* 44, WASH. Q. January 2009, at 43–59.

154. Long, *The Anbar Awakening*, at 77–78; 80–81.

155. See Thomas Ricks, *Situation Called Dire in West Iraq*, WASH. POST, Sept. 11, 2006; McCary, *The Anbar Awakening*, at 49.

156. McCary, *The Anbar Awakening*, 49–50.

157. See Long, *The Anbar Awakening*, at 81–82.

158. Dave Kilcullen, Anatomy of a Tribal Revolt, Small Wars J., Aug. 29, 2007, available at http://smallwarsjournal.com/blog/2007/08/anatomy-of-a-tribal-revolt/.

159. Id.

160. See Gant, *One Tribe at a Time*; James Dao, *Going Tribal in Afghanistan*, N.Y. Times At-War Blog, November 4, 2009, available at http://atwar.blogs.nytimes.com/2009/11/04/going-tribal-in-afghanistan; David Ignatius, *Afghan Tribes to the Rescue?*, WASH. POST, Nov. 22, 2009.

161. Gant, One Tribe at a Time, at 14, 26–29.

162. Joshua Foust, *Tribe and Prejudice: America's "New Hope" in Afghanistan*, THE NATIONAL, Feb, 11, 2010, available at http://www.thenational.ae/apps/pbcs/dll/article?AID=/20100211/REVIEW/702119988.

163. Kimberly Marten, *The Danger of Tribal Militias in Afghanistan: Learning from the British Empire*, J. INT'L AFF., 63:1 (Fall 2009) at 158–160.

164. Dexter Filkins, *Afghan Tribe, Vowing to Fight Taliban, to Get U.S. Aid in Return*, N.Y. TIMES, January 27, 2010.

165. Alissa J. Rubin, *Afghan Tribal Rivalries Bedevil a U.S. Plan*, N.Y. TIMES, March 11, 2010.

166. Rajiv Chandrasekharan, *U.S. Training Afghan Villagers to Fight the Taliban*, WASH. POST, April 27, 2010.

167. Small Wars Foundation, the U.S. Joint Forces Command Joint Irregular Warfare Center, the U.S. Marine Corps Center for Irregular Warfare, the U.S. Army/U.S. Marine Corps Counterinsurgency Center, and Noetic Group, Considerations for Tribal Engagement: A Summary of the Tribal Engagement Workshop 2010,

at 2–3 (2010), available at http://smallwarsjournal.com/events/tew/docs/TEW_Summary_Report_vi.pdf.

168.  FIELD MANUAL at ¶A-48.

169.  GHANI & LOCKHART, FIXING FAILED STATES, at 206; Ministry of Rural Rehabilitation and Development, National Solidarity Programme Frequently Asked Questions, March 6, 2010, available at http://www.nspafghanistan.org/default.aspx?Sel=26.

170.  Ministry of Rural Rehabilitation and Development, National Solidarity Programme, How Funds are Distributed, available at http://www.nspafghanistan.org/default.aspx?Sel=12.

171.  The World Bank, Afghanistan's National Solidarity Program: Overview and Challenges, available at http://web.worldbank.org/WBSITE/EXTERNAL/COUNTRIES/SOUTHASIAEXT/0,contentMDK:21166159~pagePK:14673 6~piPK:146830~theSitePK:223547,00.html.

172.  Id.

173.  Robert B. Zoellick, Op-Ed., *The Key to Rebuilding Afghanistan*, WASH. POST, August 22, 2008.

174.  Ministry of Rural Rehabilitation and Development, National Solidarity Programme, NSP Milestones, available at http://www.nspafghanistan.org/default.aspx?Sel=13.

175.  Zoellick, *The Key to Rebuilding Afghanistan*.

176.  Gregory Warner, *The Schools the Taliban Won't Torch*, WASH. MONTHLY, December 2007, available at http://www.washingtonmonthly.com/features/2007/0712.warner.html.

177.  GHANI & LOCKHART, FIXING FAILED STATES, at 206–207.

178.  Id. at 207.

179.  JOHN DEWEY, THE PUBLIC AND ITS PROBLEMS 215 (1954).

180.  Id. at 148.

181.  Id. at 149.

182.  See id. at 147, 216–217.

183.  DONALD CAMERON, PRINCIPLES OF NATIVE ADMINISTRATION AND THEIR APPLICATION 6 (2d ed. 1930).

184.  Id. at 6.

185.  The British provided the Amir with an allowance of 1.2 million rupees in 1883, which was raised to 1.8 million in 1893. During his reign, the Amir received 28.5 million rupees in grants and allowance, in addition to access to arms. See THOMAS BARFIELD, AFGHANISTAN 153 (2010).

186.  Cf. Austin Long, *The Anbar Awakening*, at 70 (describing "state tribalism"). On Kenya, see Mordechai Tamarkin, *The Roots of Political Stability in Kenya*, AFRICAN AFF., 77:308 (July 1978), at 300–301.

187.  Michael C. Dorf & Charles F. Sabel, *A Constitution of Democratic Experimentalism*, 98 COLUM. L. REV. 267 (1998).

188.  See Archon Fung & Erik Olin Wright, *Deepening Democracy: Innovations in Empowered Participatory Governance*, POL. & SOC'Y, 29:1 (March 2001), at 5–41.

189.  See Dorf & Sabel, *A Constitution of Democratic Experimentalism*.

CHAPTER 6

1.  Thomas Carothers, *The Rule of Law Revival* 3, 7, in PROMOTING THE RULE OF LAW ABROAD (Thomas Carothers, ed., 2006).

2.  BRIAN Z. TAMANAHA, ON THE RULE OF LAW 1 (2004).

3.  Special Inspector General for Iraq Reconstruction, Quarterly and Semi-Annual Report to the United States Congress 45, January 30, 2010, available at www.sigir. mil/publications/quarterlyreports/January2010.html.

4.  Liana Sun Wyler & Kenneth Katzman, Afghanistan: U.S. Rule of Law and Justice Sector Assistance 24, Cong. Res. Service, November 9, 2010, available at www.fas. org/sgp/crs/row/R41484.pdf.

5.  THE U.S. ARMY/MARINE CORPS COUNTERINSURGENCY FIELD MANUAL ¶ D-38 (2007).

6.  Andrew M. Exum, Nathaniel C. Fick, Ahmed A. Humayun, and David J. Kilcullen, Triage: The Next Twelve Months in Afghanistan and Pakistan 8 n. 10, Center for a New American Security Report, June 10, 2009, available at http://www.cnas.org/ node/976; see also Dennis C. Blair, Annual Threat Assessment of the Intelligence Community, Sen. Select Committee on Intelligence, February 12, 2009; Yochi J. Dreazen and Siobhan Gorman, *Taliban Regains Power, Influence in Afghanistan*, WALL ST. J., Nov. 20, 2008.

7.  JANE STROMSETH, DAVID WIPPMAN, & ROSA BROOKS, CAN MIGHT MAKE RIGHTS? BUILDING THE RULE OF LAW AFTER MILITARY INTERVENTIONS 56 (2006); see also TAMANAHA, ON THE RULE OF LAW, at 3 (noting that the rule of law is an "exceedingly elusive notion").

8.  Randall Peerenboom, *Human Rights and the Rule of Law: What's the Relationship?*, 36 GEO. J. INT'L L. 809, 826–827 (2005). See also TAMANAHA, ON THE RULE OF LAW, at 2 (citing statements by Vladimir Putin, Robert Mugame, Hu Jintao, and Abdul Rashid Dostum).

9.  JOSEPH RAZ, THE AUTHORITY OF LAW 210 (1983).

10. Judith N. Shklar, *Political Theory and the Rule of Law* 1, in THE RULE OF LAW (Allan C. Hutchinson & Patrick Monahan, eds., 1987).

11. Thomas Carothers, *The Problem of Knowledge*, in CAROTHERS, PROMOTING THE RULE OF LAW ABROAD, at 19, 17.

12. Id. at 21.

13. Richard H. Fallon Jr., *"The Rule of Law" as a Contested Concept in Constitutional Discourse*, 97 COLUM. L. REV. 1, 7 (1997).

14. See, e.g., TAMANAHA, ON THE RULE OF LAW 91–101; Douglas J. Simsovic, *No Fixed Address: Universality and the Rule of Law*, 35 REVUE JURIDIQUE THEMIS 739, 748–751 (2001).

15. See H. L. A. HART, THE CONCEPT OF LAW 91–99 (2nd ed. 1997).

16. See, e.g., Fallon, *"The Rule of Law" as a Contested Concept*, at 8; Brian Z. Tamanaha, *A Concise Guide to the Rule of Law* 3, in FLORENCE WORKSHOP ON THE RULE OF LAW, NEIL WALKER & GIANLUIGI PALOMBELLA, EDS., (2008); Brian Z. Tamanaha, Rule of Law For Everyone?, unpublished draft, available at http://

papers.ssrn.com/sol3/papers.cfm?abstract_id=312622, at 11; RAZ, THE AU-
THORITY OF LAW, at 212; Susan Rose-Ackerman, *Establishing the Rule of Law*
182, in WHEN STATES FAIL (Robert I. Rotberg, ed., 2004); Rachel Kleinfeld,
*Competing Definitions of the Rule of Law*, in CAROTHERS, PROMOTING THE
RULE OF LAW ABROAD, at 36.

17. Ruth Teitel, *Transitional Jurisprudence: The Role of Law in Political Transformation*, 106 YALE L.J. 2009, 2029 (1997); STROMSETH ET AL., CAN MIGHT MAKE
RIGHTS?, at 56.

18. Fallon, *"The Rule of Law" as a Contested Concept*, at 7–8, 14–17; RAZ, THE AU-
THORITY OF LAW, at 214; Peerenboom, *Human Rights and the Rule of Law*, at 876;
Kleinfeld, *Competing Definitions of the Rule of Law*, at 42.

19. Fallon, *"The Rule of Law" as a Contested Concept*, at 8; RAZ, THE AUTHORITY OF
LAW, at 214.

20. Kleinfeld, *Competing Definitions of the Rule of Law*, at 42.

21. Fallon, *"The Rule of Law" as a Contested Concept*, at 8, RAZ, THE AUTHORITY OF
LAW, at 219.

22. Tamanaha, *Concise Guide*, at 3.

23. Kleinfeld, *Competing Definitions of the Rule of Law*, at 38.

24. RAZ, THE AUTHORITY OF LAW, at 211.

25. On principled reasons, see RONALD DWORKIN, A MATTER OF PRINCIPLE 12
(1985) (stating that the rule of law must "capture and enforce moral rights"); Otto
Kirchheimer, *The Rechtsstaat as Magic Wall*, in W. E. SCHEUERMAN, ED., THE
RULE OF LAW UNDER SIEGE 254 (1996); on liberalism, see TAMANAHA, ON THE
RULE OF LAW 32 (noting that the "rule of law today is thoroughly understood in
terms of liberalism"); Tamanaha, *Rule of Law for Everyone*, at 12; see generally
Brian Z. Tamanaha, The Dark Side of the Relationship between the Rule of Law
and Liberalism, unpublished draft, available at http://papers.ssrn.com/sol3/
papers.cfm?abstract_id=1087023 (accessed April 15, 2012) (arguing that liberalism has used the rule of law to promote property rights even when averse to
democracy); on instrumentalism, see Peerenboom, *Human Rights and the Rule of
Law*, at 831.

26. Carothers, *The Rule of Law Revival*, at 5.

27. 1990 Conference on Security and Cooperation in Europe, quoted in TAMANAHA,
ON THE RULE OF LAW, at 111. See also Robert Stein, *Rule of Law: What Does It
Mean?*, 18 MINN. J. INT'L L. 293, 302 (2009) (arguing that the rule of law requires
that "[m]embers of society have the right to participate in the creation and refine-
ment of laws that regulate their behaviors"); see Allan C. Hutchinson & Patrick
Monahan, *Democracy and the Rule of Law*, in Hutchinson &Monahan, THE RULE
OF LAW; see also ALLAN C. HUTCHINSON, THE PROVINCE OF JURISPRUDENCE
DEMOCRATIZED (2008).

28. Kleinfeld, *Competing Definitions of the Rule of Law*, at 45.

29. Owen Fiss, quoted in STROMSETH ET AL., CAN MIGHT MAKE RIGHTS?, at 59.

30. American Bar Association, Rule of Law Initiative, available at http://www.abanet. org/rol/about.shtml (accessed April 15, 2012).

31. See, e.g., UN Secretary General, supra; USAID Handbook of Democracy and Government Program Indicators, no. PN-ACC-390, August 1998 ("A rule of law that contributes to the building of sustainable democracy is one that protects basic human rights"), available at www.usaid.gov/our_work/democracy_and_gover- nance/publications/pdfs/pnacc390.pdf; European Union Commission Commu- nications to the Council and the European Parliament, 1999 ("The primacy of law is a fundamental principle of any democratic system seeking to foster and promote rights, whether civil and political, or economic, social, and cultural"), available at http://europa.eu.int/comm/europeaid/projects/eidhr/pdf/presentation_rule_ of_law.pdf.

32. United Nations Peacekeeping Operations: Principles and Guidelines 98 (2008).

33. See, e.g., Stein, *Rule of Law*, at 302; Kleinfeld, *Competing Definitions of the Rule of Law*, at 44; Carothers, *The Rule of Law Revival*, at 4. The USAID once defined the rule of law as including "the basic principles of equal treatment of all people before the law, fairness, and both constitutional and actual guarantees of basic human rights." See GAO, Rule of Law Funding Worldwide for Fiscal Years 1993–1998, June 1999, at 13.

34. United Nations Development Program, Human Development Report Afghanistan 45 (2007).

35. STROMSETH ET AL., CAN MIGHT MAKE RIGHTS?, at 79.

36. Kleinfeld, *Competing Definitions of the Rule of Law*, at 38. Note that this ap- proach would imply that the rule of law certainly did not exist in the United States before the Fourteenth Amendment abolished slavery, and might not have existed in the United States before women's suffrage and the Civil Rights Acts in the 1960s.

37. Hernando De Soto, *Preface* in THE LAW AND ECONOMICS OF DEVELOPMENT xiv (Edgardo Buscaglia et al., eds., 1997); see also HERNANDO DE SOTO, THE MYSTERY OF CAPITAL (2000); DOUGLASS C. NORTH, INSTITUTIONS, INSTI- TUTIONAL CHANGE, AND ECONOMIC PERFORMANCE (1990); Carothers, *The Rule of Law Revival*, at 5 ("Basic elements of a modern market economy such as property rights and contracts are founded on law. . . . Without the rule of law, major economic institutions such as corporations, banks, and labor unions would not function").

38. Daniel Kaufmann, Aart Kraay, & Pablo Zoido-Lobaton, Governance Matters, World Bank Policy Research Working Paper 2196, at 8 (October 1999).

39. Daniel Kaufmann, Aart Kraay, & Massimo Mastruzzi, Governance Matters III: Governance Indicators for 1996–2002, World Bank Policy Research Working Paper 3106, at 4 (August 2003).

40. See Kevin E. Davis, *What Can the Rule of Law Variable Tell Us about Rule of Law Reforms*, 26 MICH. J. INT'L L. 141, 151 (2004) (criticizing this metric); see also

Stijn Claessens & Luc Laeven, *Financial Development, Property Rights, and Growth*, 58 J. FIN. 2401 (2003).

41. See Shklar, *Political Theory and the Rule of Law*, at 7.

42. Carothers, *The Rule of Law Revival*, at 7.

43. Tamanaha, *Concise Guide*, at 6; see also GAO, Rule of Law Funding Worldwide for Fiscal Years 1993–1998, GAO 99–158 (June 1999) (focusing on judicial institutions, including courts and ministries of justice); Golub, in CAROTHERS, PROMOTING THE RULE OF LAW ABROAD, at 117 (quoting a World Bank official that "[t]he rule of law is built on the cornerstone of an efficient and effective judicial system"). Ronald J. Daniels & Michael Trebilcock, *The Political Economy of Rule of Law Reform in Developing Countries*, 26 MICH. J. INT'L L. 99, 111–118 (2004) (noting the need for a judiciary and prosecutors); UN Peacekeeping Operations 25 n. 12 (citing national justice systems and institutions).

44. Stephen Golub, *A House without Foundation*, in CAROTHERS, PROMOTING THE RULE OF LAW ABROAD, at 106.

45. See, e.g., Stein, *Rule of Law*, at 302 ("Judicial power is exercised independently of either the executive or legislative powers and individual judges base their decisions solely on facts and law of individual cases"); Report of the UN Secretary General, The Rule of Law and Transitional Justice in Conflict and Post-Conflict Societies, S/2004/616, at 4 (2004) (noting that the rule of law requires the separation of powers).

46. Carothers, *The Rule of Law Revival*, at 7.

47. On accountability, see United Nations, The United Nations and the Rule of Law, available at www.un.org/en/ruleoflaw (accessed April 15, 2012). On education and reform, see American Bar Association, Rule of Law Initiative, available at http://www.abanet.org/rol/about.shtml (accessed April 15, 2012); see also Douglas Keh, Building the Rule of Law in Somaliland, UNDP CPR Newsletter (2005) (noting that the Rule of Law and Security Program focuses on "training legal professionals, establishing legal clinics, and supporting policing"), available at http://www.undp.org/cpr/newsletters/volume_1/CPRNews-Vol1-Iss1.pdf.

48. STROMSETH ET AL., CAN MIGHT MAKE RIGHTS?, at 4.

49. See, e.g., Rosa Ehrenreich Brooks, *The New Imperialism: Violence, Norms, and the "Rule of Law,"* 101 MICH. L. REV. 2275, 2285 (2003); Lan Cao, *Culture Change*, 47 VA. J. INT'L L. 357 (2007).

50. Compare Kleinfeld, *Competing Definitions of the Rule of Law*, at 40 (excluding security), with Fallon, *"The Rule of Law" as a Contested Concept*, at 7 (including security).

51. See U.S. Agency for International Development, U.S. Department of Defense, & U.S. Department of State, Security Sector Reform 3 (March 2009), available at http://www.usaid.gov/our_work/democracy_and_governance/publications/pdfs/SSR_JS_Mar2009.pdf; DFID, Security Sector Reform Policy Brief 3 (November 2003), available at http://www.dfid.gov.uk/Documents/publications/security-sector-brief.pdf; see also Kleinfeld, *Competing Definitions of the Rule of*

*Law*, at 39–41; UN Office of Rule of Law and Security Institutions (describing its operations as unifying "judicial, legal, correctional units, and mine action, disarmament, demobilization and reintegration, as well as new security sector reform functions"), available at http://www.un.org/Depts/dpko/dpko/orolsi.shtml; see also ALICE HILLS, POLICING POST-CONFLICT CITIES 70–78 (2009) (describing security sector reform).

52. PAUL W. KAHN, THE CULTURAL STUDY OF LAW 40, 6, 36 (1999); see also Teitel, *Transitional Jurisprudence*, at 2026.

53. Compare American Bar Association, Rule of Law Initiative, available at www.abanet. org/rol/about.shtml (accessed April 15, 2012) (taking a technocratic approach) with Peerenboom, *Human Rights and the Rule of Law*, at 903 (rejecting that approach).

54. Peerenboom, *Human Rights and the Rule of Law*, at 906.

55. Margaret Jane Radin, *Reconsidering the Rule of Law*, 69 B.U. L. REV. 781, 782–783, 807 (1989); Peerenboom, *Human Rights and the Rule of Law*, at 827.

56. Teitel, *Transitional Jurisprudence*, at 2020, 2025.

57. Peerenboom, *Human Rights and the Rule of Law*, at 903 n. 300; Brooks, *The New Imperialism*, at 2280.

58. Center for Law and Military Operations, Rule of Law Handbook 14 (2008).

59. Id.

60. Id. at 13.

61. FIELD MANUAL at ¶ 1–113. For an early, and classic, critique of the liberal law-and-development approach as ethnocentric, see David Trubek & Marc Galanter, *Scholars in Self-Estrangement: Some Reflections on the Crisis in Law and Development Studies in the United States*, 1974 WIS. L. REV. 1062.

62. STATHIS KALYVAS, THE LOGIC OF VIOLENCE IN CIVIL WAR 78–80 (2006).

63. See generally HART, THE CONCEPT OF LAW.

64. Sarah Sewall, *Introduction* xxxix, in FIELD MANUAL.

65. See generally SAMUEL HUNTINGTON, POLITICAL ORDER IN CHANGING SOCIETIES (1968); LEE KWAN YEW, FROM THIRD WORLD TO FIRST (2000); FAREED ZAKARIA, THE FUTURE OF FREEDOM (2003).

66. See DANI RODRIK, ONE ECONOMICS, MANY RECIPES (2008).

67. Kleinfeld, *Competing Definitions of the Rule of Law* 33–34 (arguing that institutional definitions confuse means with ends).

68. See HART, THE CONCEPT OF LAW 91–99.

69. Cf. Rule of Law Handbook, at 110.

70. United Nations Development Program, Human Development Report Afghanistan 2007, at 9 [hereafter UNDP, HDR]. For background information see Thomas Barfield, Informal Dispute Resolution and the Formal Legal System in Contemporary Northern Afghanistan, USIP (April 21, 2006), available at www.usip.org/ruleoflaw/projects/barfield_report.pdf; Thomas Barfield, Afghan Customary Law and Its Relationship to Formal Judicial Institutions, USIP (June 26, 2003), available at www.usip.org/ruleoflaw/projects/barfield2.pdf.

71. See UNDP, HDR at 95–96 (showing popular agreement on these metrics between 79 percent and 89 percent and greater acceptance than state courts by between 8 percent for human rights and 18 percent for less corrupt).

72. UNDP, HDR, at 43.

73. UNDP, HDR, at 130; Thomas Barfield, Neamat Nojumi, and J. Alexander Their, The Clash of Two Goods: State and Non-State Dispute Resolution in Afghanistan, USIP, available at http://www.usip.org/files/file/clash_two_goods.pdf (accessed April 15, 2012).

74. See UNDP, HDR, at 8 (noting the backlog of cases in Afghanistan and judges' lack of resources). Suggestions for hybrid courts have been ignored in previous transitions. In East Timor, for example, the UN ignored an East Timorese suggestion to incorporate traditional mechanisms into the new justice system. See Kings College London Conflict Security & Development Group, A Review of Peace Operations: A Case for Change: East Timor, paras. 253, 398, March 10, 2003, available at www.jsmp.minihub.org/Reports/OtherResources/Peace4Timor_10_3_03.pdf.

75. See, e.g., Brian Z. Tamanaha, The Primacy of Society and the Failures of Law and Development: Decades of Stubborn Refusal to Learn, unpublished draft, available at http://papers.ssrn.com/sol3/papers.cfm?abstract_id=1406999 (accessed April 15, 2012).

76. See, e.g., Brian Z. Tamanaha, Realistic Socio-Legal Theory 93, 104–105 (1997) (describing the state-centric and behavior-centric approaches); Max Weber, I Economy and Society 311 (Guenther Roth & Claus Wittich, eds., 1978) (describing the legal and sociological views); J. L. Comoroff & Simon Roberts, Rules and Procedures: The Cultural Logic of Dispute in an African Context 5–21 (1981); Mark Galanter, Law and Society in Modern India 32 (1989) ("Every legal system faces the problem of bridging the gap between its most authoritative and technically elaborate literary products at the 'upper' end of the system and the varying patterns of local practice at the 'lower' end. It must decide on allowable leeways—how much localism to accommodate, how to deflect local to general standards."); Roger Cotterrell, Law's Community 223 (1995).

77. See Tamanaha, Realistic Socio-Legal Theory 97 (describing the state law model and sanctions).

78. See generally J. L. Austin, The Province of Jurisprudence Determined (1832, 2000).

79. See Simon Roberts, Order and Dispute: An Introduction to Legal Anthropology 18–20 (1979) (describing the conventional approach to law and its focus on institutions); Tom R. Tyler, Why People Obey the Law 3 (2006) (describing instrumental reasons for following the law).

80. Roberts, Order and Dispute, at 19, 22.

81. See Roger Cotterrell, *Law in Social Theory and Social Theory in the Study of Law* 22, in The Blackwell Companion to Law and Society (Austin Sarat, ed., 2004) (describing the work of Niklas Luhmann).

82.  See Richard H. Fallon, *Legitimacy and the Constitution*, 118 HARV. L. REV. 1787, 1794–95 (2005) for a discussion of legal legitimacy that distinguishes between substantive and authoritative legitimacy.

83.  See ROBERTS, ORDER AND DISPUTE, at 12. See Bronislaw Malinowski, *Introduction* to H. I. HOGBIN, LAW AND ORDER IN POLYNESIA lxiii (1934) ("I personally believe that law ought to be defined by function and not by form.").

84.  TAMANAHA, REALISTIC SOCIO-LEGAL THEORY 93–95 (describing the works of legal sociologist Eugen Ehrlich and legal anthropologist Bronislaw Malinowski). For other versions, see id. at 96 (describing Ian Hamnet's "customary law" and Marc Galanter's "indigenous law").

85.  OLIVER WENDELL HOLMES JR., THE COMMON LAW 1 (1881).

86.  KAHN, THE CULTURAL STUDY OF LAW, at 6 (discussing social practice); PHILIPPE NONET & PHILIP SELZNICK, LAW AND SOCIETY IN TRANSITION 115 (1978) (considering responsiveness to social conditions).

87.  LEON LIPSON & STANTON WHEELER, LAW AND THE SOCIAL SCIENCES 2 (1986); see also Sally Falk Moore, *General Introduction* 1, in LAW AND ANTHROPOLOGY: A READER (Sally Falk Moore, ed., 2005) ("An anthropological approach to law inquires into the context of enforceable norms: social, political, economic, and intellectual. This includes, but goes further than, what Western governments and courts define as law").

88.  TAMANAHA, REALISTIC SOCIO-LEGAL THEORY, at 95.

89.  Id. at 116–117.

90.  Id. at 95.

91.  MAX WEBER, II ECONOMY AND SOCIETY 756 (Guenther Roth & Claus Wittich, eds., 1978).

92.  Fallon, *Legitimacy and the Constitution*, at 1795.

93.  HART, THE CONCEPT OF LAW, at 27–28.

94.  MOORE, LAW AND ANTHROPOLOGY, at 1 ("even in the West, formal, state-enforced law is by no means the only source of organized social order").

95.  Cf. TAMANAHA, REALISTIC SOCIO-LEGAL THEORY, at 104, 109.

96.  ROBERT C. ELLICKSON, ORDER WITHOUT LAW (1991).

97.  HART, THE CONCEPT OF LAW, at 59.

98.  Sally Falk Moore, *Introduction to the Early Classics of Legal Ethnography*, in MOORE, LAW AND ANTHROPOLOGY, at 68 (noting the challenge of holism, assuming that everything in the social and cultural context is relevant).

99.  TAMANAHA, REALISTIC SOCIO-LEGAL THEORY, at 110.

100.  TYLER, WHY PEOPLE OBEY THE LAW, at 57.

101.  Id. at 27; see also TOM R. TYLER, LEGITIMACY AND CRIMINAL JUSTICE 10 (2007).

102.  Fallon, *Legitimacy and the Constitution*, at 1792, 1805, 1848; COTTERRELL, LAW'S COMMUNITY 315 (noting that "law's political authority depends ultimately on a certain kind of moral authority").

103.  Fallon, *Legitimacy and the Constitution*, at 1792.

104. See COTTERRELL, LAW'S COMMUNITY 158.

105. Fallon, *Legitimacy and the Constitution*, at 1849.

106. See, e.g., Paul Bohannon, *Introduction* xiii, in LAW AND WARFARE: STUDIES IN THE ANTHROPOLOGY OF CONFLICT (Paul Bohannon, ed., 1967) (noting that there are two forms of conflict resolution, "administrated rules and fighting: law and war"). Sally Falk Moore, *Certainties Undone: Fifty Turbulent Years of Legal Anthropology, 1949–1999* in MOORE, LAW AND ANTHROPOLOGY 348 ("Law is a rational response to social problems").

107. CARL VON CLAUSEWITZ, ON WAR xx (Michael Howard & Peter Paret, eds., 1984).

108. That law is a mechanism of social order and power is not a new idea. See, e.g., Michel Foucault, *Disciplinary Power and Subjection*, in MOORE, LAW AND ANTHROPOLOGY, at 45 ("The system of right, the domain of law, are permanent agents of these relations of dominations, these polymorphous techniques of subjugation."). For arguments that war is politics by other means in the counterinsurgency context, see DAVID GALULA, PACIFICATION IN ALGERIA 1956–1958, at 262 (1963, RAND ed. 2006) ("War is the continuation of politics by other means. . . . Revolutionary war is no exception to this rule. One might even say that, in this sort of war, military action is but a minor factor of the conflict, a partial aspect of the operation. Give me good policy and I will give you good revolutionary war!").

109. Of course this is not always the case. One can pursue war, politics, or law for its own sake, or one for the sake of another. But it is possible to disentangle ends and means and see each as a means to the end of social order and conflict resolution.

110. CLAUSEWITZ, ON WAR 89.

111. TYLER, LEGITIMACY AND CRIMINAL JUSTICE 15.

112. This approach to popular support goes further than legal philosopher H. L. A. Hart's in *The Concept of Law*. Hart's great contribution was to demonstrate that laws were not followed because they were commanded by an authority who threatened punishment for violations. If that were true, he argued, it would be impossible to explain laws that confer powers to adjudicate or legislate, or that enable private legal relationships such as marriage or contract. Id. at 79. Rather, Hart showed that law is based on obligation, which exists "when the general demand for conformity is insistent and the social pressure brought to bear upon those who deviate or threaten to deviate is great." Id. at 86. As a result, a legal system is ultimately based on social acceptance. To be sure, not all individuals needed to accept all the laws; many would be driven to comply by fear or self-interest. But all the officials did need to embrace the rules established for creating, changing, and enforcing laws. When officials stop obeying the rules or when the population revolts, the legal system ceases to exist. Id. at 114–118. Hart says little about how a legal system can be built or rebuilt, but his central lesson, that law is based on social acceptance, actually goes further than the conventional reading of Hart that suggests that only official acceptance is needed. In fact, official acceptance

and minimal social acceptance would be necessary to maintain a stable regime. In counterinsurgency, this aligns with the need to win over the population. Without even minimal social acceptance, an insurgency would likely be more successful.

113. Matt Waldman, Community Peacebuilding in Afghanistan: The Case for a National Strategy 9, Oxfam Research Report, February 2008 (half of respondents in a survey found land to be a major cause of disputes, and over 40 percent cited water); The Asia Foundation, Afghanistan in 2007: A Survey of the Afghan People 71–72 (2007), available at http://asiafoundation.org/publications/pdf/20 (48 percent had disputes over land, 14 percent over other property issues). On the importance of land and water issues, see generally International Crisis Group, Peacebuilding in Afghanistan 2–8 (September 29, 2003).

114. See Stephen Holmes, *Lineages of the Rule of Law* 24, in DEMOCRACY AND THE RULE OF LAW (Jose Maria Maravall & Adam Przeworski, eds., 2003); Barry R. Weingast, *The Political Foundations of Democracy and the Rule of Law*, 91 AM. POL. SCI. REV. 245 (1997).

115. Ewa Wojkowska, Doing Justice: How Informal Justice Systems Can Contribute 12, UNDP (December 2006), available at http://www.undp.org/oslocentre/docs07/DoingJusticeEwaWojkowska130307.pdf; Leila Chirayath, Caroline Sage & Michael Woolcock, Customary Law and Policy Reform: Engaging with the Plurality of Justice Systems 3, World Bank Background Paper (July 2005), available at http://siteresources.worldbank.org/INTWDR2006/Resources/477383-1118673432908/Customary_Law_and_Policy_Reform.pdf.

116. Thomas Barfield, Afghan Customary Law and Its Relationship to Formal Judicial Institutions 1, USIP (June 26, 2003), available at www.usip.org/ruleoflaw/projects/barfield2.pdf.

117. Id. at 30.

118. Id.

119. Barfield, Clash of Two Goods, at 4; Masood Karokhail & Susanne Schmeidl, Integration of Traditional Structures into the State-building Process: Lessons from the Tribal Liaison Office in Loya Paktia 60, Henrich Boll Foundation, Publication Series on Promoting Democracy under Conditions of State Fragility, Issue 1: Afghanistan (2006), available at http://www.tlo-afghanistan.org/sites/default/files/About-TLO/Boell-Afghanistan-en-Integration-of-Traditional-Structures-into-the-State-building-Process.pdf; Barfield, Afghan Customary Law, at 2.

120. Barfield, Afghan Customary Law, at 3.

121. Sudhindra Sharma & Pawan Kumar Sen, Institutionalization of the Justice System 55, in The Asia Foundation, State Building, Security, and Social Change in Afghanistan (2008), available at http://asiafoundation.org/resources/pdfs/2008surveycompanionvolumefinal.pdf. Thirty-six percent of rural Afghans brought claims to a state court and 18 percent brought claims to both. Only 20 percent of urban Afghans had brought claims to a *shura* or *jirga* and only 9 percent to both state and traditional justice institutions.

122. Barfield, Afghan Customary Law, at 2, 26.

123. Id. at 1.

124. Thomas J. Barfield, *On Local Justice and Culture in Post-Taliban Afghanistan*, 17 CONN. J. INT'L L. 437, 443 (2002).

125. Barfield, Afghan Customary Law, at 5. Equality is understood as the absence of political domination.

126. Id. at 5–8.

127. Barfield, Clash of Two Goods, at 7; Christina Jones-Pauly & Neamat Nojumi, *Balancing Relations between Society and State: Legal Steps toward National Reconciliation and Reconstruction in Afghanistan*, 52 AM. J. COMP. L. 825, 838 (2004).

128. Barfield, *On Local Justice*, at 439–440.

129. Barfield, Afghan Customary Law, at 31.

130. Id. at 31.

131. Matt Waldman, Community Peacebuilding in Afghanistan: The Case for a National Strategy 9–10, Oxfam International Research Report, February 2008, available at http://www.oxfam.ca/sites/default/files/community-peacebuilding-in-afghanistan-the-case-for-a-national-strategy.pdf.

132. Islamic Republic of Afghanistan, Afghanistan National Development Strategy, Draft Summary of ANDS Justice Sector Strategy 3–4 (January 2008), available at http://lib.ohchr.org/HRBodies/UPR/Documents/Session5/AF/AFG_annexIV_Afghanistan_National_Strategies_on_Justice_Sector.pdf [hereafter Giroa, ANDS].

133. Giroa, ANDS, at 3; Neamat Nojumi, Dyan Mazurana, and Elizabeth Stites, Afghanistan's Systems of Justice: Formal, Traditional, and Customary 2, 21, 23 (June 2004), available at http://www.gmu.edu/depts/crdc/neamat1.pdf.

134. Barfield, Afghan Customary Law, at 42 (describing position of ministry of interior officials); but see Giroa, ANDS, at 4 (noting that *shira* and *jirga* can, with oversight, contribute to resolving disputes).

135. Wojkowska, Doing Justice, at 8, 11.

136. See Chirayath et al., Customary Law and Policy Reform, at 2; Wojkowska, Doing Justice, at 12.

137. See Sharma & Sen, Institutionalization of the Justice System, at 48, 57; Thomas Barfield, Informal Dispute Resolution and the Formal Legal System in Contemporary Northern Afghanistan 1, USIP (April 21, 2006), available at www.usip.org/ruleoflaw/projects/barfield_report.pdf; Wojkowska, Doing Justice, at 13.

138. Sharma & Sen, Institutionalization of the Justice System, at 48, 57 (noting fairness and trust, and presenting evidence of 2/3 satisfaction with *shuras/jirgas* and 1/3 satisfaction with state court); Barfield, Informal Dispute Resolution, at 1.

139. Barfield, Clash, of Two Goods, at 22 (noting the embeddedness of these systems).

140. Barfield, Informal Dispute Resolution, at 1–2; Wojkowska, Doing Justice, at 13, 16.

141. Barfield, Clash of Two Goods, at 17; Wojkowska, Doing Justice, at 20–23.

142. Barfield, Afghan Customary Law, at 42.

143. Id.
144. See Dept. for Int'l Dev., Non-State Justice and Security Systems 19, DFID Briefing, May 2004, available at http://www.gsdrc.org/docs/open/SSAJ101.pdf.
145. See Leigh Toomey & J. Alexander Thier, Bridging Modernity and Tradition: Rule of Law and Search for Justice in Afghanistan 4, October 2007, available at http://www.usip.org/resources/bridging-modernity-and-tradition-rule-law-and-search-justice-afghanistan; Ali Wardak, *Building a Post-War Justice System in Afghanistan*, 41 CRIME, LAW & SOCIAL CHANGE, 319, 336–337 (2004).
146. Tribal Liaison Office (TLO), Between the Jirga and the Judge: Alternative Dispute Resolution in Southern Afghanistan 2–6, March 2009, available at http://www.usip.org/files/file/jirga_judge.pdf.
147. DFID, Non-State Justice and Security Systems, at 19; Barfield, Afghan Customary Law, at 42.
148. Cf. Daryl J. Levinson, *Framing Transactions in Constitutional Law*, 111 YALE L.J. 1311 (2002).
149. Barfield, Clash of Two Goods, at 22; Jones-Pauly & Nojumi, Balancing Relations between Society and State, at 839.
150. FIELD MANUAL at ¶ 6–90.
151. See JAMES DOBBINS, SETH G. JONES, KEITH CRANE, AND BETH COLE DeGRASSE, THE BEGINNER'S GUIDE TO NATION-BUILDING xxvii (2007); Andrew Wilder, Cops and Robbers? The Struggle to Reform the Afghan National Police 49, Afghan Research and Evaluation Unit (July 2007), available at http://www.areu.org.af/index.php?option=com_docman&Itemid=&task=doc_download&gid=523; Kalev I. Sepp, *Best Practices in Counterinsurgency* MIL. REV., May–June 2005 at 9 ("an incorrupt, functioning judiciary must support the police").
152. DOBBINS ET AL., BEGINNER'S GUIDE, at 58; see also DOBBINS ET AL., BEGINNER'S GUIDE, at 50; see Wilder, Cops and Robbers?, at 54.
153. Jack Kem, Building Capacity in Iraq—Police Forces, Small Wars Journal, June 12, 2008, available at http://smallwarsjournal.com/blog/2008/06/part-2-building-capacity-in-ir/; DOBBINS ET AL., BEGINNER'S GUIDE, at 56, 58.
154. DOBBINS ET AL., BEGINNER'S GUIDE, at 62.
155. Id. at 51, 54–55, 62, 78–81, 87; see Wilder, Cops and Robbers?, at 5, 30, 32, 54.
156. Wilder, Cops and Robbers?, at 44.
157. Robert M. Perito, Afghanistan's Police: The Weak Link in Security Sector Reform 8, USIP Special Report (August 2009), available at http://www.usip.org/files/afghanistan_police.pdf.
158. Quoted in id.
159. DAVID H. BAYLEY & ROBERT M. PERITO, THE POLICE IN WAR 11–14 (2010).
160. Id.
161. Id.
162. Id. at 15; William Rosenau, "Low-Cost Trigger-Pullers": The Politics of Policing in the Context of Contemporary "State Building" and Counterinsurgency 11–12,

RAND Working Paper WR-620-USCA, Oct 2008, available at http://www.rand.org/pubs/working_papers/2009/RAND_WR620.pdf.

163. BAYLEY & PERITO, THE POLICE IN WAR, at 15.

164. See generally George L. Kelling & Mark H. Moore, *The Evolving Strategy of Policing* 101–109, in COMMUNITY POLICING (Willard M. Oliver, ed., 2000).

165. Id. at 98–99; Debra Livingston, *Police Discretion and the Quality of Life in Public Places: Courts, Communities, and the New Policing,* 97 COLUM. L. REV. 551, 566 (1997).

166. Kelling & Moore, *Evolving Strategy,* at 98–101.

167. Id. at 102–105; George L. Kelling, *Police and Communities: The Quiet Revolution* 62, in OLIVER, COMMUNITY POLICING; Livingston, *Police Discretion,* at 566–568; Mark H. Moore, Robert C. Trojanowicz, and George L. Kelling, *Crime and Policing* 41, in OLIVER, COMMUNITY POLICING; DAVID ALAN SKLANSKY, DEMOCRACY AND THE POLICE 35–36 (2008).

168. Kelling & Moore, *Evolving Strategy,* at 102, 104.

169. George L. Kelling, *Toward New Images of Policing: Herman Goldstein's "Problem Oriented Policing,"* 17 LAW & SOC. INQUIRY 539, 540 (1992).

170. Id. at 542.

171. George L. Kelling, Robert Wasserman, & Hubert Williams, *Police Accountability and Community Policing* 270, in OLIVER, COMMUNITY POLICING.

172. Kelling, *Toward New Images,* at 540.

173. Id. at 543.

174. Stuntz, Fighting Wars and Fighting Crime 10 (unpublished draft).

175. Kelling, *Toward New Images,* at 540.

176. See John. E. Eck, William Spelman, Diane Hill, Darrel W. Stephens, John R. Stedman, and Gerard R. Murphy, Problem Solving: Problem Oriented Policing in Newport News, Washington, D.C.: Police Executive Research Forum (1987) at 1–2 (quoted in Herman Goldstein, *Problem-Oriented Policing* 20 (1990)).

177. Kelling, *Toward New Images,* at 543–544, 548–550.

178. See Livingston, *Police Discretion,* at 568–571; Kelling, *Quiet Revolution,* at 63–65; Kelling & Moore, *Evolving Strategy,* at 107–108; GOLDSTEIN, PROBLEM-ORIENTED POLICING, at 11; Herman Goldstein, *Toward Community-Oriented Policing: Potential, Basic Requirements, and Threshold Questions,* 33 CRIME & DELINQ. 6, 6–10 (1987).

179. Problem-oriented and community policing are in fact two distinct approaches, see Livingston, *Police Discretion,* 573–578, but are similar enough to consider together.

180. See, e.g., Community Policing Consortium, Understanding Community Policing: A Framework for Action 128, in OLIVER, COMMUNITY POLICING; Tracey L. Meares, *Praying for Community Policing,* 90 CAL. L. REV. 1593, 1600–1601 (2002); Livingston, *Police Discretion,* at 574–575.

181. Herman Goldstein, *Improving Policing: A Problem-Oriented Approach* 23, in OLIVER, COMMUNITY POLICING.

182. GOLDSTEIN, PROBLEM-ORIENTED POLICING, at 32–35; 67–68.

183. Goldstein, *Improving Policing*, at 24–26.

184. Livingston, *Police Discretion*, at 588–589.

185. See, e.g., Community Policing Consortium, Understanding Community Policing, at 128; Moore, Trojanowicz, & Kelling, *Crime and Policing*, at 42; Kelling & Moore, *Evolving Strategy*, at 109–113; Kelling, Wasserman, & Williams, *Police Accountability and Community Policing*, at 274.

186. Community Policing Consortium, Understanding Community Policing, at 129.

187. GOLDSTEIN, PROBLEM-ORIENTED POLICING, at 24.

188. Community Policing Consortium, Understanding Community Policing, at 138; Dan M. Kahan, *Reciprocity, Collective Action, and Community Policing*, 90 CAL. L. REV. 1513, 1531–1535 (2002).

189. Kelling, *Quiet Revolution*, at 62–63.

190. GOLDSTEIN, PROBLEM-ORIENTED POLICING, at 62, 159.

191. Community Policing Consortium, Understanding Community Policing, at 134.

192. Malcolm K. Sparrow, *Implementing Community Policing* 177, 179, in OLIVER, COMMUNITY POLICING.

193. Id. at 178.

194. See Kelling, Wasserman, & Williams, *Police Accountability and Community Policing*, at 273; GOLDSTEIN, PROBLEM-ORIENTED POLICING, at 152–153.

195. On guided discretion, see Livingston, *Police Discretion*, at 658; TRACEY L. MEARES & DAN M. KAHAN, URGENT TIMES: POLICING AND RIGHTS IN INNER-CITY COMMUNITIES 23–29 (1999).

196. GOLDSTEIN, PROBLEM-ORIENTED POLICING, at 48; see also Livingston, *Police Discretion*, at 653.

197. Kelling, Wasserman, & Williams, *Police Accountability and Community Policing*, at 274.

198. GOLDSTEIN, PROBLEM-ORIENTED POLICING, at 47.

199. Livingston, *Police Discretion*, at 564, 576; Kelling & Moore, *Evolving Strategy*, at 111.

200. Stuntz, Fighting Wars and Fighting Crime, at 18–19.

201. Kahan, *Reciprocity, Collective Action, and Community Policing*, at 1518.

202. Id. at 1522–1523.

203. Id. at 1523–1525.

204. Mark H. Moore & Robert C. Trojanowicz, *Policing and the Fear of Crime* 88, in OLIVER, COMMUNITY POLICING; Wesley Skogan, *Fear of Crime and Neighborhood Change* 211, in COMMUNITIES AND CRIME, VIII CRIME AND JUSTICE: A REVIEW OF RESEARCH (Albert J. Reiss Jr. & Michael Tonry, eds., 1986).

205. James S. Corum, Training Indigenous Forces in Counterinsurgency: A Tale of Two Insurgencies 5–14, Strategic Studies Institute, March 1, 2006, available at http://www.strategicstudiesinstitute.army.mil/pubs/display.cfm?pubID=648.

206. Id. at 17, 19, 21.

207. Id. at 19; KUMAR RAMAKRISHNA, EMERGENCY PROPAGANDA: THE WINNING OF MALAYAN HEARTS AND MINDS 1948–1958, at 87 (2002).

208. ANTHONY SHORT, THE COMMUNIST INSURRECTION IN MALAYA 357 (1975); RAMAKRISHNA, EMERGENCY PROPAGANDA, at 87.

209. RICHARD STUBBS, HEARTS AND MINDS IN GUERRILLA WARFARE: THE MALAYAN EMERGENCY 1948–1960, at 157 (2004) (considering Operation Service a PR exercise); Corum, Training Indigenous Forces, at 19 (arguing for a shift, in effect, toward community policing).

210. CHARLES W. GWYNN, IMPERIAL POLICING 13–15 (1934).

211. Id. 5, 14.

212. Id. at 11.

213. Id. at 6.

214. ANTHONY A. BRAGA, PROBLEM-ORIENTED POLICING AND CRIME PREVENTION 56, 61 (2d. 2008).

215. David M. Kennedy, *Old Wine in New Bottles: Policing and the Lessons of Pulling Levers* 156, in POLICE INNOVATION: CONTRASTING PERSPECTIVES (David Weisburd & Anthony Braga, eds., 2006).

216. Id. at 164.

217. Lorraine Mazerolle & Janet Ransley, *The Case for Third-Party Policing* 191, in WEISBURD & BRAGA, POLICE INNOVATION.

218. BAYLEY & PERITO, THE POLICE IN WAR, at 76–77.

219. Rosenau, *"Low-Cost Trigger-Pullers,"* at 19.

CHAPTER 7

1. See RORY STEWART, THE PRINCE OF THE MARSHES 59 (2007) (stating that the author, who served as deputy governorate coordinator in Maysan province, Iraq, "operated at a level that had nothing to do with new constitutions"). But see David J. Kilcullen, *Countering Global Insurgency*, 28 J. STRATEGIC STUD. 597, 612 (2005) (explaining that a "constitutional path is needed, but lacking, to counter global jihad").

2. For discussion of modern constitutionalism, see JAMES TULLY, STRANGE MULTIPLICITY: CONSTITUTIONALISM IN AN AGE OF DIVERSITY 63–69 (1995).

3. SIR ROBERT THOMPSON, DEFEATING COMMUNIST INSURGENCY 66 (1966).

4. See, e.g., RUSSELL HARDIN, LIBERALISM, CONSTITUTIONALISM, AND DEMOCRACY 12–18, 82–133 (1999); Adam Przeworski, *Democracy as a Contingent Outcome of Conflicts*, in CONSTITUTIONALISM AND DEMOCRACY 59, 63–64 (Jon Elster & Rune Slagstad eds., 1993); Barry R. Weingast, *The Political Foundations of Democracy and the Rule of Law*, 91 AM. POL. SCI. REV. 245, 257–258, 261 (1997).

5. See HARDIN, LIBERALISM, CONSTITUTIONALISM, AND DEMOCRACY, at 88–89.

6. Id. at 87–88; cf. Weingast, *The Political Foundations of Democracy and the Rule of Law*, at 253 (arguing that resolution of "coordination dilemmas" leads to stable democracy and shared citizen values).

7. Weingast, *The Political Foundations of Democracy and the Rule of Law*, at 258.

8.  Barry R. Weingast, Self-Enforcing Constitutions: With an Application to Democratic Stability in America's First Century, unpublished draft, November 2005.

9.  See Weingast, *The Political Foundations of Democracy and the Rule of Law*, at 246.

10. Although the occupation constitutions of Germany and Japan stand as counterexamples, scholars hold that "[c]onstitutions written at the behest of the occupier . . . are unlikely to develop into self-enforcing bargains and as a result will depend upon the occupier for their enforcement, at least in the short run." See Zachary Elkins, Tom Ginsburg, and James Melton, *Baghdad, Tokyo, Kabul . . .: Constitution Making in Occupied States*, 49 WM. & MARY L. REV. 1139, 1146 (2008).

11. ALI A. ALLAWI, THE OCCUPATION OF IRAQ 169 (2007).

12. Noah Feldman, *The Democratic Fatwa: Islam and Democracy in the Realm of Constitutional Politics*, 58 OKLA. L. REV. 1, 6 (2005).

13. ALLAWI, THE OCCUPATION OF IRAQ, at 211.

14. See LARRY DIAMOND, SQUANDERED VICTORY: THE AMERICAN OCCUPATION AND THE BUNGLED EFFORT TO BRING DEMOCRACY TO IRAQ 51–52 (2005).

15. Jon Elster, Essay, *Forces and Mechanisms in the Constitution-Making Process*, 45 DUKE L.J. 364, 373 (1995). The distinction, he notes, is not perfect because one upstream constraint may be who constitutes the ratifiers, that is, who will become the downstream constraint. Id. at 374–375.

16. Id. at 373–374.

17. Id. at 374.

18. Id.

19. Professor Elster notes that discussion and argument may change preferences and that extrapolitical forces—the threat of "the troops and the crowds," id. at 393— can suspend constitution-making processes, but he does not explore how they influence substantive deliberations. See id. at 390–393.

20. I use "constitution" to refer to the written constitution, specifying "informal" when the informal constitution is intended.

21. Henry St. John Bolingbroke, *A Dissertation upon Parties*, in POLITICAL WRITINGS 1, 88 (David Armitage ed., 1997) (emphasis added).

22. David S. Law, *Constitutions* 1, OXFORD HANDBOOK OF EMPIRICAL LEGAL RESEARCH (Peter Cane and Herbert M. Kritzer eds., 2010). Cf. Frank I. Michelman, *Constitutional Authorship*, in CONSTITUTIONALISM 64, 70 (Larry Alexander ed., 1998) (describing the small-*c* constitution and the big-*C* Constitution); Michael J. Perry, *What Is "the Constitution"? (and Other Fundamental Questions)*, in CONSTITUTIONALISM, at 99 (distinguishing between Constitution, the text, and Constitution, norms that constitute the supreme law of the land); Ernest A. Young, *The Constitution Outside the Constitution*, 117 YALE L.J. 408, 415 (2007) (identifying the canonical and extracanonical Constitution).

23. Cf. DAVID A. STRAUSS, THE LIVING CONSTITUTION 36–37 (distinguishing between command and common law theories).

24. TULLY, STRANGE MULTIPLICITY at 60.

25. Id. at 86–87.

26. Giovanni Sartori, *Constitutionalism: A Preliminary Discussion*, 56 Am. Pol. Sci. Rev. 853, 861 (1962).

27. See Noah Feldman, *Imposed Constitutionalism*, 37 Conn. L. Rev. 857, 872 (2005). This is consistent with the idea that a constitutional "rule of recognition is a social fact." Young, *The Constitution Outside the Constitution*, at 421; see also Michelman, *Constitutional Authorship*, at 71.

28. See generally H. W. O. Okoth-Ogendo, *Constitutions without Constitutionalism: Reflections on an African Political Paradox*, in Constitutionalism and Democracy 65 (Douglas Greenberg et al. eds., 1993).

29. See Michael W. McConnell, *Textualism and the Dead Hand of the Past*, 66 Geo. Wash. L. Rev. 1127, 1130 (1998) (arguing that constitutional rules might enable, rather than constrain, self-government).

30. Edward S. Corwin, *The Constitution as Instrument and as Symbol*, 30 Am. Pol. Sci. Rev. 1071, 1072 (1936).

31. Rosa Ehrenreich Brooks, *Failed States, or the State as Failure?*, 72 U. Chi. L. Rev. 1159, 1160 (2005).

32. Cf. David A. Strauss, *Common Law Constitutional Interpretation*, 63 U. Chi. L. Rev. 877, 910–911 (1996) (analogizing the conventionalist justification for adherence to the Constitution to focal points in game theory).

33. See Stephen D. Krasner & Carlos Pascual, *Addressing State Failure*, For. Aff., July–August 2005, at 153, 159–160.

34. Zachary Elkins, Tom Ginsburg, and James Melton, The Endurance of National Constitutions 84–88 (2009).

35. For a helpful discussion of constitutions as coordination-oriented documents, see Hardin, Liberalism, Constitutionalism, and Democracy, at 85–90.

36. Afg. Const. of 1977, art. 23. See Elkins, Ginsburg, & Melton, The Endurance of National Constitutions, at 52.

37. Bangladesh Const., art. 4. See Elkins, Ginsburg, & Melton, The Endurance of National Constitutions, at 52.

38. See, e.g., McCulloch v. Maryland, 17 U.S. (4 Wheat.) 316, 415 (1819) (noting that the U.S. Constitution was intended "to endure for ages to come, and, consequently, to be adapted to the various *crises* of human affairs").

39. Elkins, Ginsburg, & Melton, The Endurance of National Constitutions, at 2.

40. U.S. Const. art. 1, § 2, cl. 3, amended by U.S. Const. amend. XIV, § 2; id. art. 1, § 9, cl. 1.

41. Elkins, Ginsburg, & Melton, The Endurance of National Constitutions, at 84–88.

42. See generally Yossi Shain, & Juan J. Linz, Between States: Interim Governments and Democratic Transitions (1995).

43. Elkins, Ginsburg, & Melton, The Endurance of National Constitutions, at 140–141.

44. See Feldman, *Imposed Constitutionalism*, at 873.

45. Noah Feldman & Roman Martinez, *Constitutional Politics and Text in the New Iraq: An Experiment in Islamic Democracy*, 75 FORDHAM L. REV. 883, 903 (2006).

46. Cf. Feldman, *Imposed Constitutionalism*, at 872–874.

47. THE U.S. ARMY/MARINE CORPS COUNTERINSURGENCY FIELD MANUAL ¶ 1–155 (2007).

48. See Kalev I. Sepp, *Best Practices in Counterinsurgency*, MIL. REV., May–June 2005, at 8, 9.

49. See ALLAWI, THE OCCUPATION OF IRAQ, at 137.

50. See id. at 240–241.

51. See id. at 73, 221–223.

52. See, e.g., AREND LIJPHART, DEMOCRACY IN PLURAL SOCIETIES (1977); EDWARD SCHNEIER, CRAFTING CONSTITUTIONAL DEMOCRACIES (2006); Arend Lijphart, *Constitutional Design for Divided Societies*, J. DEMOCRACY, April 2004, at 96, 104–105; Nancy Bermeo, *The Importance of Institutions*, J. DEMOCRACY, April 2002, at 96; John C. Calhoun, *A Disquisition on Government*, in UNION AND LIBERTY: THE POLITICAL PHILOSOPHY OF JOHN C. CALHOUN 3 (Ross M. Lence ed., 1992); Nicholas Sambanis, *Partition as a Solution to Ethnic War: An Empirical Critique of the Theoretical Literature*, 52 WORLD POLITICS 437 (2000).

53. Iraq Const. art. 2; Afg. Const. ch. 1, art. 3.

54. See Feldman & Martinez, *Constitutional Politics and Text in the New Iraq*, at 903 & n.80.

55. RAY A. MOORE & DONALD L. ROBINSON, PARTNERS FOR DEMOCRACY: CRAFTING THE NEW JAPANESE STATE UNDER MACARTHUR 49 (2002).

56. There is a tension between the idea that counterinsurgency can create and change dynamics on the ground and the suggestion that drafters incorporate existing governance structures. Context will determine which approach dominates, but even if ground-level dynamics are in flux, traditional structures may be within the historical and cultural memory of the population and thus usable as anchoring structures for governance.

57. Cf. DAVID GALULA, COUNTERINSURGENCY WARFARE 115–118 (1964) (discussing importance of census); DAVID GALULA, PACIFICATION IN ALGERIA 1956–1958, at 99 (1963, RAND ed. 2006); ROGER TRINQUIER, MODERN WARFARE: A FRENCH VIEW OF COUNTERINSURGENCY 28–29 (1964, 2006 ed.).

58. Cf. GALULA, COUNTERINSURGENCY WARFARE at 116 (discussing identification cards); Sepp, *Best Practices*, at 10 (same).

59. See Richard Briffault, *Home Rule for the Twenty-First Century*, 36 URB. LAW. 253, 258–260 (2004) (arguing that home rule advances the values of democracy, diversity, community, and innovation); Gerald E. Frug, *The City as a Legal Concept*, 93 HARV. L. REV. 1057, 1067–1073 (1980) (arguing that city power can empower individuals to participate in social decisions, creating public freedom).

60. David J. Barron, *The Promise of Cooley's City: Traces of Local Constitutionalism*, 147 U. PA. L. REV. 487, 491 (1999).

61. See Barnett R. Rubin, *Creating a Constitution for Afghanistan*, 15 J. DEMOCRACY 5, 13–16 (July 2004).

62. See Joshua Foust, Afghanistan Needs a New Constitution, not a CEO, *Registan. net*, June 24, 2009, available at: http://www.registan.net/index.php/2009/06/24/afghanistan-needs-a-new-constitution-not-ceo/.

63. S. Afr. Const. 1996 ch. 11, §§ 205–208.

64. 1 FRANCIS LIEBER, ON CIVIL LIBERTY AND SELF-GOVERNMENT 349–350 (1853).

65. See Int'l Crisis Group, Iraq: Can Local Governance Save Central Government? (2004), available at http://www.crisisgroup.org/library/documents/middle_east___north_africa/iraq_iran_gulf/33_iraq_can_local_governance_save_central_gvnt.pdf [hereafter Int'l Crisis Group, Iraq] (noting the importance of "improving communication between national ministries and local councils").

66. S. Afr. Const. 1996 ch. 7, §§ 152, 157, 160.

67. Gw. ch. 7, arts. 123–132.

68. Indon. Const. ch VI., art. 18.

69. Peter W. Chiarelli & Patrick W. Michaelis, *Winning the Peace: The Requirement for Full-Spectrum Operations*, MIL. REV., July–August 2005, at 4, 9 fig. 3.

70. Gw. ch. 7, arts. 133–134.

71. Cf. Klaus Rohland & Sarah Cliffe, The East Timor Reconstruction Program: Successes, Problems and Tradeoffs 13 (World Bank Conflict Prevention & Reconstr. Unit, Paper No. 2, 2002), available at http://siteresources.worldbank.org/INT CPR/214578-1111996036679/20482353/WP2.pdf.

72. Cf. Briffault, *Home Rule for the Twenty-First Century*, at 261–262 (arguing that fiscal capacity is one of the fundamental constraints on local home rule).

73. Int'l Crisis Group, Iraq: Can Local Governance Save Central Government?, at 29; see also Sarah Cliffe, Scott Guggenheim, & Markus Kostner, Community-Driven Reconstruction as an Instrument in War-to-Peace Transitions 21 (World Bank Conflict Prevention & Reconstr. Unit, Paper No. 7, 2003), available at http://info.worldbank.org/etools/docs/library/35122/WP7final.pdf.

74. See Cliffe, Guggenheim, & Kostner, Community-Driven Reconstruction, at 21; see also Int'l Crisis Group, Iraq: Can Local Governance Save Central Government?, at 29.

75. 1 PLUTARCH, PLUTARCH'S LIVES 130 (Dryden ed. rev., J. M. Dent & Sons 1970).

CONCLUSION

1. DAVID GALULA, PACIFICATION IN ALGERIA 1956–1958, at 168 (2006).

# Index